FIELD GUIDE
THE WILD FLOWER
WITWATERSRAND & PRE

INCLUDING THE MAGALIESBERG

Braam van Wyk
(Curator, H.G.W.J. Schweickerdt Herbarium and
Associate Professor, Department of Botany, University of Pretoria)

Sasa Malan

with the collaboration of
T. K. Lowrey
(Department of Botany, National University of Singapore)

Line drawings by
Anne Pienaar

STRUIK

To Elsa, Jaco and Jana, and to Ockert

Struik Publishers (an operating division of The Struik Group (Pty) Ltd)
Struik House
Oswald Pirow Street
Foreshore
Cape Town
8001

Reg. No.: 80/02842/07

First published 1988

Designed by Joan Sutton, Cape Town
Edited by Leni Martin
Photosetting by CTP Book Printers, Parow
Reproduction by Hirt & Carter (Pty) Ltd, Cape Town
Printed and bound by CTP Book Printers, Parow

ISBN 0 86977 814 5

Cover photographs
Top left: *Striga elegans* (600)
Top right: *Acacia karroo* (391)
Bottom left: *Merremia palmata* (287)
Bottom right: *Crinum bulbispermum* (461)

CONTENTS

Acknowledgements 4

Preface 5

Area covered by the field guide 6

Introduction 6
- Evolution of the flowering plants 6
- Flowers and their function 7
- Classification of plants 7
- The scientific names of plants 8
- Plant families and their names 9
- Plant identification made easier 9
- The flora of the field guide area 10
- Vegetation and its classification 11
- Vegetation of the field guide area 11

How to use this guide 14

Family descriptions 16

White or whitish flowers 30

Yellow or cream flowers 92

Pink to red or red-purple flowers 186

Blue or blue-purple flowers 240

Orange to brown or red-brown flowers 268

Green or greenish flowers 284

The grasses 310

Glossary 339

References and suggested reading 344

Index to scientific names 346

Index to English and Afrikaans common names 350

ACKNOWLEDGEMENTS

Dr Timothy K. Lowrey, former Curator of the C.E. Moss Herbarium, University of the Witwatersrand, furnished some of the family and species descriptions for this field guide and commented on parts of the manuscript, and we gratefully acknowledge his contribution. Unfortunately his departure to Singapore terminated his active role in this work.

Anne Pienaar, who prepared the excellent line drawings, deserves a special word of thanks.

Dr B. de Winter, Director of the Botanical Research Institute (BRI), Pretoria, kindly placed the excellent facilities of the National Herbarium at our disposal. Most of the initial identification of field collections were done by the BRI. We nevertheless take full responsibility for the correctness of all identifications in this book. For their professional assistance our gratitude is due to all staff members, particularly: Mr Aurelio Balsinhas, Mrs Cathy Clark, Mrs Mien Crosby, Mrs Lyn Fish, Mr Gerrit Germishuizen, Dr Beth Gibbs Russell, Dr Hugh Glen, Dr Kathy Immelman, Dr Otto Leistner, Mrs Barnie Pienaar, Miss Clare Reid, Miss Elizabeth Retief, Mr Brian Schrire, Mrs Estelle van Hoepen, Mrs Mariana van Wyk, and Mr Bobby Westfall. To Mrs Enid du Plessis, who gave the second author (SM) valuable guidance in the very early stages of planning this book, we also extend our thanks.

Many people helped us to find and photograph particular plants in flower. We would like to thank in particular Mr Peter Chaplin, Miss Karen Behr and Miss Beverley Steel of the Witwatersrand National Botanic Garden; the staff of the Suikerbosrand Nature Reserve; Mr Ernst Wohlitz of the Van Riebeeck Nature Reserve; Mr Wayne Matthews and Dr Danie Roos.

We also gratefully acknowledge the assistance of several other people in the preparation of this book, especially: Prof. Albert Eicker, Head of the Department of Botany, University of Pretoria, for his support of the project; Mrs Emsie du Plessis for reading parts of the manuscript and for her valuable comments and criticisms; Prof. Pieter Kok for his interest and valuable discussions on grass identification; Dr Kevin Balkwill, Mrs Mandy-Jane Balkwill and Mr Ben-Erik van Wyk for help with some identification problems; Dr B. de Winter, Mr H.G. Cameron, Mr W.S. Matthews and Mr B. Ubbink for kindly allowing us to publish some of their photographs; Mrs Jackie de Jager and Miss Thea van Rensburg for the excellent typing of the manuscript; Mr P. van Wyk of the National Parks Board and Prof. N. Grobbelaar, former Head of the Department of Botany, University of Pretoria, who were instrumental in bringing together authors and publishers; and our publishers, in particular Peter Borchert, Eve Gracie and Leni Martin for their patience, sound advice and unfailing courtesy.

Various authorities such as municipalities and the Transvaal Division of Nature Conservation provided access to and/or information on natural areas under their jurisdiction, and we thank them for their co-operation.

PREFACE

This book, the first photographically illustrated field guide to the rich flora of the south-central Transvaal, developed from the second author's (SM) hobby of photographing wild flowers in the Magaliesberg. The idea to publish her collection of photographs was initially frustrated by the difficulty of finding a professional botanist to co-operate in the project, but it began to take shape when the first author (BvW) became involved in 1986.

The layman who has no particular botanical training but likes to know something about nature around him is the intended target for this field guide. Identifying a plant is merely a means to an end, and by providing this means – in the form of a plant's scientific name – the guide opens up to the reader all published knowledge about it. We hope that professional botanists too, and in particular teachers of biology, will find this work of practical value, as we would like to see schools taking a more active role in teaching pupils the identities of plants during field work. Even at primary school level the natural inquisitiveness of the young child provides an ideal opportunity for this.

With at least 2 000 species of indigenous and naturalized alien flowering plants in the field guide area, plant identification is not an easy task. Readers should, however, find comfort in the knowledge that even experts have difficulty in dealing with the remarkable diversity of the southern African flora. Its total of about 24 000 species exceeds that of any other temperate flora in the world.

Our selection of plants has been based partly on the frequency with which species have been recorded by plant collectors, and therefore encompasses a high proportion of those most likely to be seen. In addition, we have included a few of the less common species which would probably be encountered only by the more dedicated explorer of the veld. Grasses, long neglected in general plant identification guides, do however form a major component of the vegetation of the field guide area and therefore merit a separate section.

Unlike those in many other field guides, the plants in this book are arranged not in the traditional order of their presumed evolutionary development, but are grouped firstly on the basis of floral colour and secondly according to families, in alphabetical order. We believe this approach will make it easier for the beginner to find an illustration of the plant to be identified. We have also stressed the concept of family recognition which, in our opinion, is a first step towards competence in plant identification. Formal identification keys have been avoided mainly because of our relatively incomplete coverage of the local flora, but also because the numerous, often somewhat obscure features would be of little value to the layman.

Although we have tried to use terminology that is readily accessible to the layman, the inclusion of some specifically botanical terms has been unavoidable, and a glossary has been provided to assist those unfamiliar with them. Some technical terms have been used in a generalized sense, with reference to a rootstock, for example, including structures such as roots, stems, rhizomes and tubers.

Knowledge of the names of plants inevitably leads to a greater awareness of the natural environment, and in the introduction to this book we have discussed the vegetation types and the flora of the field guide area, as well as aspects of plant classification. With a human population exceeding 5 million and still growing, the region covered by this field guide contains the greatest concentration of urban areas in southern Africa. Its natural vegetation has suffered severely from man's impact, and is constantly and inevitably being destroyed to provide for his material needs. One way to conserve it would be to cultivate local wild flower species, but so far little success has been achieved. Many of the grassland species, in particular, are highly specialized, often requiring fire in order to thrive, and normally they do not survive in cultivation for long. The only hope for their continued existence seems to lie in the protection and proper management of their natural habitat.

We trust that this book will show that there is more to the Highveld vegetation than grass, maize, cosmos, wattles and gum trees. Man, with his power of thought and ability to rise above nature, holds the key to the survival of our flora and its associated animal life. It is our sincere hope that this book will create a greater awareness of the wealth of plant life in our area, and of the need for more nature reserves where the diversity and intricacy of nature can be enjoyed.

Braam van Wyk

Sasa Malan

Pretoria, September 1988

AREA COVERED BY THE FIELD GUIDE

This field guide is intended for use in the area roughly demarcated by Rustenburg, Brits and Hammanskraal in the north, the Vaal River in the south, Potchefstroom to the west, and Witbank and Standerton in the east (Figure 1). Wild flower species of the Pretoria/Witwatersrand/Vereeniging region are particularly well covered, especially those of the Magaliesberg and the Suikerbosrand, perhaps the two most important tracts of natural land within the field guide area. Since many of the species described are widespread in grassland and bushveld regions, the field guide should also be useful in other parts of the Transvaal Highveld and in the northern Orange Free State.

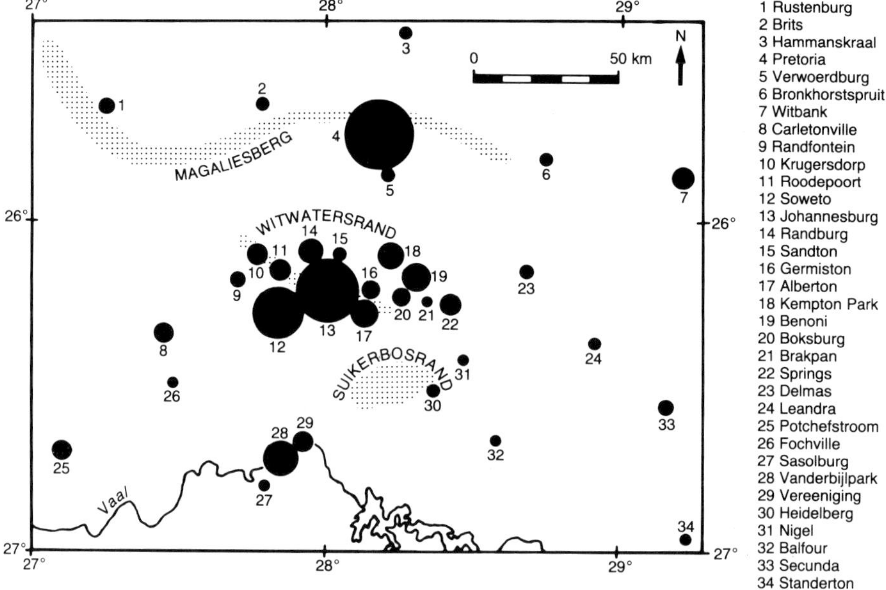

Figure 1. Map showing the area covered by this field guide.

INTRODUCTION

EVOLUTION OF THE FLOWERING PLANTS

Until well into the Cretaceous period (140 – 100 million years ago) the dominant land plants were the gymnosperms, a group of seed-bearing plants still represented today by about 650 species. These include the cycads, various conifers such as pines, cypresses and the giant redwoods (sequoias), and our own yellowwoods and cedars. The reproductive structures in the gymnosperms are cones in which the ovules, which later become the seed, are borne exposed on the surface of the cone scales at the time of pollination.

During this period of gymnosperm dominance the dinosaurs were abundant and roamed the southern continents which, at that time, were united into the supercontinent Gondwanaland. Suddenly (in geological terms) this scene changed: the dinosaurs became extinct, Gondwanaland split up into separate continents which drifted apart, and the gymnosperms were ousted by the angiosperms or flowering plants. Towards the end of the Cretaceous period the flowering plants underwent great expansion, and by the beginning of the Tertiary period (± 70 million years ago) they had become the dominant land plants they are today.

Flowering plants are seed plants, but are distinguished from the cone-bearing gymnosperms in that their ovules are enclosed in a usually roundish vessel known as an ovary. The ovary is part of the flower which, like a cone, is a short length of stem with modified leaves (sepals, petals, stamens, pistil) attached to it.

The flowering plant species of today, about 250 000 in number, are customarily divided into two main groups: the monocotyledons, which have a single embryo leaf (cotyledon) in the seed, and the dicotyledons (comprising most of the species), characterized by seeds with two embryo leaves.

FLOWERS AND THEIR FUNCTION

Although admired by man primarily for their beauty and diversity, flowers do, in fact, play an essential role in the survival of plant species. Most flowering plants depend upon external agents to carry pollen from male parts (stamens) in the flowers of one plant to the female part (pistil) of another plant.

The flowers of each species are adapted in shape, structure, colour and odour to the particular pollinating agents on which they depend, the most important being insects, birds and wind. Wind-pollinated flowers tend to be clustered in dense inflorescences, are small, dull-coloured and reduced, with an inconspicuous perianth (petals and sepals), and they lack nectar but produce abundant non-sticky and easily blown pollen. These adaptations are clearly shown by the grasses (Poaceae) which are mainly wind-pollinated; moreover, their slender erect stems (culms) sway in the slightest breeze, greatly assisting in the release of the pollen.

With the exception of the grasses and sedges (Cyperaceae), flowering plants are pollinated predominantly by insects, which are attracted by certain stimuli. Flower colour in particular signals, to birds as well as insects, the existence of a certain floral reward, usually pollen or nectar. With regard to colour it is important to note that the visual sense of the pollinator may be very different from our own. Insect colour vision has been studied by means of ingenious experiments, most of which have involved honey bees. Some of the results are mentioned in the introductory notes to each of the colour sections.

Even seasonal flowering patterns seem to be adaptations for optimizing pollinator activity. The majority of grassland herbs flower in spring, often after a fire. In the absence of tall grasses, visual floral attractants are much more easily seen by potential insect pollinators, whereas in summer, when most of the grass species are flowering, these flowers would have been less visible to the pollinator.

Daily flowering times also vary and may represent an adaptation for attracting specific pollinators or for lessening competition between species for the same pollinator. For example, flowers in species of *Kohoutia* (150, 151), *Silene* (62) and *Zaluzianskya* (168) open only at night, *Commelina* (633) during the morning, and others such as *Gynandriris simulans* (648.1) and *Talinum caffrum* (417) in the late afternoon. Differences in flowering time between species of the same genus may assist in the maintenance of specific identity by preventing possible hybridization. For example, *Aloe transvaalensis* (556) flowers in summer and the closely related *A. davyana* (554) in winter, *Anthericum cooperi* (106) opens in the morning and *A. trichophlebium* (110) in the late afternoon.

Very little is known about the pollination biology of our native flora and much useful work can still be done in this field by the patient and observant amateur. Brief notes on the significance of floral shape and colour have therefore been provided in the introduction to each colour section.

CLASSIFICATION OF PLANTS

Faced with the living world's rich diversity of plant and animal life – about 300 000 plant species and more than 1,5 million animal species – man has devised a system of classification by which this diversity can be organized. Systematic botany (also known as plant taxonomy) is the broad field concerned with the study of the diversity of plants, particularly their identification, naming, classification and evolution.

Many different kinds of classification are possible, depending to some extent on the choice of diagnostic characters employed, as well as the specific purpose of the classification. A character is any feature of an organism that can be measured, counted or otherwise assessed. In this field guide we use the so-called natural classification system which groups plants according to their overall similarity based mainly on morphological characters. Of considerable practical importance is this system's great predictive value: if one knows the outstanding features of a group, or of one member of a group of a natural classification, it is possible to predict what features are likely to be found in another member of the same group.

According to the natural classification system, plants are categorized into a hierarchical series of groups. The level at which a group stands in the hierarchy is known as its rank. Groups of any rank are known as taxa (singular taxon). The basic unit of classification is the species (abbreviated sp. when singular and spp. when plural), which is the rank customarily used by systematists to designate groups of plants that can be recognized as distinct kinds.

Species that are more like each other than like other species are grouped together in a genus. Similarly, genera are grouped into families, families into orders, orders into classes, classes into divisions, and divisions into kingdoms, the highest taxonomic rank.

Various subgroups are also used as necessary. Species may be divided into subspecies, subspecies into varieties, and varieties into forms. Variety (abbreviated var.) is a unit subordinate to the subspecies (abbreviated subsp.) when the latter category is used – otherwise it is subordinate to the species. These infraspecific categories are applied to populations of plants whose evolutionary development has not progressed to the extent of it being markedly and consistently distinct from its parent species. In other words, subspecies and varieties are recognizable morphological variations within species.

Plants are sometimes also classified according to artificial systems, which categorize them on the basis of only one or a few characters and have little or no predictive value. Such classifications are often designed to suit a special purpose, an example being the organization of plants in this field guide into six groups by the colour of their flowers. This particular system results in combining the identification benefits of an artificial system with the predictive value offered by the grouping together, within a colour group, of the species under their respective natural families.

THE SCIENTIFIC NAMES OF PLANTS

Scientific names are given to taxa so that they may be distinguished from each other and to allow for the effective communication, storage and retrieval of all information about a particular plant or group of plants. The part of systematic botany that deals with the giving of names to plants is known as nomenclature. Common names are often confusing since the same name may apply to two or more different species, or the same species may have more than one common name. Communicating in common names also presents difficulties because such a name usually applies in a specific language only. Scientific names, on the other hand, are recognized throughout the world. The scientific naming of plants is controlled by a series of rules laid down in the International Code of Botanical Nomenclature, the ultimate goal being to ensure that in any given classification a taxon can have only one correct name. A key principle underlying the provisions of the Code is that the nomenclature of a taxonomic group should be based upon priority of publication (in the case of seed plants the starting date is 1 May 1753).

A species name is made up of a combination of the generic name followed by a specific name (epithet), for example *Rhus lancea.* Once the full species name has been cited in a text, the generic name is often abbreviated to its initial letter in subsequent citations (e.g. *R. lancea*). Generic names are often based on the names of botanists or mythological figures. Specific epithets may honour or commemorate a person, or may be derived from a particular location, habitat, or a distinguishing feature of the species. The name of a subspecies or variety consists of the name of the species in which it is classified, followed by a word indicating its rank, then the subspecific or varietal epithet, for example *Crassula lanceolata* subsp. *transvaalensis*, *Cyperus obtusiflorus* var. *flavissimus* or, if both infraspecific ranks are employed, *Convolvulus sagittatus* subsp. *sagittatus* var. *phyllosepalus.*

From time to time reclassification of a plant may be required in the light of further knowledge. It may be necessary to transfer a species from one genus to another, or what has previously been considered a subspecies or variety may be given specific rank. Application of the principle of priority necessitates the displacement of a well-known specific epithet if an older published name is found. The names under which a particular plant was previously known are its synonyms and, as a considerable amount of information may be recorded in botanical literature under one or more of these names, the synonymy of a species is a key to information about it. Synonyms are often preceded by an equal sign and placed in brackets, for example [=*Rhamphicarpa tubulosa*] for *Cycnium tubulosum.* With the exception of some recent ones, very few synonyms are given in this field guide. For a more complete synonymy Gibbs Russell *et al.* (1985 and 1987) may be consulted.

Species names (or scientific names of other rank) are often followed by one or more personal names, sometimes abbreviated, for example *Erythrina lysistemon* Hutch., and *Commelina erecta* L. for John Hutchinson and Carolus Linnaeus respectively. These so-called authority citations refer to the name of the person, or persons, who formally described the plant (or proposed a particular combination) and they serve as a source of historical information regarding the name of the plant. A double author citation with some of the names in parenthesis signifies the transfer of a species from one genus to another. It is also used when a subspecies (or variety) of one author is recognized as a distinct species by another, but with retention of the original epithet. In these two cases the name of the describing author(s) (in parenthesis) is followed by that of the author(s) who made the change.

If the identity of a specimen is in doubt, the letters 'cf.' are used in the plant name, for example *Ruellia* cf. *patula*. The letters 'ined.' following a plant name signify that the name has not yet been validly published.

PLANT FAMILIES AND THEIR NAMES

Just as species are grouped into more inclusive units called genera, genera are grouped into still larger units called families. Although both reproductive and vegetative characters are used to delimit families, it is the flower that provides the most constant and convenient features for comparison. These include the fusion of petals, the number of stamens, the type of pistil, the position of the ovary, the number of carpels and ovules, the type of fruit, and the symmetry of the flower.

The flowering plants are divided into approximately 400 families. It should be noted, however, that the delimitation of some families varies considerably from one author to another. For example, some southern African taxa traditionally classified in the family Liliaceae are divided by certain modern authors among no less than eight families (the names in parenthesis refer to genera treated in this field guide):

Alliaceae (*Agapanthus*, *Nothoscordum*, *Tulbaghia*)
Anthericaceae (*Anthericum*, *Chlorophytum*, *Trachyandra*)
Asparagaceae (*Protasparagus*)
Asphodelaceae (*Aloe*, *Bulbine*, *Kniphofia*)
Colchicaceae (*Androcymbium*)
Dracaenaceae (*Sansevieria*)
Eriospermaceae (*Eriospermum*)
Hyacinthaceae (*Albuca*, *Dipcadi*, *Drimiopsis*, *Eucomis*, *Ledebouria*, *Ornithogalum*, *Schizobasis*, *Scilla*, *Urginea*)

For ease of field recognition we have accepted Alliaceae and combined the other seven families under Liliaceae.

Family names end in -aceae, with the exception of eight families whose names end in -ae. For the sake of consistency, the latter families have been given an alternative name with the -aceae ending. Although only the alternative names are used in this field guide, either usage is acceptable under the Code. These eight families and their alternative names are:

Compositae/Asteraceae
Cruciferae/Brassicaceae
Gramineae/Poaceae
Guttiferae/Clusiaceae
Labiatae/Lamiaceae
Leguminosae/Fabaceae
Palmae/Arecaceae
Umbelliferae/Apiaceae

PLANT IDENTIFICATION MADE EASIER

When plants are classified only characters that reflect differences in genetic constitution are significant. These include the so-called diagnostic characters which are used to differentiate between species or other groups. One of the secrets of identifying plants is being able to distinguish between genetic differences and those which result from variations in the environment. This ability can be developed only through careful observation and much experience.

The fact that plants are very much more variable within a species than are animals is one of the reasons why the layman often finds plant identification considerably more difficult than animal identification. Animal development is a very stable and reproducible phenomenon. In plants, however, even individuals of the same species that are growing next to each other may show considerable variation in leaf size, shape and hairiness, as well as in the number of branchlets, leaves, flowers, fruits or roots.

The value of knowing the family to which a plant belongs cannot be emphasized too strongly, and recognizing its family is usually the first essential step in the identification of the plant. Of about 135 flowering plant families represented in the field guide area, three (Poaceae, Asteraceae and Fabaceae) account for more than a third of the total number of species. The 20 most important families, representing more than 70 per cent of the species, are (ranked according to the number of species they contain): Poaceae, Asteraceae, Fabaceae, Cyperaceae, Liliaceae, Asclepiadaceae, Orchidaceae, Euphorbiaceae, Lamiaceae, Rubiaceae, Convolvulaceae, Scrophulariaceae, Acanthaceae, Malvaceae, Iridaceae, Solanaceae, Amaranthaceae, Polygonaceae, Brassicaceae and Tiliaceae.

In the family descriptions (pages 16 – 29) characters useful for the field identification of families are given in italics. Some easily recognizable characters and the families in which they predominate, or are more or less constant, are listed on the following page:

LEAVES OPPOSITE OR IN WHORLS

Acanthaceae, Aizoaceae, Apocynaceae, Asclepiadaceae, Asteraceae (infrequent), Buddlejaceae, Caryophyllaceae, Crassulaceae, Dipsacaceae, Elatinaceae, Gentianaceae, Hypericaceae, Illecebraceae, Lamiaceae, Linaceae, Loganiaceae, Loranthaceae, Lythraceae, Malpighiaceae, Melastomataceae, Mesembryanthemaceae, Molluginaceae, Nyctaginaceae, Oleaceae, Periplocaceae, Rubiaceae, Santalaceae, Scrophulariaceae, Viscaceae

LEAVES COMPOUND OR DEEPLY INCISED

Apiaceae, Araliaceae, Asteraceae, Bignoniaceae, Caesalpiniaceae, Capparaceae, Dipsacaceae, Fabaceae, Meliaceae, Mimosaceae, Passifloraceae, Ranunculaceae, Rosaceae, Rutaceae, Sterculiaceae, Verbenaceae, Vitaceae, Zygophyllaceae

LEAVES WITH STIPULES

Araliaceae, Caesalpiniaceae, Dichapetalaceae, Elatinaceae, Fabaceae, Linaceae, Malvaceae, Mimosaceae, Moraceae, Ochnaceae, Polygonaceae, Portulacaceae, Rhamnaceae, Rosaceae, Rubiaceae, Sterculiaceae, Tiliaceae, Zygophyllaceae

LEAVES WITH SECRETORY CAVITIES
(appearing as minute pellucid dots when viewed against the sun)

Fabaceae (infrequent), Myricaceae, Myrsinaceae, Myrtaceae, Rutaceae

STAMENS TRANSFORMED INTO POLLINIA
(flower without visible stamens)

Asclepiadaceae, Orchidaceae

STAMENS FEWER THAN 5

Acanthaceae, Aquifoliaceae, Cucurbitaceae, Cyperaceae, Dipsacaceae, Gesneriaceae, Iridaceae, Lamiaceae, Oleaceae, Poaceae, Proteaceae, Salicaceae, Scrophulariaceae, Selaginaceae, Ulmaceae, Verbenaceae

STAMENS NUMEROUS (more than 10)

Euphorbiaceae, Flacourtiaceae, Hypericaceae, Malvaceae, Mesembryanthemaceae, Mimosaceae, Myrtaceae, Ochnaceae, Papaveraceae, Ranunculaceae, Rosaceae, Sterculiaceae, Tiliaceae

PETALS ± UNITED

Acanthaceae, Apocynaceae, Asclepiadaceae, Asteraceae, Boraginaceae, Buddlejaceae, Campanulaceae, Convolvulaceae, Crassulaceae, Cucurbitaceae, Cuscutaceae, Dipsacaceae, Ebenaceae, Ehretiaceae, Ericaceae, Gentianaceae, Gesneriaceae, Lamiaceae, Lentibulariaceae, Lobeliaceae, Loganiaceae, Loranthaceae, Mimosaceae, Nyctaginaceae, Oleaceae, Pedaliaceae, Periplocaceae, Plantaginaceae, Plumbaginaceae, Proteaceae, Rubiaceae, Scrophulariaceae, Selaginaceae, Solanaceae, Thymelaeaceae, Verbenaceae

OVARY INFERIOR

Amaryllidaceae, Apiaceae, Araliaceae, Asteraceae, Combretaceae, Cucurbitaceae, Dipsacaceae, Gunneraceae, Hypoxidaceae, Iridaceae, Lobeliaceae, Loranthaceae, Melastomataceae, Myrtaceae, Onagraceae, Orchidaceae, Rubiaceae, Santalaceae, Velloziaceae, Viscaceae

PISTIL COMPRISING 2 OR MORE SEPARATE CARPELS WITH SEPARATE STYLES AND STIGMAS

Aponogetonaceae, Crassulaceae, Ranunculaceae, Rosaceae

MILKY OR WATERY LATEX PRESENT

Alismataceae, Apocynaceae, Asclepiadaceae, Asteraceae (uncommon), Campanulaceae, Euphorbiaceae, Lobeliaceae, Moraceae, Papaveraceae, Periplocaceae, Sapotaceae

THE FLORA OF THE FIELD GUIDE AREA

The flora of a region is the total number of plant species occurring within its boundaries. Species occurring naturally within a particular region (i.e. those not propagated or introduced accidentally by man) are referred to as indigenous or native. Naturalized plants are alien species which have become permanently established in a region, reproducing by seed or vegetative means.

On the basis of similarities in floristic composition, the flora of the world can be classified into six kingdoms, of which two concern us in southern Africa. The Cape Floristic Kingdom covers the smallest area and comprises the flora of the south-western Cape (more or less equivalent to the fynbos biome in Figure 2). Almost the whole of the remainder of Africa, including the area covered by this field guide, belongs to the Palaeotropic Kingdom.

The total number of flowering plant species and infraspecific taxa indigenous to or naturalized in the field guide area is estimated to be at least 2 000. Most naturalized aliens tend to be confined to disturbed places because they apparently cannot compete with the preadapted indigenous flora.

VEGETATION AND ITS CLASSIFICATION

Groups of individuals of the same species growing together are known as populations. Communities, on the other hand, are groups of individuals from different plant and animal species interacting in complex ways. The community and the non-living environment function together as an ecological system or ecosystem. The plant community is not merely a random aggregate of species, but an organized complex with a typical floristic composition and combination of growth forms, or structures. Every plant community is the result of a unique combination of certain environmental conditions and emanates from the interactions of species populations through time. These organized patterns allow plant communities to be classified.

All the plant communities together constitute the vegetation (often confused with the term 'flora') of a region. On a global scale the vegetation of any part of the world can be described as belonging to one of five units: forest, savanna (bushveld), grassland, desert and sclerophyllous shrub (fynbos). These broad groupings are determined by differences in climatic conditions prevailing over relatively large areas, with the result that the same kind of vegetation tends to recur in many parts of the world.

Employing as main attributes the dominant plant life form and climate (mainly rainfall seasonality, summer aridity and minimum winter temperature), Rutherford & Westfall (1986) delineated seven large vegetation units, called biomes, in southern Africa (Figure 2). These are (with percentage surface area of each given in parenthesis): the savanna (46,16%); Nama-Karoo (26,05%); grassland (16,52%); succulent Karoo (5,36%); fynbos (5,35%); desert (2,55%); and forest (0,01%) biomes.

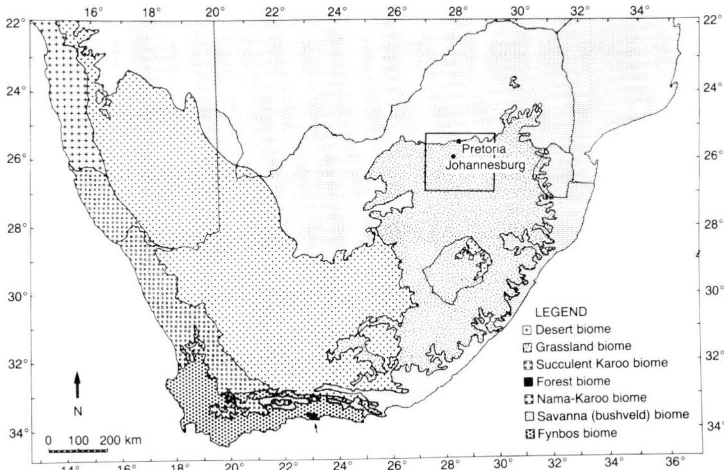

Figure 2. The biomes of southern Africa. The forest biome is represented by a single mappable unit in the Tsitsikamma area (arrowed) – most forest patches are too limited in extent to map at this scale (Rutherford & Westfall, 1986).

Biomes can often be divided into smaller, more homogeneous units (veld types) by introducing differences in floristic composition. Although the overall climatic conditions still play a major role, these smaller units often also reflect the mean annual rainfall and differences in the edaphic (soil) factors. Acocks (1953) broadly classified the southern African vegetation into 70 main veld types and a further 75 variations. After considering the agronomical potential of the veld, he defined a veld type as 'a unit of vegetation whose range of variation is small enough to permit the whole of it to have the same farming potentialities'.

Veld types can be further subdivided into a hierarchy of more specific plant communities. These often reflect very localized climatic conditions, the so-called microclimate. Other habitat conditions strongly associated with differences in plant communities include altitude, aspect, slope and rockiness of the soil surface, and soil depth, texture, structure, moisture and chemistry.

VEGETATION OF THE FIELD GUIDE AREA

The field guide area covers the transitional zone between two biomes (Figure 2): the savanna (bushveld) biome to the north and the grassland biome to the south, with the Magaliesberg roughly marking the interface between them. Several plant species are confined mainly to either one or the other of these two biomes, and this partly explains the rich diversity of species in the field guide area. The transition between the two biomes is fairly abrupt, although a narrow band south of the Magaliesberg contains a mixture of species and dominant life forms from both.

The transition matches several climatic and topographical changes roughly along a north – south gradient. These include a change from a high-altitude plateau with relatively high rainfall, temperate summers and very cold, frosty winters in the south to areas at lower altitude with lower rainfall, hot subtropical summers and mild winters in the north. Frost appears to be a major limiting factor for the southward migration of some of the more tropical elements in the savanna biome. On the other hand, the more temperate summers of the highveld account for the presence of outlier populations of a few high-altitude Drakensberg elements in the Witwatersrand and Suikerbosrand region.

The biome map of Rutherford & Westfall (1986) and the veld-type map of Acocks (1953) are used as the basis for this account (Figures 2 and 3). These two publications should be consulted for more detailed information.

Savanna biome

Savanna (known locally as bushveld) refers to a vegetation type consisting of scattered trees and shrubs and a continuous ground layer dominated by grasses. The effect is usually that of open parkland, although there is considerable variation in the density of the woody component. Bushveld trees are generally between 3 and 7 m tall, with a root system much older and more extensively developed than the aerial parts. This root system renders the woody component well adapted to the frequent periods of summer drought, whereas the generally deciduous habit of most species allows for a dormant period during the dry winter months.

Fire is important in regulating the density of the woody component, as bushveld protected from fire usually converts to dense thicket or an almost closed-canopy woodland. Much of the bushveld in the field guide area used to be much more open and grassy, but over the past century the decrease in regular burning in some areas has caused a considerable increase in, and thickening of, trees and bush, particularly on the flats between hills. In addition, overgrazing and trampling have led to a weakening of the grass cover and to local encroachment by woody and particularly spiny and unpalatable species. Bush encroachment is perhaps the most important veld management problem in the bushveld today. Complete removal of the woody component, however, would not necessarily increase the quality of the grass element. The presence of trees, with their deeper root systems, may actually be conducive to the productivity of the grass component, particularly through the transfer of plant nutrients from deeper soil layers to the more superficially located roots of the grass layer.

Invasive alien plants are less of a threat in the bushveld than they are in the grassland biome, although the syringa (*Melia azedarach*, 664) and various Australian wattles (*Acacia* spp.) do pose a problem, mainly along streams. In the bushveld the clearing of natural vegetation for cultivation is less marked than in the grassland areas, but cattle farming is practised on a large scale and often results in overgrazing. The recent upsurge in game farming may be to the advantage of the natural vegetation.

The four veld types distinguished by Acocks in the bushveld region covered by this field guide are: sour bushveld, turf thornveld, sourish mixed bushveld and mixed bushveld (Figure 3).

Sour bushveld is confined to the Magaliesberg and is an outlier of the vegetation of the Waterberg region in the central Transvaal. The soils on the north-facing slopes are generally sandy, acid, and poor in plant nutrients, whereas those on the southern side of the mountain are often better developed, less sandy and partly derived from shale. Some of the typical trees include *Acacia caffra* (388), *Bequaertiodendron magalismontanum* (426), *Protea caffra* (587), *Ochna pulchra* (400), *Strychnos pungens* (776), *Faurea saligna* (418), *Mimusops zeyheri* (161) and several species of *Combretum* and *Ficus*. Two attractive succulents, *Frithia pulchra* (566) and *Aloe peglerae* (357), are largely confined to the Magaliesberg. Of particular interest are the traces of relict forest in some of the sheltered kloofs. Forest elements include such species as *Calodendrum capense* (592), *Halleria lucida* (726), *Pittosporum viridiflorum* (415) and *Ilex mitis* (21). From a pasture point of view the grass component is referred to as 'sour', the grasses being tall, wiry and tufted, rapidly losing their nutritive value after flowering and becoming fibrous, hard and unpalatable during the dry season.

Turf thornveld is found in a narrow ± east – west belt surrounding the range of low norite hills on the flats just north of the Magaliesberg. The black turf soil, rich in clay and plant nutrients, supports a short, dense bushveld dominated by *Acacia* species. This is considered 'sweet' veld because the grasses are less hard and fibrous, and retain much of their nutritive value and palatability after flowering and through the dry season.

Sourish mixed bushveld covers the areas surrounding the previous two veld types and grades southwards into the grassland biome. The soils are heterogeneous, resulting in a mosaic of different plant communities, although *Acacia caffra* (388) is common in most of them. Sandy soil supports sourish grassland and many tree species, including *Burkea africana* (57), *Peltophorum africanum* (280) and various *Combretum* species. Lower-lying areas with soils richer in plant nutrients and clay are characterized by 'sweeter' grassland and *Acacia* species, particularly *A. karroo* (391).

Mixed bushveld replaces sourish mixed bushveld in areas where the rainfall is lower (about 500 mm per annum in parts). The northern boundary of the field guide area lies on the transition between these two veld types. The tree composition is rather mixed, with species of *Acacia* and *Combretum* prominent, but many others, such as *Peltophorum africanum* (280), also occurring. *Combretum apiculatum* (754) may become locally dominant and bush encroachment by *Acacia tortilis* subsp. *heteracantha* and *Dichrostachys cinerea* (395 and 568) is common. Many of the grasses are sweet.

Grassland biome

Over much of that part of the high central plateau known as the Transvaal Highveld the natural climax vegetation is grassland. The area's relatively high summer rainfall (up to an average of between 700 and 800 mm per annum), and winters characterized by drought, severe night frost and marked diurnal temperature variations are unfavourable to tree growth, and even most of the grasses and other herbs in the grassland die back during winter. A striking feature of many flowering plants in this biome is their perennial underground storage organs. These include bulbs, tubers and rhizomes (rootstocks), and they enable the plants to survive fire, spells of summer drought and the cold, arid winters.

Grassland soils are varied and usually conform closely to the underlying geological structure. Differences in plant communities can thus be linked especially to variations in the substrate. For example, coarse, sandy loams or sandy clay loams derived from the sedimentary Witwatersrand Supergroup are nutrient-poor and support sourish grassland. This has good grazing potential at the start of the growing season, but loses its nutritive value after flowering and becomes unpalatable during the dry season. In contrast, soils derived from the volcanic Ventersdorp Supergroup have a sandy clay or sandy clay loam texture and are rich in plant nutrients. Grass on these soils is highly palatable, even after flowering and through winter, but is prone to being overgrazed and trampled.

Fire and grazing play a major role in the grassland biome, with complete protection from both resulting in deterioration of the veld. Lack of fire, for example, is to the detriment of many bulbous plants, which are easily smothered by the accumulation of old grass remains. Excessive burning and selective grazing, on the other hand, can have a profound effect on the species composition of the various grass communities, often upsetting the balance between sweet and sour grasses.

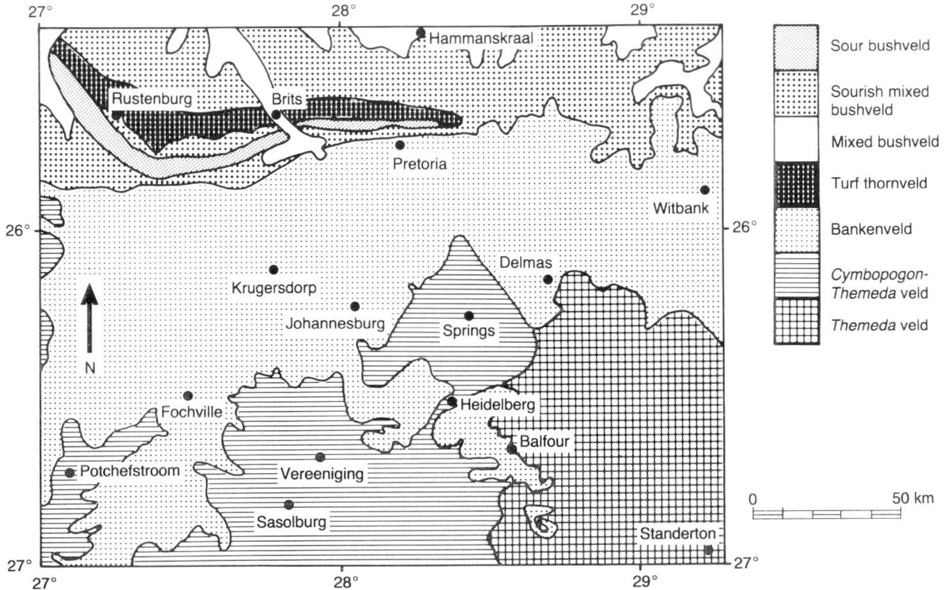

Figure 3. Veld types in the field guide area (Acocks, 1953, with slight modifications).

Much of our grassland suffers heavily from overutilization, large areas having been destroyed for the cultivation of crops, particularly maize, and for the development of extensive urban areas. The highveld landscape has also been drastically changed by the presence of alien trees, particularly species of *Eucalyptus* (136 and 570) which have been widely planted for shade and shelter. Invasive woody aliens are a major threat in open grassland, and particularly along streams. The main invaders are the black wattle (*Acacia mearnsii*, 392) and silver wattle (*A. dealbata*, 389).

The three grass-dominated veld types distinguished by Acocks in the field guide area are: Bankenveld, *Themeda* veld and *Cymbopogon-Themeda* veld (Figure 3).

Bankenveld, the largest veld type in the field guide area, lies on the transition between bushveld and grassland, and is thus fairly rich in woody plants, including bushveld elements. Most of the woody plants grow in rocky places, particularly on hillsides and in sheltered ravines, where a sparser grass layer offers less competition to their seedlings and decreases the destructive effects of fires. The microclimatic conditions prevailing on the north-facing slopes of hills are also responsible for bushveld elements penetrating quite far south into the Bankenveld. Some of the most prominent trees are *Acacia caffra* (388), *A. karroo* (391), *Protea caffra* (587), *Celtis africana* (805), *Cussonia paniculata* (748), *Euclea crispa* (81), *Diospyros lycioides* (298) and species of *Rhus*.

The soils are generally poor and sour, resulting in grassland that is of low grazing potential in winter (sourveld). The veld is particularly rich in non-grassy herbs, which contribute considerably to the wealth of plant species in this veld type. Selective grazing, trampling and the incorrect use of fire have led to a deterioration of most of the Bankenveld. Fire is an extremely important factor in this veld and many of the non-grassy herbs cannot survive for long in its absence. Late winter seems to be the best time for burning. Much of the central Bankenveld has been given over to urban development and cultivation. The area has also been encroached on by plantations of wattles – mainly *Acacia mearnsii* (392) and *A. dealbata* (389) – and naturalized aliens abound in disturbed places.

Themeda veld, also known as turf highveld, covers the south-eastern parts of the field guide area. A beautiful, very dense grassland strongly dominated by *Themeda triandra* (859), it is associated with black turf soil and dry frosty winters. Rainfall varies between 650 and 750 mm per annum. There are hardly any trees in this veld type. Fire is important and the way it is used may significantly change the species composition of the veld. The *Themeda* veld is devoted to the large-scale cultivation of maize and most of the natural vegetation has been destroyed. From the point of view of conservation, it is very sad that no significant part of this veld type, perhaps the most attractive of all our grasslands, has yet been permanently protected.

Cymbopogon-Themeda veld covers the drier southern parts of the field guide area, where the rainfall ranges between 500 and 700 mm per annum, and the winters are very cold. The soil tends to be sandy and the grasses, which are less sour than those of the Bankenveld, include *Themeda triandra* (859) and *Cymbopogon plurinodes* (852), the scattered clumps of the latter being particularly characteristic of this veld type. It merges into the Bankenveld and harbours a woody component very low in species diversity. Local encroachment of *Acacia karroo* (391) occurs, especially where the grass cover has been weakened by overgrazing. Some of the other more common trees include *Ziziphus mucronata* (793), *Rhus lancea* (740), *R. pyroides* (743), *Maytenus heterophylla* (63), *Ehretia rigida* (639) and *Diospyros lycioides* (298).

Where the soil is deep enough, most of the *Cymbopogon-Themeda* veld has been ploughed up for cultivation, and it is also used extensively for grazing for domestic stock. Fire seems to have a lower natural frequency in this area than in the previous two veld types, and invasive woody aliens do not pose a serious threat.

HOW TO USE THIS GUIDE

The flowering plants – except the grasses – have been grouped into six main colour sections. These groups are based on the general colour impression of the flower (or what the layman may take as the flower), the predominant coloration usually, but not always, being determined by the colour of the petals. In sorting flowers into colour groups, some problems may be caused by colour variation within a species, by the difficulty of faithfully reproducing some shades on film, and by differences in human colour interpretation. Cross references and alternatives have therefore been suggested under each colour section. However, most species can easily be referred to one of the following groups:

White or whitish flowers	Blue or blue-purple flowers
Yellow or cream flowers	Orange to brown or red-brown flowers
Pink to red or red-purple flowers	Green or greenish flowers

Within a colour section, the species have been grouped according to family. The families are arranged alphabetically, as are the species within each family. The grasses, which have a structure markedly different from that of other plants, are easy to recognize as a family and are treated in a separate section (page 310), where more specific instructions for identifying species are given.

Probably the most time-consuming way to identify a plant in flower is to page through the photographs, looking for one which resembles that particular plant. A quicker method is to use the guide to families at the beginning of each colour section. This guide is based on easily observed characters and narrows down by a process of elimination the families to which an unidentified plant may belong.

Using a good hand lens, examine the flower from the outside inwards, paying particular attention to the arrangement of parts (particularly the petals) and to their position of attachment. Count the floral parts if they are not numerous; note the shape of the foliage leaves and their arrangement on the stem; pick a leaf and check for the presence of milky latex oozing from the broken end of the stalk. With the aid of the contrasting statements in the guide, establish the few families to which the plant is most likely to belong, then compare the plant only with the illustrations under each of these families. Although the guide to the families is a good general reference, it does not cater for all possibilities. The best and quickest way to find the name of a plant is to learn to recognize on sight the principal plant families in the field guide area (see pages 9 and 10).

When a photograph that appears to represent the plant has been found, check carefully through the description to see whether the characters given correspond with those of the specimen. Pay particular attention to the diagnostic features printed in italics, and note the differences between closely related species. Also check the specimen against the family description (pages 16 – 29), since familial diagnostic features are usually not repeated under the individual species entries.

Leaf shape can be extremely variable, even on the same plant, and the leaf drawings supplied for many of the dicotyledons are no more than a rough guide. In some cases where the degree of variation is considerable, alternative possible leaf shapes have been depicted. For many of the Asteraceae the leaf drawn has been taken from the erect stem, not from the basal rosette. The rosette leaves usually tend to be larger and more distinctly stalked.

For ease of reference each species entry has been given a number which precedes the scientific name as accepted by the authors, and matches the number on the corresponding photograph(s) and leaf drawing. In several of the species descriptions, reference is made to closely related species, some of which have also been illustrated. Each of these species is identified by the same number as the species under which it occurs, followed by a full point and a digit (e.g. 648.1). An asterisk before the scientific name denotes a naturalized alien species. Some of the accepted scientific names are followed by a recent synonym in square brackets (see page 8). English and/or Afrikaans common names are given for the relatively few of our plants which have them.

Not intended to be complete, each species description details only those features deemed necessary for correct identification. Particularly significant diagnostic characters are italicized, and these in combination may help to distinguish between closely related species. Brief reference is made to habitat and geographical distribution within the field guide area, and a rough indication of the species' flowering time is given. Flowering behaviour generally varies from year to year and rainfall patterns can drastically influence the flowering period. Many plants – particularly the bulbous ones – flower for only a very brief period, mainly in spring. Although wild flowers can be found all year round, spring is generally the best season, with areas that have been burnt during winter providing the most colourful displays. Our seasonal concepts are very broad and intended as a general guide only:

Spring : August – November	Autumn : March – May
Summer : November – March	Winter : May – August

Important

Although most of the more common flowering plants of the field guide area are described, fewer than half of the approximately 2 000 indigenous and naturalized species are covered in this book. For the identification of plants not included in this guide, a regional Flora (see References and suggested reading) or a local herbarium which provides an identification service to the public may be helpful.

In the interests of plant conservation, please refrain from picking wild flowers or removing indigenous plants from the veld. Species legally protected under the Transvaal Nature Conservation Ordinance are indicated by ● in the index to scientific names.

FAMILY DESCRIPTIONS

ACANTHACEAE *Acanthus family*

Herbs. Leaves *opposite* from ± swollen nodes, without stipules. Inflorescence with often *large and leafy* bracts subtending individual flowers. Flowers *irregular*, 2-lipped. Petals 4 or 5, *united.* Stamens 2 or 4, attached to petals. Ovary superior, 2-chambered with *2 or more* ovules per chamber. Fruit an explosive, ± *club-shaped* capsule. Seeds often hairy, borne on small, hook-like outgrowths.

Includes flowers in the white, yellow and red colour groups.

AIZOACEAE *Brakbos family*

Herbs. Leaves alternate, opposite or whorled, with or without stipules. Flowers *small*, regular. Sepals with 4 or 5 lobes, ± persistent. Petals *absent* or small. Stamens 4 – 15, usually free. Ovary inferior or superior; styles often 2 or more, *free.* Fruit a capsule.

Includes flowers in the green colour group.

ALISMATACEAE *Water plantain family*

Aquatic or marsh herbs; milky latex present. Leaves basal; stalks *long and expanded* below to form an open sheath. Flowers regular. Sepals 3. Petals *3*, free. Stamens 3 to many. Ovary comprises 2 to many *free* carpels. Fruit a drupe, follicle or nutlet.

Includes flowers in the white colour group.

ALLIACEAE *Onion family*

Herbs with a bulb or bulb-like corm, rarely a rhizome, often with an onion smell (**Tulbaghia**). Leaves concentrated at the base, spirally set or rarely arranged in 2 ranks (**Agapanthus**). Inflorescence *umbel-like*, subtended by a whorl of 1, 2 or more membranous bracts. Flowers regular. Perianth segments 3 + 3, free or joined at the base. Stamens *6;* filaments often broad and flat, free or attached to the perianth tube. Ovary *superior.* Fruit a capsule. Seeds black.

Often included in Liliaceae (in a wide sense).

Includes flowers in the white, blue and orange colour groups.

AMARANTHACEAE *Amaranth family*

Herbs. Leaves alternate or opposite, without stipules. Flowers very *small*, regular, in *spike- or head-like* inflorescences, usually surrounded by *dry, chaffy, often spinescent* bracts. Sepals 5, free, ± *dry and membranous.* Petals *absent.* Stamens 5, *opposite* sepals; filaments *united at the base* into a short tube. Ovary superior, 1-chambered. Fruit dry, often opening by means of a lid. Seeds usually *shiny.*

Includes flowers in the white, red and green colour groups.

AMARYLLIDACEAE *Amaryllis family*

Lily-like *herbs; bulbous* or rarely rhizomatous (**Scadoxus**). Leaves mostly strap-shaped or broadly egg-shaped, generally arranged in 2 ranks, usually hairless. Flowers in *umbel* at top of leafless stalk, ± regular, subtended by 2 – 8 involucral bracts. Perianth segments 3 + 3, showy. Stamens *6.* Ovary *inferior*, often visible as a swelling at the base of a long perianth tube; 3-chambered. Fruit a capsule or fleshy berry. Seeds black.

Includes flowers in the yellow and red colour groups.

ANACARDIACEAE *Mango family*

Plants *woody*, often with *resin ducts*, particularly in the bark. Leaves alternate, *pinnately compound or trifoliolate*, without stipules. Flowers *small*, greenish or yellowish to white, regular, *unisexual* (although non-functional parts of other sex usually present). Petals 5, free. Stamens 5 or 10, free. Ovary superior, 1-chambered; styles 1 – 3, often *widely separated.* Fruit a drupe.

Includes flowers of the white, yellow and green colour groups.

APIACEAE/UMBELLIFERAE *Carrot family*

Plants *herbaceous*, rarely woody, often aromatic. Stems often with soft pith or hollow internodes. Leaves alternate, usually *much-divided*, *forming a sheath* at the base, without stipules. Inflorescence a simple or compound, flat-topped *umbel*, rarely in heads. Calyx greatly *reduced.* Petals 5, free, greenish, whitish or yellowish. Stamens 5, free. Ovary *inferior* with 2 *separate* styles. Fruit dry, dividing into 2 mericarps.

Includes flowers of the yellow and green colour groups.

APOCYNACEAE *Oleander family*

Plants *woody*, with *milky or watery latex*. Leaves *opposite* or whorled, without stipules. Flowers regular, often large and fragrant. Petals 5, *fused* into a tube, *twisted* in bud. Stamens 5, arising from the corolla tube; anthers often arrow-shaped, free or united. Ovary *1-chambered* or comprising *2 free* carpels often united by the style. Fruit large and fleshy, or dry and follicular. Seeds often plumed with *long silky hairs*.

Includes flowers of the white colour group.

APONOGETONACEAE *Cape pondweed family*

Freshwater *aquatic herbs* with a tuberous rhizome. Leaves *basal*, long and narrow, sometimes with a floating blade. Inflorescence a *forked spike*. Perianth segments 1 – 3. Stamens 6 or more. Fruit a follicle.

Includes flowers of the white and blue colour groups.

AQUIFOLIACEAE *Holly family*

Trees or *shrubs*. Leaves alternate, without stipules. Flowers regular, unisexual or bisexual; disc *absent*. Petals usually *4* and just united at the base. Stamens 4 or 5. Ovary superior. Fruit a drupe.

Includes flowers of the white colour group.

ARALIACEAE *Cabbage tree family*

Plants usually *woody*. Stems solid. Leaves alternate, usually large, *palmately or pinnately lobed or compound;* stipules *present*, often fused to the base of the leaf stalk. Inflorescence an *umbel*. Flowers regular, often greenish. Petals 5, free. Stamens 5 – 10. Ovary *inferior*. Fruit a berry or drupe.

Includes flowers of the green colour group.

ASCLEPIADACEAE *Milkweed family*

Herbs or shrublets, sometimes twining or succulent; *milky or watery latex* present. Leaves *opposite*, without stipules. Flowers regular, with a complex structure (see Figure 7, page 340), usually in *umbels*. Petals 5, *united*. Stamens ± *concealed;* filaments joined into a tube; anthers attached to the style, with pollen grains united into *waxy masses* (pollinia). *Corona* (crown-like appendages) *present* on the central column, which is made up of united stamens and carpels. Ovary comprising 2 carpels, *free* for much of their length; stigma *stalkless, disc-like*. Fruits inflated follicles, often in divergent pairs. Seeds with a coma of *silky hairs*.

Includes flowers of the white, yellow, red, orange and green colour groups.

ASTERACEAE/COMPOSITAE *Daisy family*

Herbs, rarely shrubs or trees. Leaves usually alternate, rarely opposite, often in a basal rosette, without stipules. Flowers crowded into *dense heads* subtended by an involucre of bracts arranged in 1 or more whorls, the whole resembling a single flower. Flowers of *2* types: strap-like (*ray flowers*), or ± tubular (*disc flowers*). Calyx (referred to as the 'pappus' in this family) modified into *scales, bristles, hairs*, or absent. Petals 5, *united*. Stamens 5, arising from and mostly included in the corolla tube; anthers *united* into a tube around the style; style *2-branched*. Ovary *inferior*. Fruit dry, often crowned with a *tuft of hairs* (pappus), rarely a drupe.

Based on the composition of the flower heads, 3 groups of species are recognized:

GROUP A ✳ Flower heads *radiate*, i.e. heads with central disc flowers and marginal ray flowers; ray flowers with the corolla strap-shaped, rounded or *3-toothed* at the tip. Plants rarely with milky latex. (See Figure 12, page 342.)

GROUP B ◎ Flower heads *discoid*, i.e. heads composed of disc flowers only. Plants without milky latex.

GROUP C ✹ Flower heads composed of *ray flowers only*. Corolla strap-shaped, typically *5-toothed* at the tip. Plants *with milky latex*.

The family includes flowers of the white, yellow, red, blue and orange colour groups.

BORAGINACEAE *Forget-me-not family*

Herbs or shrubs, often with *rough* hairs; stems round. Leaves *alternate*, without stipules. Flowers often in *coiled* inflorescences, *regular*. Petals 5, *united*. Stamens 5, arising from the corolla tube. Ovary 4-lobed, with 4 ovules; style often arising from *among the lobes*. Fruit comprises 4 nutlets.

See also Ehretiaceae.

Includes flowers of the white, red and blue colour groups.

BRASSICACEAE/CRUCIFERAE *Cabbage family*

Herbs, usually with sharp-tasting sap. Leaves alternate, often in a basal rosette, without stipules. Flowers regular. Petals *4*, *free;* often *stalked*, arranged in the *form of a cross*. Stamens 6: *4 long and 2 short*, free. Ovary superior, *stalkless*. Fruit a dry, 2-chambered capsule, either long and narrow or short and rounded, usually opening by means of 2 valves from below.

Includes flowers of the white and yellow colour groups.

BUDDLEJACEAE *Wild sage family*

Woody shrublets, shrubs or trees. Leaves *opposite or 3-whorled*, often united at the base by a stipular ridge. Flowers regular. Petals 4, *united* into a short tube which is often *bearded* in the throat. Stamens 4, free, arising from the throat of the corolla tube. Ovary superior. Fruit a capsule.

Includes flowers of the white and blue colour groups.

CAESALPINIACEAE *Bauhinia family*

Woody or ± herbaceous shrublets from a woody rootstock. Leaves alternate, *pinnately compound or deeply 2-lobed, with stipules*. Flowers ± *irregular*, often large and showy. Petals 5, *free*. Stamens 10, free. Ovary superior. Fruit a *pod*.

Includes flowers of the white and yellow colour groups.

CAMPANULACEAE *Bell flower family*

Herbs, usually with *milky latex*. Leaves alternate, without stipules. Flowers regular. Calyx tube usually fused to the ovary. Petals 5, *united*. Stamens 5, free from corolla; anthers free. Ovary *inferior*. Fruit a capsule, often crowned by the persistent calyx lobes.

Includes flowers of the white and blue colour groups.

CAPPARACEAE *Caper family*

Plants usually woody but sometimes herbaceous. Leaves alternate, simple or digitately compound, usually without stipules. Flowers regular or irregular (**Cleome**). Petals 4, *free*, often *stalked*. Stamens 4 to many. Ovary superior, *stalked;* style *short or absent*. Fruit a *long, narrow* capsule opening by means of 2 valves, or a berry.

Includes flowers of the white and red colour groups.

CARYOPHYLLACEAE *Carnation family*

Herbs with ± *swollen* nodes. Leaves opposite, each pair *joined* at the base around the node, usually without stipules. Flowers regular. Petals 5, *free*, tips often deeply cleft. Stamens 10, free. Ovary superior, 1-chambered, with numerous ovules; styles 5, *separate*. Fruit a capsule, opening by means of *teeth* at the tip.

Includes flowers of the white, red and orange colour groups.

CELASTRACEAE *Spike thorn family*

Plants *woody*. Leaves alternate or opposite; stipules minute. Flowers small, regular, white or greenish, with a fleshy, *nectar-secreting disc* surrounding the ovary. Petals 5, *free*. Stamens 5, free, *alternating* with the petals, arising from the margin of the disc. Ovary superior but partly sunken into the disc; style *short*, often 3-lobed. Fruit a capsule or drupe. Seeds often ± enclosed in a brightly coloured *aril*.

Includes flowers of the white and yellow colour groups.

CHRYSOBALANACEAE *Mobola plum family*

Plants *woody*. Leaves alternate, usually with 2 *glands* at base of blade or near end of stalk. Flowers regular or slightly irregular. Petals 5, free, arising from rim of *bell-shaped receptacle tube;* tube partially blocked by hairs. Stamens 6 – 10 or many, free, also *arising from rim* of receptacle tube. Ovary superior, *hairy*, often in *upper half* of receptacle tube below the mouth. Fruit a drupe.

Includes flowers of the yellow colour group.

COMBRETACEAE *Combretum family*

Plants *woody*. Leaves *opposite*, without stipules. Flowers small, regular, stalkless, with a *cup-shaped* receptacle tube, usually clustered in dense *heads or spikes*. Petals 4 or 5, *insignificant* and arising from the receptacle tube. Stamens 8 – 10, protruding; filaments bent inward in bud. Ovary *inferior* (easily mistaken for the flower stalk); style simple. Fruits *winged*.

Includes flowers of the green colour group.

COMMELINACEAE *Wandering Jew family*

Herbs with ± succulent stems and *swollen nodes*. Leaves alternate, with a *closed sheath* at the base enveloping the stem. Flowers regular or irregular, borne in *boat-shaped bracts* (spathes). Sepals 3, green. Petals *3*, blue or yellow, free or united into a tube at the base (**Cyanotis**). Stamens 6, all fertile or 3 or 4 sterile, often with *brightly coloured hairs* on filaments. Ovary superior, 3-chambered. Fruit a capsule.

Includes flowers of the yellow and blue colour groups.

CONVOLVULACEAE *Morning glory family*

Herbs, usually with long, trailing or twining stems; *milky latex* usually present. Leaves *alternate*, often lobed or ± heart-shaped, without stipules. Flowers *regular*, often subtended by 2 or more bracts. Petals 5, *united*, with distinct *midpetaline zones* (plaits), *twisted* in bud; corolla *funnel-shaped*. Stamens 5, inserted towards the base of the corolla tube. Fruit a ± 4-seeded capsule.

See also Cuscutaceae.

Includes flowers of the white, yellow, red and blue colour groups.

CRASSULACEAE *Crassula family*

Herbs or shrublets, usually *succulent*. Leaves opposite or alternate, often in a basal rosette, without stipules. Flowers regular. Petals 4 or 5, free or united. Stamens as many as or twice as many as the petals, free. Ovaries 4 or 5, *separate or slightly joined at the base only*, superior; nectar gland present at base of each ovary. Fruit usually comprising free follicles.

Includes flowers of the white, yellow, red, orange and green colour groups.

CUCURBITACEAE *Pumpkin family*

Herbs, with trailing stems, often climbing by means of spirally *coiled tendrils;* sap watery; often covered with rough hairs. Leaves alternate, usually *palmately veined*, without stipules. Flowers regular, unisexual, axillary. Petals 5, *united*, often yellow or orange. Stamens mostly 3, with anthers variously *cohering*, often curved or flexuous. Ovary *inferior;* stigma usually with 2 or 3 fleshy lobes. Fruit a large berry, with a hard or leathery wall, and sometimes spines or warts.

Includes flowers of the yellow and green colour groups.

CUSCUTACEAE *Dodder family*

Rootless, *twining* annual herbs *without* green colouring; *parasitic;* stems thread-like, attaching to the host by intrusive suckers (haustoria). Leaves *much reduced*, scale-like. Flowers small, regular, in dense heads or spike-like inflorescences. Stamens 5, attached to the corolla tube. Ovary superior, 2-chambered. Fruit a capsule.

Often included in Convolvulaceae.

Includes flowers of the white colour group.

CYPERACEAE *Sedge family*

Grass-like herbs, usually with a perennial rhizome and often growing in moist or wet places; stems often *3-angled*. Leaves often arranged in 3 ranks, grass-like, forming a sheath at the base; margins of sheath usually *fused*. Flowers small and inconspicuous, borne in the axils of conspicuous bracts which are arranged in *contracted spike- or head-like* inflorescences (spikelets). Fruit a small nut.

For comparison with Poaceae see Table 1, page 310.

Includes flowers of the white, yellow, orange and green colour groups.

DICHAPETALACEAE *Poison-leaf family*

Trees, shrubs, or shrublets with rhizomes. Leaves *alternate*, *with stipules*. Flowers regular; *disc* often comprises 5 free glands opposite petals; short *calyx tube present*. Petals 4 or 5, mostly *2-lobed*, free or united, arising from the calyx tube. Stamens 5. Ovary superior, with 2 or 3 chambers. Fruit a drupe.

Includes flowers of the green colour group.

DIPSACACEAE *Scabious family*

Herbs. Leaves opposite, mainly in a *basal rosette*, without stipules. Inflorescence a *dense involucrate head*, outer flowers often enlarged. Flowers ± irregular, somewhat 2-lipped, with a single *cup-shaped involucel* (epicalyx) below the calyx. Petals 4 or 5, *united*. Stamens 4, free, arising from the throat of the corolla tube. Ovary *inferior*. Fruit dry and indehiscent, enclosed in the epicalyx.

Includes flowers of the white colour group.

DROSERACEAE *Sundew family*

Small *herbs*, *insectivorous*, usually growing in moist places. Leaves usually in a basal *rosette*, covered with *sticky glandular hairs*. Flowers regular. Petals 5, *free*. Stamens 5, free. Ovary superior, with 1 chamber. Fruit a capsule, enclosed in the persistent calyx.

Includes flowers of the red colour group.

EBENACEAE *Ebony family*

Plants *woody*. Leaves usually alternate (in **Euclea** sometimes opposite), without stipules. Flowers *unisexual*, male and female on separate plants. Petals 3 – 8, *united*, often urn-shaped; lobes *twisted*. Stamens 3 to many; anthers *longer than* the short filaments. Ovary superior, borne on a smooth or fringed *disc*. Fruit a pulpy or fibrous berry.

Includes flowers of the white and yellow colour groups.

EHRETIACEAE *Puzzle-bush family*

Trees or shrubs. Leaves *alternate*, without stipules. Flowers *regular*. Calyx often *enlarged in fruit* and ± enclosing it. Petals 5, *united*. Stamens 5, arising from corolla tube. Ovary superior; style terminal. Fruit a drupe or berry.

Often included in Boraginaceae.

Includes flowers of the blue colour group.

ELATINACEAE *Waterwort family*

Herbs or shrublets, often aquatic or semi-aquatic. Leaves *opposite;* stipules *paired*, *interpetiolar*. Flowers usually small, regular, axillary. Petals 3 – 5, *free*. Stamens as many as or twice as many as the petals, free. Ovary *superior;* styles *3 – 5*, free. Fruit a capsule.

Includes flowers of the white colour group.

ERICACEAE *Heath family*

Woody *shrublets* or trees, often growing in acid soils. Leaves alternate, small and firm, without stipules. Flowers regular. Petals 5, *united* to form a short to conspicuous *corolla tube*. Stamens *10;* anthers opening by means of *pores*. Ovary superior. Fruit a capsule, berry or drupe.

Includes flowers of the red colour group.

EUPHORBIACEAE *Euphorbia family*

Plants herbaceous or woody, sometimes stem succulents; *milky latex* or *watery sap* present. Leaves *alternate*, with stipules. Flowers *unisexual*, regular, either borne in a modified *cup-like structure* (cyathium) or in a regular inflorescence. Sepals 5. Petals 5 (**Croton**, **Jatropha**) or absent. Ovary superior, *3-chambered* with a 3-lobed style. Fruit a capsule.

Includes flowers of the yellow, red and green colour groups.

FABACEAE/PAPILIONACEAE *Pea family*

Plants herbaceous or woody. Leaves alternate, simple or usually variously *compound*, *with stipules*. Flowers *irregular*. Corolla of 5 unequal petals, the upper one large and conspicuous (*standard*), the 2 side ones small and stalked (*wings*), the 2 basal ones united into a boat-shaped structure (*keel*) (see Figure 9, page 341). Stamens *10;* filaments free or usually *9 fused with 1 free*. Ovary superior. Fruit a *pod*.

Includes flowers of the white, yellow, red, blue and orange colour groups.

FLACOURTIACEAE *Wild peach family*

Plants *woody*. Leaves alternate, with stipules. Flowers *unisexual*, male and female on separate plants, regular. Sepals usually not clearly distinguishable from the petals, free. Petals 5, *free*. Stamens 8 – 10 or *more numerous*, free. Ovary superior, *1-chambered*. Fruit a berry or a capsule.

Includes flowers of the yellow and green colour groups.

GENTIANACEAE *Gentian family*

Herbs. Leaves *opposite* or in a basal rosette, often united at the base or connected by a transverse line. Flowers regular. Petals 4 or 5, *united*, often *twisted* in bud. Stamens as many as the petals and arising from them. Ovary superior, *1-chambered*. Fruit a capsule.

Includes flowers of the yellow and red colour groups.

GERANIACEAE *Pelargonium family*

Herbs or shrublets, often aromatic. Leaves alternate or in a basal rosette, often pinnately or palmately lobed, *with stipules*. Flowers slightly irregular or regular. Petals 5, *free*. Stamens 10 – 15, free or ± fused at the base. Ovary superior; style with 3 – 5 lobes. Fruit dry, carpels with *long persistent styles* splitting off elastically at the base of the central axis.

Includes flowers of the white and red colour groups.

GESNERIACEAE *African violet family*

Herbs of moist, usually shady places. Leaves opposite, often *basal*, without stipules. Flowers *irregular*, 2-lipped. Petals 5, *fused* into a basal tube. Stamens 4, 2 of which are *longer* than the others, attached to petals; anthers *coherent* (but not fused) in pairs. Ovary superior, *1-chambered*. Fruit a capsule with many seeds.

Includes flowers of the white colour group.

GUNNERACEAE *Gunnera family*

Herbs of moist places. Leaves alternate in a *basal rosette*, large and rounded, with *long stalks;* palmately veined; axil with a stipular scale. Inflorescence a *tall, erect spike*. Flowers *small*, unisexual, regular. Sepals 2 – 4. Petals ± absent. Stamens *2*. Ovary *inferior;* styles *2*, covered with glandular hairs. Fruit a small drupe.

Includes flowers of the green colour group.

HIPPOCRATEACEAE *Hippocratea family*

Shrublets, shrubs or trees. Leaves mostly opposite; stipules small or absent. Flowers regular, with a distinctive *nectar-secreting disc* surrounding the ovary. Petals 5, *free*. Stamens *3*, arising from *between the disc and ovary;* anthers often dehiscing *transversely*. Ovary superior but merges into the disc and appears ± inferior; style *very short*, 3-forked. Fruit a capsule or berry. Seed without an aril.

Includes flowers of the green colour group.

HYPERICACEAE *St. John's wort family*

Herbs or shrubs; hairs often *star-shaped;* sap *resinous*. Leaves *opposite*, *gland-dotted*, without stipules. Flowers mostly terminal, regular, *yellow or white*. Petals 5, *free*, *twisted* in bud. Stamens *numerous*, often *basally united* into bundles. Ovary superior. Fruit a capsule.

Often included in Clusiaceae/Guttiferae.

Includes flowers of the yellow colour group.

HYPOXIDACEAE *Star lily family*

Herbs with a *vertical tuberous rhizome*. Leaves basal, usually arranged in 3 ranks and hairy. Flowers regular, borne on an axillary, leafless, usually hairy stalk. Perianth segments 3 + 3, showy, *yellow or white*, often *green-backed*, *persistent*, *hairy* on the outer surface. Stamens 6, arising from the perianth; filaments *short*. Ovary *inferior*. Fruit a capsule, crowned by the remains of the perianth. Seeds black.

Includes flowers of the yellow colour group.

ICACINACEAE *White pear family*

Plants *woody*. Leaves *alternate*, without stipules. Flowers small, regular, white or greenish. Petals 5, *free*. Stamens 5; filaments often hairy. Ovary superior. Fruit a drupe.

Includes flowers of the white colour group.

ILLECEBRACEAE *Algerian tea family*

Herbs or rarely *shrublets*. Leaves *opposite*, often united at the base; stipules present, often *membranous*. Flowers small, regular, green or white. Sepals 4 or 5. Petals *absent*. Stamens same number as sepals and opposite them (1 or 2 in **Pollichia**). Ovary superior, 1-chambered. Fruit small, ± enclosed in the calyx.

Includes flowers of the white colour group.

IRIDACEAE *Iris family*

Herbs with *corms* or *rhizomes*. Stems often erect and leafy. Leaves *sword-shaped* and arranged in *2 ranks*. Flowers regular or *irregular*. Perianth showy with 3 + 3 segments, often united below into a tube. Stamens *3*. Ovary *inferior*, 3-chambered; style 3-lobed. Fruit a capsule.

Includes flowers of the white, yellow, red, blue and orange colour groups.

LAMIACEAE/LABIATAE *Mint family*

Herbs or *shrublets;* stems usually *4-angled*, especially when young; *aromatic*. Leaves *opposite*, each pair at right angles to the next, without stipules. Flowers *irregular*, 2-lipped or rarely bell-shaped. Petals 5, *united*. Stamens 2 – 4, attached to the corolla. Ovary deeply 4-lobed, the style arising from *between* the lobes. Fruit comprises 4 nutlets.

Includes flowers of the white, red, blue and orange colour groups.

LENTIBULARIACEAE *Bladderwort family*

Herbs of wet or damp places, mostly insectivorous. Leaves alternate or in rosettes, some modified into bladder- or bottle-like *pitchers* for catching insects. Flowers *irregular*, 2-lipped and *spurred*. Petals 5, *united*. Stamens 2, arising from the base of the corolla. Ovary superior, 1-chambered; stigma stalkless, 2-lobed. Fruit a many-seeded capsule.

Includes flowers of the white and blue colour groups.

LILIACEAE *Lily family*

Herbs or shrubs with *bulbs*, corms, rhizomes or thick fleshy roots. Leaves spirally set, mostly basal, often linear or sword-shaped, often succulent; small and reduced to scales or spines with green and needle-like stems (cladodes) in **Protasparagus**. Inflorescence variable but not umbel-like. Flowers regular or rarely irregular. Perianth segments 3 + 3, free or united. Stamens *6*. Ovary *superior*, 3-chambered. Fruit a capsule or a berry. Seeds black.

See also Alliaceae.

Includes flowers of the white, yellow, red, blue, orange and green colour groups.

LINACEAE *Flax family*

Plants herbaceous or woody. Leaves *opposite;* stipules present, often *gland-like*. Flowers regular. Petals 5, *free*, *twisted* in bud. Stamens the same number or twice as many as the petals; filaments *united* at the base. Ovary superior, usually with *5 free styles*. Fruit a capsule.

Includes flowers of the yellow colour group.

LOBELIACEAE *Lobelia family*

Herbs; milky latex often present. Leaves alternate, without stipules. Flowers *irregular*, often 2-lipped, inverted on their stalks through 180°. Petals 5, united or separate (**Cyphia**). Stamens 5; anthers *cohering* into a tube around the style. Ovary *inferior;* stigmas separate. Fruit a capsule, often crowned with the *persistent* calyx lobes.

Includes flowers of the white, red and blue colour groups.

LOGANIACEAE *Wild elder family*

Plants *woody*. Leaves *opposite or 3-whorled*, with stipules, often connected at the base by a stipular line. Flowers regular. Corolla *tubular*. Petals 4 or 5, *united*. Stamens 4 or 5, attached to the petals. Ovary superior. Fruit a capsule or berry.

Includes flowers of the white and green colour groups.

LORANTHACEAE *Showy mistletoe family*

Aerial *hemiparasitic shrubs* of other dicotyledons; branches brittle, often with swollen nodes. Leaves *opposite*, without stipules. Flowers ± *irregular*, usually large and brightly coloured. Calyx *reduced* to a low rim (calyculus). Corolla *tubular*, often split down the 1 side. Petals 5 (rarely 4), *united*. Stamens 5 (rarely 4), attached to the petals. Ovary *inferior*. Fruit a berry or drupe with an inner *sticky* layer.

Includes flowers of the white and red colour groups.

LYTHRACEAE *Pride-of-India family*

Plants herbaceous or woody, often in marshy or aquatic habitats. Leaves *opposite*, without stipules. Flowers regular; sepals *united into a calyx tube* (hypanthium), often with appendages between the lobes. Petals 4 – 8, arising from the calyx tube, usually *crumpled* in bud, wrinkled when expanded. Stamens twice the number of petals and arising at *different levels* below them, bent inward in bud. Ovary *superior*. Fruit a capsule, included in the persistent calyx tube.

Includes flowers of the red colour group.

MALPIGHIACEAE *Barbados cherry family*

Plants ± herbaceous or woody, usually twining *climbers*, often covered with *T-shaped hairs*. Leaves usually *opposite*, glands often present on either the leaf stalk or the lower surface of the blade; stipules present or absent. Flowers slightly irregular. Sepals 5, free, often with 2 glands on the outer surface. Petals 5, *free*, *stalked*, with fringed margins. Stamens *10*, free (**Triaspis**) or fused at base (**Sphedamnocarpus**). Ovary superior, 3-chambered, with *3 separate styles*. Fruit winged.

Includes flowers of the yellow and red colour groups.

MALVACEAE *Hibiscus family*

Herbs or shrubs, often covered with *star-shaped* hairs. Leaves alternate, often variously lobed, palmately veined, with stipules. Flowers regular. Calyx sometimes subtended by an *epicalyx* (lower calyx whorl). Petals 5, *free*. Stamens *numerous*, *united* into a tube around the style, joined to the petals at the base; anthers free, *with 1 chamber*. Ovary superior, with 5 or more chambers; style *branched* above. Fruit dry, breaking into segments, or a capsule.

Includes flowers of the white, yellow, red and orange colour groups.

MELASTOMATACEAE *Dissotis family*

Plants herbaceous or woody. Stems *4-angled*. Leaves *opposite*, often with 3 – 9 prominent *longitudinal* veins. Flowers ± irregular, showy. Calyx *tubular*. Petals 4 or 5, *free*. Stamens the same number or twice as many as the petals; anthers with *elongated* connectives and often sterile appendages, opening mostly by means of a *terminal pore*. Ovary *inferior*. Fruit a berry or capsule.

Includes flowers of the red colour group.

MELIACEAE *Mahogany family*

Plants *woody*. Leaves alternate, simple or mostly *pinnately compound*, without stipules. Flowers regular. Petals 5, *free*. Stamens 8 or 10, *united into a cylindrical tube* around the style. Ovary superior; stigma often *disc- or head-shaped*. Fruit a capsule or drupe.

Includes flowers of the white and blue colour groups.

MESEMBRYANTHEMACEAE *Vygie family*

Succulent herbs or shrublets. Leaves *opposite*, without stipules. Flowers regular. Calyx tube with 4 – 6 lobes, attached to the ovary. Petals *numerous*, *free*. Stamens *numerous*, free. Ovary *inferior*, usually 5-chambered; styles *absent;* stigmas ± same number as chambers. Fruit a many-seeded capsule, opening by means of valves.

Includes flowers of the white, yellow and red colour groups.

MIMOSACEAE *Thorn-tree family*

Plants *woody*, often armed with prickles or spines. Leaves alternate, *with* stipules, usually *bipinnately compound;* leaflets many. Flowers regular, small, in *tight clusters*. Petals 5, free or united into a short tube at base. Stamens *many*, long, *protruding and showy*. Ovary superior, 1-chambered. Fruit a *pod*.

Includes flowers of the yellow and red colour groups.

MOLLUGINACEAE *Carpetweed family*

Herbs. Leaves opposite, whorled or alternate, ± without stipules. Flowers *small*, regular. Sepals 5. Petals small, 3 – 5 or absent. Stamens 5 – 10, free. Ovary superior, with several chambers; styles same number as chambers. Fruit a capsule.

Includes flowers of the white colour group.

MORACEAE *Fig family*

Plants *woody*, with *milky latex* or watery sap. Leaves *alternate*, *with stipules*. Flowers tiny, unisexual, enclosed in a *hollow, vase-like receptacle* (a 'fig') or in dense heads or spikes. Fruit a small nut or drupe borne inside (e.g. fig) or outside (e.g. mulberry) the receptacle.

Includes flowers of the green colour group.

MYRICACEAE *Waxberry family*

Plants *woody*, often ± aromatic and dotted with *golden yellow* glandular hairs. Leaves alternate, without stipules. Flowers *unisexual*, male and female on same or separate plants, *stalkless* and borne in *spikes*. Perianth *absent*. Stamens with very short filaments. Ovary superior, 1-chambered, with a single ovule; stigmas *2*. Fruit often *rough* or warty and covered with a layer of wax.

Includes flowers of the green colour group.

MYROTHAMNACEAE *Resurrection plant family*

Woody *shrublets;* resinous. Leaves *opposite;* stalk sheathing at the base, forms a joint with the blade; *with stipules*. Flowers *unisexual*, male and female on separate plants, densely clustered in *erect spikes*. Calyx and corolla absent. Stamens usually 5, filaments united at the base. Ovary superior, 3-lobed with *3 free styles*. Fruit a capsule.

Includes flowers of the red colour group.

MYRSINACEAE *Myrsine family*

Plants *woody*. Leaves alternate, ± *gland-dotted*, without stipules. Flowers small, regular, borne in clusters. Petals 4 or 5, usually united towards the base. Stamens as many as and *opposite* the petals; filaments attached to the corolla. Ovary superior, 1-chambered. Fruit a berry or drupe.

Includes flowers of the white colour group.

MYRTACEAE *Guava family*

Trees and shrubs, most parts *gland-dotted*. Leaves alternate or opposite, without stipules. Flowers regular, usually with *showy* stamens. Petals 4 or 5, free, or united with calyx to form a *lid* (operculum) covering the flower in bud. Stamens *numerous, free*. Ovary *inferior*. Fruit a capsule or berry.

Includes flowers of the white and red colour groups.

NYCTAGINACEAE *'Four o'clock' family*

Plants herbaceous or woody. Leaves usually *opposite*, without stipules. Flowers regular, surrounded by *green or coloured bracts* which often resemble a calyx. Calyx tubular, *petal-like*. True petals absent. Stamens usually 5, rarely up to 30. Ovary superior, *1-chambered;* style long and slender. Fruit a nut, often enclosed in the persistent calyx tube.

Includes flowers of the yellow and red colour groups.

OCHNACEAE *Wild plane family*

Plants *woody*. Leaves alternate, often with *numerous side veins;* stipules present, often united and *occurring between the leaf stalk and the stem*. Flowers regular. Petals 5, *free*. Stamens *numerous*, free. Ovary superior, *deeply lobed* into 5 – 15 free segments united by a common style. Fruit comprises several drupes corresponding to the lobes of the ovary; borne on the enlarged and often red receptacle.

Includes flowers of the yellow and red colour groups.

OLACACEAE *Sourplum family*

Plants *woody*. Leaves alternate. Flowers regular, with a conspicuous *disc*. Calyx *small*. Petals 3 – 5, free or united. Stamens twice as many as and opposite the petals. Ovary superior or slightly sunken into the disc; stigma with 2 – 5 lobes. Fruit often a drupe.

Includes flowers of the green colour group.

OLEACEAE *Olive family*

Plants *woody*, rarely ± herbaceous shrublets. Leaves *opposite*, without stipules. Flowers regular. Petals 4, 5 or more, *united;* anthers ending in sharp points, with pollen chambers *back to back*. Stamens *2*, arising from the petals. Ovary superior. Fruit a drupe, berry or capsule.

Includes flowers of the white and yellow colour groups.

ONAGRACEAE *Evening primrose family*

Herbs. Leaves alternate or opposite, without stipules. Flowers regular. Petals *4*, *free*. Stamens *8*, free. Ovary *inferior*, 4-chambered; style *4-lobed*. Fruit a capsule.

Includes flowers of the white, yellow and red colour groups.

ORCHIDACEAE *Orchid family*

Herbs, often with rhizomes or corms. Leaves alternate, mostly basal, spirally set or in 2 ranks, with parallel veins. Flowers *irregular*, with a complex structure. Sepals 3, green or coloured. Petals 3, lower one forming a *lip*. Stamens *highly modified*, fused with style into a column; pollen *united* into waxy masses (pollinia) and *concealed* by an anther cap. Ovary *inferior*, 1-chambered. Fruit a capsule. Seeds minute, numerous.

Includes flowers of the white, yellow, blue and green colour groups.

OXALIDACEAE *Sorrel family*

Herbs. Leaves in a *basal rosette*, *palmately compound*, without stipules. Flowers regular. Petals 5, *free*, twisted in bud. Stamens 10: *5 long and 5 short;* united at base. Ovary superior, 5-chambered with *5 free styles*. Fruit a capsule.

Includes flowers of the yellow and red colour groups.

PAPAVERACEAE *Poppy family*

Herbs, often with *milky or yellow latex*. Leaves alternate, sometimes prickly, without stipules. Flowers regular, mostly *solitary* and showy. Sepals 2 or 3, often *falling quickly*. Petals 4 – 6, free, *crumpled* in bud. Stamens *numerous*, free. Ovary superior; style *absent;* stigma disc-shaped. Fruit a capsule, opening by pores or slits.

Includes flowers of the white and orange colour groups.

PASSIFLORACEAE *Granadilla family*

Herbs, shrublets, or *climbers* with axillary *tendrils*. Leaves alternate, usually *palmately lobed*, often with *glands* on stalk and blade, with stipules. Flowers regular, with a receptacle tube (hypanthium). Petals 5, *free*. *Corona* often present, comprising thread-like processes or scales. Stamens 5. Ovary superior, *1-chambered*, *stalked;* stigmas 3 – 5, free. Fruit berry-like.

Includes flowers of the yellow colour group.

PEDALIACEAE *Sesame family*

Herbs. Leaves *opposite*, often hairy and glandular (sticky), without stipules. Flowers *irregular*, weakly 2-lipped; *nectarial glands* present at base of stalk. Petals 5, *united*. Stamens *4 fertile* (2 shorter than the others) and *1 sterile*, arising from the corolla tube; anthers often *coherent in pairs*. Fruit a capsule or nut, often *2-horned* or with *spines*.

Includes flowers of the red colour group.

PERIPLOCACEAE *Khadi-root family*

Herbs, shrublets or twining climbers, with *milky latex* or watery sap. Leaves *opposite*, without stipules. Flowers regular. Petals 5, *united* into a short tube, *twisted* in bud. *Corona* of 5 entire or segmented lobes often present, arising from the corolla tube. Stamens 5, arising from the corolla tube; anthers usually *tapering in a narrow cone* above the stigma. Fruit comprises 2 follicles. Seed crowned with a tuft of *long silky hairs*.

Includes flowers of the yellow, blue and green colour groups.

PHYTOLACCACEAE *Pokeweed family*

Large, ± shrubby herbs or rarely trees. Leaves alternate, without stipules. Flowers small, regular, in terminal *spikes opposite leaves or in axils*. Sepals 4 or 5, *free*. Petals *absent*. Stamens 5 to numerous, borne on a disc. Ovary superior, comprising 4 – 12 *free or ± united* carpels; styles free, *as many as* the carpels. Fruit a berry.

Includes flowers of the yellow colour group.

PITTOSPORACEAE *Pittosporum family*

Plants *woody*, *resinous*. Leaves alternate. Flowers regular. Petals 5, *free*, with a ± *erect* basal portion and *reflexed* tips. Stamens 5, free; anthers opening by means of *pores*. Ovary superior; style simple. Fruit a capsule, opening by means of 2 valves. Seeds mostly covered with a *sticky pulp*.

Includes flowers of the yellow colour group.

PLANTAGINACEAE *Plantain family*

Herbs. Leaves alternate, clustered in a *basal rosette*, often forming a sheath at the base, *parallel-veined*, without stipules. Inflorescence stalk long, erect, leafless. Flowers small, regular, greenish or white, arranged in *dense spikes*. Petals 4, united, *papery*. Stamens 4, arising from the corolla tube; anthers *protruding* on long filaments. Ovary superior. Fruit a capsule, opening by means of a lid. Seeds often mucilaginous when wet.

Includes flowers of the white and green colour groups.

PLUMBAGINACEAE *Plumbago family*

Herbs or shrubs. Leaves alternate, often in a basal rosette, without stipules. Flowers regular. Sepals fused into a *cylindrical tube*, ribbed, often with *glandular hairs*. Petals 5, *fused* into a tube. Stamens 5, opposite and fused to the petals. Ovary superior, 1-chambered; style *divided* above into 5 branches. Fruit a nut, enclosed by the persistent calyx tube.

Includes flowers of the white colour group.

POACEAE/GRAMINEAE *Grass family*

Annual or perennial *herbs*, often with rhizomes and/or stolons; aerial stems, known as culms, generally terminate in an inflorescence; internodes ± circular and usually (in the field guide area) solid in cross-section. Leaves alternate, arranged in 2 ranks, stalkless; blade long and narrow, forming a *sheath at the base;* sheath usually *open* with the edges meeting or overlapping slightly; *ligule usually present* on upper surface at junction of lamina and sheath. Flowers small and inconspicuous, bisexual, unisexual or sterile; enclosed in 2 bracts and arranged with sterile bracts in spikelets which are the basic unit of the inflorescence. *Perianth reduced* and represented by 2 or rarely 3 microscopic scales (lodiculae) at the base of the ovary. Stamens *3;* filaments long and very slender; anthers elongate. Ovary superior, 1-chambered, with a single ovule; stigmas 2, *large and feathery*. Fruit dry, *indehiscent* (a caryopsis or 'grain'), often dispersed while still tightly enclosed in persistent bracts ('husk'). (See Figure 4, page 312 and Figure 14, page 343 for illustrations. For comparison with Cyperaceae see Table 1, page 310.)

POLYGALACEAE *Milkwort family*

Herbs or shrubs. Leaves alternate, without stipules. Flowers *irregular*. Sepals 5, *inner 2 wing-like and petal-like*. Petals ± reduced, 3 – 5, one often with a *brush-like* appendage. Stamens *8*, *united* into a tube (split above) and fused to the petals; anthers opening by means of *apical pores*. Ovary superior, *2-chambered*. Fruit usually a capsule. Seeds often covered with short hairs.

Includes flowers of the red and blue colour groups.

POLYGONACEAE *Buckwheat family*

Herbs or shrublets. Stems often with ± *swollen* nodes. Leaves alternate; stipules ± papery, forming a *tube* (ocrea) around the stem and above the node. Flowers small, regular. Sepals usually petal-like. Petals *absent*. Stamens 5 – 8, free. Ovary superior, 1-chambered; styles 2 – 4, *free*. Fruit a *lens-shaped or triangular* nut often enclosed by the persistent membranous sepals.

Includes flowers of the white, red and green colour groups.

PONTEDERIACEAE *Water hyacinth family*

Swamp or *aquatic herbs*. Stems mostly *spongy*. Leaves arranged in 2 ranks. Inflorescence a *terminal spike*, often subtended by a *spathe-like leaf*. Flowers ± *irregular*. Perianth segments 3 + 3. Stamens *6*. Ovary *superior*, 3-chambered. Fruit a capsule.

Includes flowers in the blue colour group.

PORTULACACEAE *Purslane family*

Herbs with *succulent* leaves. Leaves alternate or opposite, without stipules (**Talinum**) or with *papery or hairy* stipular appendages. Flowers regular. Sepals *2*. Petals 4 – 6, *free*. Stamens as many as and *opposite* the petals, free. Ovary superior or half inferior, *1-chambered;* style with 3 – 8 stigmatic lobes. Fruit a capsule, opening by means of valves or a lid.

Includes flowers of the yellow and red colour groups.

PROTEACEAE *Protea family*

Plants *woody*. Leaves alternate, leathery, without stipules. Flowers *irregular*, in heads, spikes or racemes, sometimes surrounded by showy bracts. Sepals 4, *petal-like*. Petals *absent* or reduced to scales. Stamens 4, *opposite* and *fused* to the sepals, often with only the anthers free or with *very short* filaments. Ovary superior with a *long* style. Fruit a nut, drupe or follicle.

Includes flowers of the white, yellow and red colour groups.

RANUNCULACEAE *Buttercup family*

Herbs or ± woody climbers. Leaves alternate or opposite, often in a basal rosette, *compound* with bases *forming a sheath*. Flowers regular, with the parts typically arranged in spirals along a rather *elongated or globular* receptacle. Sepals 5, often petal-like (petals then absent). Petals (if present) 5,

free, usually with a nectary-bearing stalk. Stamens *numerous*, free. Ovary comprising numerous *free* carpels, superior. Fruit a cluster of achenes, sometimes with plumed styles.
Includes flowers of the white, yellow and red colour groups.

RHAMNACEAE *Buffalo-thorn family*
Plants usually *woody*. Leaves alternate, *with stipules*. Flowers small, regular, usually white or greenish; *disc usually present*, nectar-secreting. Petals 5, free, often *small and reduced*. Stamens 5, *opposite to* and often embraced by the petals. Ovary superior, sometimes sunken into the disc, or inferior (**Helinus**). Fruit a drupe.
Includes flowers of the white and green colour groups.

ROSACEAE *Rose family*
Plants *woody*, rarely ± herbaceous. Leaves alternate, *with stipules*. Flowers regular, perianth and stamens *united at the base* into a cup (hypanthium). Petals 5, *free*. Stamens *numerous*, free. Ovary *inferior* or superior; carpels *free* or variously united; styles *free*. Fruit fleshy or dry.
Includes flowers of the yellow and red colour groups.

RUBIACEAE *Coffee family*
Plants herbaceous or woody. Leaves *opposite or whorled;* stipules *present, inserted between the leaf stalks* (interpetiolar), sometimes leaf-like and indistinguishable from the leaves. Flowers regular. Calyx fused to the ovary. Petals 4 or 5, united into a *tube;* mouth of the tube usually *hairy*. Stamens 4 or 5, arising from the corolla tube. Ovary *inferior*. Fruit a drupe, berry or capsule, *crowned with the persistent remains of the calyx lobes*.
Includes flowers of the white, yellow, red, blue and green colour groups.

RUTACEAE *Citrus family*
Plants usually *woody*, most parts *gland-dotted*, aromatic when crushed. Leaves alternate or opposite, without stipules. Flowers regular; *disc present* between stamens and ovary. Petals 4 or 5, *free*. Stamens 4 or 5, or up to 10. Ovary superior, with ± 4 or 5 lobes. Fruit a berry, drupe or capsule.
Includes flowers of the white and red colour groups.

SALICACEAE *Willow family*
Deciduous *trees or shrubs*. Leaves alternate, *with stipules*. Flowers small, clustered into *erect or pendulous spikes;* male and female on separate plants. Sepals and petals *absent*. Stamens 2 or more. Ovary superior, 1-chambered; stigmas usually *forked*. Fruit a capsule with 2 valves. Seeds with white *silky hairs*.
Includes flowers of the yellow and green colour groups.

SANTALACEAE *Sandalwood family*
Plants woody or ± herbaceous, usually *parasitic* (hemiparasites) on the roots of other plants. Leaves alternate or opposite, often bluish green, without stipules. Flowers *small*, regular, greenish or whitish. Sepals 3 – 6. Petals *absent*. Stamens 3 – 6, *opposite* the sepals. Ovary *inferior*, 1-chambered. Fruit a nut or drupe.
Includes flowers of the white and green colour groups.

SAPINDACEAE *Litchi family*
Trees, shrubs or climbers. Leaves *alternate*, usually compound, *without stipules*. Flowers regular, small, unisexual or bisexual, with a *disc outside the stamens* (not in **Dodonaea**). Sepals 2 – 7. Petals 3 – 5 or absent (**Dodonaea**). Stamens 4 – 8 or many, arising from the disc, often hairy. Ovary superior. Fruit a drupe or capsule, or a dry indehiscent fruit with wing-like outgrowths. Seeds often with arils.
Includes flowers of the green colour group.

SAPOTACEAE *Milkwood family*
Plants *woody; milky latex* present; young growth often with a *rusty or brownish* colour. Leaves *alternate*, without or with stipules (**Bequaertiodendron**). Flowers regular, white or cream, axillary or in *tufts on the older*, often leafless, branches. Corolla with 5 – 8 lobes, each lobe often with 2 petal-like appendages (**Mimusops**). Stamens 5 – 8, arising from and opposite the corolla lobes; filaments often *shorter* than the anthers. Fruit a berry. Seeds shiny with a broad scar.
Includes flowers of the white and yellow colour groups.

SCROPHULARIACEAE *Snapdragon family*

Herbs or rarely small trees. Leaves *opposite*, without stipules. Flowers *irregular*, often 2-lipped. Petals 4 or 5, *united*. Stamens 4, 2 of which are longer than the others, *attached* to petals. Ovary superior, 2-chambered. Fruit a *many-seeded* capsule.

Includes flowers of the white, yellow, red, blue and orange colour groups.

SELAGINACEAE *Selago family*

Herbs or shrublets. Leaves alternate, usually *narrow* and often in tufts, without stipules. Flowers *irregular*, sometimes 2-lipped. Petals 4 or 5, *united*. Stamens often *4*, attached to the corolla tube; anthers *1-chambered*. Ovary superior, with 2 chambers, 1 of which is often sterile. Fruit indehiscent, often separating into 2 nutlets, each containing 1 seed.

Includes flowers of the white, yellow, blue and orange colour groups.

SOLANACEAE *Tomato family*

Herbs, shrubs or small trees. Leaves *alternate*, often with a strong scent when crushed, without stipules. Flowers *regular*. Petals 5, *united*. Stamens *5*, arising from the corolla tube; anthers usually coherent but not fused. Ovary superior. Fruit a *many-seeded* berry or prickly capsule.

Includes flowers of the white, yellow and blue colour groups.

STERCULIACEAE *Cacao family*

Plants herbaceous or woody. Leaves alternate, with *star-shaped* hairs, often palmately lobed, *with stipules*. Flowers regular. Petals 5, *free*, *twisted* in bud. Stamens 5 and opposite petals, or up to 15, free or united into a short tube. Staminodes sometimes present. Ovary superior, with 1 – 5 chambers. Fruit a capsule.

Includes flowers of the white, yellow, red, blue and orange colour groups.

THYMELAEACEAE *Fibre-bark family*

Woody or ± woody shrublets, shrubs or small trees, often with a *tough fibrous* bark. Leaves alternate or opposite, without stipules. Flowers regular, *long and tubular*, often in dense heads. Sepals 4 or 5, *petal-like*. Petals small and *scale-like*, arising from the mouth between the calyx lobes; sometimes absent. Stamens 8 – 10, arising from the tube and *opposite* the calyx lobes; anthers often longer than filaments. Fruit 1-seeded, dry, remains closed.

Includes flowers of the yellow, red and orange colour groups.

TILIACEAE *Linden family*

Plants woody, rarely with herbaceous annual stems from a woody base, often with *star-shaped* hairs and fibrous bark. Leaves *alternate*, in *2 ranks*; usually *asymmetrical, with stipules*. Flowers regular. Petals 5, *free*, often with a glandular appendage at the base. Stamens *numerous*, free, often borne on a short column; anthers 2-chambered. Ovary superior. Fruit a drupe or capsule.

Includes flowers of the yellow and red colour groups.

TURNERACEAE *Turnera family*

Herbs or shrubs. Leaves alternate, without stipules; blade often with *nectar glands* at the base. Flowers *regular*. Petals 5, *free*, *stalked*, and twisted in bud. Stamens 5, free. Ovary superior, with *1 chamber;* styles *3*, slender. Fruit a capsule with 3 valves.

Includes flowers of the yellow colour group.

TYPHACEAE *Cat-tail family*

Herbs with creeping rhizomes; growing in *fresh water or marshes*. Leaves mostly basal, arranged in 2 ranks, long, linear, with a *flattened* blade. Flowers unisexual, *very numerous* in a very dense, *long, cylindrical spike;* male flowers in the upper and female flowers in the lower part. Perianth *reduced* to bristles or scales. Stamens 3. Ovary superior, on a *short stalk*. Fruits covered with silky hairs.

Includes flowers of the orange colour group.

ULMACEAE *Elm family*

Plants *woody*. Leaves alternate, base often with *unequal sides, with stipules*. Flowers often unisexual, regular. Sepals 4 – 8, free. Petals *absent*. Stamens same number as the sepals and *opposite* them. Ovary with 1 or 2 chambers; styles 2, *divergent*. Fruit dry or with a thin fleshy layer.

Includes flowers of the green colour group.

URTICACEAE *Nettle family*

Plants herbaceous or woody, often with *coarse or stinging* hairs; sap *watery;* bark *tough and fibrous.* Leaves alternate, rarely opposite, *with stipules.* Flowers very small, regular, greenish, *unisexual.* Calyx with 4 or 5 lobes. Petals *absent.* Stamens same number as and *opposite* the calyx lobes; filaments bent inward in bud. Ovary superior, 1-chambered. Fruit a dry nutlet or a drupe.

Includes flowers of the yellow and green colour groups.

VAHLIACEAE *Vahlia family*

Herbs or small shrublets. Leaves *opposite*, without stipules. Flowers regular, in *axillary pairs.* Calyx tube *cup-shaped*, fused to the ovary. Petals 5, *free.* Stamens 5, arising from the margin of a disc; filaments free. Ovary *inferior*, 1-chambered; styles *2, free.* Fruit a many-seeded capsule.

Includes flowers of the yellow colour group.

VELLOZIACEAE *Blackstick lily family*

Plants with fibrous, often erect stems covered with *persistent leaf sheaths.* Leaves linear, spirally set, *crowded* at the ends of stems, fibrous, forming a sheath around the stem. Flowers regular, showy. Perianth segments 3 + 3, free or basally united. Stamens *6.* Ovary *inferior*, 3-chambered. Fruit a capsule. Seed reddish brown.

Includes flowers of the white, red and blue colour groups.

VERBENACEAE *Verbena family*

Herbs, shrubs or trees. Stems often *4-angled.* Leaves *opposite*, often strongly scented, without stipules. Flowers ± *irregular*, frequently ± 2-lipped. Petals 5, *united.* Stamens *4*, arising from the corolla. Ovary superior, usually 4-chambered, each chamber containing *1* ovule. Fruit a drupe or berry, rarely 4 nutlets.

Includes flowers of the white, yellow, red, blue and orange colour groups.

VISCACEAE *Mistletoe family*

Shrubby *aerial hemiparasites* of other dicotyledons, often with swollen nodes, brittle. Leaves opposite, leathery, without stipules. Male and female flowers on the same or different plants. Flowers *minute*, regular, *unisexual;* greenish or yellowish. Sepals 2 – 4. Petals *absent.* Stamens as many as and *opposite* the sepals. Ovary *inferior*, 1-chambered. Fruit a 1-seeded berry with an inner sticky layer.

Includes flowers of the green colour group.

VITACEAE *Grape family*

Climbing shrubs or woody *vines* with *tendrils opposite the leaves*, often watery sap and ± swollen nodes. Leaves alternate, usually *palmately* compound, without stipules. Inflorescences *opposite the leaves.* Flowers small, regular, greenish; *disc present.* Petals 4 – 6, free or often ± united at the tips and falling as the bud opens. Stamens 4 – 6, free, *opposite* the petals. Ovary superior, *embedded* in the disc; style short. Fruit a berry.

Includes flowers of the yellow colour group.

XYRIDACEAE *Yellow-eyed grass family*

Herbs of moist or marshy places; rhizome usually swollen, short, thick and ± vertical. Leaves linear, basal, often in *2 ranks*, forming a sheath at the base. Flowers small, subtended by *overlapping papery bracts* and clustered in heads on a stiff, erect, unbranched shoot. Sepals 3. Petals *3*, free, *stalked*, *yellow*, fragile. Stamens 3, opposite and fused to petals. Ovary superior, usually 3-chambered. Fruit a capsule.

Includes flowers of the yellow colour group.

ZYGOPHYLLACEAE *Devil-thorn family*

Plants usually *herbaceous*, branches often jointed at the nodes. Leaves *opposite*, *with stipules*, pinnately compound. Flowers regular; disc usually present. Petals 5, *free.* Stamens 5, 10 or 15, with *scale-like appendages* at the base of the filament. Ovary superior, *5-chambered;* style 1. Fruit a capsule or divided into segments (cocci) which do not open.

Includes flowers of the yellow colour group.

WHITE OR WHITISH FLOWERS

(See also **186, 188, 193, 194, 206, 282, 286, 352, 398, 414, 418, 424, 448 – 450, 458, 464, 475, 480, 493, 506, 564, 571, 591, 611, 617, 629, 651, 676, 680, 692, 719, 722, 746, 758, 775, 784, 785**)

This section contains the pure white flowers as well as those which give the impression of being white. Some pale cream flowers appear almost white in bright sunlight and are included here. Also included are whitish flowers which have a greenish or pinkish tinge, and the many white flowers which have conspicuous nectar guides in the form of yellow centres and pink or purple stripes and spots. Some flowers that may be considered whitish are also given in the section for Green or greenish flowers (page 284).

White coloration in flowers is due mainly to multiple reflections of light by air spaces between colourless cells in the petals. It is a physical phenomenon (comparable to foaming water or snow) and no white pigments are involved. Many white flowers, however, contain a variety of flavonoid (yellowish) pigments which, to the human eye, may impart an ivory or cream coloration to the flower. These pigments absorb ultraviolet light which, although not perceptible to the human eye, is clearly visible to insects. To insects white flowers might, for example, appear blue-green or yellow. White petals with a uniform reflection of light throughout the visible and near-ultraviolet spectrum have seldom been found. This suggests that in the eyes of an insect white-coloured flowers are probably extremely rare.

White flowers are visited by a large variety of insects, especially bees and moths, but also flies, butterflies and beetles. Regular white flowers with an exposed disc are often fly-pollinated (**64**). Flowers pollinated by hawk moths (**19, 28, 118, 132, 149, 150, 151, 162, 168**) are almost always whitish (sometimes with a yellow or pink tinge) and have abundant nectar in long, narrow tubes. They lack nectar guides, emit a sweet, heavy scent at night and often close during the day. Members of the Cyperaceae, which have small, inconspicuous flowers, are wind-pollinated.

GUIDE TO THE FAMILIES WHICH INCLUDE WHITE OR WHITISH FLOWERS

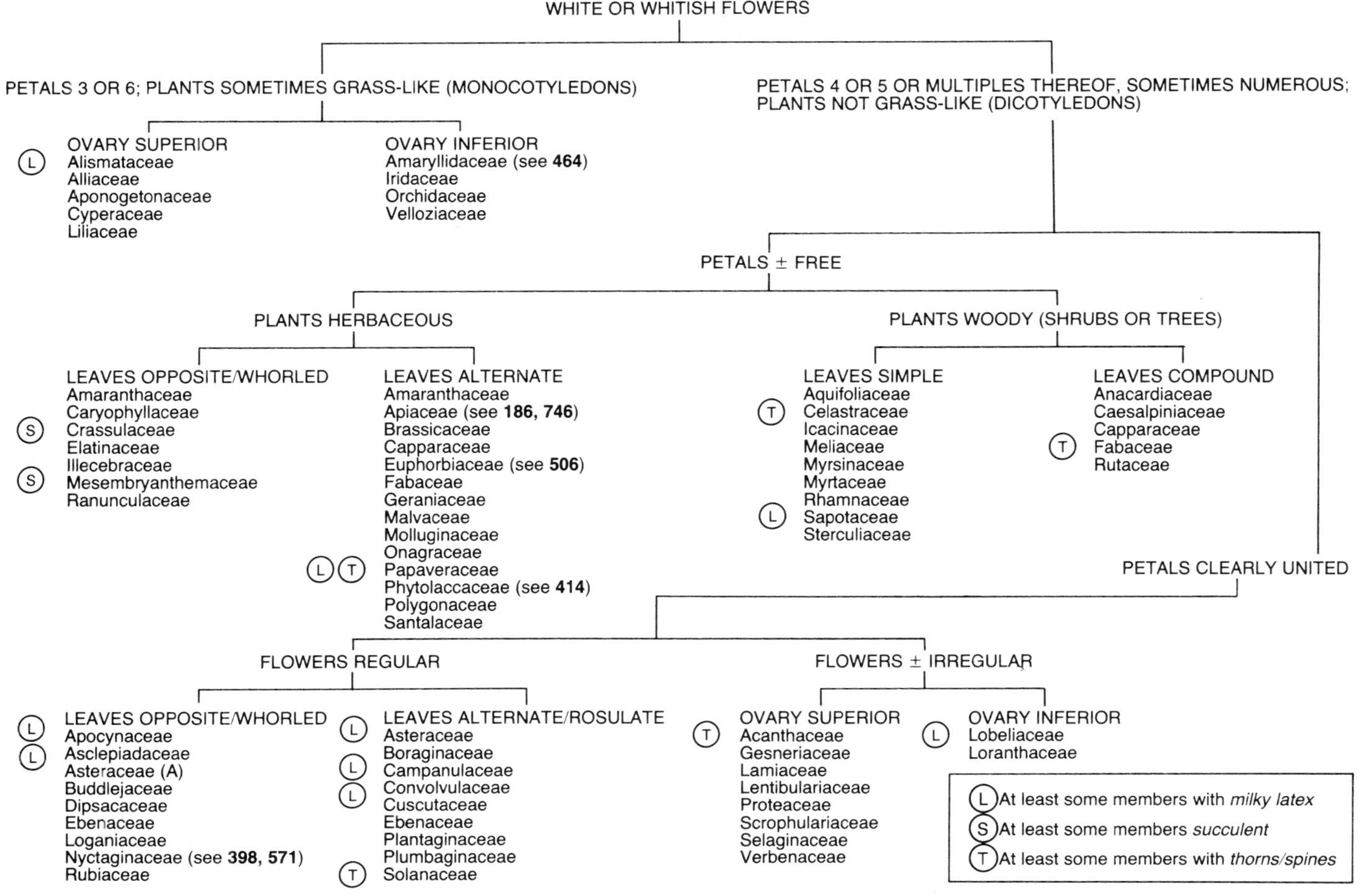

ACANTHACEAE (See page 16) See also **611**.

1 Barleria pretoriensis C.B.Cl.
Perennial shrublet with slender, ± erect stems from a woody rootstock; ± *hairless*. Leaves narrow, elliptic or lance-shaped, 30 – 60 mm long. Flowers *solitary* in axils of upper leaves, white, *turning mauve* with age. Seeds hairy.
Bushveld, on rocky hillsides. Mainly Pretoria/Magaliesberg region. Summer.

2 Chaetacanthus costatus Nees
Tufted perennial herb from a woody rootstock; shoots numerous, erect, with few branches; *sparsely covered with fine hairs*. Leaves stalkless or on short stalks, ± *narrow, elliptic*. Flowers axillary; ± *erect;* calyx lobes *narrow and fine-pointed*, about *as long as* corolla tube; corolla weakly 2-lipped, white, often tinged with pale purple.
Grassland, often in rocky places. Widespread. Spring – summer.

3 Chaetacanthus cf. **setiger** (Pers.) Lindl. (probably an undescribed species)
Perennial herb with several erect stems from a woody rootstock; *densely covered with hairs* and often ± *sticky* due to glandular hairs. Leaves on short stalks, *broadly oval to rounded*, soft-textured. Flowers in axils of upper leaves.
Grassland, often in rocky places. Mainly Pretoria/Magaliesberg region. Spring – summer.

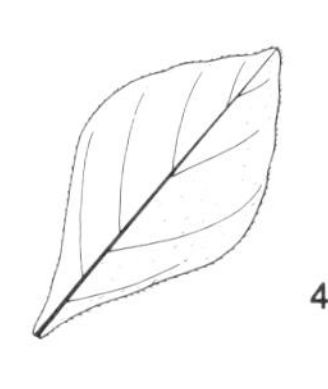

4 Crabbea acaulis N.E.Br.
Dwarf stemless herb with leaves in a *basal rosette*. Leaves *oval, flat on ground*, ± hairy. Inflorescences 1 or 2, compact, borne *in middle of leaf rosette;* bracts long and pointed, with soft, often recurved marginal spines. Flowers funnel-shaped; corolla ± 2-lipped, cream or lilac with yellow markings.
Grassland. Witwatersrand/Suikerbosrand region. Summer.

5 Crabbea hirsuta Harv.
Perennial herb with *trailing* stems; roots swollen; *hairy throughout*. Leaves stalkless, egg- to strap-shaped. Flowers borne in dense clusters amongst large bracts; bracts covered with soft hairs, with *spiny margin;* corolla white (sometimes tinged with pink) with a yellow mark in the centre.
Grassland. Widespread. Summer.

5.1 C. angustifolia Nees has trailing stems and *long, narrow* leaves. Grassland. Widespread.

5.2 C. ovalifolia Fical. & Hiern. resembles **C. hirsuta**, but the floral bracts are usually *densely covered with silky hairs* and *lack* marginal spines. Grassland. Mainly Pretoria/Magaliesberg region.

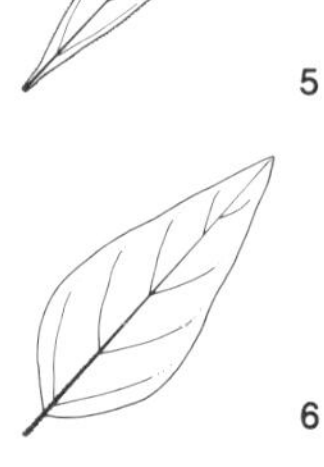

6 Hypoestes forskaolii (Vahl) R.Br.
Herb which often *spreads by stolons*. Leaves egg-shaped and covered with short hairs. Inflorescence has bracts with glandular hairs. Flowers with *dark purple nectar guides;* corolla has *glandular hairs;* lower corolla lip usually *narrow and trowel- or egg-shaped.*
Grassland, usually in rocky places. Widespread. Summer – autumn.

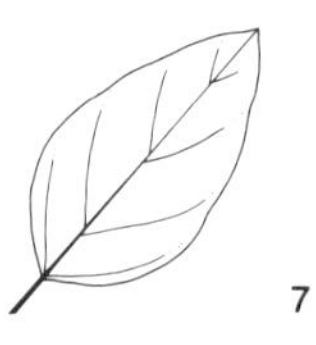

7 Isoglossa grantii C.B.Cl.
Perennial, much-branched and somewhat woody shrublet up to ± 1 m high. Leaves on short stalks, ± egg-shaped, *grey-green and hairy*. Flowers in long, compact spikes which are dense with overlapping bracts; bracts green, with *numerous glandular hairs*. Corolla 2-lipped, white, sometimes spotted with mauve or purple; lower lip with a raised, ± *pleated* surface.
Shady places, especially in clumps of bush. Mainly Pretoria/Magaliesberg and Suikerbosrand regions. Summer.

1 *Barleria pretoriensis*

2 *Chaetacanthus costatus*

3 *Chaetacanthus* cf. *setiger*

4 *Crabbea acaulis*

5 *Crabbea hirsuta*

5.1 *C. angustifolia*

5.2 *C. ovalifolia*

6 *Hypoestes forskaolii*

7 *Isoglossa grantii*

8

8 Justicia anagalloides (Nees) T. Anders.
Tufted perennial herb with *slender sprawling stems* from a woody rootstock. Leaf pairs *well spaced;* blade ± oval. Flowers borne 1 – 4 together on erect, unbranched axillary shoots; corolla *strongly 2-lipped*, upper lip notched, lower lip 3-lobed; anthers with 2 chambers at *different levels*, the lower one with a short *tail.*

Grassland. Widespread. Spring – summer.

9

9 Justicia betonica L. [=**J. pallidior** (Nees) C.B.Cl.]
Erect perennial herb from a woody rootstock. Leaves almost stalkless, ± egg-shaped, hairless. Inflorescence a *compact* terminal spike up to 100 mm long; bracts numerous, overlapping, sharply pointed, *white with green margin and venation.* Flowers 2-lipped, white with faint pinkish or purplish markings.

Bushveld, often along roadsides or in damp places. Mainly Pretoria/Magaliesberg region. Spring – summer.

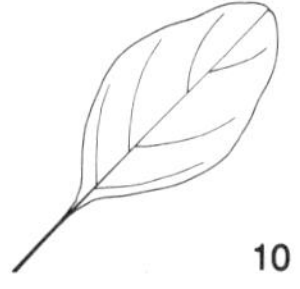

10

10 Ruellia cf. **patula** Jacq. (probably an undescribed species)
Perennial herb with ± *spreading* shoots from a woody rootstock. Leaves stalked, broadly egg-shaped; tips usually rounded; sparsely covered with hairs. Flowers *axillary, solitary;* sepals all free to the base; corolla *pure white, downy;* tube cylindrical below, widening to the shape of a bell.

Bushveld, often in shady places. Mainly Pretoria/Magaliesberg region. Spring – summer.

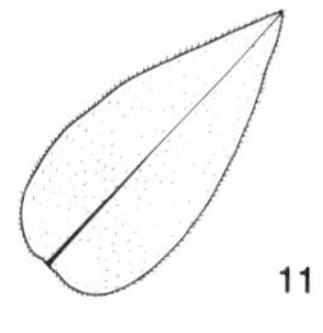

11

11 Thunbergia atriplicifolia E. Mey. ex Nees
Erect perennial shrublet up to 400 mm high; rootstock fleshy, with *milky latex;* sparsely to (usually) densely *covered with soft hairs* throughout. Leaves almost stalkless, usually oval with a *heart-shaped or rounded base;* margin usually has *1 or 2 teeth* at base. Flowers axillary, with *2 large overlapping* bracts clasping the base; corolla *dull white,* inner surface of tube *dull yellow.* Fruit 15 – 19 mm long with *globose* base surrounded by a *fringe of narrow protuberances.*

Grassland. Widespread, particularly Magaliesberg. Summer.

12

12 Thunbergia neglecta Sond.
Scrambling herb from a perennial rootstock; *covered with rough hairs.* Leaves on short stalks, *egg-shaped* with a weakly heart-shaped or *square* base; margin usually with *2 blunt teeth* on each side. Flowers and fruit very similar to those of the previous species.

Grassland, bush clumps and thornveld, often in shady conditions. Widespread. Summer.

ALISMATACEAE (See page 16)

13 *Alisma plantago-aquatica L. *Water plantain/Padda-lepel*
Robust perennial *aquatic* herb up to ± 1 m high. Leaves with *long* and erect stalks; blade egg-shaped, with a *rounded or heart-shaped* base; veins usually 5, ± parallel. Inflorescence a *much-branched* pyramidal panicle. Flowers clustered in *umbels;* carpels ± 20, free.

Along streams; probably introduced. Witwatersrand/Suikerbosrand region. Summer.

ALLIACEAE (See page 16)

14 *Nothoscordum inodorum (Ait.) Nicholson
Fragrant false garlic/Basterknoffel
Bulbous plant up to ± 500 mm high; parent bulb produces numerous loosely attached bulbils around the base. Leaves long and narrow, *flat.* Flowers in *umbels* on long stems, white to greenish white; stamens shorter than perianth segments, with *broadened* filaments.

A troublesome weed in gardens, sometimes in waste places. A native of North America. Spring – summer.

8 *Justicia anagalloides*

9 *Justicia betonica*

10 *Ruellia* cf. *patula*

11 *Thunbergia atriplicifolia*

12 *Thunbergia neglecta*

13 *Alisma plantago-aquatica*

14 *Nothoscordum inodorum*

15

AMARANTHACEAE (See page 16) See also **458**.

15 Aerva leucura Moq. *Aambeibossie*

Semi-deciduous perennial shrublet ± 1 m high; much-branched; young stems hairy. Leaves on short stalks, egg-shaped, *dull green*, sometimes densely covered with hairs; margin *wavy*. Flowers *very small*, densely crowded in white, ± *woolly, cylindrical spikes*.

Grassland and bush clumps. Widespread. Summer – autumn.

16

16 *Gomphrena celosioides Mart. *Bachelor's button/Mierbossie*

Herbaceous perennial with many *decumbent* shoots from a woody rootstock; stems ± angled, with *long silky hairs*. Leaves almost stalkless, with *long silky hairs*, mainly on the lower surface. Inflorescences *terminal*, *globose*, becoming *elongated* as the flowers mature. Flowers white, stalkless; perianth segments *papery*, *woolly* outside.

A common weed of disturbed places, particularly on pavements and along roadsides; native to tropical South America. Widespread. Spring – summer.

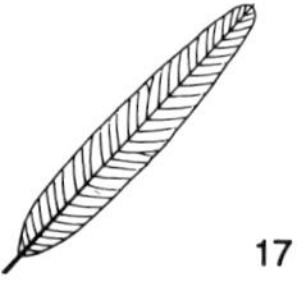

17

ANACARDIACEAE (See page 16)

17 Ozoroa paniculosa (Sond.) R. & A. Fernandes

Resin tree/Harpuisboom

Evergreen tree with a *greyish green* crown; bark dark grey to brown, rough and scaly. Leaves stalked with rounded tips; *silvery green* with side veins *parallel* and conspicuously *raised* on lower surface; margin slightly wavy. Flowers in long sprays, creamy white, strongly scented; male and female flowers on different trees. Fruit black and *wrinkled*.

Bushveld. Mainly Pretoria/Magaliesberg region. Early summer.

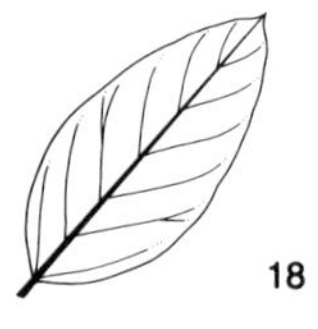

18

APOCYNACEAE (See page 17)

18 Acokanthera oppositifolia (Lam.) Codd

Bushman's poison/Boesmansgif

Evergreen shrub or small tree; sparsely branched; *hairless*. Leaves erect, *stiff and leathery* with *spiny* tip. Flowers in dense axillary clusters, sweetly scented; often *tinged with pink*. Berries red, becoming purplish black.

Wooded places, particularly kloofs and rocky outcrops. Mainly Witwatersrand/Magaliesberg region. Spring.

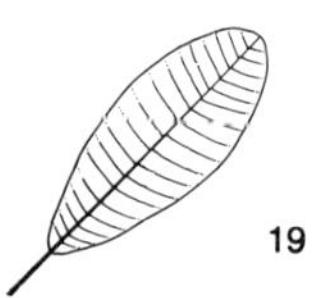

19

19 Landolphia capensis Oliv. *Wild apricot/Wilde-appelkoos*

Evergreen shrub with *trailing* branches; young growth *reddish brown*. Leaves dark green above, paler below; venation distinct. Flowers white; corolla tube *tinged with reddish orange* on the outside; sweetly scented. Fruits globose, *velvety*, pinkish orange and resembling apricots when ripe.

Grassland and bushveld, on rocky ridges. Widespread. Spring – summer.

APONOGETONACEAE (See page 17)

20 Aponogeton junceus Lehm. ex Schlechtd. subsp. **junceus**

Wateruintjie

Aquatic herb with a tuberous rhizome. Leaves basal, erect, long, *narrow and* ± *cylindrical*, sometimes with an expanded floating blade. Flowers densely crowded in *forked spikes*, white, pink or mauve, becoming green with age.

Marshy places, ponds and rivers. Widespread. Spring – summer.

For mauve-flowered form see **614**.

21

AQUIFOLIACEAE (See page 17)

21 Ilex mitis (L.) Radlk. *Cape holly/Without*

Evergreen tree up to ± 8 m high; hairless throughout; bark ± smooth. Leaves stalked, lance-shaped, ± *drooping* when mature, dark green above, *whitish green* below; stalk often *purplish*. Flowers densely clustered along branchlets. Berries bright red.

Along streams in sheltered kloofs. Widespread. Spring.

15 *Aerva leucura*

16 *Gomphrena celosioides*

17 *Ozoroa paniculosa*

18 *Acokanthera oppositifolia*

19 *Landolphia capensis*

19 *L. capensis* (fruit)

20 *Aponogeton junceus*

21 *Ilex mitis*

ASCLEPIADACEAE (See page 17) See also **188, 193** and **194**.

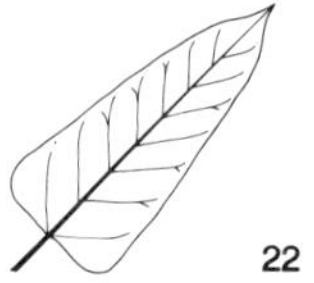
22

22 *Araujia sericifera Brot. *Moth catcher/Motvanger*
Somewhat woody perennial *climber;* stems covered with minute hairs. Leaves stalked, egg-shaped with ± *square base;* dark greyish green above, *whitish* below. Flowers in short axillary inflorescences; corolla *tubular*, white, often streaked or tinged with pink. Follicles *large*, up to 120 x 60 mm, ± egg-shaped.
A weed native to South America. Widespread. Summer.

23

23 Asclepias adscendens (Schltr.) Schltr.
Perennial herb with prostrate or spreading shoots from a woody rootstock; thinly covered with hairs. Leaves on short stalks, *narrow, triangular*, up to 40 x 10 mm. Inflorescence a *spherical* terminal umbel with ± 15 stalked flowers. Corolla reflexed, whitish, pink or mauve; corona *white*. Fruit inflated, with rough bristles.
Grassland. Widespread. Spring. □ For pink-flowered form see **466**.

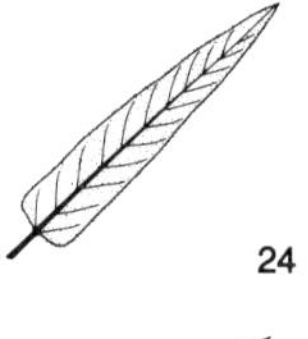
24

24 Asclepias meliodora (Schltr.) Schltr.
Low-growing perennial herb with a woody rootstock; covered with coarse hairs throughout. Stems *few*, ± stout. Leaves on short stalks, up to *120 mm* long; base ± square; tip long and tapering. Flowers borne in stalked umbels; stalk terminal, or apparently *arising from between the 2 leaves of an opposite pair;* corolla lobes reflexed; corona whitish; central column often tinged with pink.
Grassland and bushveld. Pretoria/Magaliesberg region. Spring.

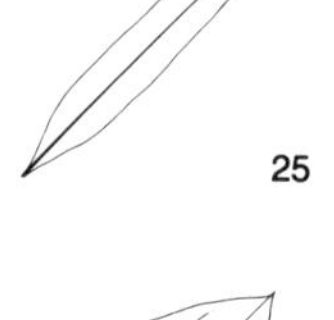
25

25 Asclepias physocarpa (E. Mey.) Schltr. *Balbossie*
Short-lived perennial or robust annual herb, often with a *single* erect stem up to *1,5 m* high. Flowers pendulous and in mainly axillary umbels; petals whitish; corona green. Fruits inflated, ± *globose* with long, wiry hairs.
Uncommon in rocky grassland and disturbed places. Mainly Suikerbosrand and Magaliesberg. Spring – summer. □ Compare **189**.

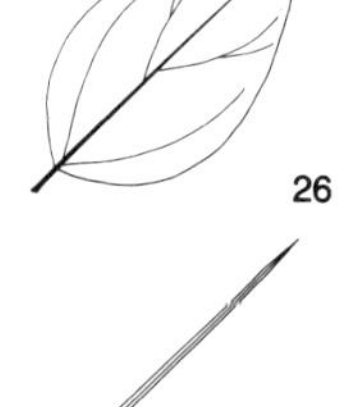
26

26 Ceropegia rendalii N.E. Br.
Delicate herb producing 1 or 2 annual stems from a ± discoid tuber; weakly twining or non-twining. Leaves stalked, broadly egg-shaped, ± fleshy, often *purplish* below and ± mottled above. Flowers axillary, 1 – 3 from a short stalk; corolla lobes fused at the tips into an *umbrella-like* canopy; canopy with 10 indentations around the circumference and supported by *5 slender struts.*
Grassland, under bushes and on rocky outcrops; rare. Widespread. Summer.

27

27 Cordylogyne globosa E. Mey.
Small herb with *1* to few rather laxly ascending to ± erect stems from a perennial rootstock. Leaves linear and hairless. Flowers in *globose* heads; corolla *urn-shaped*, white, often with a *purplish* margin.
Grassland, usually in marshy areas. Localized. Widespread. Summer.

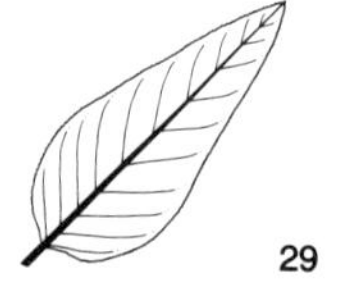
28

28 Orthanthera jasminiflora (Decne.) Schinz *Sandmelktou*
Prostrate herb with *very long* (up to ± 10 m), *trailing* stems with *few branches* from a woody perennial rootstock. Leaves on short stalks, ± egg-shaped; base rounded or *heart-shaped;* thick and rigid with a *harsh texture;* margin sometimes wavy. Flowers in axillary umbels comprising 2 – 10 flowers; corolla *hairy on the outside*, white, turning cream with age.
Grassland; uncommon. Widespread. Spring – summer.

29

29 Pachycarpus schinzianus (Schltr.) N.E. Br. *Bitterwortel*
Erect perennial herb with an underground rootstock. Leaves on short stalks, *rough-textured;* margin wavy; taste extremely *bitter*. Flowers in flat-topped *terminal umbels;* corolla cup-shaped, lobes ± erect with *recurved* tips; corona lobes white with a *violet-purple stripe* down the inner surface. Fruits inflated, spindle-shaped, with a rounded point, *6-winged*, hairless.
Grassland. Widespread. Spring.

22 *Araujia sericifera*

23 *Asclepias adscendens*

24 *Asclepias meliodora*

25 *Asclepias physocarpa*

26 *Ceropegia rendalii*

27 *Cordylogyne globosa*

28 *Orthanthera jasminiflora*

29 *Pachycarpus schinzianus*

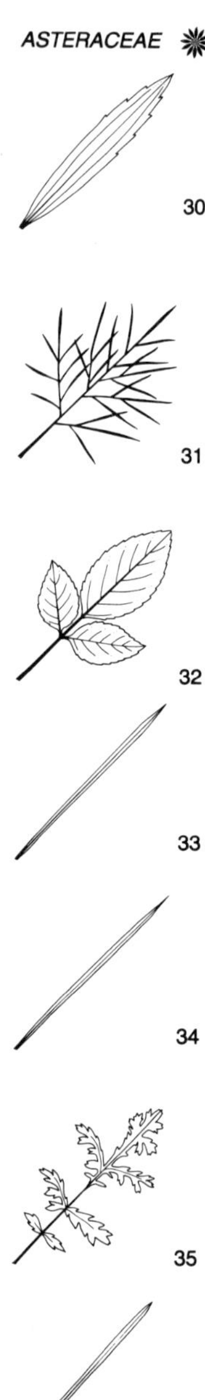

ASTERACEAE (See page 17)
Group A See also **206** and **617**.

30 Aster peglerae H. Bol.
Herbaceous perennial up to 700 mm high. Leaves alternate, with a usually prominently *toothed margin,* and *rough* to the touch. Flower heads up to 10 per branch in a ± flat-topped cluster; ray flowers white, disc flowers yellow.
Common in grassland. Widespread. Spring – summer.

31 *Bidens formosa (Bonato) Sch. Bip. *Cosmos/Kosmos*
Erect, bushy *annual* herb up to ± 2 m high. Leaves *opposite*, stalked and stem-clasping; blade *deeply and finely dissected.* Flower heads solitary on long stalks which terminate the shoots; ray flowers *red, pink or white;* disc flowers *yellow.*
Grassland; a weed of disturbed places, often in dense stands along roadsides and in old fields. A native of the southern United States and Mexico. Widespread. Summer – autumn. □ For pink/red-flowered form see **470**.

32 *Bidens pilosa L. *Blackjack/Knapsekêrel*
Erect *annual* herb; branches grooved. Leaves *opposite, compound;* leaflets usually 3, rarely 5, egg-shaped, with a sharply toothed margin. Flower heads *with or without* white ray flowers; disc flowers yellow. Fruit *long and narrow,* with 2 or 3 short *terminal awns.*
A cosmopolitan weed, possibly a native of America; common in disturbed places. Widespread. Spring – autumn. □ For discoid form see **229**.

33 Callilepis leptophylla Harv. *Bergbitterbossie*
Bushy perennial herb with a tuberous rootstock which has a strong, rather pleasant smell when cut. Leaves ± *needle-like.* Flower heads solitary, terminal; ray flowers *white;* disc flowers *purplish black.*
Grassland, often on rocky ridges. Widespread. Spring.

34 Felicia muricata (Thunb.) Nees subsp. **muricata**
Bushy perennial herb with a woody base; stems sparsely covered with rough hairs. Leaves *needle-like*, often in axillary *tufts.* Flower heads on leafless stalks at the tips of branches; ray flowers white or mauve; disc flowers yellow.
Grassland, proliferating in overgrazed places. Widespread. Summer. Compare **617**.

35 Garuleum woodii Schinz
Much-branched perennial shrublet covered with *sticky* glandular hairs; *strongly scented* when crushed. Leaves *pinnately divided* once or twice. Flower heads terminal on stalks with reduced leaves; ray flowers usually white, rarely blue or mauve; disc flowers yellow; involucral bracts with rounded points.
Grassland, on rocky ridges; rare. Suikerbosrand/Witwatersrand region. Summer – autumn.

36 Gazania krebsiana Less. subsp. **serrulata** (DC.) Roessl. *Botterblom*
Stemless perennial herb from a woody rootstock; *milky latex* present. Leaves tufted and linear with the upper surface *green* and the lower *white-felted.* Flower heads solitary, stalked; ray flowers white or yellow.
Grassland. Widespread; white-flowering form mainly Pretoria/Magaliesberg region. Spring – summer. □ For yellow-flowered form see **207**.

30 *Aster peglerae*

31 *Bidens formosa*

32 *Bidens pilosa*

33 *Callilepis leptophylla*

34 *Felicia muricata*

35 *Garuleum woodii*

36 *Gazania krebsiana*

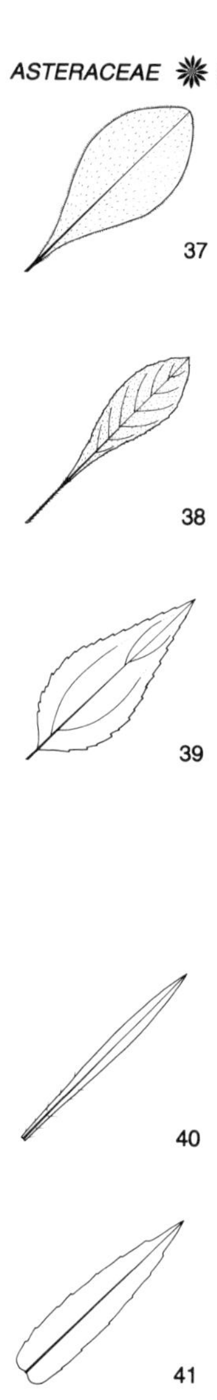

37 Gerbera piloselloides (L.) Cass. *Swartteebossie*
Stemless perennial herb with thickened roots. Leaves in a *flattened* rosette at the base, rising from a woody crown covered with silky hairs; on short stalks, ± elliptic, with a *rounded*, often *hairy* tip. Flower heads *elongated*, on long, erect and leafless stalks; stalks *swollen* below the heads and often with *golden brown hairs;* ray flowers not, or only *slightly*, longer than the bracts.
Grassland. Widespread. Spring – summer.

38 Gerbera viridifolia (DC.) Sch. Bip. subsp. **viridifolia**
Stemless herb with a perennial rootstock. Leaves basal, stalked; blade variable in shape, often ± elliptic; upper surface green with long silky hairs; lower surface of mature leaves *sparsely covered with hairs* and *green (never white-felted)* with the veins *not raised.* Flower heads solitary on long, leafless stalks; ray flowers white to pink above, usually *pinkish* below.
Grassland. Widespread. Spring – summer.
For pink-flowered form see **471**.

ASTERACEAE (See page 17)
Group B See also **475** and **480**.

39 Adenostemma caffrum DC.
Mostly hairless perennial herb up to 1 m high; sparsely branched. Leaves *opposite*, often *large* (140 x 70 mm) with coarsely toothed margin. Flower heads in groups of usually 20, sometimes fewer; ray flowers absent.
Moist places, often along streams and in seeps; rare. Widespread. Summer.

40 *Conyza bonariensis (L.) Cronq. *Flax-leaf fleabane/Kleinskraalhans*
Erect annual herb with side branches usually *as long as, or longer than* the main axis; *covered with rough hairs.* Leaves stalkless, *twisted near the base.* Flower heads arranged in rather *narrow terminal panicles* comprising disc flowers only, usually more than 10 mm across.
Common as a weed along roadsides and in other disturbed places. A native of South America. Spring – autumn.
***C. canadensis** L. and ***C. floribunda** Humb. *et al.* have side branches which are *never higher than* the main axis, the whole forming a *pyramidal* compound inflorescence. Flower heads of the former are ± 5 mm across, with minute white ray flowers, while those of the latter are usually more than 5 mm and without ray flowers. Both are weeds of disturbed places.

41 Denekia capensis Thunb.
Perennial or annual herb; usually glandular. Leaves stalkless, long and narrow, often lobed at the base; green and hairy above, *white-felted* below. Flower heads about 3 mm in diameter, in terminal clusters of up to ± 20; white or blue fading to white.
Moist places, sometimes in shallow water. Widespread. Spring – autumn.
For blue-flowered form see **618**.

42 Dicoma zeyheri Sond. *Kafferdissel*
Erect perennial herb up to 300 mm high from a woody rootstock. Stems with white *woolly* hairs. Leaves up to 30 mm wide, green above, *white-felted* below. Flower heads terminal; involucral bracts *egg-shaped*, sharply pointed, *silvery*, often tinged with purple.
Grassland. Widespread. Summer – autumn.

37 *Gerbera piloselloides*

38 *Gerbera viridifolia*

39 *Adenostemma caffrum*

40 *Conyza bonariensis*

41 *Denekia capensis*

42 *Dicoma zeyheri*

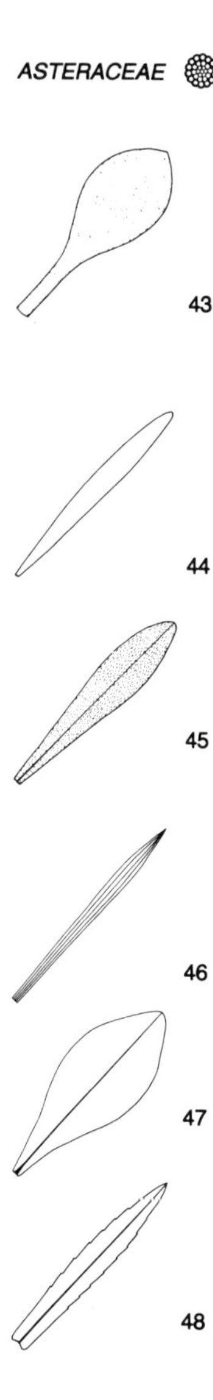

43 Helichrysum argyrosphaerum DC. *Poprosie*
Annual herb with radiating prostrate branches; sparsely covered with *grey woolly hairs* throughout. Leaves narrow into a flat, stalk-like base. Flower heads somewhat globose, *solitary* at the tips of branchlets, surrounded by leaves; involucral bracts arranged in ± 9 series, transparent, shiny, silvery white, becoming increasingly tinged with pink towards the centre, fading at maturity, tips ± *rounded*. Flowers yellow, but pink at tips.
Sandy areas, frequently growing as a weed in disturbed places. Widespread. Spring – summer. □ Also **478**.

44 Helichrysum caespititium (DC.) Harv. *Speelwonderboom*
Prostrate *mat-forming* perennial herb; branchlets about *10 mm* high, closely covered with leaves. Leaves stalkless, 5 – 10 mm long, *0,5 mm* wide; stem-clasping at the base; both surfaces ± *woolly;* margin *rolled under.* Flower heads clustered at the tips of branchlets; involucral bracts in ± 6 series, white or pink; flowers yellow, often tipped with pink.
Grassland and bushveld, usually on bare or sparsely grassed areas. Widespread. Winter – spring. □ For pink-flowered form see **479**.

45 Helichrysum cerastioides DC. var. **cerastioides** *Wolbossie*
Small bushy *perennial* herb with a woody taproot. Stems and leaves *densely covered with grey woolly hairs.* Involucral bracts (the white, petal-like leaves) arranged in ± *6 series*; tips *sharply pointed.*
Sandy grassland and rocky hillsides. Widespread. Winter – spring.

46 Helichrysum chionosphaerum DC.
Mat-forming perennial herb. Leaves long and narrow with 3 parallel veins; lower surface *white-felted along margins*, sometimes covering a larger area. Flower heads solitary, or a few clustered at branch tips; involucral bracts glossy white or creamy.
Grassland, usually on the summit of rocky ridges. Witwatersrand/ Suikerbosrand region. Spring.

47 Lopholaena coriifolia (Sond.) Phill. & C.A.Sm. *Pluisbossie*
Evergreen woody *shrub*. Leaves stalkless, ± strap-shaped, *stem-clasping* at the base and with a rounded tip; *fleshy* and *waxy grey.*
Rocky grassland, particularly on ridges. Winter – spring.

48 Senecio polyodon DC. var. **polyodon** [=**S. breyeri** S. Moore]
Erect, usually single-stemmed perennial, branching only in the upper parts; ± covered with *glandular hairs.* Stem leaves with a *broad, heart-shaped base* which clasps the stem. Disc flowers with a *usually purplish anther tube.*
Marshes or seasonally waterlogged grassland, often along streams. Rare. Summer.

49 Stoebe vulgaris Levyns *Bankrupt bush/Bankrotbos*
Intricately branched, greyish perennial shrublet; branches slender and wiry with numerous tufts of *small, heath-like leaves* (up to 4 x 0,5 mm). Leaves with upper surfaces *covered with white woolly hairs.* Flower heads minute, surrounded by *brownish yellow* inner involucral bracts; arranged in large panicles. Flowers inconspicuous, purple-tipped. Characteristic *globose galls covered with white woolly hairs* (illustrated) are usually present and frequently mistaken for the flower heads.
Grassland, proliferating in overgrazed areas. Widespread. Spring – autumn. For flowering form see **700**.

43 *Helichrysum argyrosphaerum*

44 *Helichrysum caespititium*

45 *Helichrysum cerastioides*

46 *Helichrysum chionosphaerum*

47 *Lopholaena coriifolia*

48 *Senecio polyodon*

49 *Stoebe vulgaris* (galls)

ASTERACEAE (See page 17)
Group C

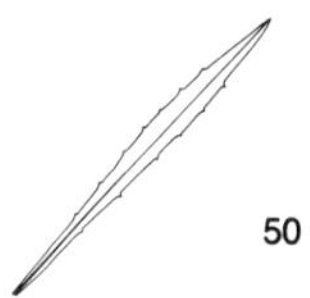
50

50 Lactuca capensis Thunb.
Low-growing perennial herb; hairless. Leaves and stem exude a *milky latex* when broken. Leaves mainly in a basal rosette, with a *bluish tinge*. Flower heads several in inflorescence with well-spaced branches, comprising ray flowers only.
Grassland and disturbed areas. Widespread. Spring – summer.

BORAGINACEAE (See page 17)

51

51 Heliotropium ciliatum Kaplan
Erect perennial shrublet, dark *greyish green* and sparsely covered with *rough hairs*. Leaves stalked, narrow and lance-shaped. Inflorescence terminal, usually *forked* into *elongated* spikes, *coiled* at the tip with flowers pointing upwards. Flowers with a long corolla tube and a very short calyx; corolla lobes with *hair-like* tips.
Bushveld, often along roadsides. Pretoria/Magaliesberg region. Spring – summer.

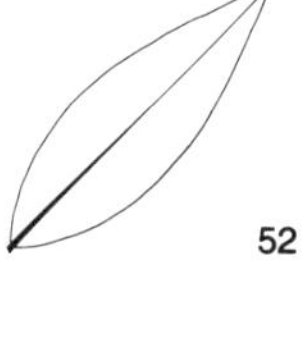
52

52 Trichodesma physaloides (Fenzl.) A.DC. *Chocolate bells/Slangkop*
Bushy herbaceous shrublet with erect annual shoots from a woody rootstock. Stems *purplish brown* with white dots; rough with short bristly hairs. Leaves stalkless; blade lance-shaped; lower surface and margin of older leaves with numerous *white dots*. Inflorescence terminal, much-branched. Flowers *bell-shaped, pendulous;* calyx dark *purplish brown*, enlarging around the fruit; corolla white with the *margin fading to brown*.
Grassland. Widespread. Spring.

BRASSICACEAE (See page 18)

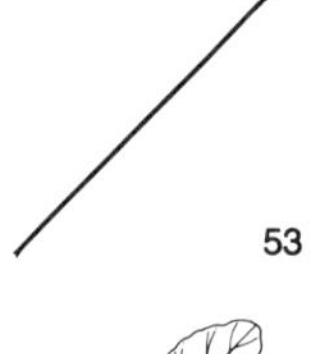
53

53 Heliophila rigidiuscula Sond.
Slender erect perennial herb up to ± 500 mm high. Leaves long and narrow. Inflorescence a terminal raceme at the end of a ± leafless stalk. Flowers with *slender* stalks, erect, becoming *recurved* in fruit; petals on short *stalks*, white. Fruits *30 – 70 mm* long, *3 – 8 mm* wide.
Grassland, in rocky places. Mainly Suikerbosrand. Spring – summer.

54

54 *Rorippa nasturtium-aquaticum (L.) Hayek *Watercress/Bronslaai*
Perennial herb with decumbent *hollow* and slightly ribbed stems. Leaves pinnately compound with the base of the stalk *flattened* and *clasping* the stem. Fruits erect, elongated and *pod-like*.
Wet places or in water. A native of Europe and Asia. Widespread. Spring – summer.

50 *Lactuca capensis*

51 *Heliotropium ciliatum*

52 *Trichodesma physaloides*

53 *Heliophila rigidiuscula*

54 *Rorippa nasturtium-aquaticum*

BUDDLEJACEAE (See page 18)

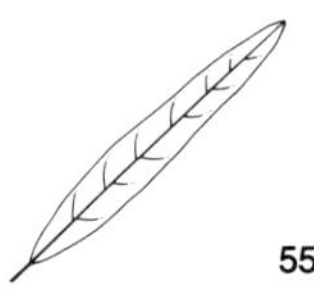
55

55 Buddleja saligna Willd. *False olive/Basterolienhout*
Evergreen shrub or tree; branchlets ± *4-angled*, with whitish scales. Leaves stalked, long and narrow, *grey-green* and ± hairless with venation impressed on upper surface; lower surface *whitish* with *prominently raised* venation; margin ± rolled under. Flowers borne in *dense terminal* and axillary panicles; stamens 4, *protruding* from the corolla. Capsules very small, surrounded by the persistent calyx.
Wooded hillsides and along streams. Widespread. Summer.

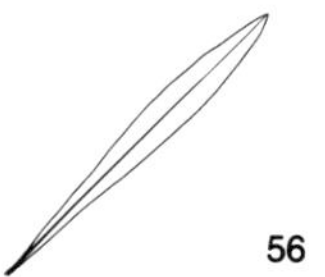
56

56 Gomphostigma virgatum (L.f.) Baill. *Otterbossie*
Evergreen perennial shrublet; ultimate branchlets very *slender*, ± *4-angled.* Leaves opposite with a *connecting ridge*, stalkless, narrow with a prominent midrib. Flowers solitary in axils of upper leaves, sweetly scented; anthers with distinct *dark purple margins;* stigma *broad and rounded.* Capsules oblong, cylindrical, faintly 2-lobed.
Along watercourses and rivers, usually growing in running water among boulders. Widespread. Spring – autumn.

CAESALPINIACEAE (See page 18)

57

57 Burkea africana Hook. *Wild seringa/Wildesering*
Deciduous tree, often with a flattened, spreading crown; bark grey-brown, rough and flaking; tips of branchlets with *velvety, reddish brown hairs.* Leaves stalked, clustered at the tips of shoots, *bipinnately compound;* leaflets alternate, ± elliptic. Flower spikes drooping, appear with the new leaves. Flowers white, often tinged greenish or with cream. Pods elliptic, wing-like, brown and woody; *1-seeded.*
Bushveld, usually in sandy soils. Mainly Pretoria/Magaliesberg region. Spring.

CAMPANULACEAE (See page 18)

58 Wahlenbergia virgata Engl.
Herb with many slender, ± erect branches from a perennial, ± woody taproot. Leaves *few and inconspicuous*, often scale-like. Inflorescence with well-spaced flowers. Corolla *8 – 10 mm* long, white or bluish. Style with *tiny glands* at base of stigmatic lobes.
Grassland. Widespread. Spring – summer. □ Compare **630**.

CAPPARACEAE (See page 18)

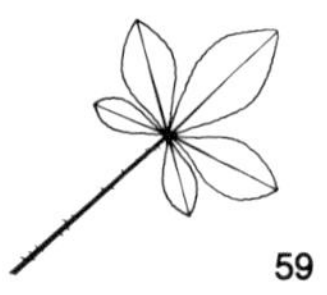
59

59 Cleome gynandra L. *Spider-wisp/Snotterbelletjie*
Much-branched *annual* covered with glandular hairs; gives off a distinctive odour when crushed. Leaves *palmately* compound with 3 – 5 leaflets; margin shallowly toothed. Petals sometimes fading to pink. Stamens borne on a *long stalk;* filaments *purplish.* Capsules narrow, 30 – 150 mm long.
Common as a weed on cultivated land and in other disturbed places. Widespread. Summer.

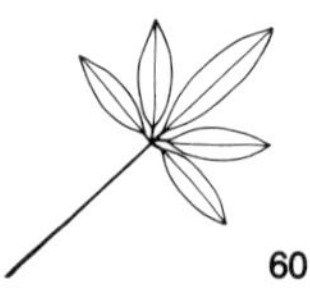
60

60 Maerua cafra (DC.) Pax *Witboshout*
Evergreen shrub with dense, dark green foliage and thick tuberous roots. Leaves usually compound with *3 – 5 leaflets*, but sometimes simple. Flowers with *numerous, white* stamens, often tinged with green; ovary *green*, borne towards the tip of a *long, slender stalk* (may be mistaken for a stigma). Berries green, slightly ribbed, each *suspended* from a *long stalk.*
Wooded areas on rocky ridges; uncommon. Widespread. Spring.

55 *Buddleja saligna*

56 *Gomphostigma virgatum*

57 *Burkea africana*

58 *Wahlenbergia virgata*

59 *Cleome gynandra*

60 *Maerua cafra*

CARYOPHYLLACEAE (See page 18)

61 Dianthus mooiensis Williams subsp. **kirkii** (Burtt Davy) Hooper

Wild pink/Wilde-angelier

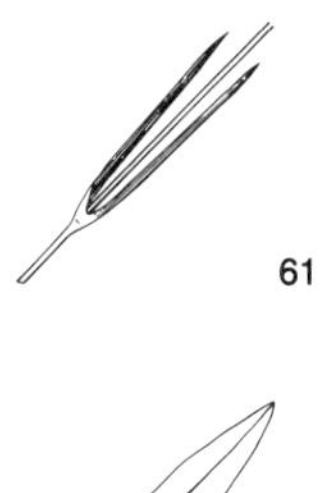

61

62

Erect *bluish green* perennial herb from a woody rootstock; hairless throughout, with the stems often tinged with purple. Leaves on flowering shoots *not rigid, 0,5 – 2 mm* wide; length of sheath 1,5 – 2 times leaf width. Flowers with the calyx 22 (rarely as short as 18 or up to 26) mm long; petals deeply *fringed*, white or pale pink.

Grassland, mainly on rocky ridges. Widespread. Summer.

Subsp. **mooiensis** has on flowering shoots more *rigid* leaves 3 – 5 mm wide; length of sheath ± equals leaf width; calyx 18 (rarely as short as 16 or up to 20) mm long. Otherwise very similar to the previous subspecies.

62 Silene bellidioides Sond.

Perennial, *sparsely branched* herb up to ± 1 m high; covered with *sticky hairs*. Stem leaves stalkless; margin sometimes wavy. Flowers in a lax, branching terminal inflorescence bearing few flowers; petals *stalked* and distinctly *forked;* ovary stalked; open in the *evening*, scented. Capsules open by means of *recurved* valves at the tip.

Grassland, usually in moist places. Widespread. Summer.

CELASTRACEAE (See page 18) See also **282**.

63 Maytenus heterophylla (Eckl. & Zeyh.) N.K.B. Robson

Spike thorn/Pendoring

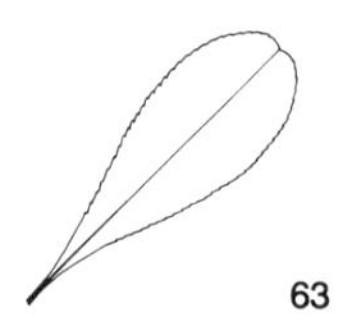

63

Semi-deciduous, much-branched shrub or small tree up to 4 m high; bark thick, *deeply ridged and fissured;* armed with *long straight spines* which often bear leaves; hairless throughout. Leaves on short stalks, often *clustered* on reduced shoots; margin shallowly toothed. Male and female flowers on different plants. Flowers produced *in profusion*, often completely covering the stems; non-functional parts of other sex always present; sweetly scented. Capsules somewhat globose, surface ± rough, brownish.

Grassland and bushveld. Widespread. Spring.

64 Maytenus polyacantha (Sond.) Marais

Kraal spike thorn/Kraalpendoring

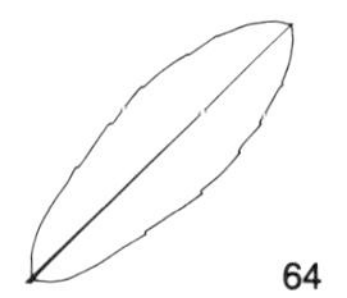

64

Dense evergreen shrublet up to ± 1,5 m high; *heavily armed* with straight spines; branchlets often tinged with red. Leaves on very short stalks, usually *clustered* in the axils of spines; *small* (about 15 x 5 mm) with ± rounded tips, leathery, dark green; margin toothless or faintly toothed. Flowers white, in sparsely branched axillary heads, sometimes produced in profusion. Capsules ± 3-lobed, reddish brown. Seed with a fleshy yellow covering.

Grassland and bushveld, usually on rocky ridges and often forming impenetrable thickets. Widespread. Summer – autumn.

61 *Dianthus mooiensis* subsp. *kirkii*

62 *Silene bellidioides*

63 *Maytenus heterophylla*

64 *Maytenus polyacantha*

CONVOLVULACEAE (Excluding Cuscutaceae; see page 19)

See also **286** and **493.**

65

65 Convolvulus sagittatus Thunb. var. **aschersonii** (Engl.) Verdc.
Perennial herb with annual *twining* stems from a woody taproot; *densely covered with short appressed silvery hairs throughout.* Leaves stalked, variable in shape; middle lobe often with wavy or scalloped margin, tip ± *rounded;* basal lobes forked or dissected. Inflorescence stalk *longer* than the leaves, bearing *2 – 6 flowers.* Flowers 8 – 10 mm long; corolla white or pale mauve-pink.
Grassland and bushveld, often twining in fences. Mainly Pretoria/ Magaliesberg region. Spring – summer.

66

66 Convolvulus sagittatus Thunb. subsp. **sagittatus** var. **hirtellus** (Hallier f.) A. Meeuse
Herb with *prostrate* annual shoots from a perennial taproot; sparsely to rather densely covered with short stiff hairs. Leaves narrow with the 2 basal lobes *forked or 2- or 3-toothed.* Inflorescences axillary; stalks bearing *1 to several flowers.* Corolla white, often tinged with pale mauve-pink.
Grassland. Widespread. Spring – summer.

C. sagittatus Thunb. var. **ulosepalus** (Hallier f.) Verdc. has leaves that are *sparsely covered with hairs* and have basal lobes redivided into *2 – 5 long or short lobes;* inflorescence stalks usually bear *2 – 6 flowers.* This often *twining* weed is widespread.

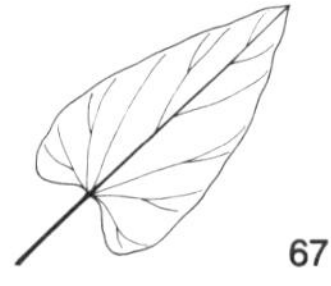

67

67 Convolvulus sagittatus Thunb. subsp. **sagittatus** var. **phyllosepalus** (Hallier f.) A. Meeuse
Herb with *prostrate* annual shoots from a perennial taproot. Stems usually branched only from the base, covered with minute hairs. Leaves stalked, ± *egg-shaped* with the base *square, heart-shaped or usually enlarged into 2 pointed lobes* like the head of an arrow, up to 10 mm wide, ± *hairless.* Flowers usually *solitary* on long stalks in the axils of the leaves, less than 20 mm long.
Grassland. Widespread. Spring – summer.

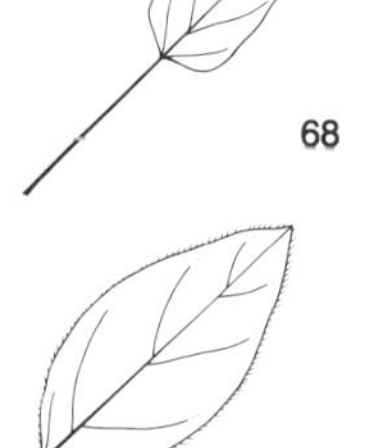

68

69

68 Falkia oblonga Bernh. ex Krauss
Dwarf, mat-forming perennial herb up to ± 60 mm high. Leaves distinctly stalked; base ± rounded. Flowers *solitary* in leaf axils; corolla white, sometimes tinged with pink or mauve on the outside; styles *2.*
Wet places in grassland, often covering large patches of ground. Mainly Witwatersrand/Suikerbosrand region. Spring – summer.

69 Seddera capensis (E. Mey. ex Choisy) Hallier f.
Mat-forming herb with several prostrate stems from a perennial taproot. Leaves *almost stalkless,* ± egg-shaped, both surfaces hairy; margin conspicuously *fringed with hairs.* Flowers axillary, *solitary, almost stalkless;* sepals with margins *fringed with hairs.*
Grassland; uncommon. Widespread. Summer.

65 *Convolvulus sagittatus* var. *aschersonii*

66 *C. sagittatus* subsp. *sagittatus* var. *hirtellus*

67 *C. sagittatus* subsp. *sagittatus* var. *phyllosepalus*

68 *Falkia oblonga*

69 *Seddera capensis*

CRASSULACEAE (See page 19) See also **758**.

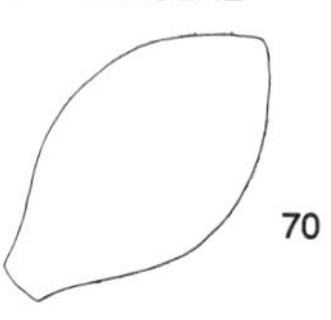

70

70 Crassula capitella Thunb. subsp. **nodulosa** (Schonl.) Toelken
Perennial *succulent* with a tuberous base. Stem erect with short *recurved* hairs. Leaf pairs spirally arranged in a usually solitary *basal rosette;* leaves *often hairy;* margin with a *fringe of hairs*. Inflorescence erect, unbranched. Flowers urn-shaped; petals have a *rounded appendage at the tip;* anthers brown to black.
Grassland, usually on gravelly slopes. Widespread. Summer.

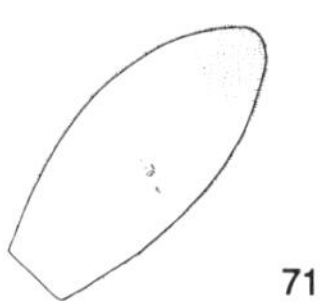

71

71 Crassula setulosa Harv. var. **setulosa**
Small perennial *succulent* herb; forms cushions of rosettes when young. Leaves in pairs, spirally arranged, old leaves *remaining* on the stem; blade *flattened;* margin densely fringed with ± *recurved whitish bristles.* Inflorescence terminal, bearing many flowers, with a *round top*. Anthers usually *dark purple or brown.*
Rocky ridges; usually on sheltered rocks or rock faces. Widespread. Summer.

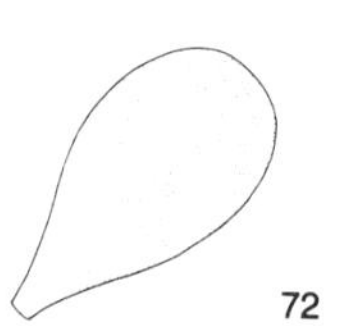

72

72 Crassula swaziensis Schonl.
Perennial *succulent* with erect or decumbent branches up to ± 200 mm long; plant consists of 1 to several rosettes, old leaves persistent. Leaves *flattened with rounded tips*, greyish green and *densely covered with fine hairs* on both surfaces. Inflorescence a terminal, ± flat-topped cluster of flowers on a solitary erect stalk. Flowers tubular, white, often tinged with pink in bud, fading to cream; anthers yellow to brown.
Grassland and bushveld, usually in rock crevices, often in exposed positions. Widespread. Summer.

CUSCUTACEAE (See page 19)

73 *Cuscuta campestris Yunck. *Dodder*
Leafless annual herb with *yellowish thread-like* (1 – 2 mm diameter) twining stems; *parasitic* and attached to annual and perennial plants by *suckers* (haustoria). Flowers minute, in compact, ± globose clusters; petals whitish, sometimes with a pinkish tinge; styles 2, free. Fruit a globose capsule, usually with 4 seeds.
A noxious weed of North American origin. Widespread. Summer.

CYPERACEAE (See page 19)

74 Ascolepis capensis (Kunth) Ridley
Tufted perennial herb. Leaves basal, *slender* and grass-like, almost *as long as* the stems. Inflorescence a terminal, *somewhat spherical* head, subtended by a *narrow leaf-like* bract up to 50 mm long, and sometimes also by a second shorter one.
Grassland, usually in swampy places. Mainly Magaliesberg. Summer.

75 Cyperus obtusiflorus Vahl var. **obtusiflorus**
Erect perennial herb from a horizontal rhizome. Leaves basal, *grass-like*, about half as long as the stem. Inflorescence comprises terminal clusters of 5 – 20 *flattened* spikelets, subtended by *2 or 3 narrow green* bracts.
Grassland. Widespread. Summer.
Var. **flavissimus** Boeck. has yellow spikelets (see **297**).
C. margaritaceus Vahl is very similar but has *less compressed* spikelets clustered in groups of *3 – 7.*

76 Kyllinga alba Nees *Witbiesie*
Slender erect herb with a perennial rhizome; hairless. Leaves basal, *grass-like.* Inflorescence *terminal, spherical*, subtended by a *few unequal, leaf-like* bracts.
Grassland, often in moist places. Widespread. Spring – summer.

70 *Crassula capitella*

71 *Crassula setulosa*

72 *Crassula swaziensis*

73 *Cuscuta campestris*

74 *Ascolepis capensis*

75 *Cyperus obtusiflorus* var. *obtusiflorus*

76 *Kyllinga alba*

DIPSACACEAE (See page 19)

77

77 Cephalaria zeyheriana Szabo

Perennial herb up to 1,5 m high with a woody rootstock; most parts usually covered with *bristly hairs*. Stems *ribbed*. Leaves mostly at base, stalkless, elongated; margin *toothed* and usually variously lobed. Flower heads at ends of branches, ± *dome-shaped to globose*, surrounded by *several rows* of rounded bracts. Calyx *without* distinctive marginal bristles.

Grassland and swampy areas. Widespread. Summer.

78

78 Scabiosa columbaria L. ***Wild scabious/Bitterbos***

Slender perennial herb with a woody rootstock; hairy throughout. Leaves in basal *rosette*, with blunt tips and toothed margin; stem leaves often deeply *lobed* once or twice. Flowers in long-stalked, *flat-topped*, terminal heads; heads encircled below by *2 rows* of soft, narrow, *pointed* bracts; peripheral flowers ± 2-lipped; sepals *bristly;* corolla *downy* outside and inside.

Grassland. Widespread. Spring – summer.

EBENACEAE (See page 20)

79

79 Diospyros austro-africana De Winter var. **microphylla** (Burch.) De Winter ***Jakkalsbos***

Much-branched deciduous shrub usually up to ± *1 m* high, with rigid branches. Leaves almost stalkless, ± egg-shaped with *rounded* tips, usually not longer than *15 mm*, stiff and thick in texture, with short *velvety hairs*, particularly on *lower* surface; venation distinctly *raised* below. Flowers solitary, axillary, *pendulous;* stalk subtended by 2 deciduous, ± opposite *boat-shaped bracts* at the base; corolla densely covered with hairs outside, lobes with tips reflexed. Berries globose, hairy, yellow or red, subtended by the persistent calyx.

Grassland, usually on rocky ridges and outcrops. Mainly Witwatersrand/ Suikerbosrand region. Spring.

80

80 Diospyros whyteana (Hiern.) F. White ***Swartbas***

Dense *evergreen* shrub, rarely a small tree; bark smooth, dark-coloured; crown usually with an occasional *orange-red* leaf. Leaves dark green and *very shiny* above, with a *hairy* margin; young leaves *densely covered with silvery hairs*. Flowers *pendent*. Berry somewhat globose, red, completely *enclosed* by the papery, enlarged and *inflated calyx*.

Rocky ridges and in the shelter of trees along streams. Widespread. Spring.

81

81 Euclea crispa (Thunb.) Guerke subsp. **crispa** ***Guarri/Gwarrie***

Much-branched evergreen tree densely covered with leaves; bark grey and smooth or rough and darker on old trunks; young growth usually with minute *rusty brown* granules (glands). Leaves on short stalks, variable in shape, tip *rounded*, leathery, rigid, *grey-green* with a *papery* texture; margin sometimes slightly *wavy*. Flowers in short axillary racemes, pendulous, fragrant. Fruit globose, with a thin layer of flesh, black, 1-seeded.

Bush clumps and bushveld, often in rocky places. Mainly Pretoria/ Magaliesberg region. Summer.

ELATINACEAE (See page 20)

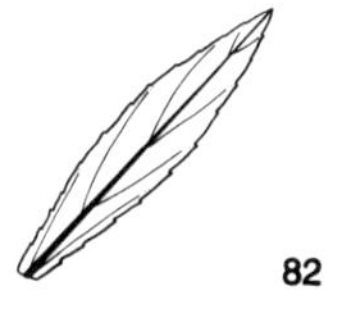
82

82 Bergia decumbens Planch. ex Harv.

Perennial shrublet with erect and decumbent annual shoots from a woody rootstock. Leaves *stalkless*, long and narrow, often reddish when young; veins fairly *broad and conspicuous;* margin with usually 4 – 9 widely spaced teeth; stipules *small* with a *toothed* margin. Flowers several in each axil; stigmas usually *purplish*.

Grassland, often along roadsides. Widespread. Spring – summer.

77 *Cephalaria zeyheriana*

78 *Scabiosa columbaria*

79 *Diospyros austro-africana*

80 *Diospyros whyteana*

81 *Euclea crispa*

82 *Bergia decumbens*

FABACEAE (See page 20)

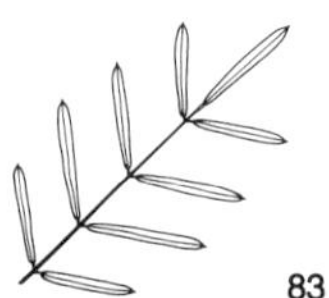

83

83 Indigofera acutisepala Conrath

Slender, *sparsely branched* perennial herb up to ± 1 m high, *greyish green.* Leaflets 5 – 7 pairs, usually *opposite.* Inflorescence *much longer* than the subtending leaf (± 40 – 80 mm), with a *slender wiry axis.* Flowers pinkish to white; buds often with *dark-coloured hairs.*

Grassland, often in moist depressions and on rocky ridges. Widespread. Spring – summer. □ Also **512**.

This is probably the same species as **I. zeyheri** Spreng. ex Eckl. & Zeyh.

84

84 *Melilotus alba Desr. *Bokhara clover/Bokhaarklawer*

Erect, much-branched annual herb up to 1,5 m high. Leaves trifoliolate; leaflets with *toothed margin* and a pungent odour when crushed; stipules fused to the leaf stalk. Flowers numerous, borne in *long slender* racemes. Pods somewhat globose.

A naturalized weed of disturbed places, particularly along streams. Native to Europe and Asia. Widespread. Summer – autumn.

85

85 *Robinia pseudo-acacia L. *Black locust/Witakasia*

Deciduous tree armed with pairs of short *stipular spines* at the nodes. Leaves *odd-pinnate* with stalked leaflets; margin toothless. Flowers in axillary *pendent* racemes on slender stalks; very *fragrant.* Pods elongate, flat, dehiscent and remaining on branches during winter.

Disturbed grassland and along streams; a garden escape of North American origin. Widespread. Spring.

86

86 Sphenostylis angustifolia Sond. *Wild sweetpea/Wilde-ertjie*

Perennial shrublet with spreading to erect branches from a woody rootstock. Leaves *trifoliolate.* Flowers pink with a yellowish spot on the standard, rarely white fading to cream; style *flattened* and almost spoon-shaped, hairy at the tip; keel *twisted.*

Grassland, particularly in rocky places. Widespread. Spring – summer. For pink-flowered form see **529**.

87

87 *Trifolium repens L. *White clover/Witklawer*

Perennial herb with *creeping* stems, hairless. Leaves palmately *trifoliolate;* leaflets often with *whitish markings* above; margins *finely toothed.* Flowers clustered into heads on erect, *long, leafless* stalks.

A widespread weed of disturbed, often moist places; forming dense colonies. A native of Europe and Asia. Spring – summer.

83 *Indigofera acutisepala*

84 *Melilotus alba*

85 *Robinia pseudo-acacia*

86 *Sphenostylis angustifolia*

87 *Trifolium repens*

GERANIACEAE (See page 21)

88

88 Monsonia attenuata Harv.
Erect single- or few-stemmed herb from a perennial rootstock; most parts with long, straight, erect *whitish hairs*. Leaves with *slender* reddish stalks up to 30 mm long, often with a *knee-like bend* at base of blade; blade long and narrow, usually folded upwards along the midrib; margin toothed; stipules *long and needle-like*. Flowers have white to yellowish or pink petals with a conspicuous greyish blue to green or blackish *network of veins*.
Grassland, rocky ridges and mountainsides. Mainly Suikerbosrand region. Summer.

89

89 Monsonia burkeana Planch. ex Harv. [=**M. biflora** DC.] *Naaldebossie*
Perennial herb with several slender, erect and sparsely branched shoots from a woody rootstock. Leaves with margin ± regularly toothed; stipules rarely ± spiny. Petals usually *14 – 24 mm* (rarely 11 mm) long, with *5 conspicuous veins* from the base; hairless, except for a few *long crinkled hairs* on the inner surface below the middle; white to pale pink, mauve or blue. Fruits tipped with a long slender beak which often becomes spirally twisted after the dried nutlets have broken up.
Grassland, often in sandy soils and on rocky ridges. Widespread. Spring. For pink-flowered form see **541**.

90

90 Pelargonium dolomiticum Knuth ex Engl.
Herbaceous, much-branched *shrublet*, dies back in winter. Leaves pinnately compound with the leaflets deeply and *irregularly dissected;* bluish grey and *densely covered with hairs*. Flowers whitish with pink *markings;* stalk of the upper 2 petals *folded lengthwise*, creating the impression of a tube.
Grassland, in well-drained sandy soil, often on dolomite, and in disturbed places. Mainly Pretoria/Magaliesberg region. Spring – autumn.

GESNERIACEAE (See page 21)

91

91 Streptocarpus vandeleurii Bak. f. & S. Moore *Olifantsoor*
Herb with a *single leaf* and no visible shoots; plants die after flowering. Leaf up to ± 300 mm long and wide; base heart-shaped; margin *bluntly toothed;* both surfaces *hairy*. Inflorescence stalk up to 300 mm long, bearing a large cluster of flowers. Flowers tubular, strongly scented, many opening together; corolla white with a pronounced yellow blotch at base of lower lip.
In crevices of rocky outcrops or on the walls of damp kloofs; rare. Widespread. Summer.

88 *Monsonia attenuata*

88 *M. attenuata* (showing venation)

89 *Monsonia burkeana*

90 *Pelargonium dolomiticum*

91 *Streptocarpus vandeleurii*

ICACINACEAE (See page 21)

92 Apodytes dimidiata E. Mey. ex Arn. subsp. **dimidiata**

White pear/Witpeer

92

Evergreen tree or shrub; bark grey, rather smooth. Leaves stalked; stalk often with *purplish tinge;* blade elliptic, dark green, sometimes with hairs on the lower surface of the midrib. Flowers small, many borne in sprays towards the ends of branchlets; ovary *densely covered with hairs.* Fruit fleshy, asymmetrical and laterally compressed, with a *hard black seed* attached to a *fleshy, orange-red bulge.*

Bushveld, often on rocky ridges and along streams. Magaliesberg. Summer.

ILLECEBRACEAE (See page 21)

93 Pollichia campestris Ait. *Waxberry/Teesuikerbossie*

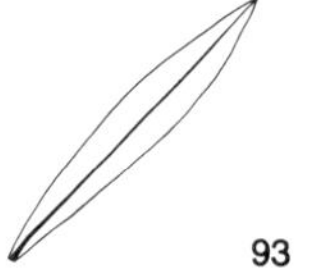

93

Perennial low-growing *shrublet* with *numerous* erect or sprawling stems from a woody rootstock. Stems covered with down. Leaves *stalkless*, narrow, paired, or apparently in whorls with *membranous* stipules at the base, greyish green. Flowers small, densely clustered in leaf axils, greenish and surrounded by *waxy white* bracts which enlarge and become *fleshy.* Fruits very small and seed-like, surrounded by the swollen, *sweet-tasting* bracts.

Grassland and rocky ridges. Widespread. Summer – autumn.

IRIDACEAE (See page 21) See also **352**.

94 Gladiolus elliotii Bak.

Erect perennial herb up to 800 mm high. Leaves ± 7, *bluish green*, ± 20 mm broad; margin yellowish. Flowers up to about 25 in an erect spike, arranged in *2 rows* pointing in *opposite* directions when open; perianth with white or milky blue background densely *speckled* with pink to maroon spots, the latter concentrated to form a *dark line* in the middle of the lobes; 3 lower lobes with a *yellow blotch.*

Grassland. Widespread. Summer. □ For pink-flowered form see **548**.

92 *Apodytes dimidiata*

92 *A. dimidiata* (fruit)

93 *Pollichia campestris*

94 *Gladiolus elliotii*

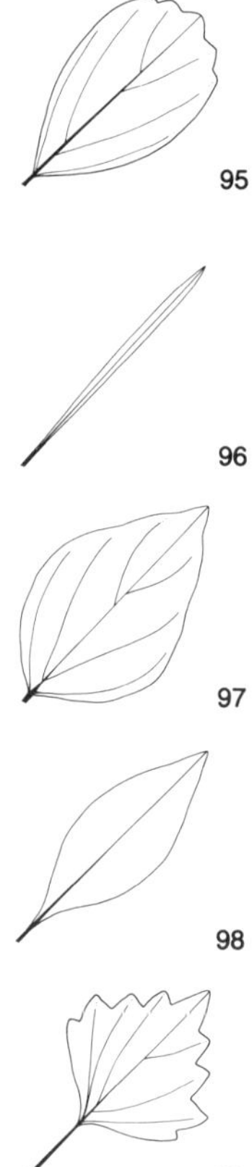

LAMIACEAE (See page 22) See also **651**.

95 Acrotome hispida Benth.
Perennial herb with few to many ± erect to spreading stems from a woody rootstock; most parts covered with *rough hairs.* Leaves on *very short stalks;* tip *rounded;* margin toothed in the upper half, or smooth. Flowers *stalkless,* densely *clustered* in the leaf axils, often developing low on the stem; calyx lobes spine-tipped; corolla 2-lipped, with the upper lip *shorter* than the lower.
Grassland, often among rocks. Widespread. Summer.
A. inflata Benth. is an *annual* erect herb with appressed and downward-pointing hairs on the stems. The leaves are covered with soft hairs and the flowers densely crowded in *globose* axillary clusters. It often becomes weedy in disturbed places. Widespread.
A. angustifolia G. Tayl. is also an annual herb, ± similar to **A. inflata** but the hairs on the stems point upwards and the leaves are narrower (5 – 14 mm wide). Magaliesberg; rare.

96 Becium angustifolium (Benth.) N.E.Br.
Erect, much-branched perennial shrublet; usually *single-stemmed* from the base; aromatic. Leaves ± stalkless, *narrow* (2 – 4 mm wide), dull grey-green, densely gland-dotted on both surfaces, often folded upward along the midrib. Inflorescences slender, *40 – 120 mm* long, with regularly spaced floral clusters. Corolla ± *4 mm* long, *pure white.*
Grassland and bushveld. Widespread. Summer.

97 Becium obovatum (E. Mey. ex Benth.) N.E.Br. var. **obovatum**
Small shrublet with several herbaceous stems arising annually from a woody rootstock. Leaves almost smooth to densely covered with hairs. Inflorescence with flowers crowded near the tip. Corolla *10 – 16 mm* long, upper lip usually with longitudinal *violet lines*, rarely pure white.
Grassland. Widespread. Spring. □ For mauve-flowered form see **650**.

98 Hemizygia pretoriae (Guerke) Ashby subsp. **pretoriae**
Erect perennial shrublet from a woody rootstock; ± hairy throughout. Leaves almost stalkless, narrowly elliptic to egg-shaped, often folded along the midrib, *gland-dotted.* Inflorescence usually unbranched. Corolla white to pale mauve with a *long, narrow tube.*
Grassland, often in rocky places. Widespread. Spring.

99 Plectranthus madagascariensis (Pers.) Benth. var. **ramosior** Benth.
Perennial *semi-succulent* shrublet; *aromatic.* Leaves 20 – 40 mm long with *scallop-toothed* margin; minutely *stippled* with reddish brown glands on the lower surface. Flowers have mature calyx with the upper sepal *much broader* than the rest; corolla white or pale mauve with purplish markings on upper lip.
Rocky grassland. Widespread. Spring – autumn. □ Also **653**.

100 Stachys natalensis Hochst var. **natalensis**
Perennial herb with several erect or decumbent stems; hairy throughout. Leaves with the base often deeply *heart-shaped;* margin *toothed.* Flowers arranged in *pairs* at the nodes; corolla with lower lip deflexed, 3-lobed and with a few *lilac markings.*
Grassy and stony hillsides. Mainly Pretoria/Magaliesberg region. Summer – autumn.

101 Teucrium trifidum Retz. [=**T. capense** Thunb.] *Koorsbossie*
Erect herbaceous perennial shrublet; covered with short *greyish hairs.* Leaves on short stalks; blade deeply *trifid,* often with more shallow lobes or teeth, lower surface densely covered with hairs and gland-dotted; margin ± *rolled under.* Inflorescence many-flowered, terminal. Corolla apparently with only 1 lip.
Wooded areas, often in groups under trees. Widespread. Summer.

95 *Acrotome hispida*

96 *Becium angustifolium*

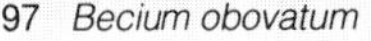

97 *Becium obovatum*

98 *Hemizygia pretoriae*

99 *Plectranthus madagascariensis*

100 *Stachys natalensis*

101 *Teucrium trifidum*

LENTIBULARIACEAE (See page 22)

102 Utricularia arenaria A. DC.

Herb with thread-like stolons and *very slender*, erect flowering stems; appears leafless, but with small *1-nerved* leaves scattered on the stolons; insectivorous, with minute, stalked, *bladder-like traps* borne in large numbers on the stolons and roots. Flowering stems 20 – 160 mm long, with *minute papillae* at the base. Flowers 1 – 5, widely spaced; corolla white or lilac with a yellowish upper lip; spur ± *twice* as long as the lower lip.

Marshy areas; rare. Widespread. Summer.

U. livida E. Mey. has also been recorded from the field guide area. It is a slightly more robust species, with the base of the inflorescence stalk *lacking papillae*. The midrib of the leaves is often *branched* near the tip. The spur is slightly *shorter* than in the previous species.

LILIACEAE (Excluding Alliaceae; see page 22)

See also **719, 722** and **775.**

103 Albuca setosa Jacq. [=**A. pachychlamys** Bak.] *Slymuintjie*

Erect herb with large fleshy underground bulb; bulb scales ending in *persistent fibres*. Leaves produced *after* the flowers, few, contain mucilage. Inflorescence up to 400 mm high. Flowers *erect*, inner 3 perianth lobes converging and hooded at the tips and outer 3 spreading; white with broad green to greenish brown central stripe on back.

Grassland. Widespread. Spring. □ Compare **104**.

103.1 A. glauca Bak. is a bulbous plant with greenish white flowers that are slightly irregular and ± horizontally arranged on an elongated raceme. It often grows in shady places under trees, and flowers in spring.

104 Albuca sp.

Erect bulbous herb up to ± 500 mm high. Leaves *well developed* at the time of flowering, ± erect, relatively *wide*, usually more than half the length of the inflorescence stalk, *fresh green*. Flowers ± crowded towards the end of a *long* inflorescence stalk; perianth segments white with a prominent green stripe.

Moist vleis in grassland. Recorded from the Witwatersrand. Summer. Compare **103**.

105 Androcymbium melanthioides Willd. var. **melanthioides**
Pyjama flower/Patrysblom

Bulbous herb with 1 – 4 narrow leaves. Flowers *stalkless*, crowded into a *head* at ground level and surrounded by leaf-like bracts; bracts white with *green veins*, often tinged with pink; styles 3.

Grassland. Widespread. Autumn – winter.

102 *Utricularia arenaria*

103 *Albuca setosa*

103.1 *A. glauca*

104 *Albuca* sp.

105 *Androcymbium melanthioides*

106 Anthericum cooperi Bak.
Slender erect perennial herb 100 – 400 mm high, with a woody rhizome. Leaves ± 8 arranged in 2 ranks, *erect*, the outer ones very small, the inner ones becoming progressively larger, usually *V-shaped* in cross-section. Inflorescence *unbranched;* stalk compressed and without bracts. Flowers clustered in axils of bracts, *opening at daybreak and fading during the morning;* filaments usually *smooth*. Capsules globose with many transverse ridges.
Grassland. Widespread. Spring. □ Compare **107**.

107 Anthericum fasciculatum Bak.
Erect perennial herb up to *600 mm* high, with a woody rootstock. Leaves few, ± arranged in 2 ranks, long and narrow (up to 5 mm wide), usually *U-shaped* in cross-section; margin with a fringe of hairs near the base. Inflorescence lax, stalk ± cylindrical. Flowers *clustered* in axils of bracts; perianth segments free, white with a central greenish band; filaments with *minute protuberances* in upper half. Capsules ± rounded.
Grassland. Widespread. Spring – summer. □ Compare **106**.

108 Anthericum longistylum Bak.
Perennial herb with a woody rhizome; *hairless*. Leaves many, in a *basal rosette*, often curled back, ± *spirally twisted* in upper half. Inflorescence with *well-spaced branches*, stalk cylindrical with bracts. Flowers open during the day, solitary in axils of bracts; stamens 6: 4 erect, 2 reclining with style. Capsules egg-shaped, with a *pointed tip*.
Grassland and bushveld. Pretoria region. Spring.

109 Anthericum transvaalense Bak.
Erect perennial herb with a woody rhizome. Leaves arranged *evenly* around stem, ± 6 mm wide, often *spirally twisted*, midrib absent, *hairy*. Inflorescence usually *unbranched*, many-flowered. Capsules pointed.
Grassland, often on rocky ridges. Widespread. Spring – summer.

110 Anthericum trichophlebium Bak.
Small perennial herb with a woody rhizome, often in clumps. Leaves ± 8 arranged in 2 ranks, *20 – 40 mm* wide, not spirally twisted, with *velvety hairs*. Inflorescence unbranched, 100 – 200 mm long, stalk flattened, hairy. Flowers congested, opening in the afternoon and fading during the night; perianth segments greenish white with a central greenish brown longitudinal band. Capsules globose.
Grassland; uncommon. Mainly Pretoria/Magaliesberg region. Spring.

111 Chlorophytum bowkeri Bak.
Robust lily-like perennial with knobbly rhizomes. Leaves basal, shiny and smooth. Inflorescence stalk erect, unbranched or with 1 branch near the base. Flowers with stalks *jointed near the middle*, star-like, petals *clear white* with prominent yellow anthers.
Shady and rocky areas. Widespread. Summer.

112 Eriospermum cooperi Bak.
Erect herb with an underground tuber. Leaf *single*, distinctly stalked and lying *flat on the ground;* blade *broadly oval* with a blunt tip; produced *at same time as or later than* the inflorescence. Inflorescence solitary, erect. Flowers with perianth segments *just joined* at the base. Seed densely covered with long, silky hairs.
Grassland. Mainly Pretoria/Magaliesberg region. Spring.

106 *Anthericum cooperi*

107 *Anthericum fasciculatum*

108 *Anthericum longistylum*

109 *Anthericum transvaalense*

110 *Anthericum trichophlebium*

111 *Chlorophytum bowkeri*

112 *Eriospermum cooperi*

113 Protasparagus cooperi (Bak.) Oberm.
Climbing or scrambling perennial herb. Stems rather soft, often twisting; armed with green to yellowish recurved spines (modified leaves). 'Leaves' (cladodes) in clusters of 8 – 20, 10 – 20 mm long, ± cylindrical. Flowers emerge from among the cladodes, borne along the length of branches. Berries red.
Wooded areas, often in rocky places. Widespread. Summer.

114 Protasparagus laricinus (Burch.) Oberm. *Wild asparagus/Katbos*
Dense, impenetrable, *multi-stemmed* shrub up to 2 m high; rootstock woody with thick fleshy roots; branches *not spine-tipped*, grey to *white*, sometimes with a zigzag appearance and fine *longitudinal grooves;* leaf function taken over by dense clusters of *cylindrical, unbranched*, needle-like stems (cladodes). Leaves modified into *curved thorns*. Flowers axillary, sweetly scented; anthers *orange*. Berries globose, bright *red* with 1 – 3 black seeds.
Bush clumps, along streams and fences, and in abandoned disturbed places. Widespread. Summer.

115 Protasparagus setaceus (Kunth) Oberm. *Asparagus fern*
Twining or sprawling perennial climber with a *soft, feathery* appearance; spines *absent* except on old main branches. 'Leaves' (cladodes) ± cylindrical, *very fine*, less than 10 mm long. Flowers borne singly or in small clusters *only at the tips* of branches.
Wooded areas, often in the shade. Widespread. Summer.

116 Protasparagus suaveolens (Burch.) Oberm.
Wild asparagus/Katdoring
Erect woody shrublet up to 1 m high with a perennial rootstock; branches *spine-tipped;* clusters of needle-like stems (cladodes) *cylindrical*, often *branched*. Leaves reduced, *not modified into thorns*. Flowers sweetly scented. Berries globose, dark green, *black* or reddish.
Rocky grassland, bush clumps and bushveld. Widespread. Spring – summer.

117 Protasparagus transvaalensis Oberm. ined. [Not yet published – previously included in **Asparagus krebsianus** (Kunth) Jessop]
Perennial *sprawling* shrub up to 2 m high; all branches with ± straight or slightly *curved* thorns (these are reduced leaves). 'Leaves' (cladodes) needle-like, ± *3-angled*, unbranched, 15 – 50 mm long. Flowers stalked, borne on *elongated leafless axes* (racemes); perianth segments white, sometimes with a purplish midrib; anthers *dark purplish black*. Berries red.
Bushveld, often in rocky places. Pretoria/Magaliesberg region. Summer.

118 Sansevieria aethiopica Thunb. *Bowstring hemp/Aambeiwortel*
Perennial, ± succulent plant with a creeping rhizome. Leaves basal, erect, *rigid*, fibrous, ± U-shaped in cross-section, with *whitish blotches;* margin reddish brown. Flowering axis erect, stout, with sterile bracts in basal half and flowers arranged in clusters above them. Flowers tubular, opening at night; perianth lobes curling back, cream, greenish white or greenish mauve. Berries globose, red.
Rocky ridges and bushveld, usually in the shelter of woody vegetation and rocks. Widespread. Spring.

119 Schizobasis intricata (Bak.) Bak. *Volstruiskos*
Bulbous perennial. Stems *wiry*, green, *much-branched*, erect or sprawling, sometimes tangled. Leaves *reduced to small scales*, with an outgrowth from the base on each side. Flowers with perianth segments white, longitudinally striped with greenish brown on lower surface.
Grassland, often in rocky places. Widespread. Spring – summer.

113 *Protasparagus cooperi*

114 *Protasparagus laricinus*

116 *Protasparagus suaveolens*

115 *Protasparagus setaceus*

117 *Protasparagus transvaalensis*

118 *Sansevieria aethiopica*

119 *Schizobasis intricata*

120 Scilla nervosa (Burch.) Jessop *Wild squill/Sandlelie*
Bulbous herb with erect leaves; upper part of bulb covered with fibrous sheaths. Leaves often ± twisted, *hairless;* veins prominently *raised* on both surfaces. Flowers on *long stalks* crowded at end of inflorescence stalk; bracts *2* per flower.
Grassland. Widespread. Summer.

121 Trachyandra asperata Kunth var. **basutoensis** (V. Poelln.) Oberm.
Grass-like perennial with a short basal rootstock; roots *thin*, fibrous, *cream to light brown.* Leaves in a basal rosette, usually 150 – 200 mm long, 1 – 4 mm wide, ± hairless; base tubular. Inflorescence erect, stalk branched or unbranched. Flowers with perianth segments free, white, with a *central brownish green band;* stalk often twisted, up to 7 mm long. Capsules covered with *short, gland-tipped protuberances* and some transverse ridges.
Grassland, usually in rocky or marshy places. Widespread. Summer.

122 Trachyandra asperata Kunth var. **nataglencoensis** (Kuntze) Oberm.
Perennial herb with a compact woody rhizome. Leaves many, basal, long and *narrow, ± hairless.* Inflorescence erect, up to 500 mm high, with side branches curving upwards. Flowers on ± erect and hairless stalks. Capsules globose, *without transverse ridges.*
Grassland, usually in marshy places. Widespread. Spring.

123 Trachyandra erythrorrhiza (Conrath) Oberm.
Perennial herb with a creeping rhizome, covered with *short hairs;* roots up to 4 mm in diameter, white at first, later becoming *orange-red.* Leaves basal, ± arranged in 2 ranks, bases of young leaves *pink;* blade *flat*, erect, ± spirally twisted, base tubular. Inflorescence erect, up to 800 mm high, unbranched or with 1 or 2 basal branches curving upward. Flowers open during the day, stalks erect. Capsules globose, covered with *short glandular protuberances.*
Grassland, usually in black turf marshes; rare. Pretoria/Witwatersrand region. Spring.

124 Trachyandra saltii (Bak.) Oberm. var. **saltii**
Grass-like perennial with an underground rhizome. Leaves of variable length, *1 – 2 mm* wide, tubular towards the base; old leaves disintegrating into *fibres.* Inflorescences often 2 or more on same plant, curving *outward and upward* at base, rarely branched. Flowers open in the afternoon and fade during the night; stalks indistinctly jointed below the flower; perianth segments white with brownish keels, fall off after flowering. Capsules without protuberances.
Grassland, often in rocky places. Widespread. Spring – summer.

125 Urginea depressa Bak.
Small bulbous plant; *leafless* at the time of flowering. Inflorescence stalk usually up to 100 mm high; flowering axis *very short and condensed*, almost an umbel. Flowers with stalks up to 15 mm long; perianth segments white inside (sometimes tinged with pink), with *brown or purplish* stripe outside.
Grassland, often in colonies. Widespread. Spring.

120 *Scilla nervosa*

121 *Trachyandra asperata* var. *basutoensis*

122 *Trachyandra asperata* var. *nataglencoensis*

123 *Trachyandra erythrorrhiza*

124 *Trachyandra saltii*

125 *Urginea depressa*

126

LOBELIACEAE (See page 22)

126 Cyphia assimilis Sond. *Baroe*

Perennial herb with slender *twining* stems from a tuberous rootstock. Leaves on short stalks, ± *narrowly elliptic;* margin shallowly toothed. Flowers widely spaced towards ends of shoots, *2-lipped*, white with pinkish markings, sometimes pale pink.

Grassland, often on rocky ridges. Mainly Pretoria/Magaliesberg region. Summer. □ Compare **558**.

127

127 Lobelia angolensis Engl. & Diels [=**L. depressa** L.f.]

Delicate, *mat-forming* annual herb. Stems prostrate or ± erect, rooting from the nodes. Leaves stalkless; margin *smooth.* Flowers solitary in leaf axils; corolla 3 – 5 mm long, white or rarely mauve; anthers 2, *tipped with hairs.*

Moist places, particularly along streams and in shallow depressions in grassland. Widespread. Summer.

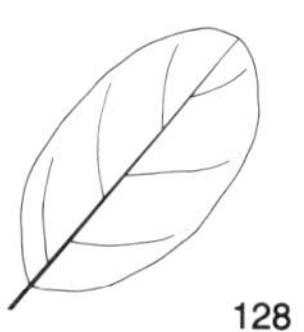

128

LOGANIACEAE (See page 22)

128 Nuxia congesta R. Br. ex Fresen. *Wild elder/Wildevlier*

Rounded *evergreen* shrub or small tree; stems *4-angled;* bark exfoliates in usually light-coloured *stringy* pieces. Leaves in *whorls of 3;* margin toothless or coarsely and bluntly toothed. Inflorescence with numerous flowers, *compact and dome-shaped.* Flowers densely covered with *hairs inside;* sweetly scented. Capsules small, hairy and ± enclosed by the *persistent* calyx.

Rocky ridges, often in exposed conditions on the summit. Widespread. Winter.

129

LORANTHACEAE (See page 22)

129 Tapinanthus natalitius (Meisn.) Danser subsp. **zeyheri** (Harv.) Wiens *Birdlime bush/Voëlent*

Deciduous shrubby perennial; hemiparasitic, growing *on branches* of **Acacia** species in particular. Leaves *thick and leathery*, oval or lance-shaped, with *grey down.* Flowers in clusters of 2 – 5; corolla tubular, up to 60 mm long, with a conspicuously swollen base, covered with *whitish down*, the lobes green and yellow-red. Berries roundish, dark red to blackish when ripe.

Common. Mainly Pretoria/Magaliesberg region. Spring.

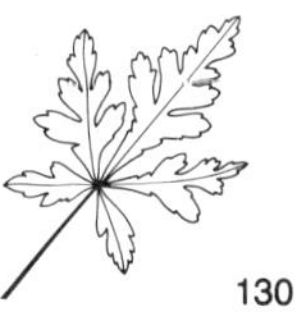

130

MALVACEAE (See page 23)

130 *Hibiscus trionum L. *Bladderweed/Terblansbossie*

Annual erect herb; stems often tinged with purple; hairy. Leaves with variable shape, usually *deeply 3-lobed* with the 2 side lobes often *re-divided;* lower surface light-coloured; margin toothed. Calyx with *conspicuous purple veins, inflated* in fruit; corolla pale cream to almost white, with a dark purple centre.

Grassland and disturbed places, often a weed in cultivated fields. A native of Europe. Widespread. Summer. □ Also **376**.

131

131 Sida ternata L.f.

Erect shrublet; sparsely branched and ± hairless. Leaves usually deeply *3-lobed* with the margin irregularly toothed. Flowers with *long slender* stalks 15 – 40 mm long. Fruit disc-shaped, with usually 5 – 9 prominent grooves radiating from the centre.

In partial shade, often near streams; uncommon. Mainly Pretoria/Magaliesberg region. Summer – autumn.

132

MELIACEAE (See page 23)

132 Turraea obtusifolia Hochst.

Evergreen erect *shrublet.* Leaves stalked, *lance-shaped*, often *clustered.* Flowers in axillary clusters of 1 – 4; style swollen at tip and protruding from the stamen tube. Capsules flattened globose, *shallowly lobed.* Seed bright *red.*

Bushveld, especially among rocks and under trees. Magaliesberg. Summer.

126 *Cyphia assimilis*

127 *Lobelia angolensis*

128 *Nuxia congesta*

129 *Tapinanthus natalitius*

130 *Hibiscus trionum*

131 *Sida ternata*

132 *Turraea obtusifolia*

MESEMBRYANTHEMACEAE (See page 23)
133 Delosperma herbeum (N.E. Br.) N.E. Br.
Highveld white vygie/Witvygie
Erect to spreading perennial *succulent*. Leaves *blue-green*, *concave* (sometimes almost grooved) above, ± triangular in cross-section, with minute papillae. Flowers white, rarely very pale pink, in axillary clusters.
Grassland. Widespread. Spring – summer.
There seems to be more than 1 species currently included under this name.

MOLLUGINACEAE (See page 23)
134 Limeum viscosum (Gay) Fenzl subsp. **viscosum** var. **glomeratum** (Eckl. & Zeyh.) Friedr.
Small *annual herb*. Stems prostrate, often *sticky* due to presence of *glandular* hairs. Leaves on short stalks, ± oval with a broad tip. Flowers small, in *dense clusters* usually *opposite a leaf;* petals 3 – 5, hood-shaped and *distinctly stalked*. Fruit black and wrinkled.
Grassland and rocky ridges, often on sandy soil. Widespread. Summer – autumn.

134

MYRSINACEAE (See page 24)
135 Myrsine africana L. *Cape myrtle/Vlieëbos*
Small, densely leaved, *evergreen shrub;* much-branched with an erect habit. Leaves on very short stalks, ± *rounded*, dark green and shiny above; margin usually *toothed*. Flowers small, white, borne in axillary clusters; petals ± 2 mm long, *gland-dotted;* anthers *protrude* beyond corolla lobes, *pink or red*. Berries slightly fleshy, purplish red when ripe.
Clumps of bush and wooded kloofs, usually in shady situations. Widespread. Spring.

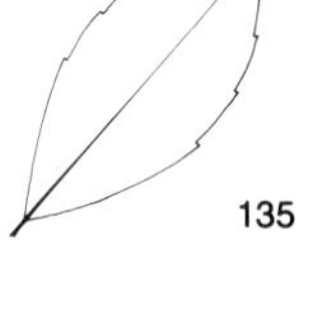
135

MYRTACEAE (See page 24)
136 *Eucalyptus camaldulensis Dehn. *River red gum/Bloekom*
Large evergreen tree up to 40 m high; bark shed in *long strips*, exposing a ± *smooth* underlayer. Adult leaves *grey-green*, stalked, alternate, *pendulous*. Inflorescences comprise *umbels* bearing up to 10 flowers, stalked, solitary in leaf axils. Buds spherical with a hemispherical lid narrowing into a *slender tip*. Open flowers *without* perianth but with numerous stamens. Capsules stalked.
A native of Australia. Although not naturalized, these large trees are widely grown in plantations and to provide shelter on farms, forming a conspicuous feature of the Highveld landscape. Widespread. Spring – summer.
Compare **570.**

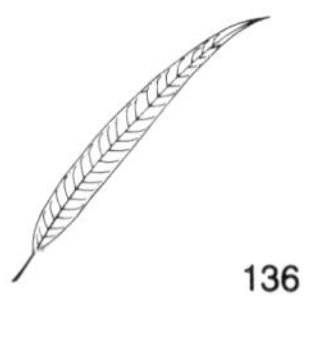
136

OLEACEAE (See page 24)
137 Olea europaea L. subsp. **africana** (Mill.) P.S. Green
Wild olive/Olienhout
Rounded *evergreen* tree; branchlets weakly 4-angled, usually with scattered *whitish dots*. Leaves *greyish green* and shiny above, *whitish green* and dull below; margin slightly rolled under. Flowers small, in many-flowered axillary sprays which are usually shorter than the subtending leaf; calyx very short. Fruit ovoid, fleshy, green with *whitish spots*, turning purple-black when ripe.
Various habitats, but particularly on rocky ridges. Widespread. Summer.

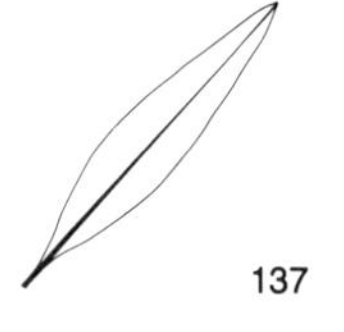
137

133 *Delosperma herbeum*

134 *Limeum viscosum*

135 *Myrsine africana*

135 *M. africana* (fruit)

136 *Eucalyptus camaldulensis*

137 *Olea europaea*

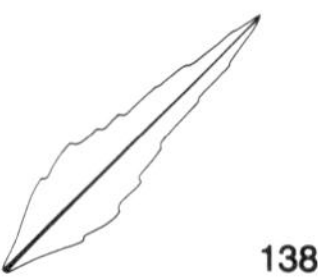
138

ONAGRACEAE (See page 24)

138 *Oenothera tetraptera Cav. ***White evening primrose/Witaandblom***

Low-growing perennial herb with many stems from a woody taproot; covered with *long hairs* throughout. Leaves variously *lobed and toothed*, at least some in a basal rosette; margin often *wavy*. Flowers *open just before sunset*, white *fading to purplish pink*. Capsules club-shaped, densely covered with hairs, with *4 broad wings* on angles.

Native to Texas and Mexico; a weed of disturbed places, common along roadsides. Widespread. Spring – autumn.

ORCHIDACEAE (See page 24) See also **784** and **785**.

139 Eulophia ovalis Lindl. subsp. **ovalis**

Robust, erect perennial herb with a creeping rhizome; leaf-bearing shoot *next* to inflorescence. Leaves ± fully developed at the time of flowering, arranged in 2 ranks, leathery, usually folded. Inflorescence unbranched. Flowers scentless and with a *flattened* appearance; petals mainly *white, speckled with blue* inside along the veins; spur ± *conical to cylindrical*.

Grassland, often on rocky ridges. Widespread. Summer.

Subsp. **bainesii** (Rolfe) A.V.Hall has yellowish flowers (see **406**).

140 Holothrix randii Rendle

Small herb with an underground tuber. *Leaf solitary*, basal and ± *flat* on the ground, ± oval, *hairless, withered* at flowering time. Inflorescence erect, slender. Flowers stalkless (inferior ovary resembles a stalk); petals *divided into numerous thread-like lobes*.

Grassland, usually on rocky ledges. Widespread. Spring.

PAPAVERACEAE (See page 25)

141

141 *Argemone subfusiformis G.B. Ownbey

Mexican poppy/Bloudissel

Robust *spiny* annual herb; hairless, with a distinctive odour when crushed. Leaves stalkless, deeply pinnately lobed, *bluish green*. Flowers solitary, terminal, pale cream to almost white. Capsules spiny, *splitting* open at the top.

A native of Mexico; common as a weed of disturbed places, often on bare ground. Widespread. Spring – summer.

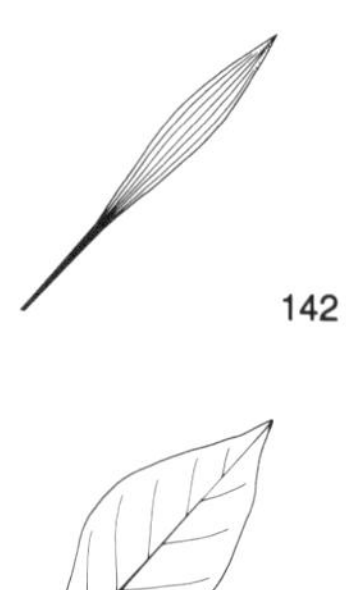
142

143

PLANTAGINACEAE (See page 25)

142 *Plantago lanceolata L. ***Narrow-leaved plantain/Oorpynhoutjie***

Perennial herb with leaves in a *basal rosette*. Leaves strap-shaped, *narrow* (length more than 4 times the width), narrowed towards the base into a wide stalk; blade with prominent, ± *parallel* veins. Inflorescences several per plant, consisting of *long* erect stalks with terminal spikes which are less than half the length of the stalk.

An introduced weed, native to Europe; usually in disturbed places, particularly on pavements. Spring – summer.

PLUMBAGINACEAE (See page 26)

143 Plumbago zeylanica L.

Climbing perennial shrublet up to ± 1 m high. Leaves stalked; stalk *stem-clasping* and slightly lobed at the base. Flowers borne in branched or unbranched many-flowered spikes; calyx covered with long, *glandular (sticky) hairs* throughout its length; corolla lobes rounded with a small *sharp* tip.

Wooded hillsides, often in shady places. Widespread. Spring – summer.

138 *Oenothera tetraptera*

139 *Eulophia ovalis* subsp. *ovalis*

140 *Holothrix randii*

141 *Argemone subfusiformis*

142 *Plantago lanceolata*

143 *Plumbago zeylanica*

POLYGONACEAE (See page 26)

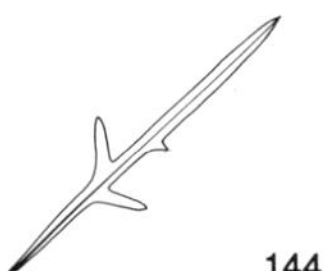

144

144 Oxygonum dregeanum Meisn. var. **canescens** (Sond.) R.A. Grah.
Low-growing perennial herb, usually with short branches from the base only; ± succulent. Leaves long and *narrow*, margin *not lobed* but often with a *pair of teeth* near the base. Ocreae with *long bristles*. Flowers in small clusters along terminal unbranched shoots; petals dirty white, often tinged with pink on the outside. Fruit ribbed, *without* spines.
Grassland and disturbed places, often on rocky ridges and along roadsides. Widespread. Spring – summer.

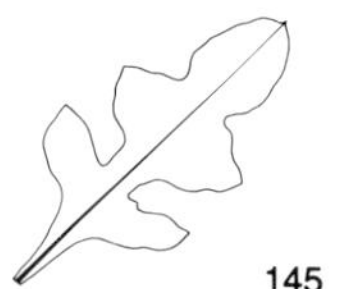

145

145 Oxygonum sinuatum (Hochst. & Steud. ex Meisn.) Damm. ***Dubbeltjie***
Low-growing annual or perennial herb with a tough taproot; hairless. Stems *deeply* grooved. Leaves *pinnately lobed;* ocreae with *long bristles*. Inflorescence terminal, elongated, spike-like with *widely spaced* white flowers. Fruit with *3 spines* at base.
Grassland, often in rocky or disturbed places. Mainly Pretoria/Magaliesberg region. Spring – summer.

PROTEACEAE (See page 26) See also **418**.

146

146 Protea gaguedi Gmel. ***White sugarbush/Witsuikerbos***
Erect, *spreading shrub;* mostly with several main stems from a woody rootstock. Leaves pale bluish green, *hairless* when mature. Flower heads terminal and usually *solitary*, borne well above the leaves; bracts spreading at maturity, densely covered with short *silky hairs*.
Rocky slopes. Mainly Pretoria/Magaliesberg region. Spring – summer.
146.1 P. welwitschii Engl. is a multi-stemmed shrublet up to 1 m high. The leaves are ± *hairy*, even when mature, and the flower heads are often in terminal *clusters*. Grassland, often in rocky places. Widespread.

RANUNCULACEAE (See page 26)

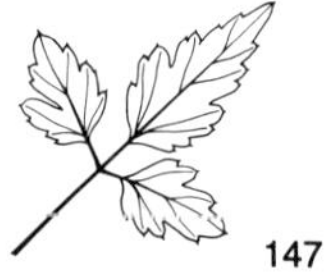

147

147 Clematis brachiata Thunb. ***Traveller's joy/Klimop***
Herbaceous or somewhat woody vine climbing vigorously by means of *twining leaf stalks*. Leaves divided into *3 – 5 leaflets*. Flowers scented; sepals showy, *densely covered with appressed hairs* and resembling petals (true petals absent); stamens numerous and showy, anthers *1,5 – 2,5 mm* long. Fruits with a long *feathery style*.
Bushy hillsides, particularly rocky places. Summer – autumn.
C. oweniae Harv. is very similar. It tends to have smaller anthers (± 1 mm long) and more leaflets (5 – 7).

RHAMNACEAE (See page 27)

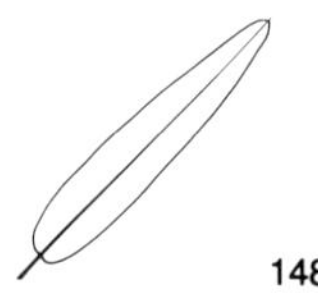

148

148 Phylica paniculata Willd.
Evergreen, much-branched and leafy shrub; twigs *velvety*. Leaves on very short stalks; blade shiny dark green above, densely *white-felted* below; base ± straight; margin *rolled under*. Flowers in terminal spikes; calyx with *white woolly hairs* on outer surface; petals very small, greenish or *cream*. Capsules shiny, brown, *crowned* with remains of calyx.
Usually along streams, often in kloofs. Mainly Magaliesberg. Summer – autumn.

144 *Oxygonum dregeanum*

145 *Oxygonum sinuatum*

146 *Protea gaguedi*

146.1 *P. welwitschii*

147 *Clematis brachiata*

148 *Phylica paniculata*

RUBIACEAE (See page 27) See also **424** and **591**.

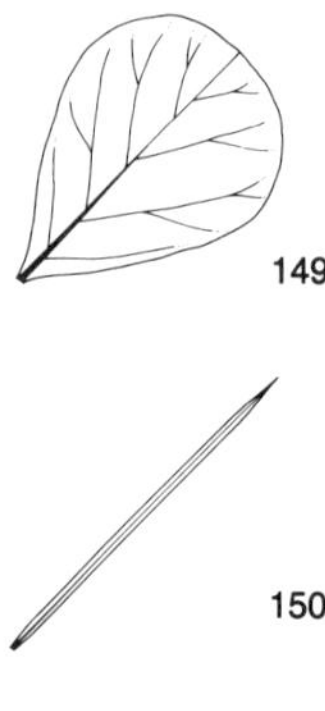
149

149 Gardenia volkensii K. Schum. subsp. **volkensii** var. **volkensii**
Bushveld gardenia/Bosveldkatjiepiering

Much-branched, twiggy, deciduous shrub; branchlets *radiating in 3s* along older branches. Leaves in *whorls of 3* at ends of branchlets, tips rounded, tapering gradually into the leaf stalk; green and glossy; lower surface with *tufts of hairs* in the axils of the side veins. Flowers have petals with ± wavy margins, white, fading to creamy yellow; calyx tube with a *slit* down 1 side. Fruit oval, strongly ribbed.

Bushveld. Pretoria/Magaliesberg region. Summer.

150

150 Kohoutia amatymbica Eckl. & Zeyh.

Slender, erect, unbranched herb from a woody perennial rootstock. Stems *almost hairless* with very few widely spaced, narrow leaves. Flowers in a *terminal cluster* (head) on the stem; petals white, cream to almost brown above, *greenish purple on lower surface.*

Common in grassland, often appearing after a fire. Widespread. Spring.

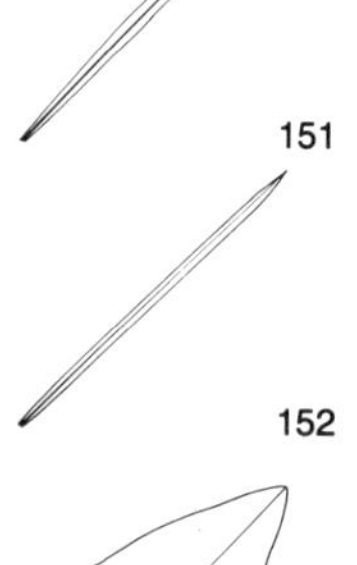
151

152

153

151 Kohoutia lasiocarpa Klotzsch

Slender, erect, ± perennial herb up to 500 mm high. Leaves stalkless, long and narrow, slightly grooved along upper surface of midrib. Flowers borne in a *branched* inflorescence, *usually arranged in pairs*, ± *stalkless*, 12 – 22 mm long, greenish or brownish white to almost white inside; open at night.

Grassland and bushveld. Widespread. Spring.

K. cynanchica DC. is similar but the flowers are usually distinctly *stalked* and *not arranged in pairs.*

152 Oldenlandia herbacea (L.) Roxb. var. **herbacea**

Annual herb with *very slender*, much-branched and intertwined wiry stems. Leaves widely spaced, *short and narrow.* Flowers axillary, ± 5 mm long; corolla tube narrow, with 4 lobes.

Grassland, usually on rocky ridges. Widespread. Summer.

153 Oldenlandia tenella (Hochst.) Kuntze

Annual, rather delicate, much-branched *creeping* herb. Leaves stalked, ± egg-shaped, 3 – 14 mm long, 2 – 7 mm wide, hairless. Corolla with a relatively *broad* tube and 4 pointed lobes, white to purplish.

Moist rock faces, often in shady places. Magaliesberg. Summer.

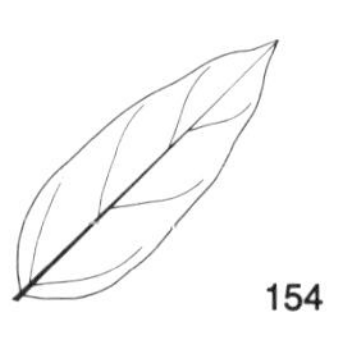
154

154 Otiophora calycophylla (Sond.) Schltr. & K. Schum. subsp. **calycophylla**

Several- to many-stemmed, somewhat woody *shrublet* with a woody rootstock; ± hairless. Stems often purplish. Leaves on very short stalks; egg- to lance-shaped, glossy green. Flowers axillary towards ends of branches, numerous and may appear head-like; calyx with *1 of the lobes enlarged and leaf-like;* corolla long with a *very narrow* tube (2,5 – 5 mm long) and spreading lobes.

Along streams and in rocky places, often rooted in crevices. Magaliesberg. Spring – summer.

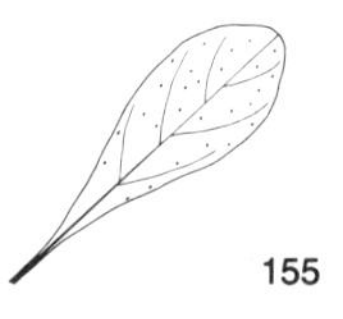
155

155 Pavetta gardeniifolia A. Rich. var. **gardeniifolia**
Christmas bush/Bruidsbos

Deciduous shrub up to 3 m high. Leaves stalked, *dotted with dark nodules* (clusters of bacteria) when held up to the light; ± hairless. Flowers in terminal or axillary clusters, sweet-scented; corolla *4-lobed*, tube *hairy* inside. Berries black, 2-seeded.

Rocky ridges, often in the shade of trees. Widespread. Summer.

149 *Gardenia volkensii*

150 *Kohoutia amatymbica*

151 *Kohoutia lasiocarpa*

152 *Oldenlandia herbacea*

153 *Oldenlandia tenella*

154 *Otiophora calycophylla*

155 *Pavetta gardeniifolia*

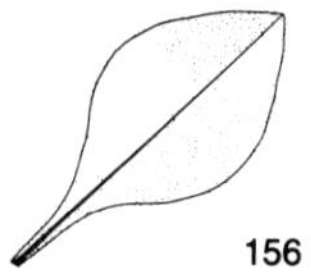
156

156 *Richardia brasiliensis Gomes *Tropical richardia/Tropiese-richardia*
Short-lived perennial herb with ± *trailing stems;* covered with *bristly hairs* throughout. Leaves narrow to broad, egg-shaped. Inflorescence comprising *stalkless* flowers *clustered* at the ends of branches, surrounded by *broad, leaf-like bracts.*

A weed from South America, naturalized in disturbed places. Widespread. Spring – summer.

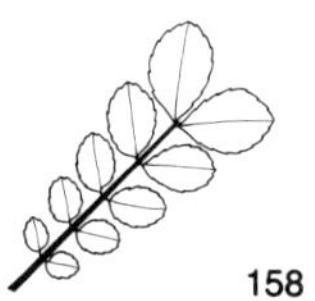
157

157 Rothmannia capensis Thunb. *Wild gardenia/Wildekatjiepiering*
Evergreen shrub or small tree; bark cracked into a grid-like pattern. Leaves on mature plants shiny, *leathery*, dark green with *prominent swellings/pockets* in the axils of the main side veins; often densely covered with hairs in young plants. Flowers trumpet-shaped with *maroon spots* on the inside of the corolla tube; sweetly scented. Fruit *large*, rounded and hard.

Rocky ridges and hillsides. Widespread. Summer.

RUTACEAE (See page 27)

158

158 Zanthoxylum capense (Thunb.) Harv. *Small knobwood/Kleinperdepram*
Deciduous shrub or small tree, armed with *straight or curved spines*; older growth often with *spines on raised knobs.* Leaves *pinnately compound*, dark green and shiny above, *gland-dotted*, strongly *lemon-scented* when crushed; midrib may bear small *sharp spines.* Flowers in short inflorescences at ends of branches, white to creamy white, scented. Capsules ± 5 mm in diameter, splitting open to reveal a single shiny black seed.

Rocky ridges, usually among other woody plants. Widespread. Spring.

SANTALACEAE (See page 27)

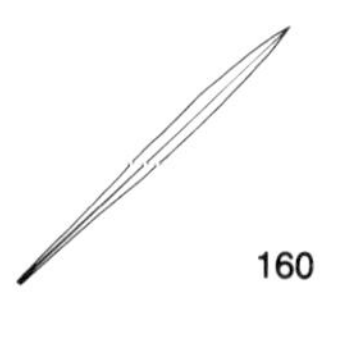
159

159 Thesium cf. **costatum** A.W. Hill
Low-growing bushy perennial herb with stiff, erect stems. Leaves well-spaced, narrow and sharply pointed, dark green. Flowers in groups of 1 – 3, relatively *large;* perianth tube *well-developed;* segments *hairless.* Fruits *with 10 distinct ribs*, crowned with the *remains of the sepals.*

Hemi-rootparasite in grassland, uncommon. Mainly Witwatersrand/ Suikerbosrand region. Spring – summer.

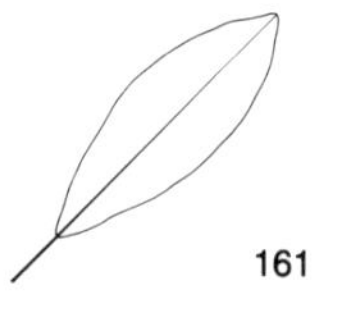
160

160 Thesium utile A.W. Hill *Besembossie*
Herbaceous perennial with numerous stiff, *yellow-green, upright* shoots. Leaves reduced and inconspicuous. Flowers minute; perianth segments with the tips *densely covered with hairs* on the inside. Fruits elliptic-globose, dry, indehiscent, *ribbed* and crowned with the *remains of the sepals.*

Hemi-rootparasite in grassland; common. Widespread. Spring – summer.

T. magalismontanum Sond. is common in the Pretoria/Magaliesberg region. It is characterized by *blue-green*, sparsely leaved stems and minute flowers in the bract axils of *lax spikes.*

Several species of **Thesium** occur in the field guide area. Distinguishing between the various species is difficult and often depends on details of the minute flowers. The group is in need of taxonomic revision.

SAPOTACEAE (See page 27)

161

161 Mimusops zeyheri Sond. *Transvaal red milkwood/Moepel*
Evergreen tree; bark rough, dark brown; young growth usually covered with short *rusty brown hairs.* Leaves stalked, leathery, borne mainly towards ends of branches. Flowers clustered in leaf axils, *drooping;* stalks rusty brown. Berries oval with *persistent calyx*, bright orange with a sweetly flavoured, mealy pulp.

Bushveld, usually in rocky places. Mainly Pretoria/Magaliesberg region. Summer.

156 *Richardia brasiliensis*

158 *Zanthoxylum capense*

157 *Rothmannia capensis*

159 *Thesium* cf. *costatum*

160 *Thesium utile*

161 *Mimusops zeyheri*

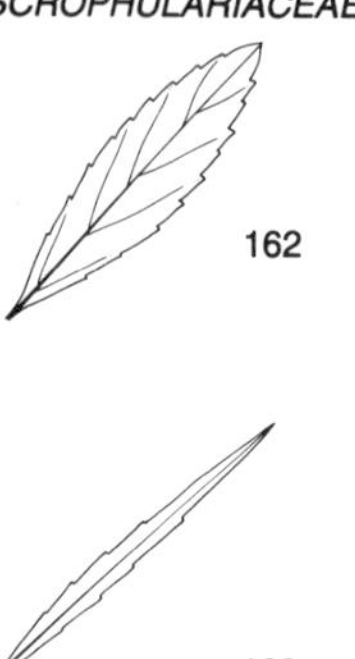
162

163

SCROPHULARIACEAE (See page 28)

162 Cycnium adonense E. Mey. ex Benth. *Ink plant/Inkblom*
Herbaceous, low-growing hemiparasitic shrublet with a perennial rootstock. Leaves covered with *rough hairs*, margin sharply *toothed.* Flowers on short stalks, solitary or paired; petals turn *black* when bruised.
Grassland, particularly on rocky slopes. Widespread. Spring – summer.

163 Cycnium tubulosum (L.f.) Engl. [=**Rhamphicarpa tubulosa** (L.f.) Benth.]
Erect perennial hemiparasitic herb; *sparsely* branched and hairless. Leaves stalkless and toothless with a *prominent midrib.* Flowers solitary in upper leaf axils; calyx lobes narrow and with fine points, *enlarging* considerably in fruit; corolla with broad and rounded lobes, the upper 2 *united higher up* than the others, white to pale pinkish purple.
Moist grassland, particularly along streams. Widespread. Summer – autumn.

164

164 Diclis reptans Benth.
Slender perennial herb with *trailing* or erect stems up to ± 200 mm high; ± fleshy. Leaves stalked, ± *rounded;* margin toothless to sharply toothed. Flowers borne on *slender* stalks in leaf axils; corolla 2-lipped, lower lip with 3 lobes, white or mauve with *pale yellow spots;* spur straight with the tip *minutely forked.*
Grassland, moist places, particularly in vleis and along streams. Widespread. Spring.

165

165 Graderia subintegra Mast. *Wild penstemon*
Perennial herb with erect or usually *trailing* shoots from a woody rootstock. Stems square in cross-section. Leaves *alternate*, stalkless and covered with short hairs; margin toothless or with 1 or 2 lobes on each side of the midrib. Flowers pink with the lower surface whitish, rarely white; corolla with the outer surface covered with *short hairs;* filaments hairy.
Common in grassland. Widespread. Spring – summer.
For pink-flowered form see **594**.

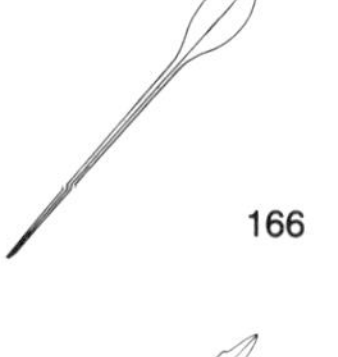
166

166 Limosella maior Diels
Small herbs with *runners*, from the nodes of which clusters of roots and erect leaves arise. Leaves variable in size; blade spatulate with ± 3 veins, gradually tapering into a *long* stalk. Flowers solitary on long, ± erect stalks which arise between the leaves; stalks usually *shorter* than the leaves; corolla white to blue.
Shallow water or marshy places. Widespread. Summer – winter.

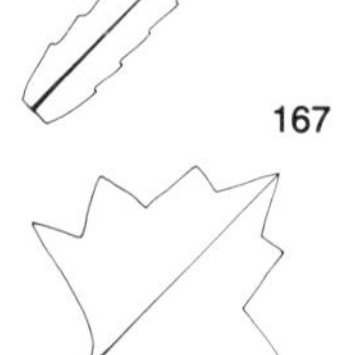
167

168

167 Mimulus gracilis R.Br.
Erect, branchless or sparsely branched herb; *hairless* throughout; often rooting at the lower nodes. Leaves well-spaced on stem, stalkless, ± clasping at base; margin faintly toothed or toothless. Flowers solitary, borne on slender stalks in the axils of upper leaves; corolla usually white (rarely mauve or purplish), with the throat *spotted yellow.*
Moist places, often along streams. Widespread. Spring – autumn.

168 Zaluzianskya katharinae Hiern *Drumsticks*
Perennial herbaceous shrublet. Leaves stalked; margin *coarsely toothed;* hairy and ± sticky. Flowers solitary in axils of upper leaves, open at dusk; corolla tube *long and cylindrical;* lobes *forked, pink below, white above.*
Grassland, on rocky ridges. Widespread. Spring – summer.

162 *Cycnium adonense*

163 *Cycnium tubulosum*

164 *Diclis reptans*

165 *Graderia subintegra*

166 *Limosella maior*

167 *Mimulus gracilis*

168 *Zaluzianskya katharinae*

168 *Z. katharinae* (buds)

SELAGINACEAE (See page 28) See also **676**.

169 Walafrida densiflora (Rolfe) Rolfe

Herb with many ± *prostrate or sprawling* stems from a perennial rootstock. Leaves needle-like, often in tufts. Flowers in *roundish* or slightly elongated heads which are borne at the *tips* of *numerous short, erect side branches* along the *length* of the main shoots.

Grassland and bushveld. Widespread. Summer.

170 Walafrida tenuifolia Rolfe

Much-branched sprawling perennial, often forming a *rounded shrublet*. Leaves fine and *needle-like*, often in *tufts*, ± hairless. Flowers small and unequally 5-lobed, borne in dense, ± *globose* heads (becoming ± elongated with age) clustered together in *rather elongated groups* at the ends of *main* branches.

Rocky ridges. Widespread. Summer.

SOLANACEAE (See page 28) See also **680**.

171 *Datura stramonium L. *Thorn apple/Olieboom*

Robust herbaceous annual up to ± 1 m high. Leaves stalked, egg-shaped; margin *coarsely and distantly* toothed or ± lobed; give off an *unpleasant smell* when crushed. Flowers solitary, axillary; calyx up to 40 mm long; corolla funnel-shaped, with *5 prominent teeth* on the rim; white to mauve-purple. Capsules covered with *relatively short* spreading spines up to *10 mm* long.

A weed of disturbed places and cultivated land. Native to North America. Widespread. Summer. □ For purple-flowered form see **677**.

***D. ferox** L., also a cosmopolitan weed, has white flowers with the calyx up to 25 mm long and the capsules covered with *very stout*, spreading spines up to *25 mm* long.

169

170

171

172 *Solanum pseudocapsicum L. *Jerusalem cherry/Bosgifappel*

Short-lived herbaceous perennial shrublet up to ± 500 mm high; unarmed and *unpleasantly scented* when crushed. Leaves with blade gradually tapering at the base into a *narrowly winged* stalk; ± *hairless* to the naked eye; margin entire or slightly and distantly scalloped. Flowers axillary, white. Berries globose, ± 15 mm in diameter, green changing through *orange to bright red*.

A native of Europe and Asia, now naturalized in disturbed places, often in the shade of trees. Summer.

172

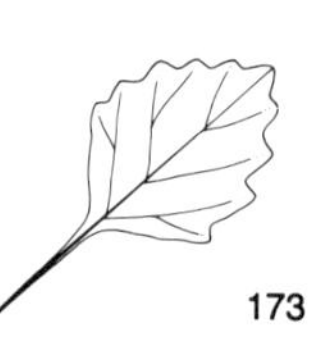

173 Solanum retroflexum Dun. *Black nightshade/Nastergal*

Erect annual or biennial herb up to ± 1 m high. Leaves stalked; margin *shallowly or deeply wavy or toothed*. Flowers in stalked, *drooping, axillary umbels* bearing few flowers; corolla white; anthers bright yellow. Berries globose, black when ripe.

Disturbed places, often under trees. Widespread. Summer.

Probably an indigenous species, although closely related to the European **S. nigrum** L. which has toothless leaves.

173

174 *Solanum sisymbrifolium Lam. *Wild tomato/Doringbitterappel*

Perennial *bushy shrublet* up to 1,5 m high. Stems densely covered with slender, *reddish brown straight spines* up to 30 mm long. Leaves deeply *pinnately lobed*, covered with star-shaped hairs and *reddish brown straight spines*, particularly on the midrib and stalk. Corolla white to pale bluish. Berry bright red, subtended by the enlarged spiny calyx (which enclosed the very young fruit).

A weed of disturbed places. Native to South America. Widespread. Summer – autumn. □ For bluish-flowered form see **685**.

174

170 *Walafrida tenuifolia*

169 *Walafrida densiflora*

171 *Datura stramonium*

172 *Solanum pseudocapsicum*

173 *Solanum retroflexum*

174 *Solanum sisymbrifolium*

STERCULIACEAE (See page 28)

175 Dombeya rotundifolia (Hochst.) Planch. var. **rotundifolia** *Wild pear/Drolpeer*

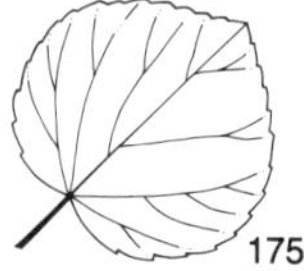

175

Deciduous tree; bark brown-black, *thick and rough.* Leaves broadly egg-shaped or *almost round;* base slightly *heart-shaped;* venation *raised* on lower surface with *5 veins* from the base; both surfaces *rough* with minute, star-shaped hairs. Flowers usually appear before the leaves, densely covering the branches, white, *fading to brown.* Capsules globose, brownish.

Open, rocky hillsides. Widespread. Spring.

VELLOZIACEAE (See page 29)

176 Xerophyta retinervis Bak. *Monkey's tail/Bobbejaanstert*

Perennial with stout, sometimes sparsely branched, erect stems which are densely covered with a thick mantle of fire-charred, *closely packed, persistent leaf bases,* and have inside many densely packed roots (the basal portion of the true stem dies off at an early stage and is replaced by the roots). Flowers usually blue or mauve, rarely white. Capsules covered with rough *hairs.*

Rocky ridges. Widespread. Spring. □ For blue-flowered form see **687**.

X. humilis (Bak.) Dur. & Schinz is a small, *mat-forming* plant with *virtually no* erect stems; leaves usually *shorter than 60 mm.* Rarely encountered in the Pretoria/Magaliesberg region.

177 Xerophyta viscosa Bak.

Perennial herb with *basal* tuft of leaves. Leaves with *stiff, sharp* hairs along the margin and keel. Flowers solitary on long stalks; stalks and base of outer perianth segments with *dark glands;* white with yellow anthers, usually with outer surface of perianth tinged pale mauve.

Rocky slopes, often in dense colonies on rock sheets. Mainly Pretoria/ Magaliesberg region. Summer. □ Also **608**.

VERBENACEAE (See page 29) See also **448, 449, 450** and **692**.

178 Clerodendrum glabrum E. Mey. var. **glabrum** *Tinderwood/Tontelhout*

178

Deciduous or evergreen shrub or small tree; twigs with scattered *small raised whitish dots.* Leaves stalked, paired or often in *whorls of 3 or 4* at the nodes; often *drooping; strongly scented* when crushed. Inflorescence a compact, terminal, *dome-shaped* head with many small, scented flowers. Fruit fleshy, ± globose, whitish or yellow, smooth and shiny.

Bushveld. Mainly Pretoria/Magaliesberg area. Summer.

179 Priva cordifolia (L.f.) Druce var. **abyssinica** (Jaub. & Spach) Moldenke *Blaasklits*

Erect soft shrublet from a perennial rootstock; most parts covered with *coarse hairs.* Stems prominently *4-angled.* Leaves with slender stalks, egg-shaped, with the base usually weakly heart-shaped or ± square; margin coarsely toothed. Flowers *lax* in *long,* slender spikes; white with purplish markings on the 2 lower lips. Fruit enclosed in the *dilated calyx tube,* covered with minute *hooked* hairs which tend to stick to clothes.

179

Among the undergrowth in clumps of bush. Mainly Pretoria/Magaliesberg region. Summer.

It is not clear whether a similar-looking plant from Suikerbosrand should be regarded as a member of this species.

175 *Dombeya rotundifolia*

176 *Xerophyta retinervis*

177 *Xerophyta viscosa*

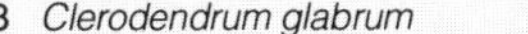

178 *Clerodendrum glabrum*

179 *Priva cordifolia*

YELLOW OR CREAM FLOWERS

(See also **11, 12, 17, 73, 141, 146, 147, 150, 157, 158, 505, 542, 586, 609, 714, 719, 722, 724, 731, 734, 735, 737 – 745, 753 – 757, 780 – 782, 795**)

Yellow flowers are easily recognizable and constitute the predominant floral colour among herbaceous plants in the grassland. A few pale orange flowers merge towards yellow and are treated in this section. Pale cream flowers may be regarded as white and some of these are presented under White or whitish flowers (page 30). See also the chapter Green or greenish flowers (page 284) for some that appear yellowish green.

Most yellow flowers owe their coloration to the carotenoid (orange or yellow) and flavonoid (yellow) groups of pigments. Often present as droplets or in granular or crystalline form, carotenoids are enclosed in numerous discrete bodies, called chromoplasts. Flavonoids are soluble in water and colour the cell sap.

Yellow flowers attract all the main groups of insect pollinators. Bees and some butterflies (particularly the nymphalids) show a strong preference for this colour group. Flowers which attract bees are usually irregular and characterized by nectar, nectar guides and few stamens. Those pollinated by butterflies have a slight scent and their nectar is well hidden in narrow tubes and spurs. Ultraviolet reflection is often found in yellow flowers. To insects yellow may appear purple, red-purple or red.

GUIDE TO THE FAMILIES WHICH INCLUDE YELLOW OR CREAM FLOWERS

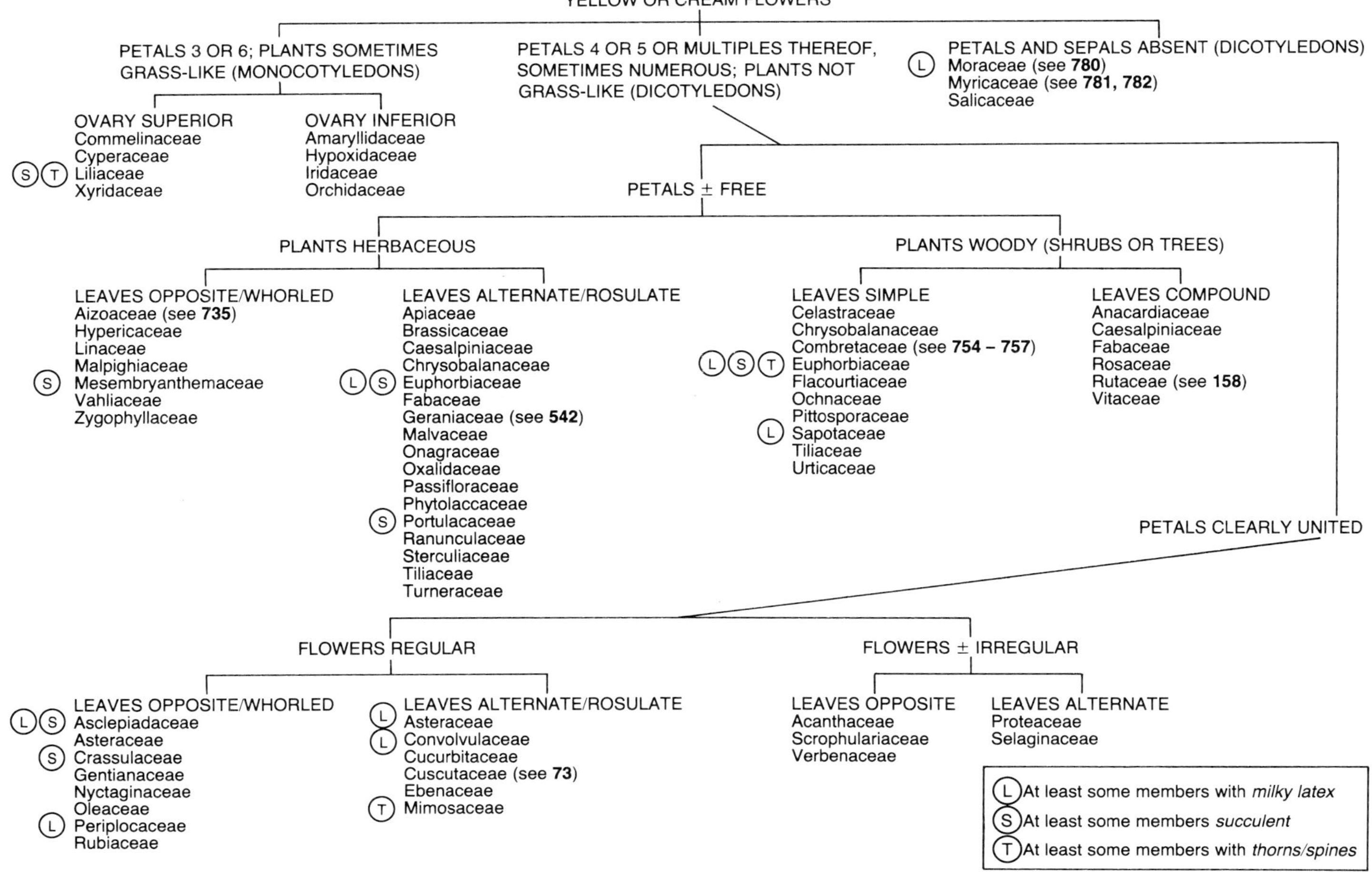

180

ACANTHACEAE (See page 16) See also **11** and **12**.

180 Justicia flava (Forssk.) Vahl

Slender erect to low spreading herbaceous shrublet. Leaf pairs *well-spaced* on stem; blade stalked, ± egg-shaped, hairless above, covered with short hairs below. Inflorescence a terminal spike; bracts *green*, with spreading hairs and *stalked* glands. Flowers 2-lipped.

Bushveld, often along roadsides and in disturbed places. Mainly Pretoria/Magaliesberg region. Spring – autumn.

AMARYLLIDACEAE (See page 16)

181 Cyrtanthus breviflorus Harv. *Yellow fire lily/Geelvuurlelie*

Perennial herb with *strap-shaped* leaves. Inflorescence erect with a terminal *umbel* comprising fewer than 6 flowers. Perianth segments hairless, united *right at the base.*

Grassland, in damp places such as vleis and along streams. Mainly Suikerbosrand/Witwatersrand region. Spring.

ANACARDIACEAE (See page 16) See also **17** and **737 – 745**.

182

182 Lannea discolor (Sond.) Engl. *False marula/Dikbas*

Small deciduous tree; bark thick, ± smooth, often reddish grey and wrinkled on younger twigs. Leaves stalked, crowded at the ends of branches, compound with 3 – 6 pairs of opposite leaflets; mature leaves green above, *white or grey* below. Flowering spikes creamy yellow, appearing at the tips of branches *before* the leaves. Fruit a drupe, ± flattened.

Bushveld, often on rocky ridges. Mainly Pretoria/Magaliesberg region. Spring.

183

183 Lannea edulis (Sond.) Engl. *Wild grape/Wildedruif*

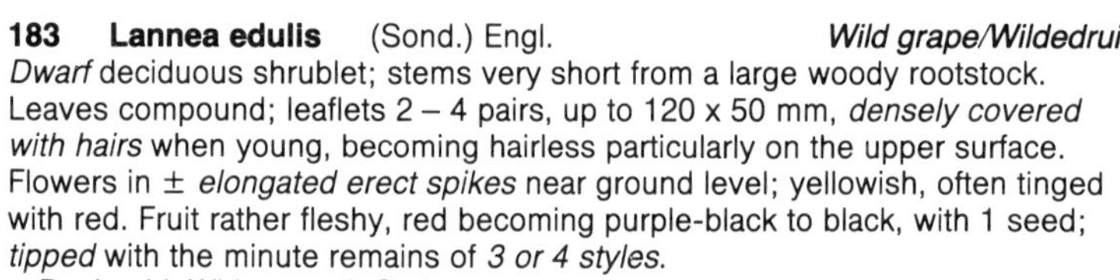

Dwarf deciduous shrublet; stems very short from a large woody rootstock. Leaves compound; leaflets 2 – 4 pairs, up to 120 x 50 mm, *densely covered with hairs* when young, becoming hairless particularly on the upper surface. Flowers in ± *elongated erect spikes* near ground level; yellowish, often tinged with red. Fruit rather fleshy, red becoming purple-black to black, with 1 seed; *tipped* with the minute remains of *3 or 4 styles.*

Bushveld. Widespread. Spring.

APIACEAE (See page 16)

184

184 Peucedanum magalismontanum Sond. *Wild parsley/Wildepietersielie*

Erect herb with *slender stems;* top of perennial rootstock covered with fibrous old leaf bases. Leaves in basal *rosette*, stalked and rather fleshy, *finely* divided into *numerous* leaflets. Flowers minute, bisexual, clustered in *twice-divided umbels* at the ends of long, ± leafless stalks. Fruit *flattened* with thickened margins, up to 12 x 8 mm.

Grassland. Widespread. Spring.

185

185 Sium repandum Welw. ex Hiern. *Water parsnip*

Erect perennial herb; stems ribbed, usually *unbranched;* hairless throughout. Leaves stalked with up to ± 12 pairs of leaflets (appearing fern-like); leaflets stalkless, usually *curved* forward; margin with *numerous forward-curving* teeth. Inflorescence (a compound umbel) terminates the main stem.

Along streams, often in water. Widespread. Summer – autumn.

186 Berula erecta (Hudson) Cov. *Tandpynwortel*

Perennial herb rather similar to the previous species but can be distinguished by *fewer* (up to 6 pairs) leaflets which stand out at *right angles* to the axis and by the margins which have a *few triangular teeth.* Flowers white.

Along streams, often in water. Widespread. Summer.

180 *Justicia flava*

181 *Cyrtanthus breviflorus*

182 *Lannea discolor*

183 *Lannea edulis*

183 *L. edulis* (fruit)

184 *Peucedanum magalismontanum*

185 *Sium repandum*

186 *Berula erecta*

ASCLEPIADACEAE (See page 17) See also **753**.

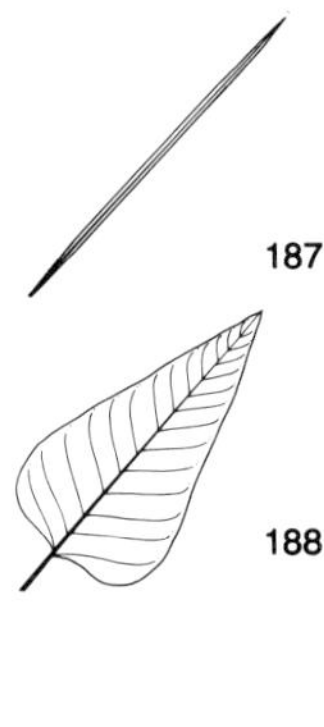

187 Asclepias aurea (Schltr.) Schltr.
Very *slender*, sparsely branched, erect herb with a woody perennial rootstock. Leaves *long and narrow;* hairless. Inflorescence a terminal umbel comprising 3 – 7 flowers, on a long stalk. Flowers with ± reflexed corolla which is *purplish brown* on the back; corona bright yellow, with *long tapering points.*
Grassland. Widespread. Summer.

188 Asclepias fallax (Schltr.) Schltr.
Perennial herb arising from a thick rootstock; almost hairless to covered with rough hairs. Flowers in ± *flat-topped* umbels on long, *rigid* stalks; petals cream to purplish brown.
Grassland. Widespread. Spring – summer.

189 Asclepias fruticosa L. *Milkweed/Melkbos*
Evergreen perennial shrublet up to 1,5 m high. Leaves on short stalks; blade long and tapering, slightly hairy; margin *not* rolled under. Inflorescences axillary, usually *pendulous*, comprising up to 10 flowers. Flowers with pale cream, reflexed corolla lobes; corona with blunt tips, greenish. Fruits inflated, *tapering* to a point; sparsely covered with soft, *bristle-like* hairs.
189 Grassland, often along roadsides and in cultivated fields that have been abandoned. Widespread. Spring – summer. □ Compare **25** and **750**.

190 Orbeopsis lutea (N.E.Br.) Leach subsp. **lutea**
Yellow carrion flower/Geelaasblom
Perennial *leafless succulent* with stems erect and *toothed* along the angles. Flowers borne in umbel-like clusters on stems, between angles; strongly *foetid;* corolla without an evident tube; petals with finely *granular* surface and margins which have slender, dark-coloured, *club-shaped hairs.*
Grassland, often in the shade of woody plants; uncommon in the field guide area. Widespread. Summer.

191 Sarcostemma viminale (L.) R.Br. *Melktou*
Vigorous, *leafless* perennial climber, often forming dense masses on other plants. Stems slightly *succulent*, trailing or twining, greyish green. Flowers in clusters at the nodes, sweetly scented; corolla with ± downward-bent margin, yellowish green; corona white.
Bushveld, often in rocky places. Pretoria/Magaliesberg region. Summer.

192 Stapelia gigantea N.E.Br. *Giant carrion flower/Reuse-aasblom*
Leafless succulent with numerous straight, erect, 4-angled stems, usually ± 150 mm high; *densely* covered with hairs. Inflorescence on a short stalk, positioned towards *base* of stem. Flowers unpleasantly scented; corolla ± flattened, yellowish with *fine wavy lines* of reddish brown to purple, *sparsely covered with hairs* which are purplish along the margin; corona dark purple.
Bushveld, rocky and often shady places. Mainly Magaliesberg. Summer.

193 Xysmalobium brownianum S. Moore
Perennial herb from a tuberous rootstock. Leaves ± 120 x 20 mm, *strongly* veined; margin conspicuously *wavy*. Flowers in stalked axillary umbels.
193 Occasional in grassland. Widespread. Spring – summer.

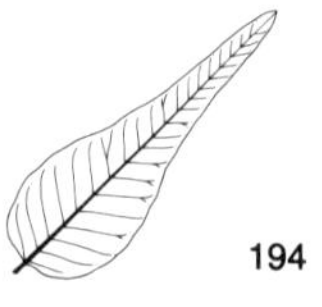

194 Xysmalobium undulatum (L.) Ait.f. *Bitterhout*
Robust, erect, perennial herb up to 1,5 m high. Stems stout, hairy. Leaves *stalkless*, up to 200 x 60 mm, both surfaces hairy and *rough* to the touch; base rounded or ± heart-shaped; margin covered with very short hairs, wavy and often reddish. Flowers in axillary umbels; corolla with a *dense beard* of white woolly hairs on the recurved tips. Fruits inflated, covered with long *curly hairs.*
Moist grassland, particularly in vleis. Widespread. Summer.

187 *Asclepias aurea*

188 *Asclepias fallax*

189 *Asclepias fruticosa*

190 *Orbeopsis lutea*

191 *Sarcostemma viminale*

192 *Stapelia gigantea*

193 *Xysmalobium brownianum*

194 *Xysmalobium undulatum*

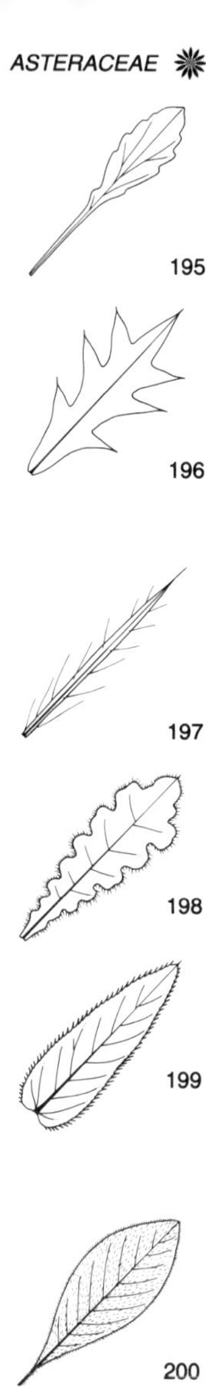

ASTERACEAE (See page 17)
Group A

195 Arctotis arctotoides (L.f.) O. Hoffm.
Mat-forming perennial herb. Leaves basal, *white-felted on lower surface*; margin ± wavy. Flower heads solitary on long stalks; ray flowers yellow, often *purplish brown* below.
Grassland, often in vleis. Witwatersrand/Suikerbosrand region. Spring – summer.

196 Berkheya carlinopsis Welw. ex O. Hoffm. subsp. **magalismontana** (H. Bolus) Roessl. *Bergdisseldoring*
Tall perennial herb or shrublet. Stems covered with *whitish felt*. Leaves coarsely toothed, the teeth *spine-tipped;* upper surface greyish green, lower surface covered with *white woolly* hairs. Seeds with dense silky covering.
Rocky grassland and bushveld. Pretoria/Magaliesberg region. Summer.

197 Berkheya insignis (Harv.) Thell.
Perennial herb with several erect stems from a woody rootstock. Leaves arranged *along the length* of the stem, stalkless, *narrow* (rarely as much as 15 mm wide), *bristle-tipped;* margin ± rolled under with *long* (up to 10 mm), *flexible bristles* along entire edge; lower surface *white-felted*. Flower heads terminal, solitary.
Grassland, often on rocky outcrops. Mainly Witwatersrand/Suikerbosrand region. Spring. □ Compare **201**.

198 Berkheya radula (Harv.) De Wild. *Boesmansrietjie*
Robust perennial herb with a woody rootstock. Stem *winged, prickly*, ± densely covered with glandular hairs. Leaves mainly in a *basal rosette*, dark green and *smooth above*, white-felted below; margin ± lobed, with *spines*.
Moist grassland and vleis. Widespread. Spring. □ Compare **200**.

199 Berkheya seminivea Harv. & Sond. *Disseldoring*
Rigid herbaceous perennial; milky latex present. Stems *unbranched*, without hairs. Leaves with *spiny margin*, green above, *white-felted* below; venation *conspicuous* and whitish above. Flower heads large.
Rocky grassland, often on koppies or hillsides. Widespread. Summer.

200 Berkheya setifera DC. *Rasperdisseldoring*
Perennial herb spreading by means of *underground runners; milky latex* present. Leaves few, mainly *basal*, ± lance-shaped, tapering to a stalk-like, clasping base; upper surface with *straw-coloured bristles;* lower surface white-felted and hairy; margin ± spiny. Flowering stem *solitary*, erect, *without wings* and ± leafless, forking above to bear *several* flower heads; involucral bracts with spiny tips and margins.
Grassland, usually in large colonies. Widespread; very common at Suikerbosrand. Spring – summer. □ Compare **198**.

201 Berkheya zeyheri (Sond. & Harv.) Oliv. & Hiern subsp. **zeyheri**
Herb with several erect stems from a woody rootstock. Stems *unbranched*, rarely forked once or twice, *leafy*. Leaves stalkless, long and *narrow* (1 – 2 mm wide); margin with *long flexible bristles* ± confined to the *lower half* of the leaf. Flower heads terminal, solitary.
Grassland. Widespread. Summer. □ Compare **197**.

195 *Arctotis arctotoides*

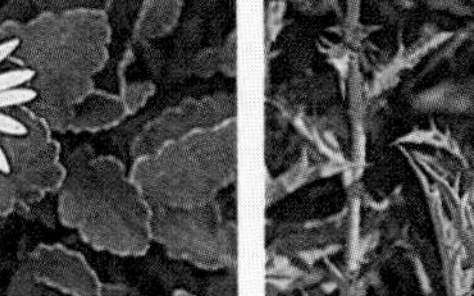

196 *Berkheya carlinopsis*

197 *Berkheya insignis*

198 *Berkheya radula*

199 *Berkheya seminivea*

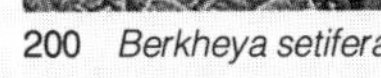

200 *Berkheya setifera*

201 *Berkheya zeyheri*

202

202 *Bidens bipinnata L. *Spanish blackjack/Spaanse knapsekêrel*
Erect annual herb up to ± 1,5 m high; sparsely branched. Leaves opposite, with a *fringe of whitish hairs* at the base between pairs; *bipinnately divided;* leaflets lance-shaped. Flower heads terminal in lax inflorescences bearing few heads; ray flowers 3 – 5, small. Seeds black, long and narrow, tipped with 3 – 4 barbed pappus awns.

A weed of Eurasian origin, now naturalized in disturbed places, often under trees on rocky ridges. Widespread. Summer.

***B. biternata** (Lour.) Merr. & Sherff also has yellow ray flowers. It differs in having *once-pinnate* leaves with usually *5 – 9* ± egg-shaped leaflets.

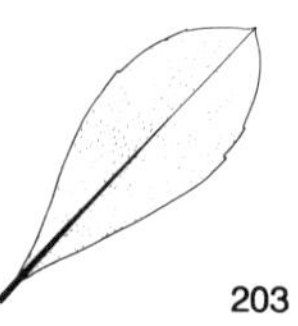
203

203 Chrysanthemoides monilifera (L.) T. Norl. subsp. **canescens** (DC.) T. Norl. *Bushtick/Bietou*
Large *bushy shrub* with *white woolly* hairs on foliage and stems. Leaves with *coarsely* toothed margin. Flower heads ± 30 mm across, few in terminal groups. Involucral bracts in 2 whorls. Seeds of ray flowers *fleshy*, purplish black when ripe.

Rocky slopes. Mainly Suikerbosrand. Nearly all year.

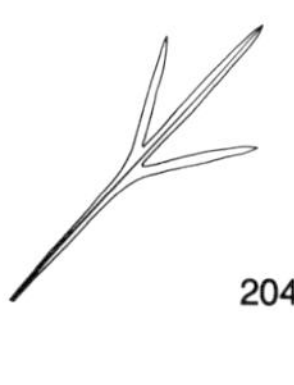
204

204 Euryops laxus (Harv.) Burtt Davy *Resin bush/Harpuisbos*
Low-growing perennial herb with annual *simple or sparsely branched* erect stems from a woody rootstock; *hairless.* Leaves ± erect, *pinnately divided* into up to 4 pairs of lobes; lobes *0,3 – 2,5 mm* wide. Flower heads *solitary* at the tips of *long, leafless stalks* borne at the ends of branches. Ray flowers usually 8 – 15, *widely spaced.*

Grassland, often on rocky ridges. Mainly Witwatersrand region. Spring.

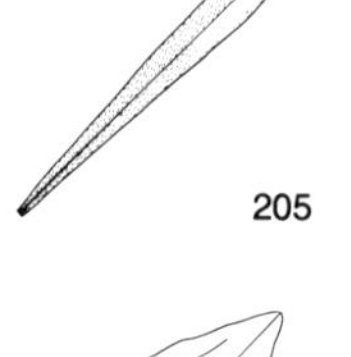
205

205 Felicia mossamedensis (Hiern) Mendonça
Much-branched perennial herb with a tough taproot; up to 300 mm high; covered with *rough hairs.* Leaves up to 6 mm wide; margin untoothed. Flower heads solitary at the tips of branches, subtended by ± 2 series of narrow bracts. Ray flowers *numerous, narrow*, yellow. Disc flowers yellow.

Bushveld, often along roadsides. Pretoria/Magaliesberg region. Spring – summer.

206

206 *Galinsoga parviflora Cav. *Gallant soldier/Knopkruid*
Slender annual herb up to ± 400 mm high; stem branching from the base. Leaves *opposite*, stalked, ± egg-shaped, *3-veined* from the base; margin often ± toothed. Flower heads in upper leaf axils or terminal groups; ray flowers 5, *very small*, white; disc flowers yellow.

A native of South America and now a cosmopolitan weed of disturbed places. Widespread. Spring – autumn.

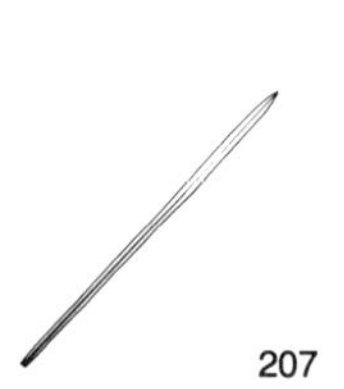
207

207 Gazania krebsiana Less. subsp. **serrulata** (DC.) Roessl. *Botterblom*
Stemless perennial herb from a woody rootstock; *milky latex* present. Leaves tufted and linear with the upper surface *green* and the lower *white-felted.* Flower heads solitary, stalked; ray flowers yellow or white.

Grassland. Widespread; yellow-flowered form mainly Witwatersrand/ Suikerbosrand region. Spring – summer. □ For white-flowered form see **36**.

202 *Bidens bipinnata*

203 *Chrysanthemoides monilifera*

204 *Euryops laxus*

205 *Felicia mossamedensis*

206 *Galinsoga parviflora*

207 *Gazania krebsiana*

208

208 Geigeria burkei Harv. subsp. **burkei** var. **intermedia** (S. Moore) Merxm. *Vermeerbos*

Perennial herb with a woody rootstock. Stems prostrate to ± erect. Leaves long and *narrow* (± 1 mm), with minute and indistinct gland dots. Flower heads *stalkless, solitary at each fork* of the stem; bracts in many series, those of the outermost series with *leaf-like appendages;* corolla of ray flowers with 3-toothed tip.

Grassland, often on rocky ridges. Widespread. Summer.

209

209 Gerbera ambigua (Cass.) Sch. Bip.

Stemless herb with a perennial rootstock. Leaves *basal*, stalked; blade variable in shape, often ± elliptical; upper surface green and hairy; lower surface of mature leaves *densely white-felted* with the veins ± *raised.* Flower heads solitary on long, leafless stalks; ray flowers yellow.

Grassland. Widespread. Spring.

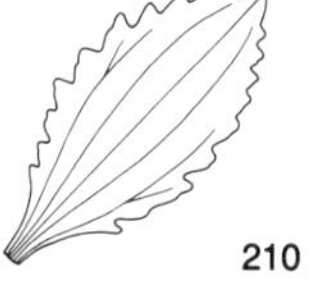

210

210 Haplocarpha lyrata Harv.

Stemless perennial herb. Leaves in a *basal rosette;* upper surface green, *smooth* to the touch, lower surface *white-felted;* margin *deeply lobed.* Flower heads solitary on leafless stalks, at 100 – 300 mm *2 – 3 times* the length of the leaves; outer involucral bracts *taper to a point.*

Grassland, often in moist places. Widespread. Summer. □ Compare **211**.

211

211 Haplocarpha scaposa Harv. *Tonteldoosbossie*

Stemless perennial herb. Leaves in a *basal rosette*, broadly elliptic, narrowing to a stalk-like base; upper surface green, often *rough* to the touch; lower surface *white-felted;* margin sometimes very shallowly toothed but *not lobed.* Flower heads solitary on leafless stalks, at 300 – 450 mm *many times* longer than the leaves; outer involucral bracts with ± *blunt* tips.

Grassland, often in moist places. Widespread. Summer. □ Compare **210**.

212

212 Osteospermum muricatum E. Mey. ex DC. subsp. **muricatum**

Evergreen, much-branched shrublet with an underground rootstock; with *sticky* glandular hairs; strongly *scented* (± of citrus oil). Leaves stalkless, some with the margin toothed or pinnately cleft. Flower heads solitary at ends of leafless stalks; ray flowers *short*, barely longer than the sharply pointed involucral bracts. Fruiting heads *erect.* Seeds ± triangular to *globose*, hard.

Grassland. Widespread. Spring – summer.

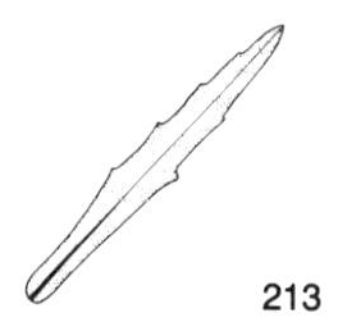

213

213 Osteospermum scariosum DC. var. **scariosum**

Erect herb with several ± *unbranched* annual shoots from a woody perennial rootstock; sparsely covered with *rough hairs;* aromatic; greyish green. Leaves mainly basal; margin with *widely spaced* teeth and ± *rounded* spaces between; sticky glandular hairs present mainly on lower surface. Flower heads terminal on erect stalks; solitary; ray flowers with corolla *much longer* than the involucral bracts, usually with *reddish or purplish veins* below. Fruiting heads *drooping.* Seeds large, oval, with 3 *broad* papery *wings* often tinged with purple.

Grassland. Widespread. Spring.

208 *Geigeria burkei*

210 *Haplocarpha lyrata*

209 *Gerbera ambigua*

211 *Haplocarpha scaposa*

212 *Osteospermum muricatum*

213 *Osteospermum scariosum*

214

215

214 Senecio achilleifolius DC. *Slootopdammer*
Perennial herb. Stems long, *prostrate*, stiff and *rod-like*, *freely rooting*. Leaves *deeply and finely* lobed, woolly when young, hairless at maturity. Flower heads solitary or several arranged in a flat-topped cluster at branch tips; involucral bracts *gland-dotted*.

In rocky streambeds or along streams in moist hollows. Widespread. Summer.

215 Senecio affinis DC.
Erect perennial herb up to ± 1,5 m high; *hairless* at the base, sometimes also higher up. Stems *unbranched* below inflorescence. Leaves long and narrow, ± erect; stem leaves stalkless and often ± *lobed* at the base; margin *closely and minutely* toothed. Ray flowers *8*, ± *reflexed*.

Grassland. Widespread. Summer. ☐ Compare **221**.

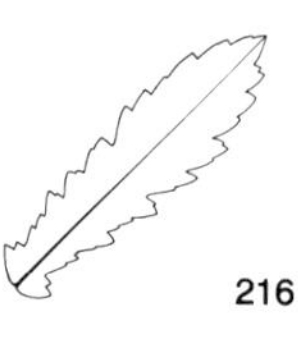
216

216 Senecio consanguineus DC.
Starvation senecio/Hongerbos-senecio
Bushy annual or perennial herb, branching from or near the base; most parts have *glandular hairs*. Leaves stalkless, elongated; margin *sharply and coarsely* toothed; base *stem-clasping* with 2 lobes. Flower heads in laxly branched terminal inflorescences; ray flowers *6 – 8*, becoming reflexed at an early stage; involucral bracts ± 14, with short *glandular hairs*.

Grassland, rocky ridges, sometimes a weed of cultivated land. Spring – summer. ☐ Compare **218** and **219**.

217

217 Senecio coronatus (Thunb.) Harv. *Sybossie*
Erect herb with a perennial rootstock covered with *silky hairs*; most parts (even the roots) ± covered with *woolly* hairs. Basal leaves with *broad stalks*, ± elliptic, 100 – 400 mm long. Flowering stems 1 to several, rather *stout*. Flower heads *2 – 20* in a rounded terminal cluster.

Grassland, usually in large colonies. Widespread. Spring.

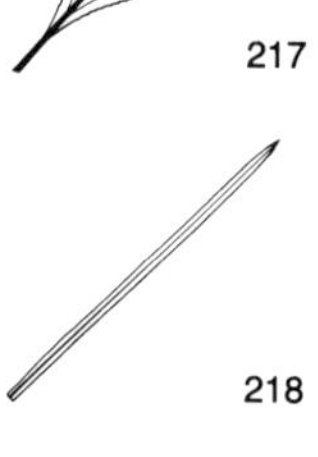
218

218 Senecio harveianus MacOwan
Bushy perennial herb, ± hairless. Leaves stalkless, long and narrow; margin ± *smooth*. Flower heads solitary at the ends of stems, *large and showy;* ray flowers often *rolled under*.

Grassland, often on rocky ridges; uncommon and localized. Widespread. Early spring. ☐ Compare **216** and **219**.

219

219 Senecio inaequidens DC. [=**S. burchellii** DC. *p.p.*]
Canary weed/Geelopslag
Bushy perennial herb, much-branched from the base. Leaves narrow with pointed tips; base half-clasping or stalk-like; margin *toothed*. Ray flowers ± *13*, often *rolled under*.

Grassland, often in trampled and disturbed areas. Widespread. Spring – summer. ☐ Compare **216** and **218**.

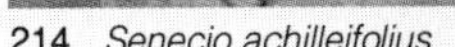

214 *Senecio achilleifolius*

215 *Senecio affinis*

216 *Senecio consanguineus*

217 *Senecio coronatus*

218 *Senecio harveianus*

219 *Senecio inaequidens*

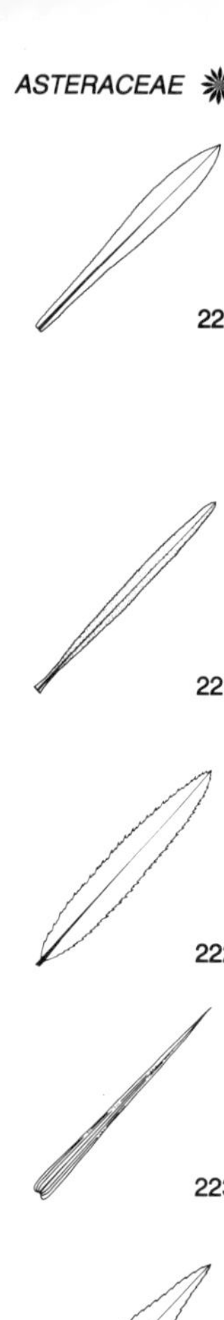

220 Senecio inornatus DC.
Erect perennial herb up to ± *2 m* high from a woody rootstock. Basal leaves long and elliptical, tapering to a long stalk at the base, often with *traces* of a white woolly covering; margin ± toothed. Flowering stem *solitary*, robust. Flower heads many, in a branched, flat-topped inflorescence; ray flowers *5*, short, appearing somewhat later than the disc flowers, becoming reflexed at an early stage.
Grassland, often in moist places, particularly in vleis. Widespread. Summer.

221 Senecio lydenburgensis Hutch. & Burtt Davy
Erect perennial herb up to ± 1,4 m high; crown of rootstock covered with *fibrous bases* of old leaves; stems usually *unbranched* below, densely leafy; most parts *sparsely and loosely covered with whitish woolly hairs.* Leaves on stem stalkless, half-clasping at base; margin closely and minutely toothed. Flower heads in loosely branched terminal panicles; stalks with *sparse covering of woolly hairs;* ray flowers ± *8*, becoming *reflexed* at an early stage; bracts ± 12, *shorter* than the disc flowers, with *whitish woolly hairs*, particularly towards the base.
Grassland, often in rocky places. Widespread. Summer. □ Compare **215**.

222 Senecio pentactinus Klatt
Perennial herb with several erect, usually unbranched stems from a woody rootstock, up to about 1,5 m high; ± hairless. Leaves on short stalks; blade ± narrowly elliptic or lance-shaped, with *12 or more* side veins; margin toothed, teeth often *unequal.* Flower heads numerous, arranged in ± *flat-topped* terminal panicles; ray flowers 5, spreading, *pale yellow.*
Grassland, often in rocky places. Widespread. Spring.

223 Senecio scitus Hutch. & Burtt Davy
Slender erect herb with a perennial rootstock. Leaves leathery, length of large ones *6 – 10 or more* times their width, tapering *sharply* towards the tip, ± *clasping* at the base; margin thickened; *hairless.* Flowering stems unbranched. Flower heads with usually *8*, rarely up to 10 ray flowers.
Grassland, often in groups. Widespread. Spring – summer.

224 Senecio serratuloides DC. var. **gracilis** Harv.
Erect perennial herb with 1 or a few flowering shoots from a woody rootstock; ± *hairless.* Leaves *long and narrow* (up to 120 x 15 mm); margin *toothed.* Flower heads many, congested in terminal groups; ray flowers 8 – 13, corolla *recurving* at an early stage.
Along streams and *in marshes*, often growing in water. Widespread. Summer – autumn.

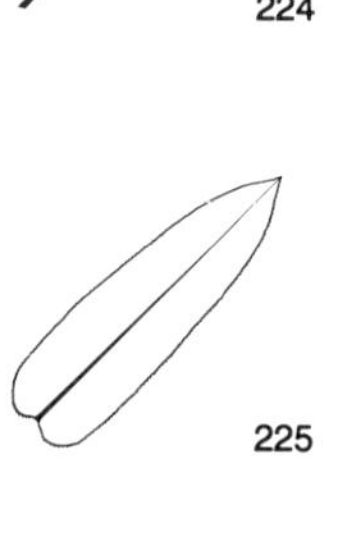

225 Senecio venosus Harv.
Erect herb up to 1 m high with a woody rootstock; *hairless*, except for wool hidden deep in leaf axils. Stems usually *unbranched* below the inflorescence. Leaves stalkless, *blue-green;* base *heart-shaped;* venation very *conspicuous* when leaf is held up to the light. Flower heads numerous, arranged in a spreading terminal cluster; ray flowers 5 – 7, sometimes absent.
Grassland and bushveld, often in rocky places; common. Widespread. Spring. □ For discoid form see **261**. Compare **257**.

220 *Senecio inornatus*

221 *Senecio lydenburgensis*

222 *Senecio pentactinus*

223 *Senecio scitus*

224 *Senecio serratuloides*

225 *Senecio venosus*

226 *Tagetes minuta L. *Khaki weed/Kakiebos*

Erect annual herb up to ± 2 m high; *strongly* scented. Leaves *pinnately* divided; leaflets hairless, with the margins *sharply* toothed. Flower heads in congested terminal groups, *narrow, cylindrical*, yellowish green with a few short and broad white ray flowers.

A native of South America. Common as a weed in disturbed places and cultivated fields. Widespread. Summer – autumn.

227 Ursinia nana DC. subsp. **nana**

A bushy *annual* herb. Leaves divided into *narrow* segments, hairless. Flower heads solitary on long leafless stems, drooping when young; bracts around head have *broad papery* tips. Fruits with white, *petal-like* scales at tip.

A weedy plant in dry disturbed areas. Widespread. Spring – summer.

ASTERACEAE (See page 17)

Group B See also **46**.

228 Brachylaena rotundata S. Moore *Bergvaalbos*

A tree of small to medium size. Leaves and young twigs covered with *greyish white* hairs. Flower heads in tight *globular* clusters, sexes on separate plants; male flowers bright lemon yellow; female flowers pale yellow. Fruits with white bristles on top.

Rocky north-facing slopes of quartzite ridges and koppies. Widespread. Early spring.

229 *Bidens pilosa L. *Blackjack/Knapsekêrel*

Erect *annual* herb; branches grooved. Leaves *opposite, compound;* leaflets usually 3, rarely 5, egg-shaped, with a sharply toothed margin. Flower heads *with or without* white ray flowers; disc flowers yellow. Fruit *long and narrow*, with 2 – 3 short *terminal awns.*

A cosmopolitan weed, possibly a native of America; common in disturbed places. Widespread. Spring – autumn. □ For radiate form see **32**.

230 Conyza podocephala DC.

Perennial herb covered with *rough hairs;* often with leafy *runners.* Basal leaves tapering to a broad stalk-like base; margin coarsely scalloped in the upper half. Flower heads solitary on long *leafless* stalks, pale yellow, often with tiny ray flowers.

Roadsides and disturbed grassland. Widespread. Summer.

231 Cotula anthemoides L. *Gansgras*

Delicate, ± *fleshy* annual herb; much-branched from the base; *hairless.* Leaves stalkless; base *stem-clasping;* margin *dissected, forming sharp points.* Flower heads solitary on long stalks, *flat-topped.*

Marshy places, often in dense stands. Widespread. Spring – summer.

232 *Flaveria bidentis (L.) Kuntze *Smelter's bush/Smelterbossie*

Erect annual herb up to ± 1 m high; hairless. Stems *yellowish.* Leaves *opposite*, stalk-like bases of each pair ± *joined* around the stem; margin toothed. Flower heads bearing few flowers, clustered in terminal and axillary groups (*secondary heads*) on short stalks; involucral bracts 2 – 4, closely arranged in a single whorl to form a *cylindrical* tube.

A weed of disturbed places, often along roadsides. Native to tropical America. Widespread. All year.

226 *Tagetes minuta*

227 *Ursinia nana*

228 *Brachylaena rotundata*

229 *Bidens pilosa*

230 *Conyza podocephala*

231 *Cotula anthemoides*

232 *Flaveria bidentis*

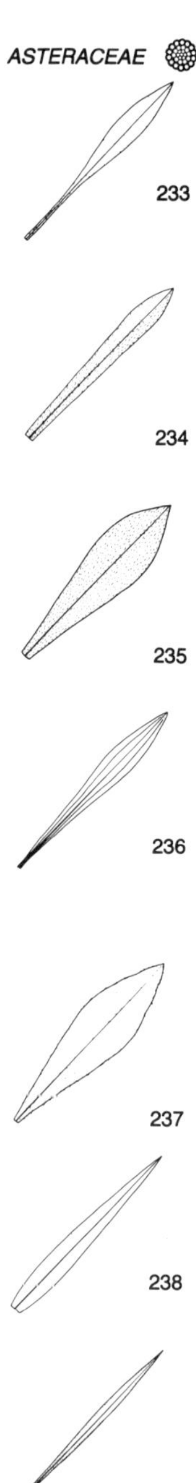

233 Helichrysum acutatum DC. *Sticky everlasting/Taaisewejaartjie*
Erect perennial herb with a woody rootstock. Leaves *stalked*, mainly tufted at base of plants, covered with *glandular hairs*, and often with very *thick, greyish white wool.* Flower heads in dense clusters; bracts *closely overlapping*, bases straw-coloured, woolly, with *sharply* pointed tips, *bright yellow.*
Grassland. Widespread. Spring – summer. ☐ Compare **237**.

234 Helichrysum aureonitens Sch. Bip.
Erect perennial herb up to ± *300 mm* high, from a *creeping* rootstock; covered with *greyish white appressed woolly hairs* throughout. Stems slender, *simple* or *sparsely* branched. Leaves stalkless with a broad base. Flower heads in compact clusters at the ends of branchlets; bracts *woolly* at base, yellow, often tinged with *pale brown* at tips.
Grassland, often forming extensive populations. Widespread. Spring – summer.

235 Helichrysum cephaloideum DC.
Perennial herb with a woody rootstock; basal leaves often *wither* at flowering. Leaves at base lance-shaped, with a thin covering of *grey woolly* hairs. Flowering stem erect, with *small erect* leaves *along its length;* also covered with *grey woolly* hairs. Flower heads in a *compact cluster*, usually *webbed together* at the base with densely interwoven hairs.
Grassland. Widespread. Summer.

236 Helichrysum coriaceum Harv. ***Vaalteebossie***
Erect perennial herb; base woody, covered with *brown silky wool.* Flowering stem leafy, mainly in the *lower half.* Leaves leathery, *smooth* and green above, *white-felted* below. Flower heads with *straw-coloured*, ± woolly involucral bracts; flowers cream or yellow.
Grassland. Widespread. Spring – summer. ☐ Compare **239** and **242**.

237 Helichrysum dasymallum Hilliard
Perennial herb with 1 or more erect stems from a woody rootstock. Leaves up to *140 x 60 mm*, diminishing in size up the stem; base broad, stalk-like; *thickly covered* with *greyish white* wool, not sticky. Flower heads arranged in small clusters in a ± flat-topped panicle, ± *10 mm* long, surrounded by *sharply* tapering, *loosely* arranged and ± *spreading* bracts which are bright lemon yellow; disc flowers few, *orange.*
Grassland, usually on rocky (often dolomite) slopes. Mainly Pretoria region. Summer. ☐ Compare **233**.

238 Helichrysum epapposum H. Bol.
Herbaceous. Stems very slender, with *greyish white* woolly hairs. Leaves rigid; margins *rolled under.* Flower heads numerous in *flat-topped* clusters, bright canary yellow. Seeds *without* coma of hairs.
Marshes or along streams; rare. Magaliesberg. Summer.

239 Helichrysum harveyanum Wild
Erect perennial herb with a woody rootstock. Flowering stems ± *leafy throughout.* Leaves on stem stalkless, *long and narrow;* ± *rough* above and on lower surface of midrib; margin often *rolled under.* Flower heads with *tawny* involucral bracts which have ± *rounded* tips; flowers yellow or cream.
Grassland and bushveld, often on rocky ridges. Mainly Pretoria/ Magaliesberg region. Spring – summer. ☐ Compare **236** and **242**.

233 *Helichrysum acutatum*

234 *Helichrysum aureonitens*

235 *Helichrysum cephaloideum*

236 *Helichrysum coriaceum*

237 *Helichrysum dasymallum*

238 *Helichrysum epapposum*

239 *Helichrysum harveyanum*

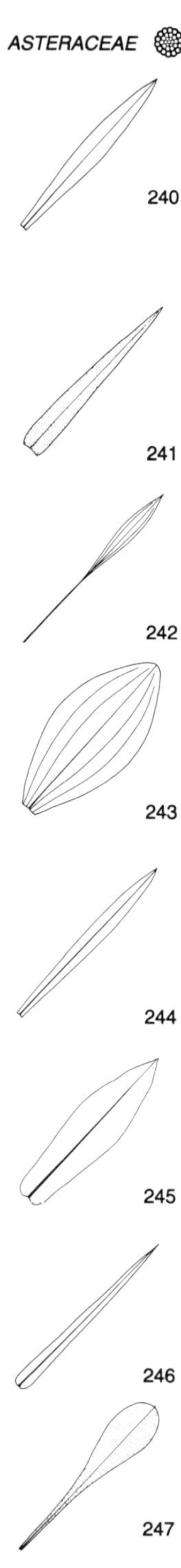

240 Helichrysum kraussii Sch. Bip.
Perennial *shrublet* up to 1 m high; much-branched, *densely covered with leaves; aromatic.* Leaves stalkless, narrow; margin *strongly rolled under;* lower surface *white-felted.* Flower heads cylindrical, in numerous *flat-topped* clusters at ends of branches.
Grassland and bushveld, usually in dense stands, particularly on the summits of rocky ridges. Widespread. Autumn – spring.

241 Helichrysum melanacme DC. [=**H. kuntzei** (Kuntze) Moeser]
Multi-stemmed perennial shrublet, often forming *tangled clumps.* Stems sparsely branched, lax, wiry. Leaves stalkless, ± lance-shaped; base *broad,* ear-clasping; upper surface sparsely covered with appressed woolly hairs; lower surface more densely covered with appressed *whitish woolly hairs.* Flower heads ± cylindrical, in small, terminal, *flat-topped* clusters; bracts greenish yellow, tips of inner ones (and sometimes others) *straw-coloured* and minutely *crisped* (visible with hand lens); disc flowers deep yellow.
Rocky grassland. Suikerbosrand. Summer.

242 Helichrysum nudifolium (L.) Less. ***Hottentot's tea/Hottentotstee***
Perennial herb; spreading by means of *underground runners.* Leaves ± rigid, narrow to oval; upper surface *rough.* Flowering stems leafy, mainly in *lower half.* Flower heads many, in a *tight, rounded cluster;* bracts closely overlapping, woolly at base, *blunt-tipped,* pale yellow to *lemon yellow.*
Grassland. Widespread. Summer. □ Compare **236** and **239**.

243 Helichrysum pilosellum (L.f.) Less.
Perennial herb; crown covered with *brown silky 'wool'.* Leaves ± *3, flat* on the ground, with 3 prominent parallel veins; *rough* and *dark green* above, *white-felted* below. Flower heads closely packed in a ± *flat-topped* cluster on a long, woolly and ± *leafless* stalk, bright yellow; involucral bracts *pale brown.*
Grassland, often in vleis. Widespread. Spring.

244 Helichrysum rugulosum Less.
Perennial herb with many *erect stems* from a *creeping* rootstock. Stems *densely covered with leaves* and sparsely *white-felted.* Leaves stalkless, *2 – 5 mm* wide, greyish green; margin ± rolled under; lower surface *white-felted.* Flower heads in compact clusters; involucral bracts with tips ± *curled and toothed,* pinkish, becoming creamy with age; disc flowers yellow.
Grassland, in dense groups. Widespread. Spring – summer.

245 Helichrysum setosum Harv. ***Yellow everlasting/Geelsewejaartjie***
Bushy perennial or shrublet. Leaves ± egg-shaped, with short, often *sticky, glandular hairs.* Flower heads solitary at tips of *long leafy* branches, rather *large* (20 – 30 mm across); disc flowers bright yellow; bracts yellow, radiating *outward,* like miniature sunflower rays.
Rocky grassland, often on the summits of ridges. Widespread. Summer.

246 Nidorella anomala Steetz
A somewhat weedy, stiffly erect perennial herb with *sticky* stems. Leaves narrow, covered with short, *rough hairs,* ± *sticky.* Flower heads *small* (± 2 mm across), numerous, in tight, flat or rounded clusters; outer flowers *with 3 or 4 lobes;* bright yellow.
Grassland, often in groups along roads and in vleis. Widespread. Summer.

247 Nidorella hottentotica DC.
Erect, *sparsely branched* perennial herb up to ± 1,5 m high. Leaves narrow, undulating, densely covered with *white woolly hairs.* Flower heads arranged in ± flat-topped terminal groups; bright yellow; ray flowers *small,* 2-lipped.
Grassland, often along roadsides. Widespread. Summer.

240 *Helichrysum kraussii*

241 *Helichrysum melanacme*

242 *Helichrysum nudifolium*

243 *Helichrysum pilosellum*

244 *Helichrysum rugulosum*

245 *Helichrysum setosum*

246 *Nidorella anomala*

247 *Nidorella hottentotica*

248 Nolletia rarifolia (Turcz.) Steetz
Slender erect herb from a perennial rootstock. Stems *wiry*, up to 300 mm high, *sparsely* branched above, ± hairless. Leaves *widely spaced*, erect, *less* than 1 mm wide. Flower heads comprise disc flowers only; solitary at the tips of branches; involucral bracts with embedded orange *gland dots*.
Grassland. Widespread. Spring.

249

249 Pentzia pilulifera (L.f.) Fourc. *Stinkkruid*
Bushy annual herb; *strongly aromatic*. Leaves stalkless, *deeply dissected* with 2 stipule-like lobes at the base. Flower heads solitary on long, erect and *leafless* stalks, *globose*, with numerous tightly packed disc flowers, subtended by *closely arranged* green bracts forming a plate.
Grassland, usually in disturbed places; uncommon. Mainly Suikerbosrand/ Witwatersrand region. Spring.

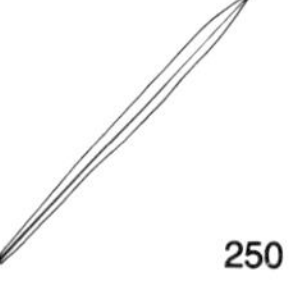
250

250 Phymaspermum athanasioides (S. Moore) Källersjö
[=**Brachymeris athanasioides** (S. Moore) Hutch.]
Small slender shrub up to ± 2 m high; *sparsely* branched. Leaves *narrow*, numerous, crowded towards the tips of stems. Flower heads in *flat-topped* terminal clusters.
Koppies and rocky ridges, usually between summit rocks. Widespread. Winter.

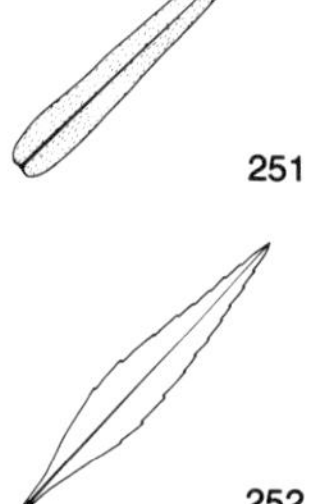
251

252

251 *Pseudognaphalium luteo-album (L.) Hilliard & Burtt
[=**Gnaphalium luteo-album** L.] *Cud weed/Roerkruid*
Annual herb with 1 to several ± erect stems from the base; covered with *greyish woolly hairs* throughout. Leaves *stem-clasping* at the base, long and narrow, *both surfaces alike in colour*. Flower heads in dense clusters at the ends of flowering stems; involucral bracts ± *as long as* the flowers, *shiny*.
Grassland, mainly disturbed and moist places, often along streams. Probably a native of Europe and Asia. Widespread. Summer.

252 Psiadia punctulata (DC.) Vatke
Small *hairless* shrub with *sticky and shiny* leaves and young branches. Leaves narrow, lance-shaped. Flower heads with *marginal flowers female* and *disc flowers bisexual*, arranged terminally in *flat-topped* clusters.
Bushveld, along dry sandy or rocky river beds and on rocky ridges, often under trees. Magaliesberg. Summer.

253

253 Schistostephium crataegifolium (DC.) Fenzl. ex Harv. *Bergkruie*
Tufted *aromatic* perennial herb with *unbranched* erect stems from a spreading rootstock. Leaves with *long, grey silky* hairs; margin deeply and irregularly cut into *pointed* segments often tipped by a *bristle*, the lower pair of segments *stipule-like*. Flower heads up to 30, clustered at the tips of branches.
Grassland, especially in moist places and around rocky outcrops. Widespread. Summer. □ Compare **254**.

254

254 Schistostephium heptalobum (DC.) Oliv. & Hiern.
Perennial *aromatic* shrublet; branches slender, often ± *decumbent* and supported by other vegetation. Leaves stalkless, pinnately *lobed* (3 – 4 pairs), the lower pair *stipule-like*, *sparsely* covered with hairs (*not* with grey silky hairs). Flower heads small, in terminal groups of about 20.
In clumps of bush, particularly on rocky ridges. Widespread. Summer. Compare **253**.

248 *Nolletia rarifolia*

249 *Pentzia pilulifera*

250 *Phymaspermum athanasioides*

251 *Pseudognaphalium luteo-album*

252 *Psiadia punctulata*

253 *Schistostephium crataegifolium*

254 *Schistostephium heptalobum*

255 Senecio barbertonicus Klatt

A much-branched, vine-like *succulent* shrub up to ± 2 m high; old stems *rough* with leaf scars. Leaves *cylindrical* and succulent, slightly curved. Flower heads in clusters at branch tips, *narrow* and bell-shaped.

Bushveld, usually in ± sandy areas among rocky outcrops and summit rocks, rarely clambering over shrubs or small trees. Mainly Pretoria/Magaliesberg region. Spring – summer.

256 Senecio glanduloso-pilosus Volkens & Muschl.

Low-growing perennial herb from a woody rootstock, covered with *rough glandular hairs* which are often *sticky*. Leaves crowded towards the base, narrow and elliptic, ± fleshy; margin *coarsely and irregularly* toothed. Flower heads in a terminal compound inflorescence; comprising disc flowers only; purple or *dull yellow*.

Grassland. Widespread. Spring. □ Compare **482**.

257 Senecio isatideus DC. *Dan's cabbage/Blouvleibossie*

Erect perennial herb up to 1,5 m high, with a woody rootstock; *bluish green*. Leaves on the lower part of the stem have the base tapering into a *wide, flat and winged* stalk which is half-clasping; tips ± *blunt;* margin ± toothed. Flower heads with *disc florets only*, congested in terminal clusters on the unbranched flowering stem.

Moist grassland, usually in large groups, particularly in vleis. Widespread; very common at Suikerbosrand. Summer. □ Compare **225** and **261**.

258 Senecio longiflorus (DC.) Sch. Bip. *Sjambok bush/Sambokbos*

Perennial shrublet with erect *succulent* stems. Leaves *absent* or very small. Flower heads solitary, *elongated;* flowers *protrude* far beyond the bracts.

Bushveld. Mainly Rustenburg region. Winter.

259 Senecio othonniflorus DC.

Perennial herb with *rigid*, usually *unbranched* erect stems up to ± 1 m high; hairless. Stems with ± *translucent* longitudinal stripes. Leaves crowded on lower half of stem, stalkless, ± erect, long, narrow and tapering to a point, ± *fleshy* and *greyish green;* margin slightly rolled back; midrib prominent on lower surface. Flower heads surrounded by ± *12 broad* and ± *fleshy* bracts.

Grassland. Widespread. Spring – summer.

260 Senecio oxyriifolius DC. [=**S. orbicularis** Sond.] *False nasturtium/Kappertjieblaar*

Fleshy perennial herb with a tuberous rootstock; *bluish green;* hairless. Leaves ± *rounded*, with a *slender* stalk up to 150 mm long; blade often attached to the stalk by *the lower surface* (instead of the margin); margin variable but usually ± *coarsely* toothed. Flowering stem solitary, erect, up to 1 m high, *leafless*, with a few heads clustered at the end. Flower heads with disc flowers only.

Grassland, mainly amongst rocks. Widespread. Spring – summer.

261 Senecio venosus Harv.

Erect herb up to 1 m high, with a woody rootstock; *hairless*, except for wool hidden deep in leaf axils. Stems usually *unbranched* below the inflorescence. Leaves *stalkless, blue-green;* base *heart-shaped;* venation very *conspicuous* when leaf is held up to the light. Flower heads numerous, arranged in a spreading terminal cluster; ray flowers 5 – 7, sometimes absent.

Grassland and bushveld, often in rocky places; common. Widespread. Spring. □ For radiate form see **225**. Compare **257**.

255 *Senecio barbertonicus*

256 *Senecio glanduloso-pilosus*

257 *Senecio isatideus*

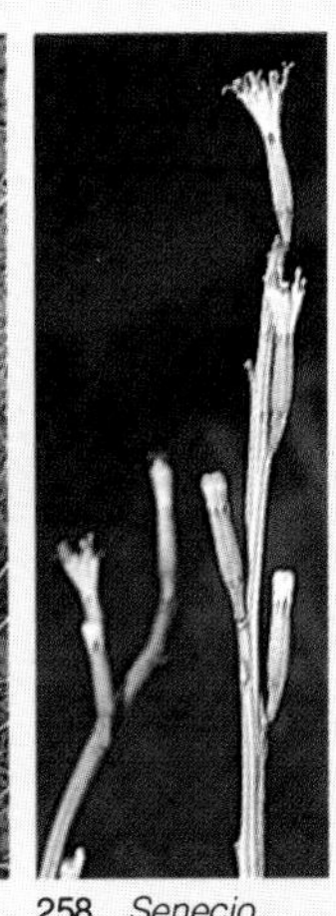
258 *Senecio longiflorus*

259 *Senecio othonniflorus*

260 *Senecio oxyriifolius*

261 *Senecio venosus*

262

262 *Xanthium strumarium L. *Large cocklebur/Kankerroos*
Erect *annual* herbaceous shrublet. Stems stout, *ribbed*, often brownish or reddish. Leaves stalked, ± heart-shaped and often with 3 – 5 lobes; *3-veined* from base; with short *bristly hairs* on both surfaces; margin *toothed.* Flower heads unisexual, inconspicuous, in *axillary clusters;* male and female flowers on the same plant. Fruit dry, brown, *ellipsoid*, up to 20 mm long, covered with stout *hooked* spines and with 2 conspicuous *horns* at the tip.
A cosmopolitan weed, probably a native of tropical America; disturbed places, often along streams. Widespread. Summer.

ASTERACEAE (See page 17)
Group C

263

263 Crepis hypochoeridea (DC.) Thell.
Perennial herb up to 500 mm high, with a woody rootstock. Leaves mostly *basal;* margin ± *distantly* toothed. Flowering stems ± *without* leaves. Flower heads solitary or in an open cluster of few heads; involucral bracts in *2* whorls, the inner *much longer* than the outer, with *long ± dark-coloured bristly hairs* on the outside. Seeds narrowed into a long beak tipped with white bristles.
Grassland. Widespread. Spring. ☐ Compare **264**.

264

264 *Hypochoeris radicata L. *Hairy wild lettuce/Harige skaapslaai*
Perennial herb with a thick fleshy rootstock. Leaves in a *basal rosette*, ± *hairy* above; margin *deeply pinnately lobed.* Flower heads solitary at the tips of *long* inflorescence branches; involucral bracts in *3 or 4* whorls.
Disturbed places, often on pavements. A native of Europe. Widespread. Spring. ☐ Compare **263** and **271**.

265 Launaea rarifolia (Oliv. & Hiern) L. Boulos
Low-growing perennial herb with a thick fleshy rootstock and *milky latex.* Leaves *absent* at the time of flowering. Flower heads erect, comprising ± 10 strap-like ray flowers; each ray corolla tipped with 5 teeth; involucral bracts form an *elongated* cylindrical 'stalk' below the flowers.
Grassland; rare. Widespread. Early spring.

262 *Xanthium strumarium*

263 *Crepis hypochoeridea*

264 *Hypochoeris radicata*

265 *Launaea rarifolia*

266 Sonchus dregeanus DC.
Erect perennial herb. Leaves all or most *crowded towards the base*, variable, usually *long and narrow* with a few *coarse* teeth. Inflorescence stalk *with leaves* which become progressively smaller upwards; bearing up to 5 heads. Flower heads have *white woolly hairs* at the base.
Grassland, often on rocky ridges. Widespread. Spring. □ Compare **269**.

267 Sonchus nanus Sond. ex Harv.
Dwarf perennial herb with *milky latex*. Leaves crowded in a *basal rosette;* bluish green; margin irregularly lobed and toothed. Flower heads *almost stalkless* at flowering time; comprising numerous ray flowers.
Grassland. Widespread. Spring.

268 *Sonchus oleraceus L. *Sow thistle/Sydissel*
Annual herb with erect, *hollow* stems; *milky latex* present. Leaves originally in a basal rosette; lower leaves with a winged stalk; upper leaves stalkless; blade *deeply incised* with the lobes pointing ± *towards the base*, terminal lobe *triangular;* margin *sharply* toothed. Flower heads in terminal umbels; involucral bracts green with a membranous margin.
A native of Eurasia and North Africa, now a cosmopolitan weed; common in disturbed places. Widespread. All year.

269 Sonchus wilmsii R.E. Fr. *Milk thistle/Melkdissel*
Erect herb with 1 or 2 *stout hollow* stems; somewhat *bluish*. Leaves arranged ± *evenly along the length* of the stem, stalkless; with large, *ear-like appendages* at stem attachment; margin coarsely and deeply toothed. Flower heads terminal, rather large; bright yellow inside, often *pink or reddish* outside, particularly when old; involucral bracts with *white woolly hairs* at base.
Disturbed grassland and along roadsides. Widespread. Spring – summer. Compare **266**.

270 *Taraxacum officinale Weber *Common dandelion/Perdeblom*
Perennial herb with a long stout taproot and basal *rosette* of leaves. Leaves elongate; margin deeply and *sharply* incised, the teeth pointing *towards the base;* apical lobe *triangular.* Flower heads solitary on stalks that are usually slightly longer than the leaves; bracts at base of mature heads arranged in *several* rows, those of the outer rows usually *reflexed* and those of the inner rows *erect.*
A troublesome weed, particularly in lawns and other places subjected to trampling; probably a native of Europe. Widespread. Spring – autumn.
The name **T. officinale** is used here in a wide sense for a complex group of microspecies.

271 Tolpis capensis (L.) Sch. Bip.
Perennial herb with a stout woody rootstock. Stem usually *leafless.* Leaves in a *basal rosette*, smooth or sparsely covered with hairs; margin often deeply toothed. Flower heads borne on long *hollow* stalks; 6 – 10 mm across; yellow.
Grassland, often in disturbed places. Widespread. Spring – summer. Compare **264**.

272 *Tragopogon dubius Scop. *Yellow goat's beard/Geelbokbaard*
Erect semi-perennial herb with a thick, fleshy taproot; *hairless* throughout. Leaves *grass-like, forming a sheath* at the base, *bluish green.* Flower heads terminal, solitary, encircled by ± 8 *long, pointed* bracts; stalk *swollen* and hollow below the head.
A weed of disturbed places; originally from Europe. Widespread. Spring – autumn.

266 *Sonchus dregeanus*

267 *Sonchus nanus*

268 *Sonchus oleraceus*

269 *Sonchus wilmsii*

270 *Taraxacum officinale*

271 *Tolpis capensis*

272 *Tragopogon dubius*

272 *T. dubius* (fruiting head)

BRASSICACEAE (See page 18)

273

273 *Raphanus raphanistrum L. *Wild radish/Ramenas*
Erect annual or biennial herb up to 800 mm high. Leaves at base stalked, deeply *pinnately* lobed, the terminal lobe *large;* stalk *grooved*. Flowers with petals stalked, yellow (rarely white), sometimes with *dark* veins. Fruits *pod-like*, at least 4 times as long as they are wide, *deeply constricted* between the seeds, eventually breaking at the constrictions into 1-seeded portions.
Native to Europe; widespread, often in moist places. Spring – summer.

274

274 Rorippa nudiuscula Thell.
Perennial herb up to 600 mm high; ± *hairless* throughout. Leaves mainly in a *basal rosette*, very variable in shape, often ± *pinnately* lobed. Flowers in *bractless* terminal racemes; petals 3 – 4,5 mm long. Fruits pod-like, ± *erect*, tipped with the persistent style which is 0,8 – 1,5 mm long.
Grassland, in moist places. Widespread. Spring.

275

275 Sisymbrium thellungii O.E. Schulz *Wild mustard/Wildemosterd*
Erect annual or biennial herb with a stout taproot. Leaves mainly in a *basal rosette*, variously lobed; both surfaces covered with *rough* hairs. Flowers in a *branched* terminal inflorescence *with bracts;* corolla ± 8 mm long. Fruits pod-like, ± *compressed*, up to 100 mm long, covered with *rough* hairs and tipped with a beak 2 – 4 mm long.
Often a weed in disturbed places. Widespread. Spring.

CAESALPINIACEAE (See page 18)

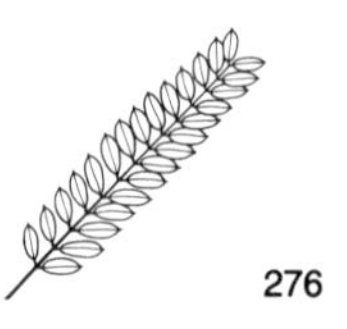
276

276 *Cassia didymobotrya Fresen. *Wild senna*
Multi-stemmed perennial shrub; *unpleasantly scented* when bruised. Leaves compound with 10 – 22 pairs of leaflets; leaf stalk and rhachis without glands; stipules persistent, *broadly egg-shaped* with the base ± *heart-shaped* and tip sharply pointed. Inflorescences of *many-flowered, erect racemes* in axils of upper leaves; bracts dark *brownish green*, ± *sticky*. Pods *flattened*.
Native to tropical Africa, now naturalized in disturbed places. Mainly Pretoria/Magaliesberg region. Spring – summer.

277

277 Cassia italica (Mill.) Lam ex F.W. Andr. subsp. **arachoides** (Burch.) Brenan *Eland's pea/Elandsertjie*
Perennial herb with several *trailing stems* from a woody taproot; young stems at times covered with *glandular hairs*, sticky. Leaves pinnately compound with usually *4 – 6* pairs of leaflets; stalk 6 – 10 mm long; small *finger-like glands* in axils of leaflets. Inflorescences comprise stalked axillary racemes. Flowers with bright yellow petals which become brown-veined with age. Pods *flattened*.
Grassland and bushveld, usually in sandy soils. Mainly Pretoria/Magaliesberg region. Spring – summer.

278

278 Cassia comosa (E.Mey.) Vogel var. **capricornia** Steyaert
Perennial herb with ± spreading stems from a *woody rootstock*. Leaves compound with 15 – 35 pairs of leaflets; main axis (rhachis) *grooved* above, margin of groove covered with fine hairs; gland on leaf stalk just below junction of first pair of leaflets *elliptic and without a stalk*. Inflorescences borne above the leaf axils, usually comprising 2 – 3 flowers; petals 8 – 13 mm long.
Grassland. Widespread. Spring – summer. ☐ Compare **279**.

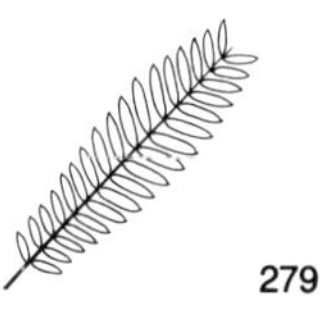
279

279 Cassia mimosoides L. *Fishbone cassia/Boesmanstee*
Erect or prostrate annual or perennial herb; much-branched; *without* a woody rootstock. Leaves stalked, with a *circular* or *circular-elliptic* gland on the stalk below the basal pair of leaflets; leaflets *35 – 65* pairs; axis with a long, narrow *ridge* along upper surface. Inflorescence of 1 – 3 flowers borne on internode *above* the leaf axil. Flowers with sepals brownish, often tinged with red.
Grassland. Widespread. Summer. ☐ Compare **278**.

273 *Raphanus raphanistrum*

273 *R. raphanistrum* (habit)

274 *Rorippa nudiuscula*

275 *Sisymbrium thellungii*

276 *Cassia didymobotrya*

277 *Cassia italica*

278 *Cassia comosa*

279 *Cassia mimosoides*

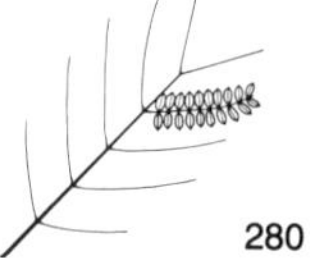
280

280 Peltophorum africanum Sond. ***African wattle/Huilboom***

Deciduous or semi-deciduous tree with a dense leafy crown; young shoots densely covered with fine, *rusty brown* hairs. Leaves *bipinnate*, feathery, with *numerous* leaflets, each ± 4 – 8 mm long; densely covered with hairs on the lower surface, sometimes also on the upper one. Inflorescence an erect terminal raceme. Flowers with *crinkled* yellow petals. Pods flat, *winged*, with fine velvety hairs.

Bushveld. Mainly Magaliesberg. Summer.

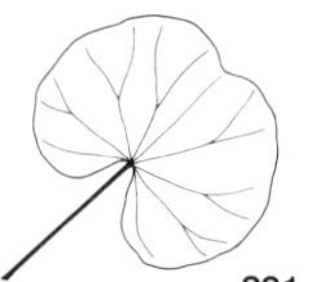
281

281 Tylosema fassoglense (Schweinf.) Torre & Hillc.
Gemsbok bean/Gemsbokboontjie

Shrublet with long, prostrate and *trailing* stems from a very large, woody underground tuber; tendrils axillary, *forked*. Leaves stalked; blade *2-lobed* at tip and with *heart-shaped* base. Flowers borne in short axillary racemes; petals *stalked*, 1 small and 4 large, yellow fading to pink, surface *crinkled*. Pods flat and woody, containing 1 or 2 seeds.

Grassland, often on dolomite. Pretoria/Magaliesberg region. Summer.

CELASTRACEAE (See page 18)

282

282 Maytenus tenuispina (Sond.) Marais

Deciduous, often multi-stemmed shrub up to ± 1,5 m high; branchlets often *reddish* and covered with *minute hairs*, armed with slender *spines* (reduced branchlets) up to 10 mm long. Leaves stalked, often in tufts, narrowly elliptic, pale green; margin shallowly toothed. Flowers yellowish or greenish white. Capsules ± *3-angled, pendulous*, yellowish sometimes tinged with red. Seed with a fleshy white covering at the base.

Wooded areas, often on rocky hillsides. Widespread. Summer.

CHRYSOBALANACEAE (See page 18)

283

283 Parinari capensis Harv. subsp. **capensis**
Dwarf mobola/Grysappeltjie

Dwarf deciduous shrublet which forms *large stands* from an extensive underground stem and root system; aerial shoots usually *less than 200 mm* high. Leaves on short stalks, ± elliptic; lower surface covered with *silvery whitish hairs*, venation *prominently raised*. Inflorescence terminal and axillary, many-flowered; axes and outer surface of flowers covered with *whitish hairs*. Fruit fleshy, ellipsoid, greyish yellow and aromatic when ripe.

Grassland, often on rocky ridges. Widespread. Spring.

COMMELINACEAE (See page 19)

284 Commelina africana L.

Spreading herb with erect or trailing stems from a small woody perennial rootstock with long thick roots; hairless to hairy. Leaves stalkless, long and narrow, forming a sheath at the base. Flowers borne in *stalked, boat-shaped* spathes; petals 3, the upper 2 well developed and *stalked*, the lower petal *reduced* and ± colourless.

A common and very variable grassland species, often on rocky outcrops. Widespread. Summer.

At least 4 varieties occur in the field guide region: var. **africana** has flat, usually hairless leaves; var. **barberae** (C.B.Cl.) C.B.Cl. (**284.1**) has folded, ± hairless leaves, spathes which taper narrowly to a sharp point, and large flowers with upper petals ± 15 mm long; var. **lancispatha** C.B.Cl. is similar to the previous variety but has smaller flowers (upper petals ± 8 mm long); and var. **krebsiana** (Kunth) C.B.Cl. (**284.2**) has folded, hairy leaves and short, broad spathes.

C. subulata Roth is the only other yellow-flowered **Commelina** in our area. It is a slender, erect, short-lived *annual* with ± *stalkless* spathes, and is confined to seasonally wet areas, even growing in water.

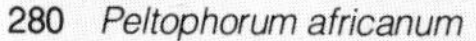

280 *Peltophorum africanum*

281 *Tylosema fassoglense*

282 *Maytenus tenuispina*

282 *M. tenuispina* (fruit)

283 *Parinari capensis*

284.1 *Commelina africana* var. *barberae*

284.2 *Commelina africana* var. *krebsiana*

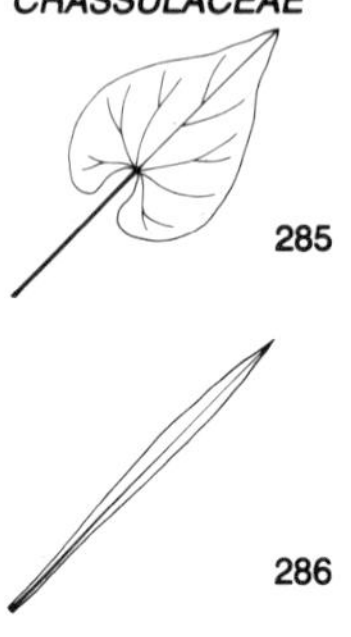
285

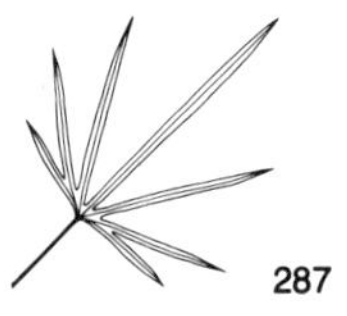
286

287

288

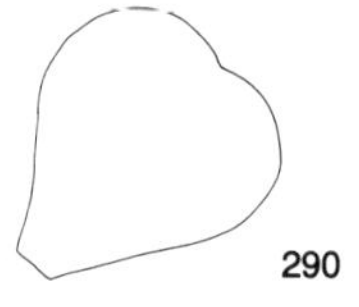
289

290

CONVOLVULACEAE (See page 19)

285 Ipomoea obscura (L.) Ker-Gawl. var. **fragilis** (Choisy) A. Meeuse *Wild petunia/Wildepatat*

Perennial herb with *trailing* or twining stems from a tuberous rootstock. Leaves *heart-shaped;* both surfaces with *fine, soft hairs;* margin often fringed with hairs. Flowers solitary or in groups of 2 or 3.

Grassland. Widespread. Summer.

286 Ipomoea simplex Thunb.

Small, usually *unbranched* erect herb up to *100 mm* high, with a tuberous rootstock; *hairless.* Leaves almost stalkless, *long, narrow* and *tapering.* Flowers *solitary* in leaf axils, usually opening 1 at a time; corolla pale cream to almost white.

Grassland, often on rocky ridges. Widespread. Spring.

287 Merremia palmata Hallier f.

Perennial herb with long *trailing* or twining stems; *hairless* throughout. Leaves stalked, deeply *palmately divided* into 5 – 7 narrow (0,5 – 8 mm) finger-like lobes. Flowers axillary, often solitary; sepals *leathery;* corolla up to *30 mm* long, pale yellow with a *deep red or maroon centre*, outside often purplish along the midpetaline areas; anthers ± *spirally twisted.*

Grassland and bushveld. Pretoria/Magaliesberg region. Spring – summer.

288 Merremia tridentata (L.) Hallier f. subsp. **angustifolia** (Jacq.) Ooststr.

Slender, straggling perennial herb; shoots often *twining; hairless* throughout. Leaves widely spaced, on *very short* stalks, long and narrow (± 2 mm), with *2 small, lobed* basal wings. Flowers axillary, *solitary* on long slender stalks; corolla yellowish, with or without a reddish centre.

Grassland and bushveld, often in rocky places. Widespread. Spring – autumn.

CRASSULACEAE (See page 19)

289 Kalanchoe paniculata Harv. *Krimpsiektebossie*

Succulent with a rosette of fleshy leaves and usually only 1 erect stem; rootstock swollen. Leaves usually *stalked* (first ones stalkless), *green* to *yellowish green* and ± tinged with red at the tip; margin untoothed. Inflorescence *flat-topped* with numerous deep yellow flowers.

Grassland, usually on rocky ridges. Widespread. Autumn – winter.

290 Kalanchoe thyrsiflora Harv. *White lady/Geelplakkie*

Succulent with a rosette of fleshy leaves from a slightly swollen rootstock; plants die after flowering. Leaves *stalkless*, *greyish green*, covered with a *whitish* bloom; margin often tinged with red. Inflorescence terminal, stout, erect, bearing clusters of numerous short-stalked flowers; corolla tube with *powdery white* outer surface.

Grassland, usually on rocky ridges. Widespread. Autumn.

285 *Ipomoea obscura*

286 *Ipomoea simplex*

287 *Merremia palmata*

288 *Merremia tridentata*

289 *Kalanchoe paniculata*

290 *Kalanchoe thyrsiflora*

CUCURBITACEAE (See page 19)

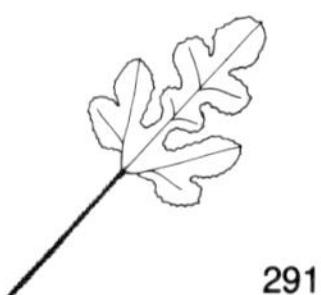
291

291 Citrullus lanatus (Thunb.) Matsumura & Nakai *Tsamma/Karkoer*
Annual herb with several stout *trailing* stems up to ± 3 m long; usually *greyish green;* tendrils usually *forked*. Leaves *stalked*, heart-shaped at base, deeply lobed, ± *rough* on both surfaces. Flowers axillary; corolla greenish on the outside, pale yellow inside. Fruit *globose*, up to 200 mm in diameter, pale green or greyish green, usually *mottled* with longitudinal irregular bands of dark green.
Grassland and bushveld, usually in disturbed places, particularly cultivated fields. Widespread. Summer.

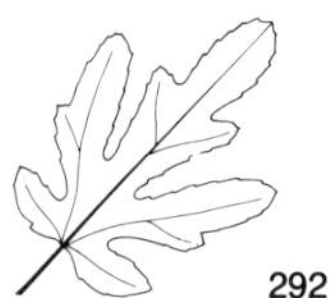
292

292 Coccinia adoensis (A. Rich.) Cogn.
Perennial climber with *hairy* stems and tendrils; roots tuberous. Leaves stalked, very variable in shape; mostly with 3 (sometimes up to 7) lobes, middle lobe usually *longer* than the others; both surfaces rough; margin *finely* and *regularly toothed*. Male and female flowers on separate plants. Flowers with pointed calyx lobes. Fruits oval, orange-red, with a smooth surface.
Bushveld and wooded areas in grassland, usually climbing in shrubs and trees. Widespread. Spring – summer.

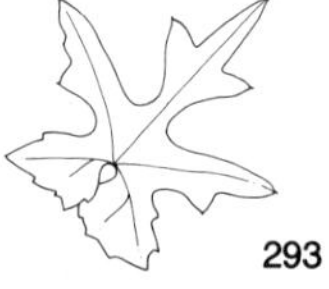
293

293 Coccinia sessilifolia (Sond.) Cogn. *Muisvoëlkomkommer*
Herbaceous perennial *climber* with a tuberous rootstock; *hairless;* tendrils unbranched. Leaves *stalkless*, *deeply* palmately 5-lobed, *bluish green*. Male and female flowers on separate plants. Corolla pale yellow to nearly white, *strongly veined*. Fruit elongated, green mottled with white, ripening to red from the tip.
Grassland and bushveld. Widespread. Summer.

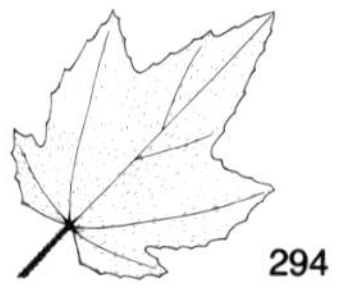
294

294 Cucumus hirsutus Sond. *Wild cucumber/Suurkomkommer*
Perennial with *trailing* annual stems from a woody rootstock; densely covered with *rough* hairs. Leaves usually *longer than they are wide;* base ± heart-shaped; margin *shallowly lobed or unlobed*. Male and female flowers on separate plants. Fruits ± globose, yellow, *hairy* but *spineless*.
Grassland and bushveld; often in sandy places. Widespread. Spring – summer. ☐ Compare **295**.

295

295 Cucumus zeyheri Sond.
Herb with long *trailing* stems from a woody rootstock; stems covered with *coarse hairs;* tendrils unforked. Leaves stalked, *deeply dissected into 3 – 7 lobes;* covered with *coarse hairs*. Male and female flowers on the same plant. Flowers yellow, stalked, solitary in leaf axils. Fruit ellipsoid, yellow, covered with *soft spines*.
Grassland. Widespread. Summer. ☐ Compare **294**.

296

296 Momordica balsamina L. *Laloentjie*
Perennial *climber* with a tuberous rootstock; tendrils not forked; *unpleasantly scented* when bruised. Leaves stalked, deeply dissected into 5 – 7 lobes; margin distinctly and irregularly toothed. Male and female flowers on the same plant. Fruit ± *spherical*, orange-red, *with rounded projections; spontaneously dehiscent* when picked; seed has a fleshy, *bright red* and sweet-tasting covering.
Sandy soil, often in disturbed places. Widespread. Summer – autumn.

291 *Citrullus lanatus*

292 *Coccinia adoensis*

292 *C. adoensis* (leaf variant)

293 *Coccinia sessilifolia*

294 *Cucumus hirsutus*

295 *Cucumus zeyheri*

295 *C. zeyheri* (fruit)

296 *Momordica balsamina*

CYPERACEAE (See page 19)

297 Cyperus obtusiflorus Vahl var. **flavissimus** Boeck. *Geelbiesie*

Erect perennial herb from a horizontal rhizome. Leaves basal, *grass-like*, ± half as long as the stem. Inflorescence comprises terminal clusters of *flattened* spikelets, subtended by *2 or 3 narrow green* bracts.

Grassland. Widespread. Summer.

Var. **obtusiflorus** has white spikelets (see **75**).

EBENACEAE (See page 20)

298 Diospyros lycioides Desf. subsp. **guerkei** (Kuntze) De Winter *Bloubos*

Rounded deciduous shrub; bark *smooth*, grey to brownish. Leaves on short stalks, usually *hairy;* veins impressed on upper surface, *distinctly raised below.* Flowers solitary, axillary, *pendulous*, fragrant; petals with strongly *reflexed* tips. Berries ± elliptic-globose, yellow, turning deep red; calyx *persistent*, lobes strongly reflexed.

Grassland and bushveld, often associated with quartzite outcrops. Widespread. Spring.

Subsp. **lycioides** has *hairless* mature leaves with the veins *not raised*, except for the midrib. It is rather rare in the field guide area.

298

EUPHORBIACEAE (See page 20) See also **505**.

299 Acalypha angustata Sond. var. **glabra** Sond. *Copper leaf/Katpisbossie*

Perennial shrublet with many *erect* annual shoots from a woody rootstock; *unpleasantly scented* when crushed. Leaves *almost* stalkless, lance-shaped, usually *less than 10 mm* wide; margin slightly toothed. Sexes on different plants. Male flowers densely clustered in erect, axillary inflorescences; yellowish tinged with red (illustrated). Female flowers terminal, with long *red feathery* styles forming a brush above lobed floral bracts.

Grassland. Widespread. Spring – summer.

For female flowers see **504**. Compare **505**.

A. caperonioides Baill. is very similar but has *stalkless*, less conspicuously toothed leaves, *10 – 30 mm* wide; the female flowers have long red styles which are *barely feathery.*

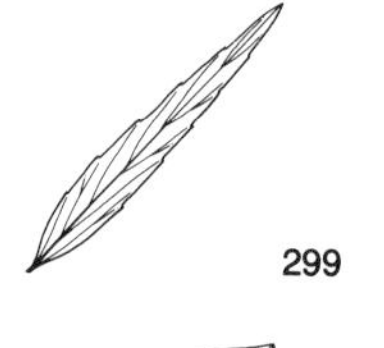

299

300 Clutia pulchella L. *Lightning bush/Weerligbos*

Small shrubs with green, often *warty*, branchlets. Leaves thinly textured, *blue-green* below, with *translucent* veins; minutely *dotted* when viewed against light. Often with a few *bright orange* leaves scattered on the plant. Male and female flowers on separate plants. Capsules green, 3-chambered and dehiscent.

Mainly on hillsides and in thickets along streams. Widespread. Summer.

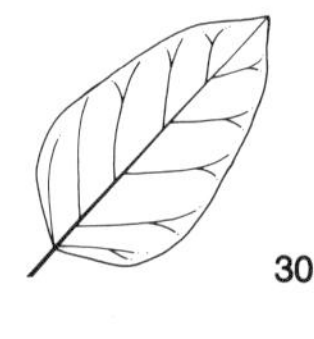

300

301 Croton gratissimus Burch. var. **subgratissimus** (Prain) Burtt Davy *Lavender fever-berry/Laventelkoorsbessie*

Deciduous shrub or small tree up to 4 m high. Leaves *drooping;* dark green above, *silvery* and dotted with *golden-brown scales* below; *lavender-scented.* Often with bright *yellow or red leaves* scattered on the tree. Flowers either male or female, in *drooping spikes;* both sexes on the same tree.

Rocky ridges. Mainly Pretoria/Magaliesberg region. Spring.

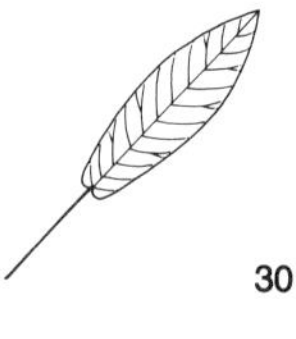

301

302 Dalechampia capensis Spreng.f.

Herbaceous perennial *climber* or scrambler with *twining stems;* sparsely covered with hairs throughout. Leaves stalked, *deeply divided into 3 – 5 lobes;* margin toothed. Flowers of both sexes on same plant; *enveloped by 2 showy floral bracts*, enlarged and resembling petals, with a lobed and toothed margin, and *strongly veined.* Capsule surrounded by *stiff, feathery calyx lobes* with stinging hairs.

Bushy slopes. Magaliesberg. Summer.

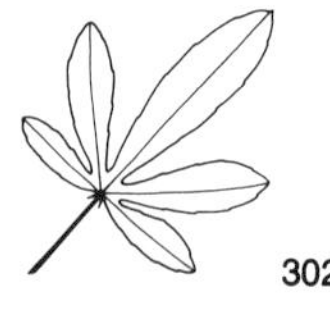

302

297 *Cyperus obtusiflorus* var. *flavissimus*

298 *Diospyros lycioides* subsp. *guerkei*

298 *D. lycioides* subsp. *guerkei* (fruit)

299 *Acalypha angustata* (male)

300 *Clutia pulchella*

301 *Croton gratissimus*

302 *Dalechampia capensis*

303 Euphorbia clavaroides Boiss. var. **truncata** (N.E.Br.) White, Dyer & Sloane *Vingerpol*

Perennial *succulent* with main stem underground. Branches erect, arranged in a dense, *flat-topped cushion* at ± ground level. Leaves minute, fall soon after appearing. Inflorescences (cyathia) resembling flowers produced at the tips of branches; yellowish.

Grassland, often in stony places. Mainly Witwatersrand/Suikerbosrand region. Spring – autumn.

304 Euphorbia cooperi N.E. Br. ex Berger *Candelabra euphorbia/Kandelaarnaboom*

Succulent tree shaped *like a candelabra;* single-stemmed. Branches grow at right angles to stem, then *curve* upwards; deeply *constricted* into *heart-shaped segments; 5- or 6-angled,* with paired spines on a continuous horny strip along each ridge; lower branches *die away annually.* Flowers clustered along ridges between spines. Fruits *3-lobed*, reddish or purplish brown.

Bushveld, in rocky places. Magaliesberg. Winter.

305 Euphorbia ingens E. Mey. ex Boiss. *Tree euphorbia/Naboom*

Succulent, short-stemmed tree with a dense crown. Branches *erect*, much-divided; usually *4- or 5-angled*, not deeply constricted; segments widest towards the middle, ridges with paired spines but *without* a continuous horny strip; lower branches *not shed with age.* Flowers clustered next to spines, yellowish green, often tinged with red. Capsules ± *globose.*

Bushveld, often in rocky places. Magaliesberg. Autumn – winter.

306 Euphorbia schinzii Pax *Klipmelkbossie*

Spiny dwarf *succulent* which forms a *compact clump* of *erect branches* 100 – 150 mm high. Branches usually *4-angled*, ± flat or grooved down the sides, dark green; *spines paired*, straight, dark brown, borne together with a leaf at the tips of greyish brown protuberances; leaf minute, drops off soon after appearing. Flower-like structures in *groups of 3.*

Rocky hillsides, often in rock fissures. Pretoria/Magaliesberg region. Winter.

307 Euphorbia striata Thunb. var. **striata** *Melkgras*

Herb with *slender*, erect annual stems from a woody rootstock; *almost leafless.* Leaves on main stems sparse, *narrowly triangular* gradually *tapering* to a sharply pointed tip (not to be confused with the conspicuous, *oppositely* arranged leaf-like bracts subtending the flowers).

Infrequently scattered in grassland, often in seasonally inundated seepage areas and vleis. Widespread. Spring.

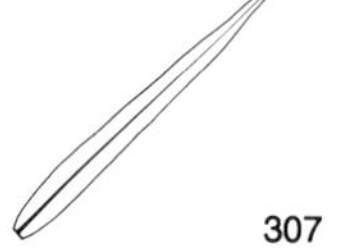

307

303 *Euphorbia clavaroides*

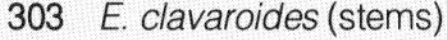

303 *E. clavaroides* (stems)

304 *Euphorbia cooperi*

305 *Euphorbia ingens* (habit)

306 *Euphorbia schinzii*

307 *Euphorbia striata*

308

308 Jatropha lagarinthoides Sond.
Herbaceous shrublet from a woody rootstock, young stems often tinged with red. Leaves *stalkless*, long and narrow (4 – 10 mm), often with a reddish margin when young, *hairless*. Flowers axillary, male and female on same plant; bracts and sepals fringed with *conspicuous glandular hairs*, often reddish; petals 5, cream; stamens usually 8, absent in female flowers.
Grassland, often in rocky places. Mainly Pretoria/Magaliesberg region. Spring.

FABACEAE (See page 20)

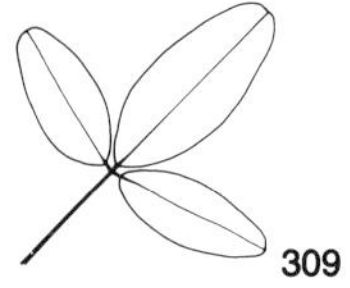
309

309 Argyrolobium pauciflorum Eckl. & Zeyh. var. **pauciflorum**
Erect perennial herb with a woody taproot; *densely covered* with short *appressed silvery hairs*. Leaves stalked, trifoliolate; stipules *triangular*. Flowers *single* or *irregularly spaced* on inflorescence axis, usually *distinctly stalked;* calyx *2-lipped*. Pods ± densely covered with hairs.
Rocky grassland. Widespread. Summer.

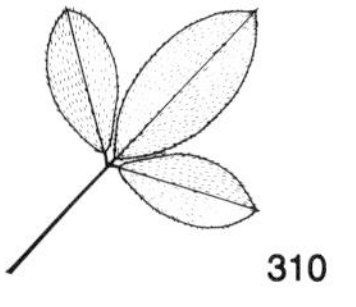
310

310 Argyrolobium cf. **velutinum** Eckl. & Zeyh.
Perennial herb with slender *trailing* stems from a woody taproot. Leaves densely covered with *silvery hairs*, often ± *folded* along the midrib; stipules ± *linear*. Flowers axillary towards tips of stems, each stalk usually bearing 2 flowers.
Rocky grassland. Suikerbosrand. Spring.

311

311 Calpurnia villosa Harv. var. **intrusa** (R.Br. ex Ait.f.) E. Mey.
Bushy perennial shrublet; young branches covered with *minute appressed hairs*. Leaves compound with 5 – 13 pairs of leaflets; leaflets elliptic, *base rounded*, tip with a *short sharp point*, ± hairy on both surfaces or hairless. Racemes many-flowered, 60 – 150 mm long (*longer* than the leaves). Flowers yellow, turning cream or brown with age.
Rocky grassland, often in dense stands. Mainly Suikerbosrand. Summer.

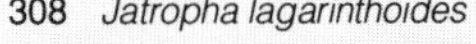

308 *Jatropha lagarinthoides*

309 *Argyrolobium pauciflorum*

310 *Argyrolobium* cf. *velutinum*

311 *Calpurnia villosa*

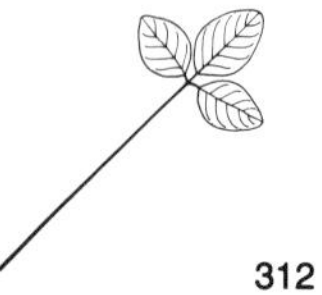
312

312 *Crotalaria agatiflora Schweinf. *Bird flower/Voëltjiebos*
Bushy shrub or small tree up to ± 3 m high. Leaves on long stalks, compound with 3 leaflets, each on a *short stalk;* stipules usually deciduous on older shoots. Racemes usually terminal, on stout stalks and *many-flowered.* Flowers resemble birds hanging on to the axis; calyx often tinged with purple; corolla greenish yellow, keel with a *projecting greenish or purplish beak.* Pods *inflated.*
Native to East and north-east Africa. Naturalized in disturbed places, particularly along roads. Mainly Pretoria region. Spring – autumn.

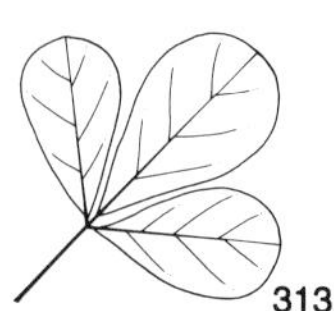
313

313 Crotalaria brachycarpa (Benth.) Burtt Davy ex Verdoorn *Jaagsiektebossie*
Perennial shrublet with numerous erect stems from a woody rootstock. Stems *hairless* to the naked eye, but with minute erect hairs under magnification. Leaves stalked, trifoliolate. Flowers 16 – 25, in terminal racemes 50 – 100 mm long; corolla bright yellow, keel *angular,* with a narrow twisted tip. Pods ± *globose, thick-walled,* covered with minute appressed hairs; bearing 2 – 4 seeds.
Grassland and bushveld, often in moist places and along roadsides. Mainly Pretoria/Magaliesberg region. Spring – summer.

314

314 Crotalaria eremicola Bak.f.
Small perennial shrublet with rigid branches from a woody rootstock; *armed with distinct straight spines* that are slender and project at ± right angles all along the branches. Leaves on short stalks, *trifoliolate,* ± hairless. Flowers *solitary* along the branches; petals 6 – 7 mm long, keel turned upwards and narrowed into a slender tip. Pods ± globose, inflated and covered with short hairs; 1-seeded.
Grassland. Pretoria/Magaliesberg region. Spring – summer.

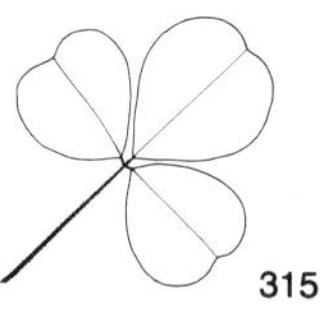
315

315 Crotalaria lotoides Benth. *Klapperbossie*
Spreading or decumbent perennial shrublet. Stems with *spreading hairs.* Leaves stalked, trifoliolate; leaflets *broadly egg-shaped* to ± *circular,* hairy or hairless. Inflorescence comprises 1 – 3 flowers. Flowers light yellow, often with a tinge of pink (pale salmon), keel *turning upwards* well below the middle and with a straight projecting tip. Pods *elongated,* up to 30 mm long, ± *cylindrical,* hairy, pointed.
Grassland and disturbed places, often along roadsides. Mainly Pretoria/Magaliesberg region. Spring – summer.

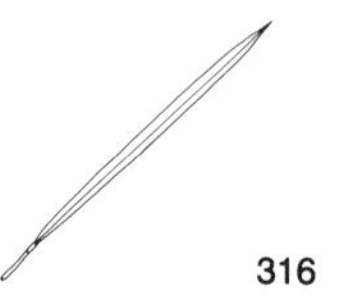
316

316 Crotalaria orientalis Burtt Davy ex Verdoorn subsp. **orientalis**
Shrublet up to ± 800 mm high, from a woody perennial rootstock; mature growth *hairless.* Stems erect, much-branched and *wiry.* Leaves *simple, 0,5 – 1,5 mm* wide. Flowers on *slender* stalks and *widely spaced* along branches; standard *cream* with *reddish brown* parallel veins; wings *yellow;* keel turned upwards and narrowed into a slender tip. Pods *inflated.*
Bushveld, often along roadsides. Pretoria region. Spring.

317

317 Crotalaria sphaerocarpa Perr. ex DC. *Mealie crotalaria/Mielie-crotalaria*
Erect *annual* herb up to 500 mm high; covered with short hairs. Leaves stalked, trifoliolate; leaflets with *rounded* tip. Inflorescence comprises *long, slender, many-flowered* racemes. Corolla *5 – 6 mm* long, pale yellow and *hairy.* Pods ± *globose,* up to 5 mm in diameter, *hairy.*
Bushveld, common in sandy soil and disturbed places, particularly roadsides and cultivated fields. Mainly Pretoria/Magaliesberg region. Spring – summer.

312 *Crotalaria agatiflora*

313 *Crotalaria brachycarpa*

314 *Crotalaria eremicola*

315 *Crotalaria lotoides*

316 *Crotalaria orientalis*

317 *Crotalaria sphaerocarpa*

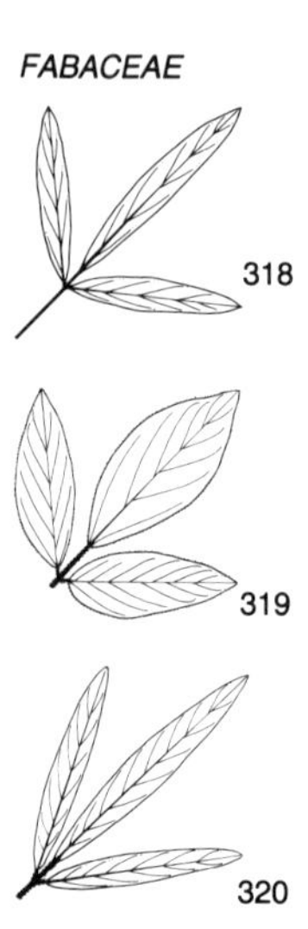

318 Eriosema burkei Benth.
Erect, sparsely branched perennial herb; densely covered with *silvery hairs.* Leaves *trifoliolate;* venation *prominent* on lower surface; stalk of terminal leaflet *longer than 10 mm.* Flowers crowded into inflorescences borne on *long,* leafless stalks; petals often with *reddish veins.*
Grassland. Widespread. Spring. □ Compare **320**.

319 Eriosema cordatum E. Mey.
Perennial herb with *prostrate stems* from a woody rootstock. Stems with tips often *growing upwards*, covered with spreading hairs. Leaves stalked, simple or trifoliolate; leaflets usually 50 – 70 mm long, dark green, with some spreading hairs; stipules *longer than 5 mm.* Inflorescence an erect, many-flowered axillary spike. Corolla yellow, *standard with red veins.* Pods round in outline, flat, hairy.
Grassland. Widespread. Spring.

320 Eriosema salignum E. Mey.
Erect, *sparsely branched*, perennial herb; covered with *silvery hairs.* Leaves trifoliolate; leaflets with *prominent veins* and *silvery hairs* on lower surface; stalk of terminal leaflet *up to 6 mm* long. Flowers crowded into inflorescences borne on long, leafless stalks; petals often with *reddish veins.*
Grassland, often in clayish soil. Widespread. Spring. □ Compare **318**.

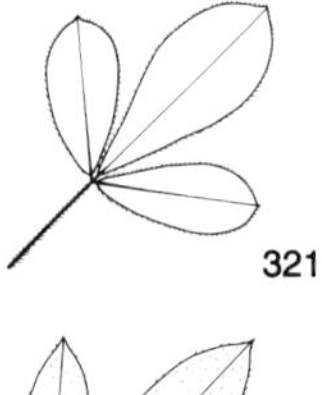

321 Lotononis calycina (E. Mey.) Benth. var. **hirsutissima** Duemmer
Low-growing, much-branched perennial herb; *densely* covered with *long spreading hairs*, particularly on the lower leaf surface. Leaves trifoliolate; leaflets lance-shaped; stipules leaf-like. Flowers single or in few-flowered inflorescences near the ends of branchlets; calyx *as long as, or longer* than the keel; corolla yellow, often tinged with brown.
Grassland and bushveld. Widespread. Spring.
Var. **calycina** Duemmer has leaflets with *scattered hairs* on the lower surface.

322 Lotononis eriantha Benth. var. **eriantha**
Perennial shrublet with a woody rootstock. Stems much-branched, *straggling*, prostrate or *curving upwards* from the base. Leaves on short stalks, *trifoliolate;* leaflets oval with *spreading hairs.* Flowers in *dense terminal clusters;* corolla covered with *short hairs*, yellow, turning *reddish brown* with age. Pods hairless.
Grassland. Widespread. Summer.

323 Lotononis foliosa H. Bol.
Herbaceous, densely leafy perennial with erect, sparsely branched shoots from a woody taproot. Leaves on short stalks; leaflets *tapering at both ends* and with *long (2 – 3,5 mm)*, spreading hairs; stipules free, *leaf-like*, 10 – 12 mm long. Flowers in dense, *dome-shaped*, terminal clusters; corolla with very *blunt* keel; all parts *blacken* with age.
Grassland, particularly rocky ridges. Widespread. Spring.
Flowers of **L. lanceolata** Benth. also *blacken* with age. This plant differs from the previous species in that its leaves are *almost hairless*, glossy and ± fleshy. Rarely recorded from the Pretoria region. Summer.

318 *Eriosema burkei*

319 *Eriosema cordatum*

320 *Eriosema salignum*

321 *Lotononis calycina* var. *hirsutissima*

322 *Lotononis eriantha*

323 *Lotononis foliosa*

324

324 Lotononis laxa Eckl. & Zeyh. var. **multiflora** Duemmer
Perennial herb with *creeping* to ± *erect* branches; covered throughout with *appressed silvery hairs.* Leaflets 5 – 12 (occasionally 20) mm long. Inflorescence axillary with flowers in *groups of 2 – 5.* Petals 7 – 8 (occasionally 6) mm long, keel *shorter* than the wings, yellow fading to *orange.* Pods covered with appressed silvery hairs.

Grassland. Widespread. Spring.

Var. **laxa** differs in that its flowers are *solitary* in the axils of leaves. Grassland. Widespread.

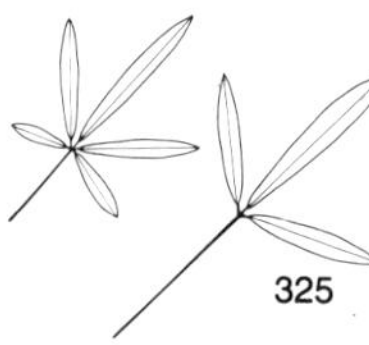
325

325 Lotononis listii Polhill [=**Listia heterophylla** E. Mey.]
Creeping herbaceous perennial, often forming dense mats; branches often rooting at the nodes; *hairless* throughout. Leaves stalked, with usually 3 or 4 leaflets. Flowers clustered in few- or many-flowered racemes; petals yellow *tinged with brown.* Pods *flattened, twisted and folded.*

Grassland, particularly moist areas. Widespread. Summer – autumn.

326

326 Macrotyloma axillare (E. Mey.) Verdc.
Twining herb from a woody rootstock. Stems covered with appressed hairs. Leaves trifoliolate, with minute *hair-like stipules* at the bases of the leaflets. Flowers with *narrow, elongated appendages* on the standard and very narrow wings; *greenish yellow.* Pods compressed, with sharp tips.

Often climbing in low bushes. Mainly Pretoria/Magaliesberg region. Summer.

327

327 *Melilotus indica (L.) All. ***Yellow sweet clover/Geelstinkklawer***
Herbaceous shrublet with a *distinctive odour* when crushed. Leaves trifoliolate; leaflets with *shallowly toothed* margin and *translucent* side veins on the lower surface.

Along streams and in cultivated or disturbed areas; often favouring moist conditions. Native to Europe and Asia. Widespread. Spring – summer.

328

328 Melolobium wilmsii Harms ***Heuningbossie***
Erect shrublet with many annual stems from a woody perennial rootstock; *hairless.* Leaves on *short stalks* (2 – 8 mm long), trifoliolate; leaflets *narrow,* 10 – 25 mm long; stipules free, *bristle-like.* Flowers axillary towards the ends of branches; calyx *2-lipped;* corolla with the keel *shorter* than the wings. Pods flattened, hairless.

Grassland, often in rocky places. Mainly Witwatersrand/Suikerbosrand region. Summer.

329

329 Pearsonia cajanifolia (Harv.) Polhill subsp. **cajanifolia**
Shrublet with several erect annual stems from a woody perennial rootstock. Stems hairy. Leaves on short stalks (10 – 20 mm), trifoliolate; leaflets ± densely covered with *brownish or greyish hairs,* particularly on the lower surface; stipules free, bristle-like. Flowers in *dense terminal clusters;* calyx with lowest tooth separate, upper teeth joined in pairs. Pods flattened, densely covered with hairs.

Grassland, usually in rocky places. Widespread. Summer.

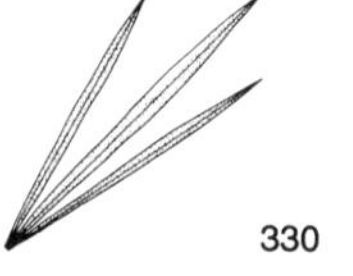
330

330 Pearsonia sessilifolia (Harv.) Duemmer subsp. **sessilifolia**
Herb with slender erect shoots from a perennial rootstock; most parts *densely covered with appressed silvery hairs.* Leaves trifoliolate, ± *stalkless;* stipules fall off early. Flowers *stalkless,* clustered *near the ends* of branchlets, yellow, *fading to orange-brown;* standard erect; keel straight. Pods cylindrical.

Grassland. Widespread. Spring.

324 *Lotononis laxa* var. *multiflora*

325 *Lotononis listii*

326 *Macrotyloma axillare*

327 *Melilotus indica*

328 *Melolobium wilmsii*

329 *Pearsonia cajanifolia*

330 *Pearsonia sessilifolia*

331

331 Rhynchosia adenodes Eckl. & Zeyh.
Erect shrublet with a perennial rootstock; sometimes with ± prostrate stems. Leaves stalked, trifoliolate; leaflets usually ± *as long as they are wide*, hairless or with short hairs, and minute glandular dots on the lower surface. Inflorescence with stalk up to 50 mm long and usually 3 – 6 flowers. Pods with scattered stout hairs.
Rocky grassland. Widespread. Spring.

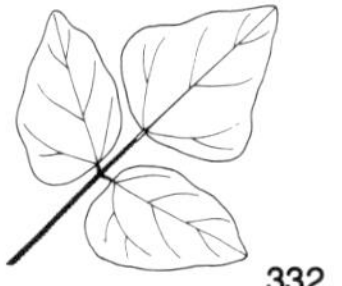

332

332 Rhynchosia caribaea (Jacq.) DC.
Perennial with herbaceous *twining* stems; sparsely covered with hairs. Leaves stalked, trifoliolate; leaflets *tapering* towards the tip. Inflorescences axillary, with flowers *widely spaced*. Flowers yellow with conspicuous *brownish veins*. Pods flattened, *sickle-shaped*, covered with silky hairs.
Grassland and bushveld, usually climbing in woody vegetation. Pretoria/Magaliesberg region. Spring – summer.

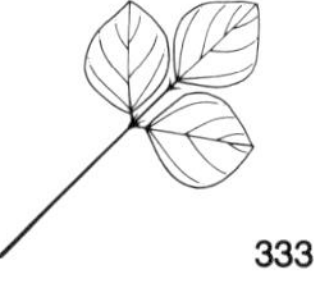

333

333 Rhynchosia minima (L.) DC. var. **prostrata** (Harv.) Meikle
Perennial herb with *creeping or twining* branches from a woody rootstock; ± *hairless* except for minute hairs mainly on the stems and young leaves. Leaves on *long stalks*, trifoliolate, middle leaflet ± *as long as it is wide;* lower surface dotted with *minute glands*. Inflorescences *longer* than the leaves, bearing 8 – 25 flowers. Petals 6 – 8 mm long, yellow tinged with brown.
Moist grassland, often on clayish soils. Mainly Pretoria/Magaliesberg region. Summer.

334

334 Rhynchosia monophylla Schltr.
Perennial herb with long *trailing* stems. Leaves *simple* or with up to 3 leaflets; blade with *3 – 5 prominent veins from the base*. Flowers with calyx densely covered with glandular hairs; corolla with *yellow standard*, often with brownish red or red veins or markings, and *bright pinkish red wings*.
Rocky grassland. Widespread. Spring.

335

335 Rhynchosia nitens Benth. *Vaalboontjie*
Erect silvery grey perennial *shrublet* up to ± 1 m high. Leaves with distinct stalks, trifoliolate; leaflets broadly egg-shaped, with rounded tips; lower surface *densely covered with silvery hairs*. Inflorescences axillary, bearing *1 – 3 flowers;* petals yellow, with back of standard *downy* and glandular.
Grassland and bushveld, usually on the summits of rocky ridges. Widespread. Spring.

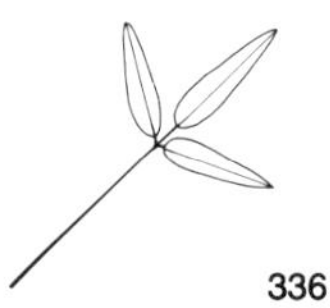

336

336 Rhynchosia totta (Thunb.) DC.
Slender perennial herb; stems *creeping* to twining; young growth often with yellowish hairs. Leaves trifoliolate; leaflets up to 35 x 10 mm, with *prominent* veins on lower surface. Flowers usually *1 or 2* on a *slender* axis; corolla 6 – 12 mm long.
Grassland. Widespread. Spring.

331 *Rhynchosia adenodes*

332 *Rhynchosia caribaea*

333 *Rhynchosia minima*

334 *Rhynchosia monophylla*

335 *Rhynchosia nitens*

336 *Rhynchosia totta*

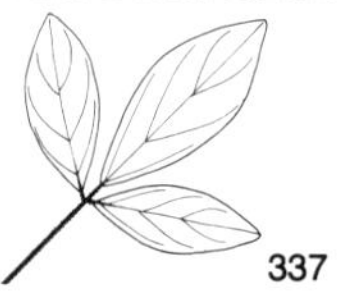
337

337 Stylosanthes fruticosa (Retz.) Alston
Much-branched perennial shrublet. Leaves trifoliolate; leaflets with *whitish side veins conspicuous on lower surface*, tips ± *pointed*, terminal leaflet *stalked;* stipules *united around the stems*, *sharply* pointed. Flowers borne at the ends of branches, partly hidden by leaf-like bracts and *facing upwards*. Pods flattened, *constricted* between seeds.

Grassland and bushveld. Mainly Pretoria/Magaliesberg region. Spring – summer.

338

338 Zornia linearis E. Mey.
Much-branched herb with ± *prostrate* stems from a perennial taproot. Leaves compound with 3 or 4 *very narrow* (0,5 – 1,5 mm) leaflets, dotted with *minute glands*. Flowers borne in erect spikes between *leaf-like bracts*, yellow, often with *reddish veins;* bracts with minute glands and *hairy* margins. Pods *spiny*.

Grassland and bushveld, often along roadsides and in disturbed places. Widespread. Spring – summer. □ Compare **339**.

339 Zornia milneana Mohlenbr.
Much-branched herb with *prostrate* stems and a woody rootstock. Leaves compound with 3 or 4 leaflets, each *3 – 6 mm* wide; lower surface *gland-dotted*. Flowers borne terminally, each enclosed between 2 *prominent green bracts* with *hairy margins*. Pods conspicuously constricted between seeds, flattened, with 1 straight edge and the other wavy, and a prominent *network of spreading hairs* (spines absent).

339

Grassland. Widespread. Spring – summer. □ Compare **338**.

Z. capensis Pers. has leaflets with numerous glands, bracts *without hairs* on the margin, and pods *without spines*.

Z. glochidiata Reichenb. is an erect *annual*. The leaves have only *2* leaflets, and gland dots are absent.

FLACOURTIACEAE (See page 20)

340 Dovyalis zeyheri (Sond.) Warb. *Wild apricot/Wilde-appelkoos*
Deciduous shrub or tree up to 4 m high; armed with *spines*, particularly on coppice shoots and young growth; young twigs *hairy;* bark light-coloured; plants emit a carrion smell at certain times of the year. Leaves stalked, *3-veined from base*, usually *velvety;* margin toothed or toothless. Male and female flowers on different trees. Female flowers insignificant; male flowers in clusters of 3 – 6, with *green, hairy*, sepal-like petals and numerous stamens. Berries oblong, yellow, *velvety*.

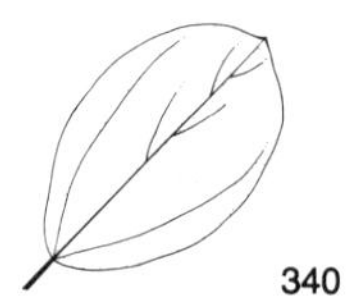
340

Rocky ridges and kloofs, often along streams. Mainly Pretoria/Magaliesberg region. Spring.

337 *Stylosanthes fruticosa*

338 *Zornia linearis*

339 *Zornia milneana*

340 *Dovyalis zeyheri* (male)

GENTIANACEAE (See page 20)

341 Sebaea grandis (E. Mey.) Steud.
Slender erect herb up to ± 250 mm high, often *unbranched.* Stems *square* in cross-section. Leaves stalkless, *lance-shaped.* Flowers terminal, *solitary or few,* with long stalks; sepals with keel *winged* towards the base; corolla *cream* or pale yellow; stigma *2-lobed.*
Grassland. Widespread. Summer.

341

342 Sebaea leiostyla Gilg
Slender erect *annual* herb. Stem usually solitary, unbranched below, *square* in cross-section. Leaves in *widely spaced* pairs, stalkless, ± *rounded,* ± 10 mm diameter, leathery. Flowers in a dense, *many-flowered* terminal inflorescence, *bright yellow;* filaments arising from the gaps between the petals; style with a minute *stigmatic swelling* below the middle.
Grassland, usually in moist vleis. Widespread. Spring – summer.

342

HYPERICACEAE (See page 21)

343 Hypericum aethiopicum Thunb. subsp. **sonderi** (Bred.) N.K.B. Robson *St John's wort/Vlieëpisbossie*
Erect herb with a perennial rootstock. Stems *unbranched, cylindrical* with *black dots* (glands). Leaves *stalkless,* broadly egg-shaped, *4 – 15 mm* wide, base ± *heart-shaped;* margin usually with *dark dots.* Flowers usually with sepals and petals obviously *black-dotted;* stamens numerous, clustered into several bundles around the ovary.
Grassland. Widespread. Spring – summer.

343

344

344 Hypericum lalandii Choisy
Erect herb with a perennial (sometimes annual) underground rootstock. Stems slender, *4-angled,* hairless, up to 400 mm high. Leaves stalkless, ± *lance-shaped, 0,5 – 6 mm* wide; margin *recurved.* Flowers pale yellow to pale orange; sepals and petals *without dark dots.* Stamens numerous in 5 bundles around the ovary.
Swampy and moist grassland. Widespread. Summer.

341 *Sebaea grandis*

342 *Sebaea leiostyla*

343 *Hypericum aethiopicum*

344 *Hypericum lalandii*

HYPOXIDACEAE (See page 21)

345 Hypoxis acuminata Bak.
Erect perennial herb up to 500 mm high, with tufts of leaves from a branched rootstock; *basal parts stem-like;* often in *tussocks of 3 – 40* shoots. Leaves spirally arranged, 5 – 12 mm wide with fewer than 15 ribs; *V-shaped* in cross-section, with numerous *long hairs* on both surfaces. Inflorescence *usually with 2 – 6 flowers.*
Grassland, particularly damp places. Widespread. Spring – summer. Compare **351**.

346 Hypoxis argentea Harv. ex Bak.
Small perennial herb with an underground tuberous rootstock. Leaves *2 – 7 mm* wide, V-shaped in cross-section, *densely covered with silky hairs mainly on the lower surface*, but sometimes also on the upper one. Inflorescence slender, branched, often ± *decumbent*, bearing 2 – 6 flowers.
Grassland. Widespread. Spring – summer.
H. filiformis Bak. is a small plant with leaves up to 3 mm wide, ± shallowly *U-shaped* in cross-section and with very fine hairs mainly on the *margin*. Grassland, often in moist places. Spring – summer.

347 Hypoxis hemerocallidea Fisch. & Mey. [=**H. rooperi** S. Moore] *Gifbol*
Perennial herb with the basal portion *not elongated and stem-like;* rootstock fleshy, vertical, yellow when cut. Leaves appear above ground *before the flowers*, arranged in *3 ranks*, rather stiff and *broad*, arching outwards, sparsely covered with *hairs*; margin fringed with hairs. Inflorescence with 5 – 13 flowers. Petals 10 – 25 mm long.
Grassland. Widespread. Spring. □ Compare **350**.

348 Hypoxis interjecta Nel
Perennial herb with the basal portion *not elongated and stem-like;* rootstock fleshy, vertical. Leaves appear above ground late in spring *after the flowers*, wider than 8 mm, with more than 20 ribs, *completely hairless.* Inflorescence with *2 – 4* flowers.
Grassland. Widespread. Spring.

349 Hypoxis multiceps Buchinger
Perennial herb with a swollen vertical rootstock. Leaves arranged in *3 ranks*, with *more than 25 ribs*, covered with *rough hairs*, poorly developed at the time of flowering. Inflorescence appears above ground *before the leaves.* Flowers 2 – 4 in ± opposite pairs.
Grassland. Widespread. Winter – spring.

350 Hypoxis obtusa Burch. ex Edwards
Perennial herb with a tuberous rootstock. Leaves appear above ground *before* the flowers, *not distinctly 3-ranked*, ± erect, rather stiff, ± *spirally twisted* when mature; margin and keel with a *thick band of white hairs.*
Grassland, often in sandy places. Widespread. Spring. □ Compare **347**.

351 Hypoxis rigidula Bak. *Kaffertulp*
Perennial herb usually with a *single, stiffly erect shoot* up to 1 m high from a fleshy rootstock; basal parts *stem-like*, up to 200 mm long; sparsely or densely covered with *white hairs* throughout; plants not in tussocks. Leaves 0,8 – 1,4 m long, *U-shaped* in cross-section, strongly ribbed. Inflorescence usually with *6 – 13* flowers.
Grassland. Widespread. Spring – summer. □ Compare **345**.

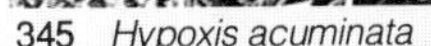

345 *Hypoxis acuminata*

346 *Hypoxis argentea*

347 *Hypoxis hemerocallidea*

348 *Hypoxis interjecta*

349 *Hypoxis multiceps*

350 *Hypoxis obtusa*

351 *Hypoxis rigidula*

IRIDACEAE (See page 21) See also **714**.

352 Gladiolus permeabilis Delaroche subsp. **edulis** (Burch. ex Ker-Gawl.) Oberm. *Patrysuintjie*

Slender herbaceous perennial. Leaves present at flowering time, 3 – 5, erect, long and narrow. Flowers with tips of perianth lobes drawn out into *long points*, giving flowers a spidery appearance; colour variable, usually creamish tinged with pink or mauve, lobes sometimes with a dark maroon or pinkish central line or with yellow blotches.

Grassland. Widespread. Summer – autumn.

353 Gladiolus woodii Bak.

Perennial herb with an underground corm. Leaves that are well developed *absent* at the time of flowering (a *single*, ± hairy leaf appears after flowering). Inflorescence erect, with 2 – 4 reduced, closely sheathing leaves towards the base; bearing 4 – 12 flowers spaced or close together. Flowers small, 2-lipped, deep purple-maroon or dark brown (mainly Witwatersrand) to *greenish yellow* (mainly Pretoria).

Grassland, usually among rocks. Mainly Pretoria/Witwatersrand region. Spring. □ For brownish-flowered form see **714**.

354 Homeria pallida Bak. *Yellow tulip/Geeltulp*

Erect perennial herb; underground corm with a fibrous covering. Leaf *solitary, trailing, much longer than the stem* (up to 1 m), 5 – 15 mm wide, grooved. Flowers borne on an erect axis; style branches *flattened* and petal-like.

Grassland, often on clayish soils in moist places. Widespread. Spring – summer.

LILIACEAE (See page 22)
See also **719** and **722**.

355 Albuca shawii Bak. *Lantern flower/Lanternblom*

Slender erect bulbous herb; most parts densely covered with short *glandular* (sticky) hairs, *smell of liquorice* when crushed. Flowers in terminal racemes, *pendulous*, fragrant; perianth segments yellow with a *green central stripe*.

Grassland, on rocky ridges. Witwatersrand/Suikerbosrand region. Spring – summer.

356 Aloe mutabilis Pillans *Geelkransaalwyn*

Succulent with a relatively short, usually *trailing* stem, rarely up to 1 m long. Leaves *greyish or bluish green;* margin with yellowish teeth. Inflorescence with 1 or *2 branches*, usually *curving outwards and upwards;* stalk with several brownish membranous bracts.

Rocky places, often on rock faces. Localized on the Witwatersrand ridge and Magaliesberg. Winter.

Sometimes considered a variation of **A. arborescens** Mill.

357 Aloe peglerae Schonl. *Bergaalwyn*

Succulent with the leaves *curving inwards* and forming a compact basal rosette. Leaves *without spots*, but with a number of prickles on the medial line of the lower surface near the leaf tip; margin with reddish brown prickles. Inflorescence *unbranched.* Flowers dull red in bud, becoming greenish cream when open.

Rocky places, often on gravelly quartzite. Confined mainly to the Magaliesberg range, usually on the northern slopes and summit. Winter.

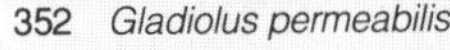

352 *Gladiolus permeabilis*

353 *Gladiolus woodii*

354 *Homeria pallida*

355 *Albuca shawii*

356 *Aloe mutabilis* (habit)

356 *A. mutabilis*

357 *Aloe peglerae*

358 Bulbine abyssinica A. Rich.
Perennial herb with a hard, compact rootstock. Leaves basal, ± erect, straight, circular in cross-section, *not twisted*, with white marginal wing at base. Flowers borne *close together* in a spike-like inflorescence; stamens with *filaments densely covered with hairs;* stalks of old flowers and fruit straight and projecting at ± right angles from the central axis; bracts ± 14 mm long, narrow.
Rocky grassland. Widespread. Spring. □ Compare **359**.

359 Bulbine angustifolia V. Poelln. [=**B. tortifolium** Verdoorn]
Robust herb with a perennial rhizome. Leaves basal, arranged evenly around the stem, up to 300 mm long, ± circular in cross-section, *spirally twisted.* Flowers in long terminal racemes up to ± 700 mm high, each subtended by a small bract; filaments *densely covered with hairs*. Capsules globose.
Grassland, often in rocky places. Widespread. Spring. □ Compare **358**.

360 Bulbine capitata V. Poelln. [=**B. stenophylla** Verdoorn]
Slender erect perennial herb with a 30 – 40 mm long, *stem-like portion* (formed by the overlapping leaf bases) at the base of each shoot. Leaves cylindrical, straight. Inflorescence *compact*, ± *flat-topped*. Stamens with *filaments densely covered with hairs*.
Rocky grassland. Widespread. Spring.

361 Bulbine narcissifolia Salm-Dyck *Wildekopieva*
Erect perennial herb; rootstock short with fleshy roots; plants solitary or growing in clumps. Leaves *flattened*, 5 – 20 mm wide, *greyish green*, slightly *fleshy* with a *yellowish sap*. Flowers numerous, *densely clustered* at the end of a long erect stalk; filaments with a *dense beard* of yellow hairs.
Grassland, often common in localized areas, particularly in overgrazed veld. Widespread. Spring.

362 Eriospermum abyssinicum Bak. [=**E. luteo-rubrum** Bak.]
Perennial herb with an underground tuber. Leaf *solitary*, erect, on a long stalk, with a distinct, narrowly elliptic blade; usually produced *later* than the inflorescence and often a few centimetres away from it. Inflorescence up to 600 mm high, axis *slender and wiry* with lowest flower stalks *greatly elongated and curving upwards*. Petals yellow, with a greenish midpetaline band. Seeds covered with silky hairs.
Grassland, on rocky ridges. Widespread. Spring.

363 Eriospermum tenellum Bak.
Slender, erect herb arising from a fleshy tuber; sometimes leafless at the time of flowering. Leaves up to 3, erect, ± narrowly elliptic. Inflorescence up to ± *150 mm* high, with 7 – 10 well-spaced flowers; lower flower stalks *not conspicuously longer than the upper ones*. Fruit a *capsule;* seeds densely covered with white hairs.
Grassland, usually in damp shallow soil on rocky ridges. Widespread. Spring.

358 *Bulbine abyssinica*

360 *Bulbine capitata*

359 *Bulbine angustifolia*

361 *Bulbine narcissifolia*

362 *Eriospermum abyssinicum*

363 *Eriospermum tenellum*

364 Kniphofia ensifolia Bak. subsp. **ensifolia**
Erect perennial herb with fibrous roots. Leaves basal, *V-shaped* in cross-section; margin *finely toothed.* Flowers crowded into dense spike-like inflorescences, tubular and ± drooping, *red* in bud and *greenish white to cream* when open.
Marshy places. Widespread. Spring – summer.

365 Kniphofia porphyrantha Bak. *Red-hot poker/Vuurpyl*
Erect perennial herb with fibrous roots. Leaves basal, ± flat with a *smooth* margin. Flowering stem *longer* than the leaves. Flowers crowded into dense, spike-like inflorescences; tubular and ± drooping; buds *orange;* open flowers *lemon yellow.*
Swampy places. Widespread. Spring – summer.

366 Protasparagus virgatus (Bak.) Oberm.
Erect, *non-spiny* perennial shrublet from a woody rootstock. Stems *slender*, ± rigid, *straight* and *green;* needle-like stems ('leaves') cylindrical, in clusters of 2 – 4. Leaves reduced to blunt spurs, *not spine-like.* Flowers mainly axillary, not in racemes, borne along the length of branches, *pendulous*, pale greenish cream. Berries red.
Clumps of bush, often in semi-shade. Mainly Pretoria/Magaliesberg region. Spring.

LINACEAE (See page 22)
367 Linum thunbergii Eckl. & Zeyh. *Wild flax/Wildevlas*
Erect perennial herb. Stems usually *unbranched for most of their length; hairless*. Leaves stalkless, opposite at the base of the stem, becoming alternate higher up, ± 10 mm long, narrow, *sharply pointed; gland-like stipules* at base *dark brown*. Flowers terminal in branched, many-flowered inflorescences; buds often with a *reddish tinge*; styles 5, *free*.
Grassland and bushveld. Widespread. Summer.

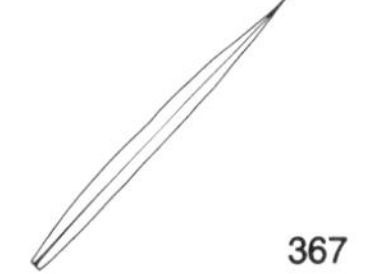
367

MALPIGHIACEAE (See page 23)
368 Sphedamnocarpus galphimiifolius (Juss.) Szyszyl.
Deciduous *climbing shrublet* with *twining* stems. Leaves with stalks, up to ± 75 x 50 mm; base rounded or heart-shaped; *hairless or sparsely covered with hairs* along the margin and principal veins. Flowers in axillary *umbels* bearing few flowers; petals *pale yellow*, margins often ± *folded under;* styles usually 3, free. Fruit *3-winged*, with *rusty brown hairs* which cause irritation.
Grassland and bushveld. Widespread. Summer.
Sometimes treated as **S. pruriens** (Juss.) Szyszyl. var. **galphimiifolius** (Juss.) P.D. de Villiers & D.J. Botha.

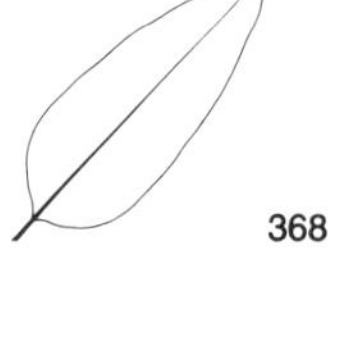
368

369 Sphedamnocarpus pruriens (Juss.) Szyszyl. var. **pruriens**
Deciduous climbing shrublet or climber with *twining stems*. Leaves stalked; base rounded or heart-shaped; *densely covered with greyish or silvery hairs* on both surfaces; stalk with 2 glands in upper half. Flowers in axillary *umbels* bearing 2 – 6 flowers, *bright yellow;* petals *wrinkled* and on short stalks; styles usually 3, free. Fruit comprises ± 3 single-seeded, *winged* units covered with *rusty brown hairs* which cause irritation.
Clumps of bush and open bushveld, often on rocky ridges. Widespread. Summer – autumn.

369

364 *Kniphofia ensifolia*

365 *Kniphofia porphyrantha*

366 *Protasparagus virgatus*

367 *Linum thunbergii*

369 *Sphedamnocarpus pruriens*

368 *Sphedamnocarpus galphimiifolius*

MALVACEAE (See page 23) See also **724**.

370

370 Hibiscus aethiopicus L. var. **ovatus** Harv.
Low-growing perennial herb with a woody rootstock; stems and leaves with *bristly, star-shaped* hairs. Leaves *oval*, with a *blunt tip;* margin usually toothless. Flowers solitary, with a lower calyx whorl (epicalyx) of 7 – 9 *very narrow*, pointed segments, ± 5 mm long; petals usually *pale yellow*, rarely pinkish red; stigmas *bright red*.
Grassland. Widespread. Spring – summer.
For pink-flowered form see **562**.

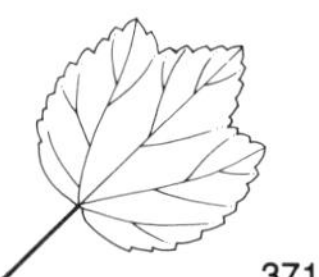
371

371 Hibiscus calyphyllus Cav. *Wild stockrose/Wildestokroos*
Shrubby perennial herb up to 2 m high. Leaves with stalk up to 50 mm long; blade ± *circular*, rarely with 3 – 5 lobes, base *heart-shaped;* with soft *velvety* hairs on both surfaces; margin toothed. Flowers on short stalks, with dark brown or maroon centre; lower calyx whorl of *5 segments*, relatively *broad* in the middle, tapering to a long, *hair-like* tip, ± 20 mm long.
Grassland, bushveld and clumps of bush, often in shady or moist places. Summer. □ Compare **379**.

372

372 Hibiscus engleri A. Schum. *Wild hibiscus/Wildehibiskus*
Erect shrublet up to 1 m high; most parts with star-shaped hairs which are *extremely irritating*. Leaves *3-lobed* with *elongated* middle lobe, base *heart-shaped;* margin deeply and irregularly *toothed*. Flowers yellow with dark reddish centre; lower calyx whorl of *narrow* lobes about *2 mm* long; upper whorls up to 15 mm long.
Bushveld. Mainly Pretoria/Magaliesberg region. Summer – autumn.

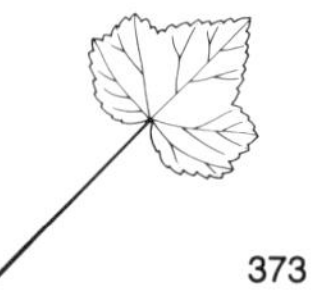
373

373 Hibiscus lunarifolius Willd.
Erect, sparsely branched shrublet up to 1 m high. Leaves stalked, ± *rounded*, with *3 shallow lobes*, base *heart-shaped;* margin toothed. Flowers solitary in leaf axils at ends of branches, yellow, *without a dark centre;* epicalyx comprises 5 segments; petals with *hairy* outer *surface* when in bud.
Rocky hillsides. Widespread. Summer.

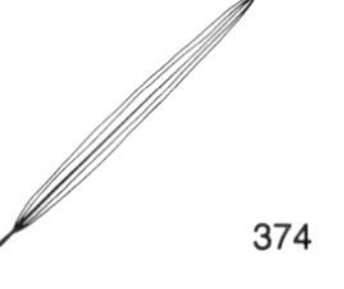
374

374 Hibiscus microcarpus Garcke
Low-growing herb from a woody perennial rootstock; covered with *rough hairs* throughout. Leaves *unlobed*, *long* and relatively *narrow* (1 – 15 mm); margin with star-shaped hairs, toothless or with a few coarse teeth. Flowers yellow or pink; maroon centre absent or present; epicalyx comprises 7 or 8 segments.
Grassland and disturbed places. Widespread. Summer.
For pink-flowered form see **563**.

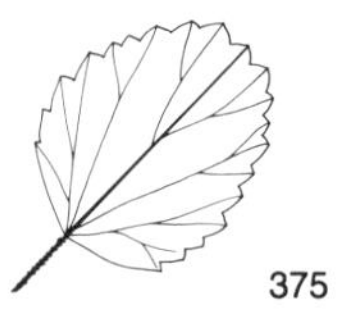
375

375 Hibiscus pusillus Thunb.
Perennial herb with *slender straggling* branches from a woody perennial rootstock; sparsely covered with hairs. Leaves variable in shape, some circular, others lobed; all with *sharply toothed* margins. Flowers on *long, slender* stalks up to 200 mm long; lower calyx whorl with *8 – 11* segments, *narrow*, ± 10 mm long; petals yellow with dark base, rarely pink.
Grassland, usually in stony places and sandy soil. Widespread. Summer.

376

376 *Hibiscus trionum L. *Bladderweed/Terblansbossie*
Erect *annual* herb; hairy. Stems often tinged with purple. Leaves ± variable in shape, usually *deeply 3-lobed*, with the 2 side lobes often *re-divided;* lower surface light-coloured; margin toothed. Flowers have calyx sometimes with *conspicuous purple veins*, *inflated* in fruit; corolla pale cream to almost white, with a dark purple centre.
Grassland and disturbed places, often a weed in cultivated fields. A native of Europe. Widespread. Summer. □ Also **130**.

370 *Hibiscus aethiopicus*

371 *Hibiscus calyphyllus*

372 *Hibiscus engleri*

373 *Hibiscus lunarifolius*

374 *Hibiscus microcarpus*

375 *Hibiscus pusillus*

376 *Hibiscus trionum*

377

377 *Malvastrum coromandelianum (L.) Garcke *Prickly malvastrum*
Erect, semi-woody, ± perennial shrublet up to 1 m high. Stems often purplish, with long *silvery appressed hairs.* Leaves stalked, ± elliptical; blade with venation *conspicuously sunken* on upper surface; margin *coarsely toothed.* Flowers clustered in leaf axils; calyx surrounded by *3 sepal-like bracts.* Fruit comprises ± 13 segments, hairy.

A native of North America, now a weed of disturbed places. Widespread. Spring – summer.

378

378 Melhania prostrata DC.
Somewhat woody perennial shrublet with erect, spreading or prostrate branches; usually *branched near the base;* new growth densely covered with greyish hairs, interspersed in parts with scattered *red-brown bunched hairs* which appear as minute dots. Leaves with upper surface which soon becomes ± hairless, *lower surface retains velvety grey hairs;* blade more or less *folded upward* along the midrib, both ends rounded. Flowers solitary or in pairs; stamens 5 fertile and 5 sterile; ovary *densely covered with whitish hairs.*

Grassland and bushveld, often in shady conditions. Widespread. Summer.

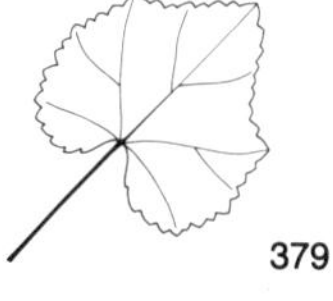

379

379 Pavonia senegalensis (Cav.) Leistner
Low-growing perennial shrublet; stems ± decumbent to erect, *densely covered* with short erect hairs. Leaves on long stalks; blade *broadly rounded*, usually slightly 3-angled in the upper half, densely covered with short, ± appressed hairs on lower surface; base deeply heart-shaped; margin toothed. Flowers axillary, on long stalks, yellow with a deep maroon centre; calyx surrounded by ± *12 very narrow lobes* (epicalyx), the latter *as long as or slightly longer* than the calyx lobes.

Bushveld, often along roadsides. Recorded from the Springbok Flats north of Pretoria. Summer.

The leaf shape of this species superficially resembles that of **Hibiscus calyphyllus** (**371**).

380

380 Pavonia transvaalensis (Ulbr.) A. Meeuse
Perennial herb up to 1 m high, with a woody rootstock; usually *sticky.* Leaves stalked, *deeply divided into 3 – 5 lobes;* margin toothed. Epicalyx comprises 8 – 17 *narrow* segments which are *much longer* than the calyx.

Bushveld, often in sandy places or amongst rocks. Mainly Pretoria/ Magaliesberg region. Spring – summer.

377 *Malvastrum coromandelianum*

378 *Melhania prostrata*

379 *Pavonia senegalensis*

380 *Pavonia transvaalensis*

381

381 Sida alba L. *Spiny sida/Stekeltaaiman*
Slender annual or short-lived perennial shrublet up to 600 mm high. Leaves stalked, dark green above, *dull green* below; base slightly heart-shaped; margin closely toothed; stalk usually subtended by *3 small spine-like protuberances.* Flowers 1 – 4 in leaf axils.
Disturbed places and in the shade of trees. Probably indigenous. Widespread. Spring – summer.

382

382 Sida cordifolia L. *Flannel weed/Koekbossie*
Herbaceous perennial shrublet with a stout woody taproot; covered with *velvety grey hairs* throughout. Leaves *broadly oval,* ± *heart-shaped* at base; *often yellowish, particularly the venation;* margin coarsely toothed. Flowers in dense, many-flowered clusters.
A weed in waste places and old cultivated fields, particularly in sandy soils. Widespread. Summer – autumn.

383

383 Sida dregei Burtt Davy *Spider-leg*
Slender, much-branched twiggy shrublet. Leaf with oval blade and a blunt tip; margin has a few *coarse, blunt teeth.* Flowers *solitary* in leaf axils, with flower stalks *much longer* than the leaves (usually more than 30 mm). Epicalyx *absent.*
Usually in light shade under trees. Widespread. Spring – summer.

384

384 Sida rhombifolia L. *Arrowleaf sida/Taaiman*
Erect branched shrublet with a strong taproot; bark *very tough.* Stems often purplish towards the base. Leaves with upper surface dark green, lower surface *greyish green;* margin finely toothed. Flowers solitary on stalks that are usually *shorter than 30 mm.*
A weed of disturbed places, common along roadsides. Widespread. Summer.

MESEMBRYANTHEMACEAE (See page 23)

385 Delosperma leendertziae N.E.Br.
Leendertz's yellow vygie/Geelbergvygie
Succulent perennial herb; erect to spreading. Leaves 10 – 25 mm long, *semi-cylindrical.* Flowers few in a *lax inflorescence;* petals ± 20.
On rocky ridges. Mainly Pretoria/Magaliesberg region and Suikerbosrand. Spring – summer.

386 Lithops lesliei (N.E.Br.) N.E.Br.
Transvaal stone plant/Kwaggaballetjies
Succulent with only the oval *tips of 2 leaves visible at ground level;* top surface *brownish* with complex *markings.* Flowers solitary.
In brown shale on hilltops, rare, localized and very difficult to spot when not in flower. Widespread. Summer.

381 *Sida alba*

382 *Sida cordifolia*

383 *Sida dregei*

384 *Sida rhombifolia*

385 *Delosperma leendertziae*

386 *Lithops lesliei*

MIMOSACEAE (See page 23)

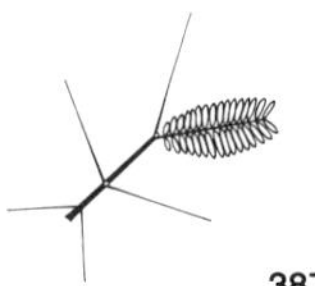

387

387 *Acacia baileyana F. Muell. ***Bailey's wattle/Bailey-se-wattel***

Evergreen tree up to ± 5 m high; *unarmed*. Leaves on *very short* (2 – 8 mm) stalks, bipinnately compound; leaflets *less than 2 mm* wide, *densely crowded, bluish green*, ± *hairless*. Inflorescences of bright yellow *globose heads* in axillary racemes or panicles which are *longer* than the leaves. Pods brown, straight or slightly curved.

Introduced from Australia, occurs as a garden escape. Mainly in the Pretoria/Magaliesberg region. Spring.

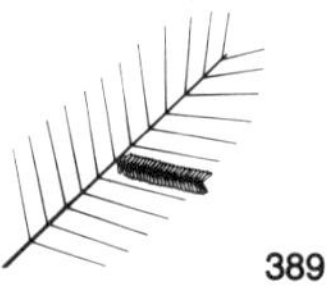

388

388 Acacia caffra (Thunb.) Willd. ***Common hookthorn/Gewone haakdoring***

Tree armed with *recurved thorns in pairs* at nodes. Leaves pale green and ± feathery. Flowers in *elongated spikes*, creamy white, turning yellow with age. Pods light brown to reddish brown, usually straight.

Thornveld and rocky ridges. Widespread. Spring.

A. ataxacantha DC. (Flamethorn/Rank wag-'n-bietjie) is a similar shrub or tree with a tendency to *climb* and with *curved* thorns *scattered* along the branches. It flowers *midsummer – autumn* and has conspicuous *red to purple* pods. Mainly Magaliesberg, sometimes forming impenetrable thickets.

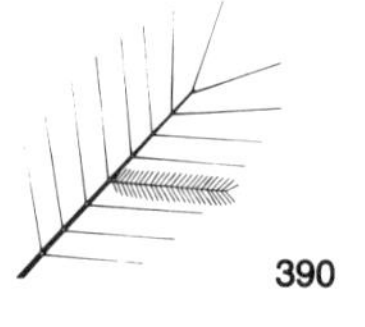

389

389 *Acacia dealbata Link ***Silver wattle/Silwerwattel***

Evergreen tree with hairy branchlets; *spines absent*. Leaves have *raised glands* on the upper surface of the main axis (rhachis) *only where it is joined* by pairs of lateral axes; leaflets *2 – 5,5 mm* long, *bluish green*, hairless to ± *densely covered with hairs* on lower surface. Inflorescences *spherical* on short axillary branches; flowers *bright yellow*.

An invader of grassland and riverbanks, native to Australia. Widespread. Autumn – spring. □ Compare **392**.

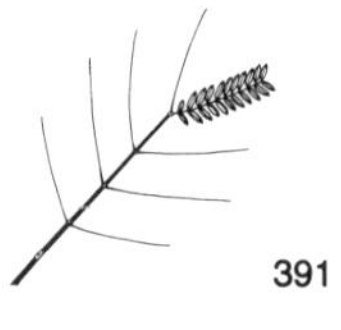

390

390 *Acacia decurrens Willd. ***Green wattle/Groenwattel***

Evergreen tree with young branches usually prominently ridged and *hairless; spines absent*. Leaflets very narrow (± 0,5 mm), 6 – 15 mm long, *green, hairless*. Inflorescences *spherical* and on *axillary* branches; flowers *bright golden yellow*.

An invader of grassland and riverbanks, native to Australia. Widespread. Spring.

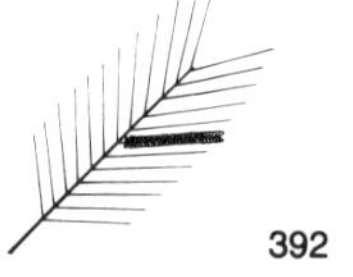

391

391 Acacia karroo Hayne ***Sweet-thorn/Soetdoring***

Deciduous shrub or tree; bark dark brown or *black, rough and fissured*. Thorns paired, stipular; *straight and white;* more abundant and longer on young plants. Inflorescences *globose*, clustered towards the ends of branches, sweet-scented. Pods brown, *sickle-shaped*, dehiscent.

Grassland, bushveld and thornveld; common. Widespread. Summer.

392

392 *Acacia mearnsii De Wild. ***Black wattle/Swartwattel***

Evergreen tree with young branches usually angular and *densely covered with hairs; spines absent*. Leaves with *numerous raised glands* along the main axis (rhachis); leaflets 1,5 – 4 mm long, covered with minute hairs. Inflorescences *spherical* and at the ends of branches. Flowers *pale yellow*.

An invader of grassland and riverbanks, native to Australia. Widespread. Spring. □ Compare **389**.

387 *Acacia baileyana*

388 *Acacia caffra*

389 *Acacia dealbata*

390 *Acacia decurrens*

392 *Acacia mearnsii*

391 *Acacia karroo*

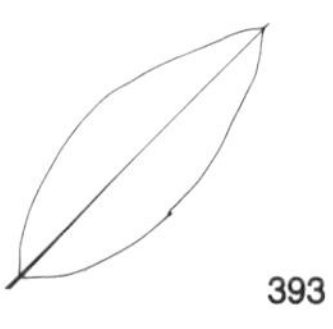
393

393 *Acacia podalyriifolia A. Cunn. ex G. Don *Pearl acacia/Pêrelakasia*

Medium-sized evergreen tree with a dense *greyish green* crown, branchlets densely covered with grey hairs, *unarmed.* Leaves (phyllodes) on very short stalks, ± *egg-shaped*, tapering to a slender *hair-like tip;* densely covered with hairs; margin with *1 or 2 minute glands.* Flowers *bright yellow*, clustered in *globose* heads borne in axillary racemes towards the ends of branchlets. Pods straight, flattened, with ± wavy margin.

A native of Australia, naturalized in disturbed places. Mainly Pretoria region. Autumn – winter.

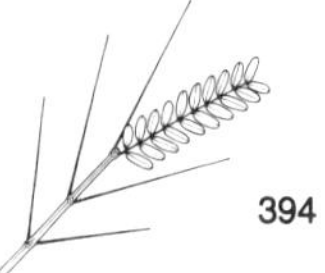
394

394 Acacia robusta Burch. subsp. **robusta** *Enkeldoring*

Robust tree armed with *paired straight thorns* at nodes. Leaves borne on prominent *swellings or cushions.* Flowers clustered in *spherical* heads, *creamy white.* Pods brownish, straight to slightly curved, *woody, 20 – 30 mm* wide.

Thornveld, river valleys and wooded hillsides. Widespread. Early spring.

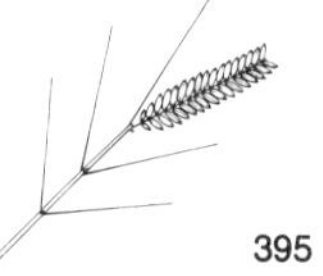
395

395 Dichrostachys cinerea (L.) Wight & Arn. subsp. **africana** Brenan & Brumm. *Sickle bush/Sekelbos*

Much-branched deciduous *shrub* or small tree; often *flat-topped;* armed with *unpaired spinescent branchlets*, the latter often with leaves. Leaves feathery, bipinnate. Inflorescence a *pendulous spike*, the upper part with *pink sterile flowers*, the lower part with *yellow fertile flowers.* Pods *curly and twisted*, densely clustered in heads.

Bushveld. Mainly Pretoria/Magaliesberg area. Summer. □ Also **568**.

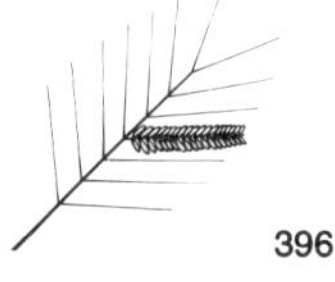
396

396 Elephantorrhiza burkei Benth. *Sumach bean/Basboontjie*

Branched shrub or small tree up to ± *3 m* high; *unarmed* and ± hairless. Leaves bipinnate, *blue-green;* leaflets only slightly asymmetrical at the base. Inflorescence axillary, *spike-like.* Flowers *pale yellow*, becoming darker with age; stalks with *minute reddish glands* at the base.

Bushveld, usually on rocky ridges. Pretoria/Magaliesberg region. Spring.

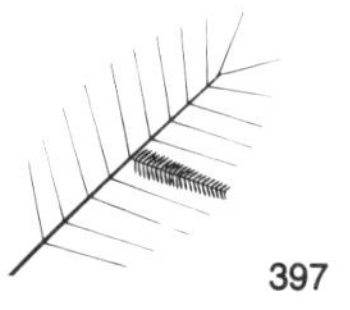
397

397 Elephantorrhiza elephantina (Burch.) Skeels *Elephant's root/Olifantswortel*

Shrublet with erect, usually unbranched, *annual* stems *up to 500 mm* high from a *large*, red, woody underground rootstock; branchlets usually hairless. Leaves bipinnate, fern-like. Flowers in dense elongated *spikes, arising near ground level;* flower stalks with a *zone of weakness near the middle* and with *minute reddish or reddish brown glands* at the base. Pods compressed, transversely veined; the valves separate from the persistent margins when the pods open.

Grassland, often forming extensive stands. Widespread. Spring.

NYCTAGINACEAE (See page 24)

398

398 *Mirabilis jalapa L. *Four o'clock/Vieruurtjie*

Erect shrubby herb with annual aerial parts from a perennial tuberous taproot; *hairless.* Stems ± *square* in cross-section, brittle. Leaves stalked, ± *heart-shaped.* Flowers clustered at *branch tips;* calyx *tubular*, with a spreading 5-lobed limb, white, yellow, red or variegated; surrounded by *5 calyx-like green bracts.*

A native of South America. Cultivated as a garden ornamental and now naturalized in disturbed and often moist places. Widespread. Spring – summer. For red-flowered form see **571**.

393 *Acacia podalyriifolia*

394 *Acacia robusta*

395 *Dichrostachys cinerea*

396 *Elephantorrhiza burkei*

397 *Elephantorrhiza elephantina*

398 *Mirabilis jalapa*

OCHNACEAE (See page 24)

399

399 Ochna pretoriensis Phill. *Bergpruim*

Deciduous or ± evergreen *shrub* up to about 2 m high; much-branched, with a ± spreading habit; bark *rough*, brownish. Leaves on very short stalks, *10 – 15 mm* wide; margin *shallowly toothed*. Flowers appear before the leaves, usually *solitary* on short shoots; petals yellow, *stalked;* anthers open by means of *pores;* calyx becomes ± reflexed and pinkish green to *bright red* at fruiting stage. Fruit elliptic-globose, ± fleshy, shiny black.

Bushveld, on rocky, often north-facing hillsides. Mainly Pretoria/Magaliesberg region. Spring. □ For fruits see **572**.

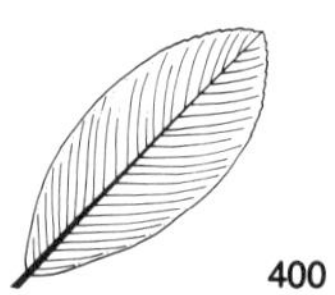

400

400 Ochna pulchra Hook. *Peeling plane/Lekkerbreek*

Deciduous shrub or small tree; sometimes dwarfed, with numerous erect shoots from underground stems; branches brittle; bark grey, *flakes* in membranous pieces to expose *smooth, creamy white patches* on stem. Leaves on short stalks, ± elliptic, 20 – 40 mm wide, shiny green (bronze or red in spring); margin *shallowly toothed in upper half*. Inflorescences terminate short branches, *many-flowered, pendulous*, appear with the young leaves. Flowers fragrant; calyx becomes ± reflexed and turns *bright pinkish red* in fruit. Seed kidney-shaped, ± fleshy, shiny black.

Bushveld, on rocky hillsides and in sandy soils. Mainly Pretoria/Magaliesberg region. Spring. □ For fruits see **573**.

OLEACEAE (See page 24)

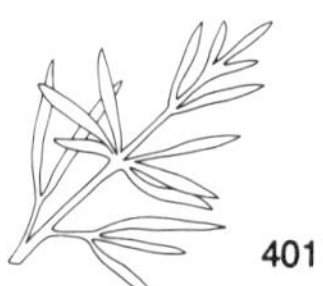

401

401 Menodora africana Hook. *Balbossie*

Somewhat herbaceous shrublet with many slender branches from a woody perennial rootstock; stems *ridged*. Leaves *deeply divided* into *narrow segments;* margin rolled under, with rough hairs. Flowers solitary, yellow, tinged with brownish red on the outer surface; calyx lobes *divided;* corolla *red in bud*. Capsule globose, often 2-lobed, with a papery wall.

Grassland, often in rocky places. Widespread. Spring – summer.

ONAGRACEAE (See page 24)

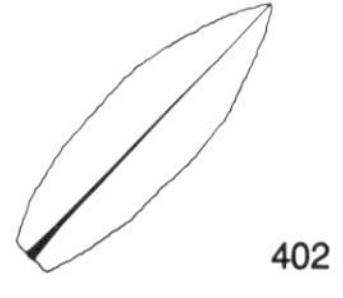

402

402 *Oenothera indecora Cambess. *Small evening primrose/Nagblom*

Herbaceous annual or perennial with shoots ± *bending downwards* from a stout taproot; most parts covered with fine appressed hairs. Leaves *stalkless;* midrib and principal side veins *whitish* and *particularly conspicuous below;* margin with ± shallow and widely spaced teeth, *wavy*. Flowers solitary in the axils of reduced leaves near the ends of branches; *open just before sunset;* petals *3 – 6 mm* long, *pale yellow*, fading to reddish.

A weed of South American origin, usually in disturbed places. Widespread. Spring – summer.

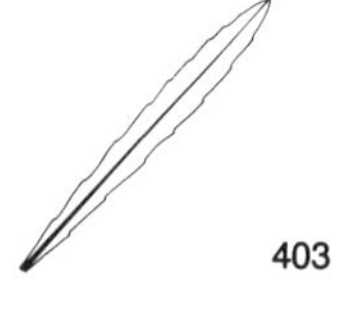

403

403 *Oenothera stricta Ledeb. ex Link *Yellow evening primrose/Geelaandblom*

Perennial herb with a few ± *erect* and usually *unbranched* shoots from a stout taproot; hairy. Stems often tinged with red. Leaves (some, if not all) in a basal rosette, stalkless, base ± square to rounded, side veins *indistinct;* margin with shallow and widely spaced teeth. Flowers solitary in the axils of upper leaves, *open at night* and fade to *orange then dark pink*; petals *20 – 35 mm* long.

A weed of waste places, particularly roadsides. Native to southern Chile and Argentina. Widespread. Spring – summer.

399 *Ochna pretoriensis*

400 *Ochna pulchra*

401 *Menodora africana*

402 *Oenothera indecora*

403 *Oenothera stricta*

ORCHIDACEAE (See page 24)

404 Disa woodii Schltr.
Erect *unbranched* herb up to ± 500 mm high. Leaves evenly spaced along stem, becoming smaller towards the tip; *stem-clasping;* tips often drying to *reddish brown*. Flowers numerous, densely arranged in a *cylindrical* terminal spike.
Grassland, always in marshy places; rare. Mainly Pretoria/Magaliesberg region. Spring.

405 Eulophia clavicornis (Lindl.) var. **inaequalis** (Schltr.) A.V. Hall
Erect deciduous herb with a perennial creeping rhizome. Leaves usually *absent* at the time of flowering. Flowers with sepals *as long as or longer* than the petals; petals ± elliptic, bright yellow; spur *cylindrical*, *± 5 mm* long, with a blunt tip.
Grassland, often on rocky ridges. Widespread. Spring.
Var. **clavicornis** has deep purple flowers (see **665**). □ Compare **408**.

406 Eulophia ovalis Lindl. subsp. **bainesii** (Rolfe) A.V. Hall
Robust, erect, perennial herb with a creeping rhizome; leaf-bearing shoot *adjacent to* the inflorescence. Leaves ± *fully developed* at the time of flowering, arranged in *2 ranks*, leathery, usually *folded*. Inflorescence unbranched. Flowers scentless and with a *flattened* appearance; petals mainly *cream to pale straw yellow;* spur ± *flattened*.
Grassland, often in rocky places. Widespread. Summer.
Subsp. **ovalis** has whitish flowers (see **139**).

407 Eulophia streptopetala Lindl.
Robust erect perennial herb with a pseudobulb partly above ground. Leaves thin and *prominently ribbed longitudinally*, up to 750 x 110 mm. Inflorescence an elongated raceme with *widely spaced* flowers. Flowers with sepals and petals *wide apart;* sepals *green* with dark *purplish brown markings;* petals ± *round*, bright lemon yellow.
Grassland and thornveld, often along streams. Mainly Magaliesberg. Summer.

408 Eulophia tuberculata H. Bol.
Deciduous herb developing from a perennial creeping rhizome with swollen tuberous internodes. Leaves usually *develop only after flowering*, spreading, stiff. Inflorescence erect, ± 400 mm long. Flowers with petals *bright yellow* and distinctly *reddish-veined* on inner surface, usually *larger* than the sepals; lip ± deflexed; spur *very short (almost absent)*.
Grassland, often in groups among quartzite rocks. Widespread. Spring. Compare **405**.

409 Eulophia welwitschii (Reichb.f.) Rolfe
Erect perennial herb with an underground rhizome. Leaves stiff, erect, *ribbed and folded* like a fan. Flowers in dense terminal clusters, drooping, *cream-coloured*, with the sepals and petals *not wide apart;* petals slightly *smaller* than the sepals; lip with 2 *dark maroon side lobes*.
Rocky or marshy grassland; rare. Widespread. Summer.

404 *Disa woodii*

405 *Eulophia clavicornis* var. *inaequalis*

406 *Eulophia ovalis* subsp. *bainesii*

407 *Eulophia streptopetala*

408 *Eulophia tuberculata*

409 *Eulophia welwitschii*

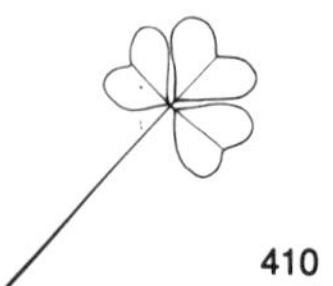
410

OXALIDACEAE (See page 25)

410 *Oxalis corniculata L. *Creeping sorrel/Ranksuring*

Small herb with the stems *prostrate*, brownish, densely covered with hairs and *rooting at the nodes*. Leaves on slender stalks, divided, with 3 leaflets; leaflets *indented* at the tip, *almost hairless above, densely covered with hairs below*. Flowers clustered on long erect stalks.

A troublesome weed of disturbed places, often along roads and in gardens. A native of Europe and Asia. Widespread. All year.

PASSIFLORACEAE (See page 25)

411 Adenia digitata (Harv.) Engl. *Wild granadilla/Bobbejaangif*

Herbaceous climber from a fleshy *underground tuber;* with *tendrils*. Leaves stalked; blade deeply divided into 3 – 5 lobes, with *2 glands* where the stalk joins the blade; leaflets ± lance-shaped, often *deeply lobed, greyish or bluish green below*. Inflorescences stalked, bearing 1 – 20 flowers, *ending in a tendril* up to 150 mm long. Fruit berry-like, ellipsoid to oblong, *orange to red*, splitting into 3 – 5 valves.

Bushveld, often in clumps of bush. Pretoria/Magaliesberg region. Summer.

411

412 Adenia glauca Schinz

Deciduous perennial climber; basal part *considerably thickened*, ± bottle-shaped and mostly above ground, *shiny green*. Leaves stalked, roundish in outline, divided into *5 broadly elliptic lobes* with *2 paired, flap-like glands* at the base of the lobes; *bluish green*. Inflorescences axillary, stalked, bearing 2 – 5 flowers, usually *ending in a tendril*. Fruit berry-like, ± globose, splitting into 3 valves.

Bushveld, in rocky places; rare. Pretoria/Magaliesberg region. Spring – summer.

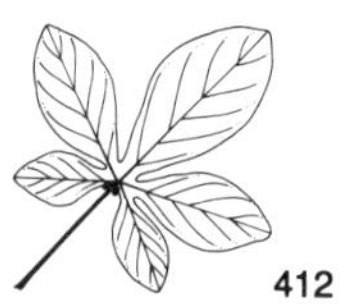
412

PERIPLOCACEAE (See page 25)

413 Cryptolepis oblongifolia (Meisn.) Schltr. *Bokhoring*

Evergreen *multi-stemmed shrub* up to 1 m high, sometimes tending to climb. Leaves in *well-spaced pairs*, elliptic. Flowers in few-flowered axillary clusters, creamy white to yellow; anthers with *long points* converging towards the flower centre. Fruit consists of *paired follicles* ± joined at the base and resembling horns. Seed with a tuft of hairs.

Rocky hillsides. Mainly Pretoria/Magaliesberg region. Summer.

C. transvaalensis Schltr. (Bobbejaantou) is a twining climber with rounded, sharp-tipped leaves. Mainly Magaliesberg.

413

PHYTOLACCACEAE (See page 25)

414 *Phytolacca octandra L. *Inkberry/Bobbejaandruif*

Sparsely branched herbaceous shrublet; some branches tinged with *purplish pink*. Flowers essentially *stalkless* on *upright* spikes. Fruit *flattened*, comprising a ring of *several tightly fused* carpels; fleshy and dark purple-black when ripe.

Probably exotic. Mainly confined to disturbed places, particularly roadsides. Widespread. Spring – summer.

414

410 *Oxalis corniculata*

411 *Adenia digitata*

412 *Adenia glauca*

413 *Cryptolepis oblongifolia*

414 *Phytolacca octandra*

PITTOSPORACEAE (See page 25)

415

415 Pittosporum viridiflorum Sims *Cheesewood/Kasuur*
Small *evergreen* tree; bark smooth when young, roughening with age, smells of liquorice and has a bitter taste. Leaves stalked, clustered at the *ends of branches*, shiny green and ± hairless, with a *resinous smell* when crushed. Flowers in dense, *flat-topped terminal clusters*, fragrant. Capsules ± divided into 2 lobes, with a sharp tip, yellowish orange when ripe, splitting to expose seeds with an *orange-red*, moist and shiny covering.
Wooded areas on rocky ridges and along streams. Widespread. Summer.

PORTULACACEAE (See page 26) See also **586**.

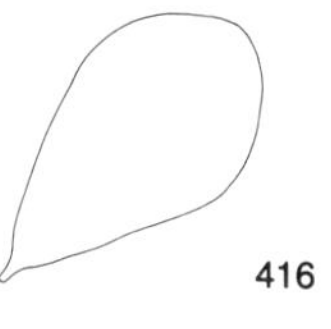

416

416 *Portulaca oleracea L. *Purslane/Varkkos*
Prostrate *annual succulent* with a deep taproot; *hairless*. Leaves ± stalkless; tips *broadly rounded*. Flowers terminal, solitary or up to 5 surrounded by a cluster of leaves.
A native of Europe, now a cosmopolitan weed of disturbed places. Widespread. Summer. □ Compare **586**.

417

417 Talinum caffrum (Thunb.) Eckl. & Zeyh. *Ystervarkwortel*
Erect or decumbent perennial herb from a thick fleshy tuber; *hairless*. Leaves *semi-succulent*, with margin often rolled under. Flowers with stalks *thickened towards the end* and a *pair of small bracts* in the upper half; petals ± twice the length of the sepals. Capsules ± globose.
Grassland and bushveld. Widespread. Spring – summer.

PROTEACEAE (See page 26) See also **146**.

418

418 Faurea saligna Harv. *Beechwood/Boekenhout*
Slender deciduous tree with an *upright* shape and *drooping* branches; bark *blackish*, rough, vertically grooved; young branchlets reddish. Leaves with *reddish stalks*, lance-shaped, grey-green, *drooping;* margin often wavy. Flowers in *drooping spikes*, cream or light green, becoming silvery grey with a reddish tinge. Fruits surrounded by whitish *silky hairs*.
Bushveld, often in sandy soils. Magaliesberg. Spring – summer.

RANUNCULACEAE (See page 26) See also **147**.

419

419 Ranunculus multifidus Forssk. *Buttercup/Botterblom*
Herbaceous perennial with at least some of the leaves in a *basal rosette; hairy* throughout. Leaves stalked, divided into *2 or 3 pairs* of leaflets which are themselves *divided and deeply toothed*. Flowers on long, *hollow* stems, with numerous stamens and a *dome-shaped* structure (receptacle) in the centre.
Swampy grassland, along streams and in vleis. Widespread. Spring – summer.
R. meyeri Harv. is a small herb with *trailing* stems and *heart-shaped* leaves.

415 *Pittosporum viridiflorum*

416 *Portulaca oleracea*

417 *Talinum caffrum*

418 *Faurea saligna*

418 *F. saligna* (fruits)

419 *Ranunculus multifidus*

ROSACEAE (See page 27)

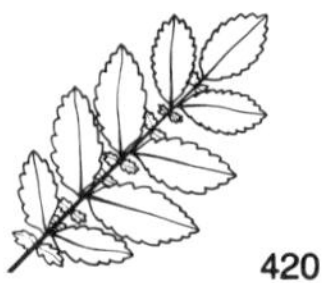

420

420 *Agrimonia odorata Mill. *Agrimony/Akkermonie*

Erect perennial herb up to 1 m high, from a woody rootstock; *hairy throughout.* Leaves *pinnately divided* into 4 or 5 pairs of toothed leaflets; these *interspersed with smaller, toothed, leaflets*. Flowers well-spaced in *long narrow terminal inflorescences;* calyx covered with *hooked bristles*, persistent, and encloses the fruit.

Moist grassland and disturbed places, often in dense stands. A native of Europe. Widespread. Summer – autumn.

421

421 *Duchesnea indica (Andr.) Focke *Wild strawberry/Wilde-aarbei*

Mat-forming perennial herb with prostrate branches rooting at the nodes. Leaves *trifoliolate;* stipules *membranous*, irregularly cleft. Fruit a bright red, ± globose strawberry, surrounded by *leaf-like bracts*.

A garden escape in moist shaded places, particularly along streams. Native to Europe and Asia. Widespread. Spring – autumn.

422

422 Leucosidea sericea Eckl. & Zeyh. *Oldwood/Ouhout*

Crooked evergreen shrub or small tree; bark *rough and flaky;* young shoots reddish and covered with *persistent hairy stipules*. Leaves *compound*, dark green above, covered with *whitish hairs* below; emit a *strong odour* when crushed; leaflets deeply *toothed.* Flowers borne in dense, usually upright spikes; corolla yellow; calyx green and ± *persistent.*

In kloofs and along streams, particularly on high-lying plateaux. Mainly Suikerbosrand and Magaliesberg. Spring.

RUBIACEAE (See page 27) See also **150, 157** and **795**.

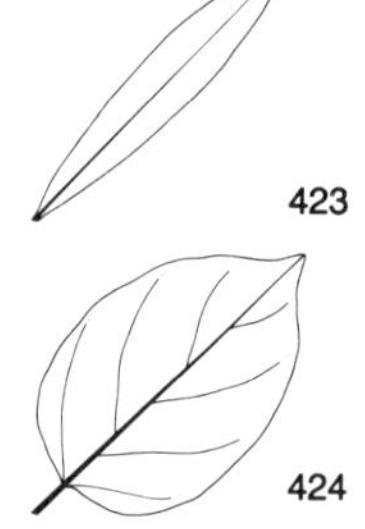

423

424

423 Fadogia homblei De Wild. [=**F. monticola** Robyns] *Wildedadel*

Perennial shrublet up to ± 500 mm high, with many erect, *unbranched annual shoots* from a woody rootstock. Stems *4-angled.* Leaves stalkless, in *whorls of 3 – 5, dark shiny green* above, *greyish white* below. Flowers clustered in leaf axils. Fruits fleshy, shiny black.

Bushveld and rocky ridges, mainly in sandy soils. Pretoria/Magaliesberg region. Spring.

424 Psydrax livida (Hiern) Bridson [=**Canthium huillense** Hiern]

Evergreen shrub or small tree. Leaves stalked, *hairless.* Flowers cream or greenish white, borne in many-flowered *axillary clusters;* sepals *4;* petals *4;* stamens *4.* Fruit a ± globose drupe.

Bushveld, often on rocky ridges. Pretoria/Magaliesberg region. Spring.

SALICACEAE (See page 27)

425

425 Salix mucronata Thunb. subsp. **woodii** (Seemen) Immelman [=**S. woodii** Seemen] *Wild willow/Wildewilger*

Deciduous *shrub or small tree* up to ± 3 m high; branches *spreading* and somewhat drooping. Leaves lance-shaped, pale green above, with a *greyish bloom* below; margin toothed or smooth. Male and female flowers on separate plants. Flowers in ± *erect* spikes. Seeds with a tuft of hairs.

Along streams, often growing almost in the water. Widespread. Summer. Compare **802**.

420 *Agrimonia odorata*

421 *Duchesnea indica*

422 *Leucosidea sericea*

425 *Salix mucronata*

423 *Fadogia homblei*

424 *Psydrax livida*

SAPOTACEAE (See page 27)

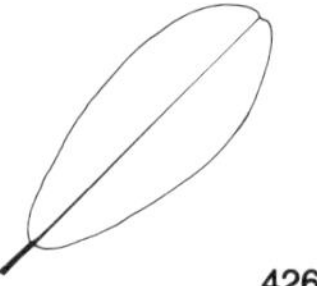
426

426 Bequaertiodendron magalismontanum (Sond.) Heine & J.H. Hemsl. *Transvaal milkplum/Stamvrug*
Evergreen, densely leaved shrub or small tree up to ± 3 m high; young growth with *golden brown* hairs. Leaves stalked, ± drooping, shiny and dark green, often with a *greyish bloom* above, dull green with fine *golden brown* hairs below. Flowers in dense clusters mainly on the *old leafless parts* of the main stem and branches; strongly scented; corolla cream, turning reddish or brown. Berries ellipsoid, bright red when ripe.
Grassland and bushveld, on rocky ridges. Widespread. Spring.

SCROPHULARIACEAE (See page 28) See also **598**.
427 Alectra orobanchoides Benth.
Erect hemiparasitic herb attached to the roots of other plants; *unbranched* or sparsely branched from the base; roots *bright orange*. Leaves reduced to stalkless, green, *scale-like* structures. Flowers solitary in the axils of bracts, disposed in a spike; petals with *reddish parallel veins*, which are usually more conspicuous on the lower surface.
Mainly in shady conditions under trees. Localized but widespread. Autumn.

428

428 Alectra sessiliflora (Vahl) Kuntze *Verfblommetjie*
Erect hemiparasitic herb on the roots of other plants; underground parts *bright orange; sparsely covered with rough hairs* throughout. Leaves stalkless or with stalk up to 3 mm long; blade up to *30 x 20 mm;* margin irregularly toothed. Inflorescence with prominently toothed, leaf-like bracts. Flowers with corolla protruding just beyond the calyx.
Grassland. Widespread. Summer – autumn.

429 Harveya pumila Schltr. *Geelinkblom*
Dwarf parasitic herb with shortened stems. Leaves reduced to *scale-like* structures. Flowers *stalkless;* corolla whitish with a yellow throat (forms with pink flowers reported from outside the field guide area).
Damp grassland, usually near streams; very rare. Recorded from the Magaliesberg. Spring – summer.

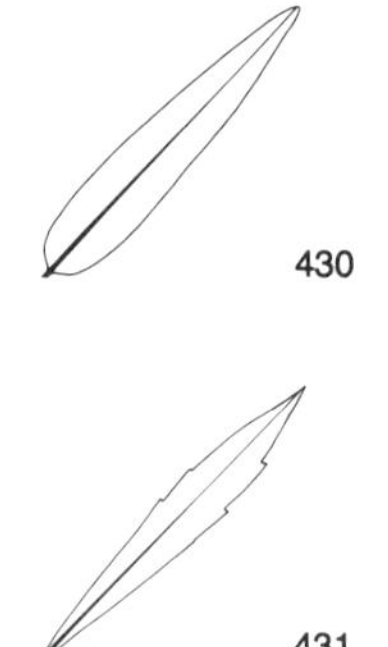
430

431

430 Melasma scabrum Berg
Erect, sparsely branched perennial herb; covered with *rough* hairs. Leaves *stalkless*, with smooth or faintly toothed margin. Flowers on long stalks, with 2 *narrow bracts* ± halfway up; corolla dark *purplish brown* on outer surface.
Moist vleis and along streams. Mainly Magaliesberg. Summer.

SELAGINACEAE (See page 28)
431 Hebenstretia comosa Hochst. *Katstert*
Herbaceous shrublet with many *unbranched* stems from a woody perennial rootstock. Leaves stalkless, *long and narrow;* margin toothless, or with a few inconspicuous teeth. Flowers numerous, in *elongated terminal spikes;* corolla yellow with an *orange blotch*, distinctly 4-lobed.
Grassland. Widespread. Spring – summer. ☐ Compare **730**.

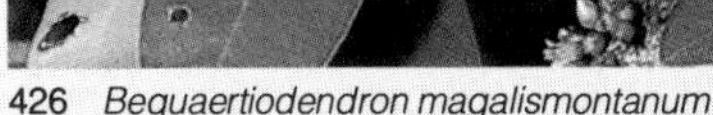

426 *Bequaertiodendron magalismontanum*

426 *B. magalismontanum* (fruit)

427 *Alectra orobanchoides*

428 *Alectra sessiliflora*

429 *Harveya pumila*

430 *Melasma scabrum*

431 *Hebenstretia comosa*

SOLANACEAE (See page 28)

432

432 *Physalis viscosa L. *Sticky gooseberry/Klewerige appelliefie*

Erect bushy herb sending up annual shoots from an extensive system of underground stems; densely covered with *short* (often rather sticky) *hairs* throughout. Leaves yellowish green. Flowers on slender stalks, solitary in leaf axils, *drooping;* stamens *converging into a pointed cone.* Berries completely enclosed by the *inflated calyx.*

A common weed of disturbed grassland and waste places. Native to tropical America. Widespread. Spring – summer.

STERCULIACEAE (See page 28) See also **731**.

433

433 Hermannia floribunda Harv.

Perennial shrublet with long erect or sprawling branches; branched mainly *at the base;* ± *densely* covered with star-shaped hairs, each with a minute bulbous base. Leaves stalked, ± egg-shaped, usually *broader than they are long* and *5-veined* from the base; margin with blunt, irregularly spaced teeth. Inflorescences *many-flowered,* mainly in the axils of leaves towards the ends of shoots. Flowers drooping; calyx ± *inflated.*

Grassland and stony hillsides. Widespread. Summer – autumn.

434

434 Hermannia grandistipula (Buchinger ex Hochst.) K. Schum.

Erect shrublet from a woody perennial rootstock. Leaves dull green, *densely covered with soft hairs,* tips rather *blunt;* margin with *blunt teeth;* stipules *deeply divided* into narrow leaf-like segments. Inflorescences mainly axillary towards the ends of stems. Flowers pendulous; *calyx inflated,* densely covered with hairs, whitish green; corolla lobes *just protruding* beyond the calyx.

Grassland. Widespread. Summer.

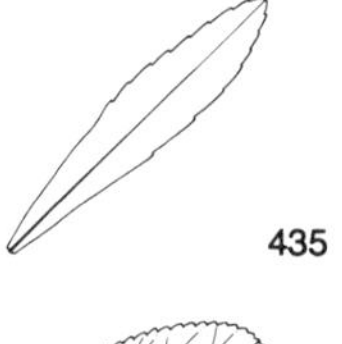

435

435 Hermannia lancifolia Szyszyl.

Small erect herb from a woody rootstock; spreading by means of underground stems to form *dense patches.* Leaves elongated, *grey-green,* lower surface densely covered with short greyish hairs; margin *finely toothed in upper half.* Inflorescences usually bearing 2 flowers. Flowers on *long stalks,* pendulous.

Grassland. Widespread, but apparently not yet recorded from the Magaliesberg. Spring – summer.

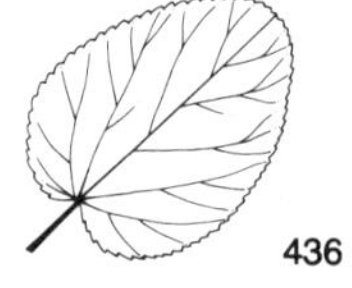

436

436 Hermannia transvaalensis Schinz

Herb with *trailing* stems from a perennial rootstock. Leaves *widely spaced;* blade broadly oval; base *heart-shaped;* tip rounded; with *rough texture* and sparsely dotted, star-shaped hairs; margin finely and bluntly toothed; *stipules lobed.* Inflorescence erect with widely spaced flowers. Flowers pendulous.

Grassland. Widespread. Summer.

437

437 Waltheria indica L. *Meidebossie*

Erect perennial shrublet up to ± 500 mm high; covered with short hairs, some of which glisten in sunlight. Leaves stalked, with margin shallowly and *irregularly* toothed. Flowers in *dense axillary clusters* which are stalked or stalkless.

Grassland and bushveld, often on rocky ridges and in disturbed places. Mainly Pretoria/Magaliesberg region. Summer – autumn.

432 *Physalis viscosa*

433 *Hermannia floribunda*

434 *Hermannia grandistipula*

436 *Hermannia transvaalensis*

435 *Hermannia lancifolia*

437 *Waltheria indica*

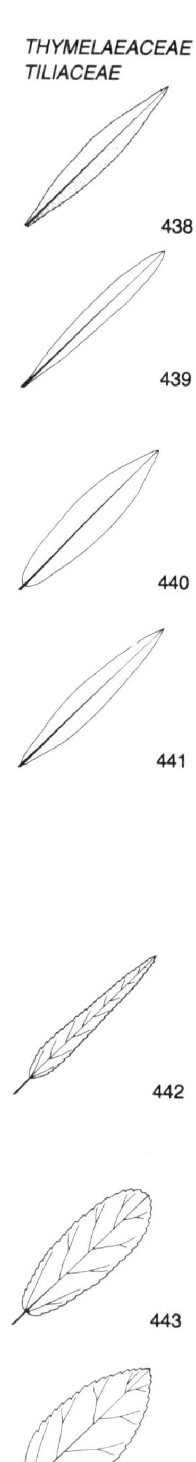
438
439
440
441
442
443
444

THYMELAEACEAE (See page 28)

438 Gnidia caffra Meisn. *Gifbossie*

Shrublet with tough erect stems arising from a fleshy underground tuber. Leaves ± densely arranged along stems, *sparsely covered with hairs*, ± 6 mm wide and *sharply pointed*. Inflorescence a *many-flowered* terminal head, *without* an elongated leafless stalk. Flowers *lemon yellow;* tube less than 15 mm long.

Grassland. Widespread. Spring. □ Compare **439**.

439 Gnidia capitata L.f. *Kerrieblom*

Herbaceous shrublet with a fleshy rootstock. Leaves stalkless, sharply pointed, often *bluish green* and ± hairless. Flowers in *lax, few-flowered* heads which *lack* an elongated leafless stalk; *mustard yellow*, more than 20 mm long.

Grassland. Widespread. Spring. □ Compare **438**.

440 Gnidia kraussiana Meisn. var. **kraussiana** *Harige gifbossie*

Small robust shrublet with several erect *hairy stems* from a thick perennial underground tuber. Leaves with stalk 1 – 2 mm long; usually *densely covered with silky hairs;* margin often fringed with hairs. Flowers covered with silky hairs; *18 – 45* borne in compact, terminal heads carried on an ± *elongated leafless stalk; mostly 5 of each* floral part.

Grassland. Widespread. Spring.

441 Gnidia sericocephala (Meisn.) Gilg ex Engl.

Slender perennial herb with erect shoots from a woody rootstock; *hairy*. Leaves alternate, ± stalkless, narrow, *bluish green*. Flowers borne in stalked globose heads surrounded by a ring of *broad, sharply pointed, overlapping* bracts; calyx tubular with *silky hairs* on the outer surface, *greenish yellow;* petals *absent*.

Grassland. Widespread. Spring – summer.

TILIACEAE (See page 28)

442 Corchorus confusus Wild

Herb with *prostrate or spreading* branches from a woody perennial rootstock; branchlets covered with *bristles*, at least when young. Leaves stalked, lance- to egg-shaped, *3-veined* from the base, hairy on both surfaces; margin *scalloped*. Petals *slightly shorter* than the sepals and tapered at the base into a short stalk. Capsules *pod-like* and bristly, carried on a straight stalk.

Grassland and bushveld; mainly on rocky ridges. Widespread. Summer.

C. asplenifolius Burch. is similar to the previous species and is very common in the field guide area. It has *hairless* stems or sometimes a line of curly hairs on *1 side* of the stem only, and pod-like capsules with a *twisted or curved* stalk.

443 Grewia flava DC. *Raisin bush/Rosyntjiebos*

Deciduous *shrub* up to ± 2 m high; young branchlets covered with *greyish hairs;* bark grey to black, smooth. Leaves with pale green and slightly hairy upper surface, *grey-green and velvety* lower surface; margin finely toothed. Sepals with *greyish hairs on outer surface, inner surface yellow and hairless.* Fruit a globose or 2-lobed drupe; reddish brown.

Bushveld, thornveld and clumps of bush. Widespread, but uncommon in the field guide area. Summer.

444 Triumfetta sonderi Ficalho & Hiern *Maagbossie*

Much-branched perennial shrublet from a woody rootstock. Leaves covered with *rough, star-shaped* hairs; margin *finely and irregularly* toothed. Sepals with *hood-shaped* tips and a *short, horn-like protuberance*. Fruit globose with *numerous long red bristles.*

Grassland and rocky ridges. Widespread. Summer.

438 *Gnidia caffra*

439 *Gnidia capitata*

440 *Gnidia kraussiana*

441 *Gnidia sericocephala*

442 *Corchorus confusus*

443 *Grewia flava*

444 *Triumfetta sonderi*

444 *T. sonderi* (fruit)

TURNERACEAE (See page 28)

445 Piriqueta capensis (Harv.) Urb. *Haarbossie*

445

Perennial shrublet from an underground rootstock; *hairy* throughout. Leaves ± stalkless; blade narrowly egg-shaped with *1 – 3 pairs of circular glands on the lower surface near the margin;* margin *toothed.* Flowers axillary, solitary; petals on short stalks; styles *3.*

Bushveld. Pretoria/Magaliesberg region. Spring – summer.

URTICACEAE (See page 29)

446 Obetia tenax (N.E.Br.) Friis [=**Urera tenax** N.E.Br.] *Mountain nettle/Bergbrandnetel*

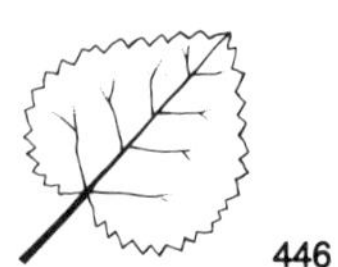

446

Multi-stemmed deciduous shrub up to ± 3 m high; bark with *tough fibres.* Stems ± fleshy and armed with *stinging hairs* when young. Leaves on long stalks, ± *heart-shaped, 3-veined* from the base; both surfaces with *stinging hairs;* margin toothed. Flowers borne in short axillary sprays, *very small,* greenish yellow or whitish.

Bushveld, usually in rocky places. Mainly Pretoria/Magaliesberg region. Spring.

VAHLIACEAE (See page 29)

447 Vahlia capensis (L.f.) Thunb.

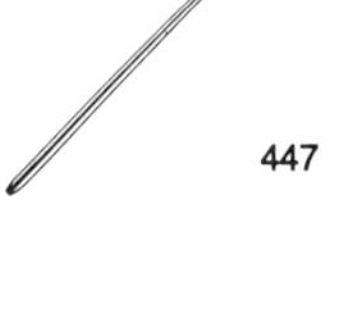

447

Small erect herb with a perennial taproot. Leaves stalkless, long and *narrow.* Flowers in *axillary pairs;* sepals *sharply pointed;* petals *shorter* than the sepals; styles *2,* long and *spreading.* Capsule ± globose, tipped with the persistent remains of the flower.

Grassland, often in moist places. Widespread. Spring.

VERBENACEAE (See page 29) See also **609** and **734**.

448 Lippia javanica (Burm.f.) Spreng. *Fever tea/Beukesbossie*

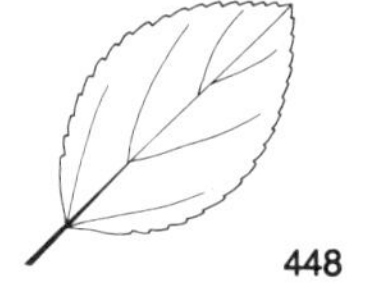

448

Erect, much-branched shrub *up to 2 m* high; covered with *rough hairs; aromatic,* emits a strong *verbena-like* scent when crushed. Stems ± square in cross-section. Leaves often ± *folded upward* along the midrib; margin toothed. Flowers in *dense,* ± *globose, stalked heads;* calyx distinctly *2-lobed;* corolla slightly 2-lipped; bracts less than 4 x 3 mm (not longer than the flowers).

Grassland and bushveld. Widespread. Summer – autumn.

449 Lippia rehmannii H. Pearson *Laventelbossie*

449

Erect shrublet up to ± *500 mm* high, with shoots sprouting from *ground level.* Leaves *aromatic,* emitting a strong *lemon-like* scent when crushed; margin toothed. Flowers in *dense,* ± *globose heads*; bracts longer than 4 mm.

Grassland and bushveld. Mainly Pretoria/Magaliesberg region. Spring – summer.

L. scaberrima Sond. is also a small bushy plant ± *500 mm* high. It has a strong *verbena- or mint-like* smell and the bracts are conspicuous, more than 4 x 3 mm, *longer than* the flowers. Grassland. Mainly Witwatersrand/ Suikerbosrand region.

450 Plexipus hederaceus (Sond.) R. Fernandes [=**Chascanum hederaceum** (Sond.) Moldenke]

450

Perennial herb from a woody rootstock; covered with short rough hairs. Stems ± *prostrate, turning up at the ends* to become inflorescences. Leaves mostly basal, wedge-shaped to ± rounded; tips *rounded or blunt;* margin *deeply toothed.* Inflorescence an erect terminal spike with the axis capable of *continuous extension.* Flowers densely arranged between small pointed bracts; corolla with a *long tube,* 2-lipped, pale cream to almost white; style with a heel-like bend.

Grassland. Widespread. Summer.

P. adenostachyus (Schauer) R. Fernandes is very similar to the previous species, but has more *elongated* leaves with ± *sharply pointed* tips.

445 *Piriqueta capensis*

446 *Obetia tenax*

447 *Vahlia capensis*

448 *Lippia javanica*

449 *Lippia rehmannii*

450 *Plexipus hederaceus*

VITACEAE (See page 29)

451 Cyphostemma lanigerum (Harv.) Descoings ex Wild & Drum. ***Wildedruif***

Bushy perennial with ± *climbing* stems and tendrils; *densely covered with hairs* throughout. Leaves stalked, with *3 – 5 leaflets* arising from the same point; margins ± toothed; stipules up to 10 mm long. Inflorescence *opposite* a leaf, much-branched, ± *flat-topped.* Buds cylindrical, *constricted* in the middle.

Rocky ridges. Pretoria/Magaliesberg region. Summer.

452 Rhoicissus tridentata (L.f.) Wild & Drum. subsp. **cuneifolia** (Eckl. & Zeyh.) N.R. Urton ***Bushman's grape/Boesmansdruif***

Deciduous *climber or sprawling shrub.* Stems with tendrils *opposite* some leaves. Leaves stalked, *trifoliolate;* leaflets ± hairy, margin *toothed*, terminal leaflet on a short stalk and usually with a blunt tip. Flowers inconspicuous, creamy white, often tinged with red; borne in *clusters opposite leaves* or tendrils. Fruit fleshy, red to purple when ripe, sometimes with small white spots (lenticels).

Grassland and bushveld, usually on rocky ridges or along streams. Spring.

XYRIDACEAE (See page 29)

453 Xyris capensis Thunb.

Densely tufted perennial up to 300 mm high. Leaves *basal*, erect, flat, *long and narrow* (grass-like), arranged *like a fan* from a small, weakly developed rootstock. Inflorescence stalk long and *wiry*, golden brown at the base. Flowers clustered in a *roundish*, ± 6-flowered spike; bracts conspicuous, overlapping, scaly, brown and shiny; petals very delicate, withering quickly.

Swampy places and along streams. Widespread. Spring – summer.

X. congensis Buettn. is a densely tufted perennial with a *hard rootstock* covered with *persistent, shiny reddish brown, twisted leaf bases.* Flowering spikes are *egg-shaped.* Along streams in the Magaliesberg.

ZYGOPHYLLACEAE (See page 29)

454 Tribulus terrestris L. ***Dubbeltjie***

Annual herb with much-branched *prostrate* shoots; covered with long *whitish hairs* throughout. Leaves opposite, usually with 1 of a pair *shorter* than the other; pinnately compound, *without a terminal leaflet;* leaflets with lower surface *densely covered with hairs.* Flowers solitary in leaf axils; petals 5; stamens 10; *style absent.* Fruit with *sharp spines.*

Grassland, usually a weed of disturbed places. Widespread. Spring – autumn.

451 *Cyphostemma lanigerum*

452 *Rhoicissus tridentata*

452 *R. tridentata* (fruit)

453 *Xyris capensis*

454 *Tribulus terrestris*

PINK TO RED OR RED-PURPLE FLOWERS

(See also **2, 4, 5, 18, 61, 90, 98, 105, 163, 168, 188, 256, 334, 356, 357, 364, 612, 619, 620, 625, 646, 657 – 660, 666, 686, 696, 731**)

Pink and red flowers are easily recognizable, but in some instances it is difficult to separate red-purple flowers from blue-purple ones. It is also difficult to record faithfully purplish colours on film, and in photographs the colours often come out with pinkish tones. Red-purple flowers are included in this group, but if a purple flower cannot be found here, also consult the section on Blue or blue-purple flowers (page 240).

Colours of flowers in the range from pink to red to purple to blue usually result from the presence of anthocyanins, a group of pigments belonging to the same class of chemicals as the yellow flavonoids. Anthocyanins dissolve in the cell sap and can vary, depending on the pH of the solution. If it is very acid, the colouring is most likely to be red, whereas if it is more alkaline, the pigment tends towards blue. Purple comes in many shades which fall between red and blue.

Red flowers are most often associated with pollination by sunbirds (**509, 510**) and certain butterflies, particularly the swallowtails (**549**) and the whites (**600**). Bees and most other insect pollinators are red-blind and in theory should not be attracted to pure red colours. However, in nature many red flowers are visited by bees which are attracted by the ultraviolet light the flowers reflect rather than by the red. In addition, red-purple and most red flowers contain a blue component and this is visible to bees. It has also been shown that bees can be trained to respond to red colours, even those of flowers which typically attract birds.

Birds have a colour vision very similar to that of humans except that they react less strongly to blue or violet and are more sensitive to red. They also resemble humans in that they are blind to ultraviolet light. To most insects bright red flowers which do not reflect ultraviolet might, for example, appear dull grey, while those reflecting ultraviolet are likely to be perceived by them as blue.

GUIDE TO THE FAMILIES WHICH INCLUDE PINK TO RED OR RED-PURPLE FLOWERS

PINK TO RED OR RED-PURPLE FLOWERS

- PETALS 6 (MONOCOTYLEDONS)
  - OVARY SUPERIOR
    - (S) (T) Liliaceae
  - OVARY INFERIOR
    - Amaryllidaceae
    - Iridaceae
    - Velloziaceae
- PETALS 4 OR 5, RARELY NUMEROUS (DICOTYLEDONS)
  - PETALS CLEARLY UNITED
    - FLOWERS REGULAR
      - LEAVES OPPOSITE
        - (L) Apocynaceae (see **18**)
        - Asclepiadaceae
        - Asteraceae
        - (S) Crassulaceae
        - Gentianaceae
        - Nyctaginaceae
        - (L) Periplocaceae (see **666**)
        - Rubiaceae
        - Thymelaeaceae
      - LEAVES ALTERNATE/ROSULATE
        - (T) Asteraceae
        - Boraginaceae
        - (L) Convolvulaceae
        - Ericaceae
        - (T) Mimosaceae
        - Thymelaeaceae
    - FLOWERS ± IRREGULAR
      - OVARY SUPERIOR
        - (T) Acanthaceae
        - Lamiaceae
        - Pedaliaceae
        - Proteaceae
        - Scrophulariaceae
        - Verbenaceae
      - OVARY INFERIOR
        - (L) Lobeliaceae
        - Loranthaceae
  - PETALS ± FREE
    - PLANTS HERBACEOUS
      - LEAVES OPPOSITE
        - OVARY SUPERIOR
          - Amaranthaceae
          - Caryophyllaceae
          - Lythraceae
          - Malpighiaceae
          - (S) Portulacaceae
          - Ranunculaceae
        - OVARY INFERIOR
          - Melastomataceae
          - (S) Mesembryanthemaceae
          - Onagraceae
      - LEAVES ALTERNATE/ROSULATE
        - FLOWERS REGULAR
          - LEAVES WITHOUT STIPULES
            - Amaranthaceae
            - Droseraceae
            - Onagraceae
            - Oxalidaceae
          - LEAVES WITH STIPULES
            - (L) Euphorbiaceae
            - Geraniaceae
            - Malvaceae
            - Polygonaceae
            - (T) Rosaceae
            - Sterculiaceae
            - (S) Portulacaceae
        - FLOWERS ± IRREGULAR
          - Capparaceae
          - Fabaceae
          - Geraniaceae
          - Polygalaceae
    - PLANTS WOODY (SHRUBS OR TREES)
      - (T) Fabaceae
      - Ochnaceae
      - (T) Rosaceae
      - Rutaceae
      - Tiliaceae
- PETALS AND SEPALS ABSENT (DICOTYLEDONS)
  - (L) Moraceae (see **777 – 779**)
  - Myricaceae (see **781, 782**)
  - Myrothamnaceae
  - Myrtaceae

(L) At least some members with *milky latex*
(S) At least some members *succulent*
(T) At least some members with *thorns/spines*

ACANTHACEAE (See page 16) See also **2, 4, 5** and **612**.

455 Crossandra greenstockii S. Moore

455

Erect herb from a woody perennial rootstock. Leaves ± oval and mostly in a *basal rosette*. Flowers in *dense spikes;* inflorescence stalk usually unbranched; bracts green, up to *30 mm* long, overlapping, hairy with *spiny* margin and tip.

Bushveld, often in the shade of trees and shrubs on rocky hillsides. Mainly Pretoria/Magaliesberg region. Spring.

456 Dicliptera eenii S. Moore

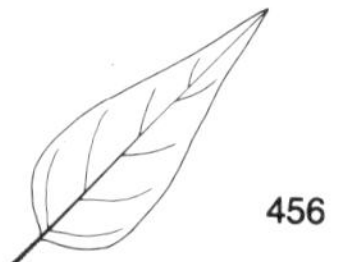
456

Herbaceous shrublet with *straggling* branches. Leaves stalked, elliptic and *well-spaced* in opposite pairs. Flowers in axillary clusters; subtended by green, *sharply pointed*, hairy bracts; corolla distinctly *2-lipped;* stamens 2, protruding.

Bushveld, usually in shady places on rocky ridges and along streams. Mainly Pretoria/Magaliesberg region. Summer – autumn.

AMARANTHACEAE (See page 16)

457 *Achyranthes aspera L. *Chaff flower/Langklits*

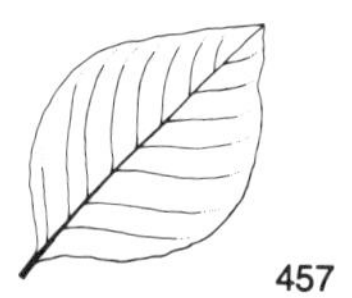
457

Erect to climbing perennial herb. Stems *4-ribbed*. Leaves stalked, elliptic to egg-shaped, dark green above, pale green below, ± hairy; margin *slightly wavy;* veins prominent on lower surface. Flowers ± *7 mm* long when mature, arranged in *erect, elongated terminal* spikes.

Grassland and bushveld, often in the shade. Origin uncertain. Widespread. Summer.

***A. sicula** (L.) All. has *very slender* terminal spikes with *widely spaced* flowers ± *4 mm* long. Native to North America.

458 Hermbstaedtia odorata (Burch.) T. Cooke var. **odorata** *Rooiaarbossie*

458

Slender, erect and irregularly branched herb from a perennial rootstock. Leaves usually *alternate*, on short stalks, considerably longer than they are broad. Inflorescence a terminal *spike* with numerous flowers *densely arranged* on the axis. Flowers white, often *tinged with pink or red.*

Grassland. Widespread. Summer.

AMARYLLIDACEAE (See page 16)

459 Ammocharis coranica (Ker-Gawl.) Herb. *Seeroogblom*

Bulbous plant with *decumbent*, *strap-shaped* leaves. Leaves smooth with *hairy* margins; older leaves with *blunt* (died-back) tips. Inflorescence with a *flattened* stalk and silvery pink, *sweetly scented* flowers with *white* anthers and recurved perianth segments.

Grassland, usually in groups. Widespread. Spring.

460 Boophane disticha (L.f.) Herb. *Poison bulb/Kopseerblom*

Bulbous plant with neck of bulb usually *exposed* above ground level. Leaves greyish green, erect and arranged in a conspicuous *fan;* usually produced after flowering. Flowers sweetly scented. Flower stalks *lengthen considerably* during the fruiting stage, thereby transforming the inflorescence into a *large sphere* which eventually breaks off and is blown around by the wind.

Grassland, often in rocky places. Widespread. Spring.

455 *Crossandra greenstockii*

456 *Dicliptera eenii*

457 *Achyranthes aspera*

458 *Hermbstaedtia odorata*

459 *Ammocharis coranica*

460 *Boophane disticha*

461 Crinum bulbispermum (Burm.f.) Milne-Redh. & Schweick.
Orange River lily/Vleilelie

Bulbous plant. Leaves smooth, folded upward along the midrib, *bluish green;* basal portion erect, the tip arching over to touch the ground; margin often wavy with a narrow cartilaginous border. Flowers tend to hang down when open; anthers *greyish or light brown.* Fruits ± large, with many green and roundish, fleshy seeds.

Moist grassland, usually along rivers and in vleis. Mainly Witwatersrand/ Suikerbosrand region. Spring.

C. lugardiae N.E.Br. has ± narrow leaves (up to 25 mm wide in the middle) whereas **C. macowanii** Bak. has leaves up to 50 mm wide in the middle. Both species have *black* anthers. They are rare and confined mainly to the Pretoria/ Magaliesberg region.

462 Crinum graminicola Verdoorn *Graslelie*

Bulbous plant. Leaves *flat, dark green,* strap-shaped and spreading at ground level; margin *hairy.* Flowers with *yellow* anthers. Fruits globose, each with a *pointed* tip.

Grassland, usually in sandy soil; localized and rather rare. Widespread. Summer.

463 Cyrtanthus tuckii Bak. var. **transvaalensis** Verdoorn
Fire lily/Vuurlelie

Erect bulbous plant up to ± 300 mm high. Leaves *appear after the flowers.* Flowers clustered at the tip of a rigid erect stalk, *pendulous;* perianth segments united into a *tube* which gradually widens from the base to the throat; perianth lobes *not spreading.*

Grassland, often in vleis; uncommon. Widespread. Spring.

464 Haemanthus humilis Jacq. subsp. **hirsutus** (Bak.) Snijman

Bulbous plant with *2* (rarely 3) leaves appearing ± with the inflorescence. Leaves broadly elliptic, usually recurved to ± erect; margin and either the lower or upper surface *hairy.* Flowers with filaments protruding 5 – 15 mm. Berries cream or orange.

In shady places between rocks, often with the bulbs tightly wedged in crevices. Widespread. Summer.

465 Scadoxus puniceus (L.) Friis & Nordal *Red paintbrush/Rooikwas*

Bulbous plant. Leaves erect, clasping at the base to form a short *pseudostem;* leaf stalk *purple-spotted;* margin *wavy.* Flowers in dense clusters, short-tubed, with conspicuous scarlet filaments and yellow anthers. Berries scarlet.

Shady places. Widespread. Spring.

461 *Crinum bulbispermum*

462 *Crinum graminicola*

463 *Cyrtanthus tuckii*

464 *Haemanthus humilis*

464 *H. humilis* (whitish variant)

465 *Scadoxus puniceus*

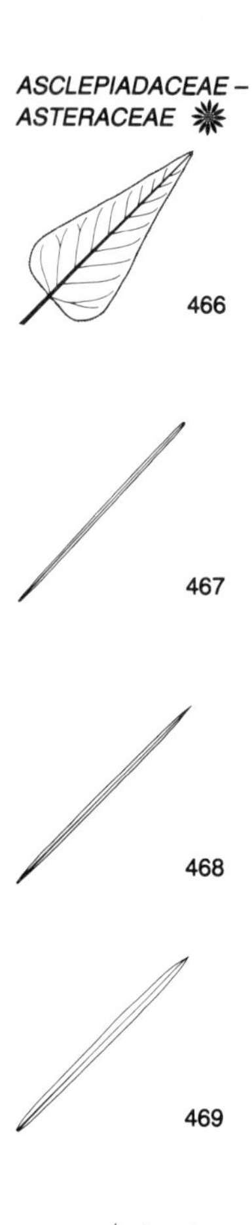

ASCLEPIADACEAE (See page 17) See also **188** and **696**.

466 Asclepias adscendens (Schltr.) Schltr.

Perennial herb with prostrate or spreading shoots from a woody rootstock; sparsely covered with hairs. Leaves on short stalks, *narrow and triangular*, up to 40 x 10 mm. Inflorescence a *spherical* terminal umbel comprising ± 15 stalked flowers. Corolla reflexed, whitish, dull pink or mauve; corona white. Fruit inflated, with rough bristles.

Grassland. Widespread. Spring. ☐ For white-flowered form see **23**.

467 Asclepias brevipes (Schltr.) Schltr.

Sparsely branched perennial herb; stems *decumbent or procumbent.* Leaves long and narrow with margin *rolled under;* covered with minute *rough hairs.* Flowers in ± 4-flowered umbels; corolla lobes spreading, with incurved tips, greyish white above, tinged with pinkish purple below, *3 – 4 mm* long; corona lobes elongated into a *narrow channelled* point, *3 – 4 mm* long.

Grassland. Widespread. Spring.

Very similar to the following species (**468**) but with smaller flowers.

468 Asclepias stellifera Schltr. *Spring stars*

Herb with erect or spreading branches from a perennial rootstock. Leaves almost stalkless, *long* (up to 100 mm) and *narrow* with ± parallel margins; sparsely covered with *rough hairs.* Flowers in groups on long inflorescence stalks; calyx recurved; corolla lobes ± delicate in texture, ± reflexed, *5 – 7 mm* long; corona lobes *very prominent, triangular*, spreading, *5 – 7 mm* long. Fruits spindle-shaped, up to 60 mm long, held erect on *twisted or looped* stalks.

Grassland. Widespread. Spring. ☐ Compare **467**.

ASTERACEAE (See page 17)

Group A ❋

469 Athrixia elata Sond. *Daisy-tea bush/Wildetee*

Much-branched perennial shrublet. Stems *slender.* Leaves narrow; margin *curled under*, almost covering the *white* lower surface. Flower heads terminal; surrounding bracts with *long pointed tips* and loosely covered with woolly hairs.

Rocky slopes. Widespread. Spring – summer.

470 *Bidens formosa (Bonato) Sch. Bip. *Cosmos/Kosmos*

Erect, bushy *annual* herb up to ± 2 m high. Leaves *opposite*, stalked and stem-clasping; blade *deeply and finely dissected.* Flower heads solitary on long stalks which terminate the shoots; ray flowers *red, pink or white;* disc flowers *yellow.*

Grassland, a weed of disturbed places; often in dense stands along roadsides and in old fields. A native of the southern United States and Mexico. Widespread. Summer – autumn. ☐ For white-flowered form see **31**.

471 Gerbera viridifolia (DC.) Sch. Bip. subsp. **viridifolia**

Stemless herb with a perennial rootstock. Leaves basal, stalked; blade variable in shape, often ± elliptic; upper surface green with long silky hairs; lower surface of mature leaves *sparsely covered with hairs* and *green* (*never white-felted*), with the veins *not raised.* Flower heads solitary on long, leafless stalks; ray flowers white to pink above, usually *pinkish* below.

Grassland. Widespread. Spring. ☐ For white-flowered form see **38**.

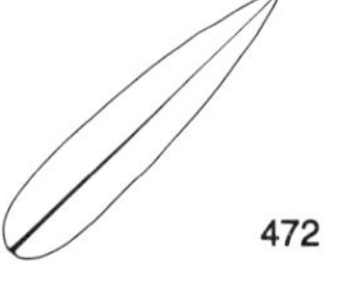

472 *Zinnia peruviana (L.) L. *Wildejakobregop*

Erect *annual* herb. Leaves *opposite*, stalkless, widely spaced, covered with *rough hairs.* Flower heads solitary, terminal on stalks which gradually *thicken towards the end.* Ray flowers red or pale orange, *persistent*, drying to purplish or brown.

A naturalized weed from South America, often found in disturbed places and in the shade of clumps of bush. Widespread. Summer – autumn.

466 *Asclepias adscendens*

467 *Asclepias brevipes*

468 *Asclepias stellifera*

469 *Athrixia elata*

470 *Bidens formosa*

471 *Gerbera viridifolia*

472 *Zinnia peruviana*

ASTERACEAE (See page 17)
Group B See also **256**, **619**, **620** and **625**.

473

473 Blumea mollis (D.Don) Merr.

Perennial herb up to 900 mm high. Stem and lower leaves sparsely covered with hairs; young leaves and flower heads covered with *silky white hairs*. Leaves with *toothed* margins. Flower heads in compact clusters; ray flowers absent; pink to purple.

Moist places, especially along streams. Mainly Pretoria/Magaliesberg region. Spring – summer.

474

474 *Cirsium vulgare (Savi) Ten. *Scottish thistle/Skotse-disse*

Robust, erect biennial herb up to 1,5 m high. Stems grooved, with interrupted *spiny wings* extending from leaf bases. Leaves in a basal rosette in the first year of growth; stem leaves deeply *pinnately lobed* with the segments ending in *strong spines*. Flower heads clustered at the tips of flowering shoots, red-purple; involucral bracts numerous with *spiny tips*.

A native of Europe, western Asia and North Africa. Grassland, often in moist, overgrazed areas such as vleis; also in disturbed places. Widespread. Summer.

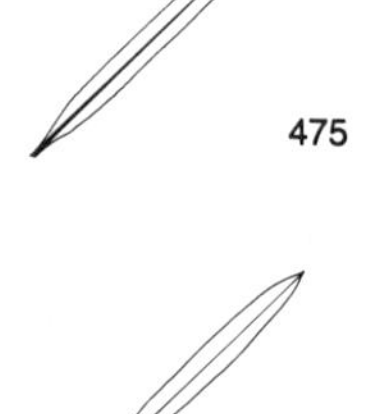

475

475 Dicoma anomala Sond. subsp. **circioides** (Harv.) Wild *Maagbitterwortel*

Perennial herb with several ± *erect* stems from a stout woody rootstock. Leaves *narrow* (± 2 mm), alternate, with the upper surface green and the lower *white-felted*. Flower heads thistle-like; bracts *narrow* and with *very sharp points* but *not spreading* at the tips; disc flowers pale pinkish mauve to almost white.

Common in stony grassland. Widespread. Summer – autumn.

Subsp. **anomala** has ± *prostrate* branches and flower heads with the tips of involucral bracts spreading.

476

476 Epaltes gariepina (DC.) Steetz *Blougifbossie*

Erect perennial herb up to ± 500 mm high; often sticky. Stems *stiff*, ± solitary below, branched above. Leaves long and narrow, *stalkless*, with the base continuing as long *narrow wings along the stem*. Flower heads ± 4 x 3 mm, in clusters at the tips of branches, apparently discoid (ray flowers very small), pinkish purple.

Bushveld, often in disturbed places. Pretoria/Magaliesberg region. Summer.

477

477 *Eupatorium macrocephalum Less.

Erect perennial herb up to 1 m high, with a woody rootstock; covered with *rough hairs* throughout. Leaves narrow to a stalk-like base; margin toothed. Flowering stem branches at the end to form a compound inflorescence of numerous heads. Flower heads *fluffy*, with disc flowers only.

A native of South America; naturalized in grassland. Mainly Pretoria region. Summer.

473 *Blumea mollis*

474 *Cirsium vulgare*

475 *Dicoma anomala* subsp. *circioides*

476 *Epaltes gariepina*

477 *Eupatorium macrocephalum*

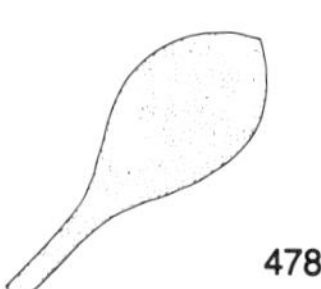
478

478 Helichrysum argyrosphaerum DC. *Poprosie*
Annual herb with radiating prostrate branches; sparsely covered with *grey woolly hairs* throughout. Leaves narrowing into a flat, stalk-like base. Flower heads ± globose, *solitary* at the tips of branchlets, surrounded by leaves; involucral bracts arranged in ± 9 series, transparent, shiny, silvery white, becoming increasingly tinged with pink towards the centre, fading at maturity, tips ± *rounded*. Flowers yellow, but pink at tips.
Sandy areas, frequently growing as a weed in disturbed places. Widespread. Spring – summer. ☐ Also **43**.

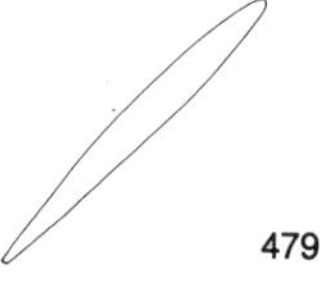
479

479 Helichrysum caespititium (DC.) Harv. *Speelwonderboom*
Prostrate *mat-forming* perennial herb; branchlets ± *10 mm* high, closely covered with leaves. Leaves stalkless, 5 – 10 mm long, *0,5 mm* wide; stem-clasping at the base; both surfaces ± *woolly;* margin *rolled under*. Flower heads clustered at the tips of branchlets; involucral bracts in ± 6 series, white or pink; flowers yellow, often tipped with pink.
Grassland and bushveld, usually on bare or sparsely grassed areas. Widespread. Winter – spring. ☐ For white-flowered form see **44**.

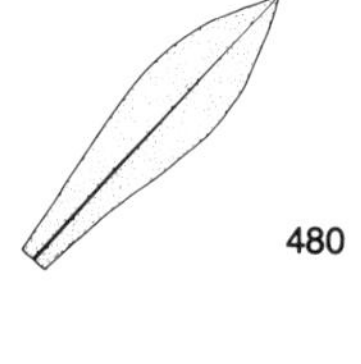
480

480 Helichrysum candolleanum Buek
Perennial herb with a stout woody taproot; branches trailing or erect; covered with *soft greyish woolly hairs throughout*. Leaves stalkless, 1,5 – 5 mm wide. Flower heads many, arranged in *tight globose clusters* at the tips of branchlets and surrounded by woolly leaves that are usually *longer* than the compound head. Involucral bracts slightly longer than the flowers, *sharply* pointed, ± *transparent*, inner bracts *tipped with pink*, fading to white; flowers *yellow*.
Bushveld, often in sandy soil and disturbed places; uncommon. Pretoria/ Magaliesberg region. All year.

481

481 Senecio anomalochrous Hilliard
Slender, erect perennial herb up to 1 m high; patches of *white woolly hairs* present in leaf axils. Leaves mostly in a *basal rosette*, stalked; blade up to 160 x 10 mm; stem leaves stalkless and smaller. Flower heads with disc flowers only, wine-red; involucral bracts *sharply* pointed with a *tuft of hairs* at the tip.
Grassland, usually on rocky ridges. Mainly Suikerbosrand. Summer.

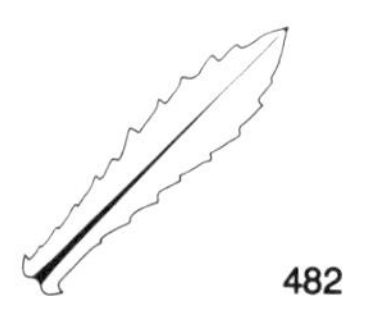
482

482 Senecio erubescens Ait. var. **crepidifolius** DC.
Erect perennial herb; most parts covered with *glandular hairs* (often sticky). Stems *decumbent then erect*, branched in the upper half and leafy mainly in the lower half. Leaves ± *point to the same side* of the stem; stem leaves ± lance-shaped, stalkless, clasping at the base; margin *coarsely toothed*. Flower heads bell-shaped.
Grassland, often in moist places. Widespread. Spring – summer. Compare **256**.

478 *Helichrysum argyrosphaerum*

479 *Helichrysum caespititium*

480 *Helichrysum candolleanum*

481 *Senecio anomalochrous*

482 *Senecio erubescens*

BORAGINACEAE (See page 17)

483 Cynoglossum hispidum Thunb. *Hound's tongue/Ossetongblaar*
Erect, sparsely branched herb from a perennial rootstock; covered with short *rough hairs*. Leaves at base lance-shaped and stalked; stem leaves stalkless. Inflorescence terminal, *loosely branched*, with well-spaced flowers. Flowers minute, *drooping*, red-purple; corolla bell-shaped with *swollen appendages* at the mouth, these formed by the corolla tube being pushed inward; stamens not protruding. Fruit comprises *4 rounded nutlets* up to 12 mm in diameter, on drooping stalks up to 20 mm long, covered with small *hooked spines*.

Grassland. Widespread. Spring.

C. lanceolatum Forssk. is very similar but has numerous *large* stem leaves *reaching the base* of the inflorescence, and *small* fruits on stalks *less than 5 mm* long. Widespread.

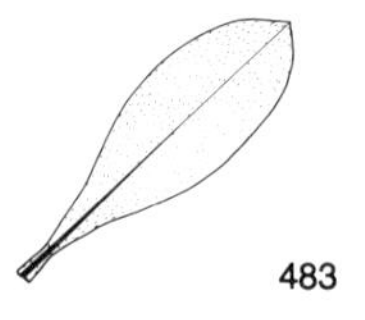
483

CAPPARACEAE (See page 18)

484 Cleome maculata (Sond.) Szyszyl.
Erect annual herb with *almost hairless* stems. Leaves *palmately* compound with *3 – 5 narrow* leaflets; *hairless* or with minute rough hairs. Flowers irregular; the 2 upper petals have a *yellow band with a purple margin* down the centre. Fruit a narrow capsule, 40 – 100 mm long.

Grassland, often a weed of disturbed sandy places. Widespread. Summer.

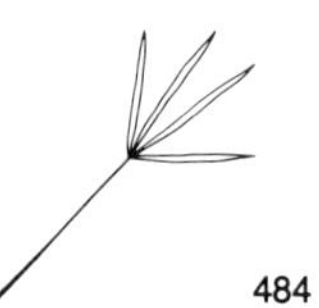
484

485 Cleome monophylla L. *Spindlepod/Rusperbossie*
Erect annual herb with *hairy* stems. Leaves *simple;* blade with *rough* (often sticky) *hairs* on both surfaces. Flowers irregular; the 2 upper petals sometimes have a *yellow band with a purple margin* across the centre. Fruit a narrow capsule, 50 – 110 mm long.

Disturbed places, often a weed in dense stands, particularly in sandy soils. Widespread. Summer.

485

486 Cleome rubella Burch. *Pretty lady/Mooinooientjie*
Erect annual herb covered with *sticky glandular hairs*. Leaves aromatic, compound; leaflets 5 – 9, usually folded upward along the midrib. Flowers borne in the axils of *bracts* which *resemble leaves*; stalks ± absent.

Common, particularly as a weed in cultivated fields or waste places. Widespread. Spring – summer.

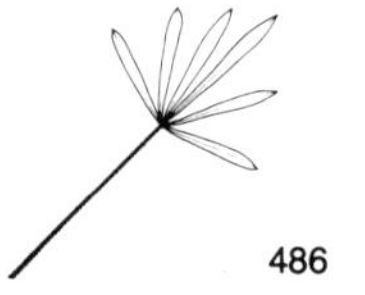
486

CARYOPHYLLACEAE (See page 18) See also **61**.

487 Silene burchellii Otth. var. **burchellii** *Gunpowder plant/Kruitbossie*
Herb with erect annual shoots from a swollen perennial taproot; all aerial parts covered with short but *not sticky* hairs. Leaves obovate or oblong-obovate. Inflorescence with all the *flowers turned to 1 side*. Flowers open in the evening; petals *forked* at the apex, greenish with the inner surface often pinkish.

Common in grassland, particularly on rocky ridges. Widespread. Spring – summer.

Var. **angustifolia** Sond. has leaves which are *long and narrow* with ± parallel margins, or are narrowly lance-shaped. Widespread in grassland. Summer.

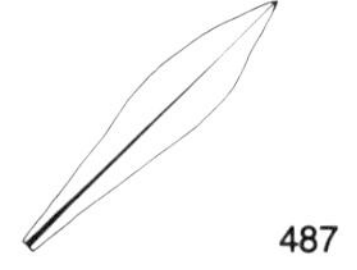
487

483 *Cynoglossum hispidum*

485 *Cleome monophylla*

484 *Cleome maculata*

486 *Cleome rubella*

487 *Silene burchellii* var. *burchellii*

CONVOLVULACEAE (See page 19)

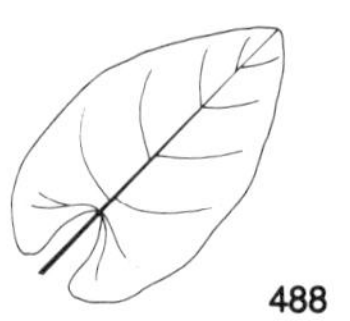
488

488 Ipomoea bathycolpos Hallier f. var. **bathycolpos**

Veldsambreeltjies

Perennial herb from a long, thin, woody taproot. Stems long, *trailing*, with a *rough texture*. Leaves ± fleshy; base *deeply heart-shaped;* apex *rounded;* surface *rough to the touch*. Inflorescence stalk bears *1 flower* which is subtended by 2 bracts; corolla pink or white with a *dark pink centre*.

Grassland. Widespread. Summer.

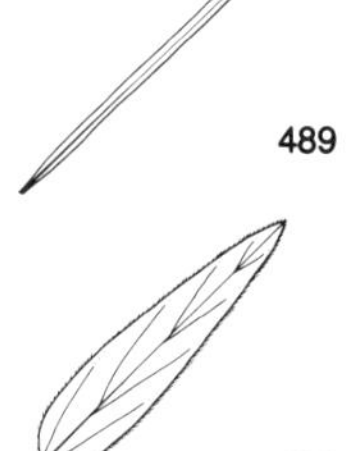
489

489 Ipomoea bolusiana Schinz subsp. **bolusiana**

Tuberous herb with *erect* or prostrate stems. Leaves *hairless*, *deeply dissected* into 3 – 9 very narrow segments which radiate from a *distinct* stalk, occasionally simple and apparently stalkless.

Grassland. Widespread. Spring – summer. ☐ Compare **496**.

490

490 Ipomoea crassipes Hook.

Herb with ± erect or trailing stems from a perennial tuberous rootstock. Leaves unlobed, egg- to lance-shaped; *hairy*, often with a purplish margin. Flowers *solitary; calyx surrounded by leaf-like bracts;* rarely white with dark purple centre. Fruit a *dehiscent* capsule.

Grassland. Widespread. Spring – summer. ☐ Compare **494** and **495**.

491

491 Ipomoea magnusiana Schinz var. **magnusiana**

Perennial with annual twining or prostrate stems from a thin woody taproot. Leaves deeply *palmately divided into 3 – 7 lobes;* green and sparsely covered with appressed hairs above, densely covered with *white woolly hairs* below, except on the main veins which are covered with yellowish hairs. Flowers usually in *dense heads*; corolla *12 – 15 (occasionally 20) mm* long.

Grassland and clumps of bush. Widespread. Summer.

Var. **eenii** (Rendle) A. Meeuse is very similar, but the corolla is longer (*20 – 25 mm*).

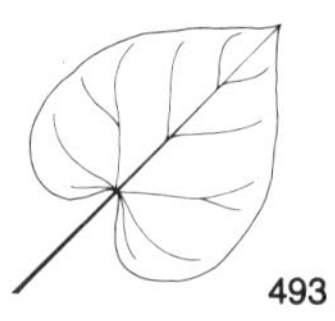
492

492 Ipomoea ommaneyi Rendle *Beespatat*

Perennial with large tuberous taproot and *robust* annual *trailing* stems. Leaves up to 300 x 120 mm, both surfaces *densely covered with silvery white hairs;* margin closely *wavy* with a dense *yellowish fringe of hairs*. Flowers several together in a *dense head*.

Grassland. Widespread. Summer.

493

493 *Ipomoea purpurea (L.) Roth *Morning glory/Purperwinde*

Twining annual herb. Stem hairy. Leaves stalked; blade broadly *heart-shaped* with pointed tip; both surfaces sparsely covered with hairs. Inflorescences axillary, bearing 1 to a few flowers. Calyx with *bristly hairs* at the base. Corolla variable in colour: purplish blue with reddish midpetaline areas, pale purple, pink to white.

A native of tropical and subtropical America. Cultivated in gardens and now naturalized as a weed in disturbed places. Widespread. Summer – autumn. For purple-flowered form see **637**.

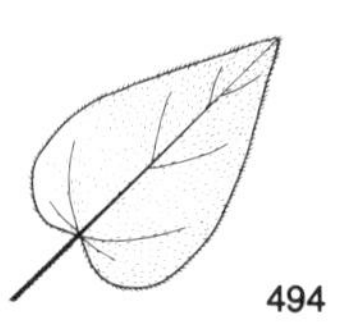
494

494 Ipomoea transvaalensis A. Meeuse

Perennial with annual prostrate or erect stems from a tuberous rootstock. Leaves *simple*, distinctly *heart-shaped* at the base, hairy (particularly on lower surface) and clearly stalked. Inflorescence bearing 1 or 2 flowers, usually *shorter* than the leaves. Flowers subtended by minute bracts; corolla with a few short hairs towards the tops of the midpetaline areas and dense *tufts of hairs* protruding from the tips. Fruit a *dehiscent* capsule.

Grassland, mainly on rocky slopes. Widespread. Spring – summer. Compare **490** and **495**.

488 *Ipomoea bathycolpos*

489 *Ipomoea bolusiana*

490 *Ipomoea crassipes*

491 *Ipomoea magnusiana* var. *magnusiana*

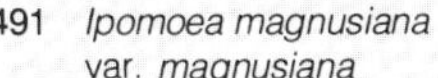

492 *Ipomoea ommaneyi*

493 *Ipomoea purpurea*

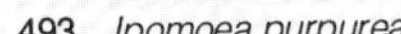

494 *Ipomoea transvaalensis*

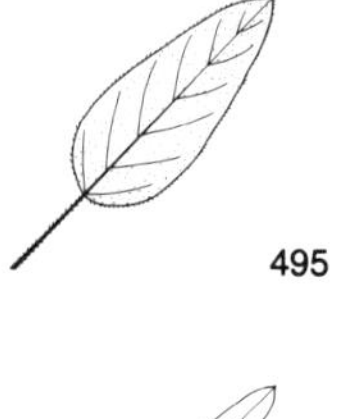

495

495 Turbina oblongata (E. Mey. ex Choisy) A. Meeuse
Perennial herb with annual *prostrate stems* from a large tuberous rootstock. Stems ± angular, with *stiff yellowish or brownish hairs*. Leaves on short stalks, ± erect, variable in shape but often egg-shaped to elliptical; upper surface sparsely covered with *yellowish hairs*, lower surface also sparsely covered or more densely so; margin ± *wavy, with a fringe of hairs*. Flowers usually *solitary* on erect stalks; outer sepals ± densely covered with *stiff yellowish hairs*. Fruit ± globose with a leathery, *indehiscent* wall.

Grassland. Widespread. Summer. ☐ Compare **490** and **494**.

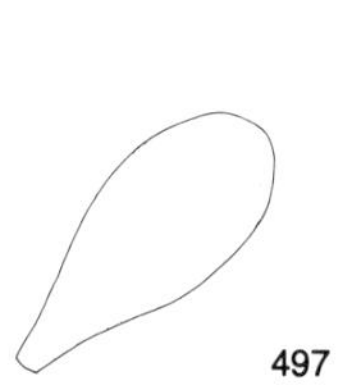

496

496 Turbina oenotheroides (L.f.) A. Meeuse *Krismisblom*
Erect, *much-branched shrublet* from a perennial rootstock; most parts covered with *short, appressed silvery hairs*. Leaves *narrow* (2 – 8 mm), ± stalkless. Flowers axillary, solitary on *very short* stalks; corolla with very short *appressed silvery hairs*.

Grassland. Mainly Vereeniging/Potchefstroom region. Summer. Compare **489**.

CRASSULACEAE (See page 19)

497 Adromischus umbraticola C.A. Sm. subsp. **umbraticola** *Bontplakkie*

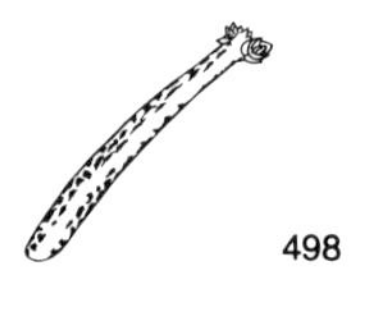

497

Succulent with branched tuberous base. Leaves *spirally* arranged, flattened and usually *slightly convex* on both surfaces; grey-green or bluish green, often *tinged with brown* and sometimes dotted with faint *purplish spots*. Corolla with *hairs in throat* and a *powdery bloom* on the outer surface.

Rocky places or in the shade of other vegetation. Widespread. Spring – summer.

498

498 *Bryophyllum delagoense (Eckl. & Zeyh.) Schinz
Succulent with 1 or a few erect stems. Leaves stalkless, *cylindrical, grey-green with darker spots;* tips with 5 – 8 teeth, in the axils of which *small plantlets* are produced. Flowers clustered at the tips of stems, ± *drooping*.

A native of Madagascar. An occasional garden escape in disturbed places near areas of habitation; often growing in dense stands. Mainly Pretoria/ Magaliesberg region. Winter.

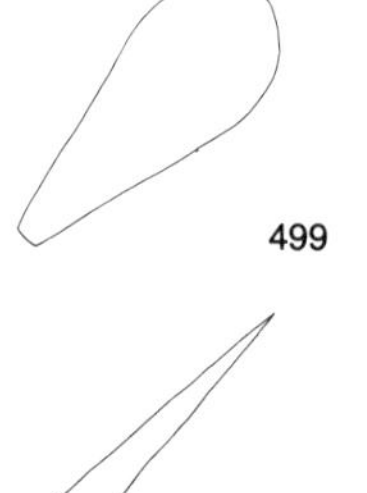

499

499 Cotyledon orbiculata L. var. **oblonga** (Haw.) DC. *Plakkie*
Robust succulent with decumbent branches. Leaves ± flattened, greyish green with a *white powdery bloom* and *reddish* margins. Flowers pendulous, with a ± *cylindrical* corolla tube and hairless petals.

Uncommon on rocky ridges. Mainly Magaliesberg. Winter – spring.

C. barbeyi Schweinf. ex Bak. has narrower, greyish to brownish green leaves, and flowers with *hairy* petals and the corolla tube *bulging* at the base. Bushveld, rarely in rocky places. Magaliesberg; rare. Winter.

500

500 Crassula alba Forssk. var. **alba**
Short-lived perennial succulent; usually *unbranched*. Leaves mainly in a basal *rosette;* margin densely *fringed with minute hairs*. Inflorescence erect, many-flowered and ± *flat-topped*. Stamens with *dark brown* anthers.

Grassland, often on rocky ridges. Widespread but never common. Summer – autumn.

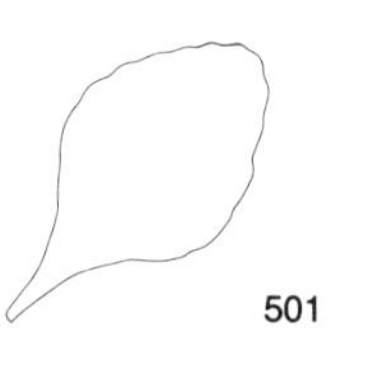

501

501 Kalanchoe rotundifolia (Haw.) Haw. *Nentabos*
Sparsely branched, erect *succulent* herb. Leaves elliptical to rounded, sometimes slightly lobed; *blue-green* with a *whitish bloom*. Flowers borne in ± flat-topped inflorescences with a long erect stalk; *4* of each floral part; corolla tubular, *twisting* with age, orange-red.

Grassland and bushveld; shady positions, often forming dense stands among rocks or under trees or shrubs. Widespread. Autumn. ☐ Also **702**.

495 *Turbina oblongata*

496 *Turbina oenotheroides*

497 *Adromischus umbraticola*

498 *Bryophyllum delagoense*

499 *Cotyledon orbiculata*

500 *Crassula alba*

501 *Kalanchoe rotundifolia*

DROSERACEAE (See page 20)

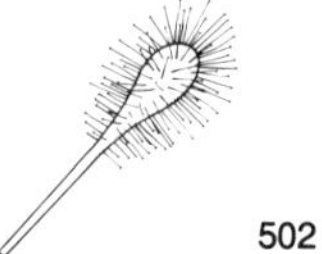

502

502 Drosera madagascariensis DC.

Slender insectivorous herb with *leafy stems* which are also covered with old leaf remains. Leaves distinctly *stalked;* blade with knob-shaped, *glandular hairs* above, hairless below. Inflorescence stalk axillary near growing tip of stem, wiry and *sharply curved* at the base. Flowers 4 – 12, all *pointing in the same direction.*

In marshy places, uncommon. Widespread. Summer.

ERICACEAE (See page 20)

503

503 Erica woodii H. Bol. *Pink heath/Pienkheide*

Shrublet up to ± 600 mm high; branches *hairy.* Leaves narrow, with the lower surface ± *grooved;* covered with coarse hairs or almost hairless. Flowers *numerous,* solitary in leaf axils towards the ends of branchlets; style protruding beyond the petal lobes, with a *stigma swollen* like the head of a pin.

Mountainous areas, usually along streams. Mainly Magaliesberg. Summer – winter.

EUPHORBIACEAE (See page 20)

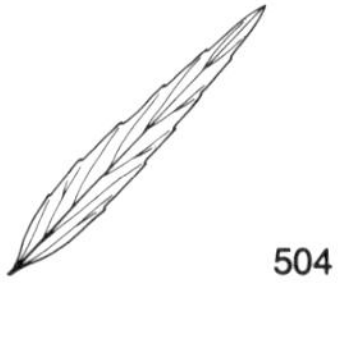

504

504 Acalypha angustata Sond. var. **glabra** Sond. *Copper leaf/Katpisbossie*

Perennial shrublet with many *erect* annual shoots from a woody rootstock; *unpleasantly scented* when crushed. Leaves *almost* stalkless, lance-shaped, usually *less than 10 mm* wide; margin slightly toothed. Sexes on different plants. Male flowers densely clustered in erect, axillary spikes; yellowish tinged with red. Female flowers terminal, with long, *red, feathery* styles (illustrated) forming a brush above lobed floral bracts.

Grassland. Widespread. Spring – summer. ☐ For male flowers see **299**.

A. caperonioides Baill. is similar but has *stalkless* and less conspicuously toothed leaves, *10 – 30 mm* wide; the female flowers have long red styles which are *barely feathery.*

505

505 Acalypha petiolaris Hochst.

Bushy perennial from a woody rootstock. Leaves distinctly *stalked;* thin and *densely covered with hairs;* blade often turned backwards at an angle to the stalk. Male and female inflorescences usually *on the same plant;* male spikes axillary and yellowish; female spikes terminal with slender red styles.

Grassland, mainly in rocky places with sandy soil. Widespread. Summer.

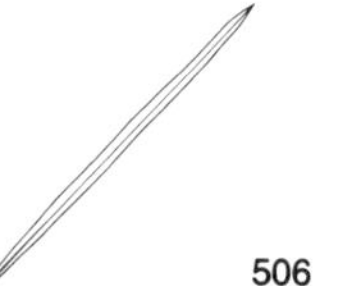

506

506 Euphorbia trichadenia Pax ***Melkbol***

Small erect perennial herb from an underground tuber. Leaves stalkless, *long and narrow,* slightly curved, ± fleshy and *folded upward* along the midrib. Inflorescences *cup-shaped,* borne in *forks of branches,* surrounded by *much-divided* petal-like structures, white or yellow-green, often with a reddish tinge.

Bushveld, often in sandy places. Pretoria/Magaliesberg region. Spring.

502 *Drosera madagascariensis*

503 *Erica woodii*

504 *Acalypha angustata* (female)

505 *Acalypha petiolaris*

506 *Euphorbia trichadenia*

FABACEAE (See page 20) See also **334**.

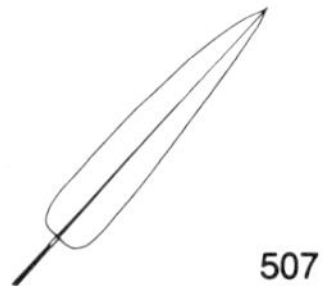

507

507 Alysicarpus rugosus (Willd.) DC. subsp. **perennirufus** J. Leonard
Herbaceous perennial with sparsely branched stems *spreading* from a woody rootstock. Leaves *simple;* stipules membranous and ± the *same length* as the leaf stalk. Flowers on long-stalked, densely clustered terminal racemes; calyx fringed with *brown hairs*. Pods with transverse ridges and *constricted* between seeds.

Grassland, often in sandy or gravelly soil. Spring.

Subsp. **rugosus** is more *erect* and tends to be *annual*. Calyx fringed with *white hairs*. Grassland, often in damp places with clayish soils.

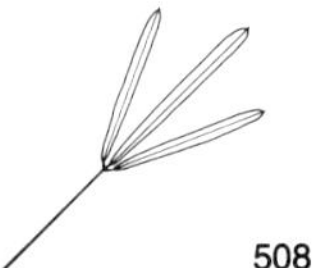

508

508 Argyrolobium tuberosum Eckl. & Zeyh.
Herbaceous perennial with tuberous roots; sparsely covered with silky hairs throughout. Stems slender, erect, usually *unbranched*. Leaves with stalk up to 20 mm long; leaflets taper to a *fine point*, ± hairless above. Inflorescence with a few *irregularly spaced*, ± stalkless flowers; calyx *2-lipped, silvery;* petals yellow tinged with reddish brown. Pods 40 – 60 mm long, with short hairs; seeds red.

Grassland, usually in moist places. Widespread. Summer.

509

509 Erythrina lysistemon Hutch.
Common coral tree/Gewone kafferboom
Deciduous shrub or small tree with *hooked thorns* on the young shoots and occasionally also on the leaf stalk and rhachis. Leaves trifoliolate, hairless. Flowers usually appear before the leaves. Pods *constricted* between seeds and often twisted; seeds *bright red* with a small black spot (hilum).

Rocky hills and ravines in sheltered, almost frost-free places. Mainly Magaliesberg. Spring.

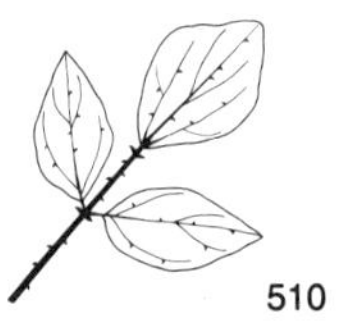

510

510 Erythrina zeyheri Harv. *Ploegbreker*
Dwarf deciduous shrublet from a large tuberous rootstock; aerial stems very short, annual, armed with *short, sharp, recurved prickles*. Leaves *trifoliolate, very large*, often appearing after the inflorescences; covered with rough hairs; leaflets with *recurved prickles on the midrib and larger side veins*. Inflorescences with longitudinally ridged stalks; flowers arranged in *whorls*, drooping, very rarely white. Pods with hard, *orange-red* seeds.

Grassland, frequently in moist vleis with clay soils; usually in colonies. Widespread. Spring.

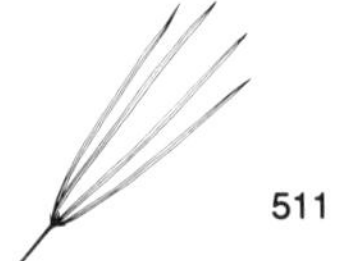

511

511 Dolichos angustifolius Eckl. & Zeyh. *Wild pea/Wilde-ertjie*
Perennial with *slender*, erect and ± coiling stems from a woody rootstock; *leafless or almost so* at the time of flowering. Leaves on new growth comprise 3 *long, narrow* leaflets, each *tightly folded upward* along the midrib.

Grassland. Widespread. Spring.

507 *Alysicarpus rugosus* subsp. *perennirufus*

508 *Argyrolobium tuberosum*

509 *Erythrina lysistemon*

511 *Dolichos angustifolius*

510 *Erythrina zeyheri*

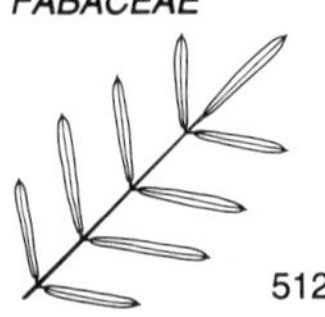
512

512 Indigofera acutisepala Conrath
Slender, *sparsely branched* perennial herb up to ± 1 m high, *greyish green.* Leaflets 5 – 7 pairs, usually *opposite.* Inflorescence *much longer* than the subtending leaf (± 40 – 80 mm), with a *slender wiry axis.* Flowers pinkish to white; buds often with *dark-coloured hairs.*
Grassland. Widespread. Spring – summer. ☐ Also **83**.
This is probably the same species as **I. zeyheri** Spreng. ex Eckl. & Zeyh.

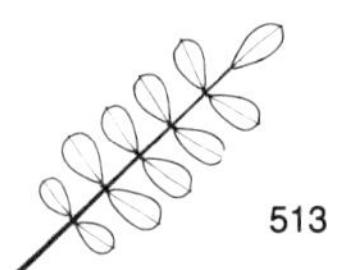
513

513 Indigofera adenoides Bak.f.
Perennial shrublet from a woody rootstock. Stems covered with *glandular hairs.* Leaves compound, with 3 – 6 pairs of leaflets which are usually *opposite.* Petals 2 – 4 mm long. Pods covered with *glandular hairs.*
Grassland, usually on rocky slopes. Widespread. Spring – summer.

514

514 Indigofera comosa N.E.Br.
Much-branched perennial shrublet from a woody rootstock. Stems erect or prostrate, ± hairy but *without glandular hairs.* Leaflets on most leaves *opposite*, 2 – 4 times longer than they are broad, with reddish brown to black *glands* where pairs of leaflets meet; upper surface *hairless*, lower surface with *long erect hairs;* often folded along the midrib. Flowers with calyx 3 – 5 mm long; corolla *4 – 6 mm* long, deep pinkish red. Pods with erect, non-glandular hairs.
Grassland, mainly on rocky ridges. Widespread. Spring – summer.
Compare **520** and **522**.

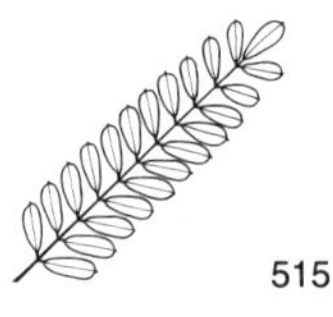
515

515 Indigofera cryptantha Benth. ex Harv.
Shrublet up to 500 mm high with a few erect stems from a woody rootstock. Stems *densely* covered with leaves. Leaves up to *80 mm* long; leaflets 5 – 12 *opposite* pairs, *without glands*, ± hairless or with appressed hairs mainly on lower surface. Inflorescences *much shorter* (± 20 mm long) and *partially concealed* by the leaves, clustered along the length of the stem. Petals 3 – 4 mm long. Pods *sickle-shaped, deeply constricted between the seeds.*
Grassland and bushveld. Mainly Pretoria/Magaliesberg region. Spring – summer.

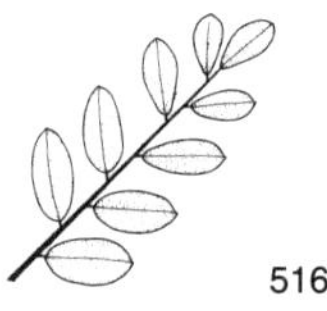
516

516 Indigofera daleoides Benth. ex Harv. var. **daleoides**
Perennial herb with ± *prostrate* stems, *densely covered with hairs throughout.* Leaves stalked, pinnately compound; leaflets mostly *alternate;* stipules narrow, sharply pointed, hairy. Inflorescence erect, axillary, densely flowered. Flowers with sepals hairy and ± *as long as the petals;* corolla red with dark reddish maroon wings. Pods *pointing downwards*, hairy.
Grassland and disturbed places, often along roadsides. Widespread. Spring.

517

517 Indigofera filipes Benth. ex Harv.
Erect *annual* shrublet with *wiry* stems branching mainly at the base. Leaves almost stalkless, with 3 – 6 *opposite* pairs of leaflets; length of each leaflet *more than 10 times the width.* Inflorescence *longer* than the accompanying leaf, usually with fewer than 10 flowers; axis wiry, often reddish; calyx often dark. Pods ± cylindrical, sparsely covered with hairs.
Grassland, often in disturbed places. Widespread. Summer.

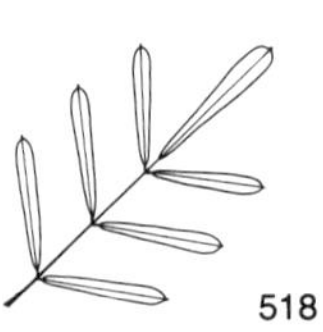
518

518 Indigofera hedyantha Eckl. & Zeyh. *Aambeibossie*
Perennial shrublet up to ± 300 mm high, with many erect stems from a woody rootstock. Leaves compound with 2 – 4 pairs of leaflets, each often folded upward along the midrib; hairless above, covered with *silky hairs* below. Inflorescence a short, compact spike; 1 – 5 on each stem; *longer* than the leaves. Flowers with corolla 8 – 12 mm long, dark red; standard as seen in bud, with *black or brownish appressed hairs* on outer surface. Pods cylindrical.
Grassland, often in rocky places. Widespread. Summer.

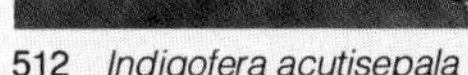

512 *Indigofera acutisepala*

513 *Indigofera adenoides*

514 *Indigofera comosa*

515 *Indigofera cryptantha*

516 *Indigofera daleoides*

517 *Indigofera filipes*

518 *Indigofera hedyantha*

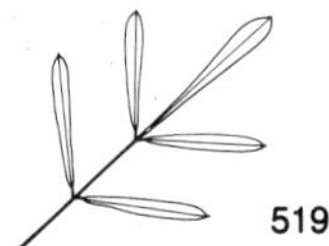
519

519 Indigofera hilaris Eckl. & Zeyh.
Perennial shrublet with *erect, sparsely branched* stems from a woody rootstock. Stems with *non-glandular* appressed hairs. Leaves usually *greyish green;* leaflets on most leaves *opposite.* Inflorescences axillary and often *shorter* than the leaves. Petals *6 – 8 mm* long.
Grassland; very common. Widespread. Spring.

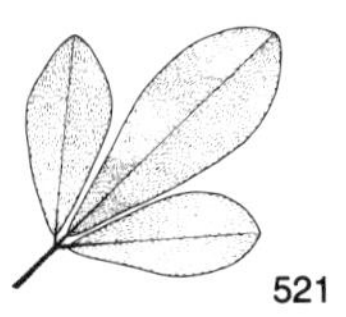
520

520 Indigofera melanadenia Benth. ex Harv.
Perennial shrublet up to ± 1,5 m high with *upright habit* and a rounded to spreading, much-branched crown (often resembling *miniature trees*). Stems *reddish brown.* Leaflets *opposite*, with *dark glands* where a pair meets, and *silvery appressed hairs on both surfaces.* Flowers with awn-like calyx lobes; corolla *3 – 5 mm* long.
Common on rocky slopes in grassland. Widespread. Summer.
Compare **514** and **522**.

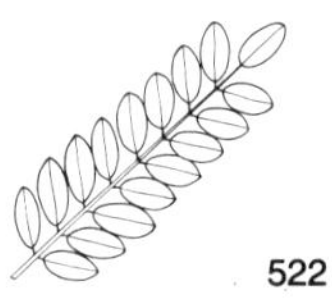
521

521 Indigofera newbrowniana J.B.Gillett
Much-branched, ± *woody* shrublet up to ± 500 mm high. Stems covered with minute *whitish hairs* when young. Leaves divided into *3 (sometimes up to 5) leaflets*, densely covered with appressed hairs on both surfaces. Inflorescences axillary, *very short* and usually *3-flowered.*
Bushveld, often in rocky or sandy places. Pretoria/Magaliesberg region. Spring.

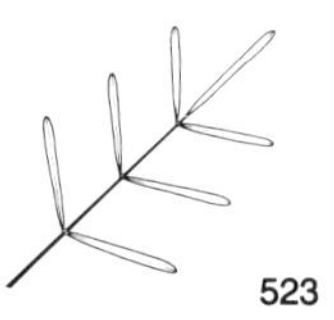
522

522 Indigofera oxytropis Benth. ex Harv.
Shrublet with ± *prostrate* and often reddish stems from a woody rootstock. Leaflets *opposite*, with conspicuous *reddish glands* where pairs meet, densely covered with *appressed hairs below*, *hairless above*, often folded upward along the midrib. Flowers in dense, axillary, stalked spikes; corolla *10 – 15 mm* long, dark reddish pink.
Grassland and bushveld, often in rocky places. Spring – summer.
Compare **514** and **520**.

523

523 Indigofera setiflora Bak. [=**I. pretoriana** Harms]
Perennial herb with erect, much-branched shoots from a woody rootstock. Leaves compound; leaflets 2 – 4 pairs, *opposite*, with *dark glands* where pairs meet, *very narrow* (± 1,5 mm) and *folded upward* along the midrib. Inflorescences axillary. Petals 6 – 8 mm long; standard dark pink with a *whitish spot* on the inner surface near the base. Pods hairy, *5 – 8 mm* long.
Grassland, often in rocky places. Widespread. Spring – summer.
This species will probably become **I. confusa** Prain & Bak.f.

524

524 Indigofera sordida Benth. ex Harv.
Perennial shrublet with *rough erect hairs.* Stems often *sticky.* Leaves with 4 – 6 pairs of leaflets. Inflorescence axillary, up to 200 mm long, with a distinct stalk. Corolla ± *15 mm* long; standard cream, *hairy* on the outer surface.
Bushveld, often in sandy soil and along roadsides. Mainly Pretoria/Magaliesberg region. Spring.

525

525 Indigofera spicata Forssk.
Perennial with *creeping* stems from a woody rootstock. Leaves compound, leaflets usually *alternate;* stipules *broad* and *hairless.* Pods straight or slightly curved downwards, ± *cylindrical*, sometimes constricted between the seeds.
Grassland, often in sandy soil and rocky places. Mainly Pretoria/Magaliesberg region. Summer.
I. oxalidea Welw. ex Bak. is very similar but has pods *flattened* sideways and slightly *curved upwards.*

519 *Indigofera hilaris*

520 *Indigofera melanadenia*

521 *Indigofera newbrowniana*

522 *Indigofera oxytropis*

523 *Indigofera setiflora*

524 *Indigofera sordida*

525 *Indigofera spicata*

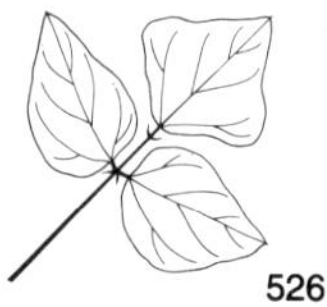
526

526 *Lablab purpureus (L.) Sweet subsp. **uncinatus** Verdc. *Lablab bean/Lablab-boontjie*

Creeping or twining herb with a perennial rootstock; ± *hairless.* Leaves trifoliolate; stipules *reflexed.* Flowers in axillary racemes which are *longer* than the leaves; *axis swollen* where the flower stalks join it; corolla with keel curved inward at a right angle, pink-purple. Pods with an *irregularly toothed* horny margin. Seeds ± compressed, dark brown with a white attachment (aril).

Grassland and bushveld, often in moist places. Indigenous elsewhere in Africa. Mainly Pretoria/Magaliesberg region. Summer.

527

527 Lessertia stricta L. Bol. *Blaasertjie*

Herbaceous, rather *weak-stemmed* shrublet from a perennial rootstock. Leaves stalked, compound, with 4 – 6 pairs of leaflets. Flowers in stalked axillary racemes, pinkish purple, *fading to violet or blue;* style *bearded around stigma.* Pods *flattened,* with ± *membranous* walls.

Grassland, often in vleis and rocky places. Mainly Pretoria/Magaliesberg region. Summer.

528

528 Ophrestia oblongifolia (E. Mey.) H.M. Forbes var. **oblongifolia**

Herb with *creeping* stems from a perennial rootstock. Leaves compound; leaflets *hairy on lower surface,* usually 40 – 50 mm long. Calyx with *brownish hairs.* Petals 8 – 10 mm long, pale to dark pink. Pods flattened.

Grassland, often in sandy, stony soil. Widespread. Spring – summer.

529

529 Sphenostylis angustifolia Sond. *Wild sweetpea/Wilde-ertjie*

Perennial shrublet with spreading to erect branches from a woody rootstock. Leaves *trifoliolate.* Flowers pink with a *yellowish spot* on the standard, rarely white fading to cream; style *flattened* and ± spoon-shaped, hairy at the tip; keel *twisted.*

Grassland, particularly in rocky places. Widespread. Spring – summer.
For white-flowered form see **86**.

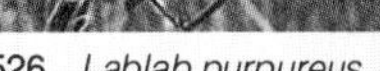
526 *Lablab purpureus*

527 *Lessertia stricta*

528 *Ophrestia oblongifolia*

529 *Sphenostylis angustifolia*

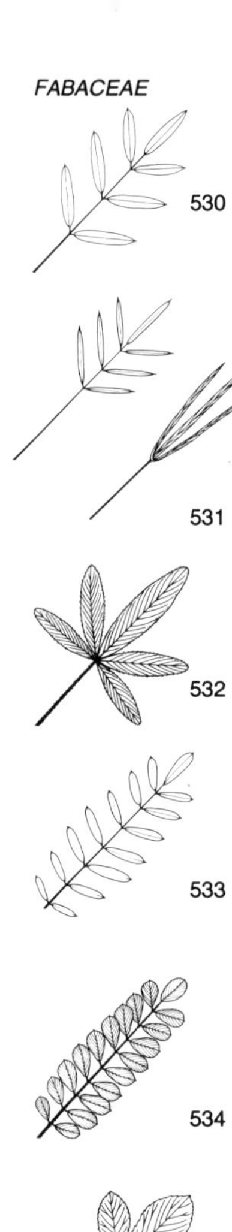

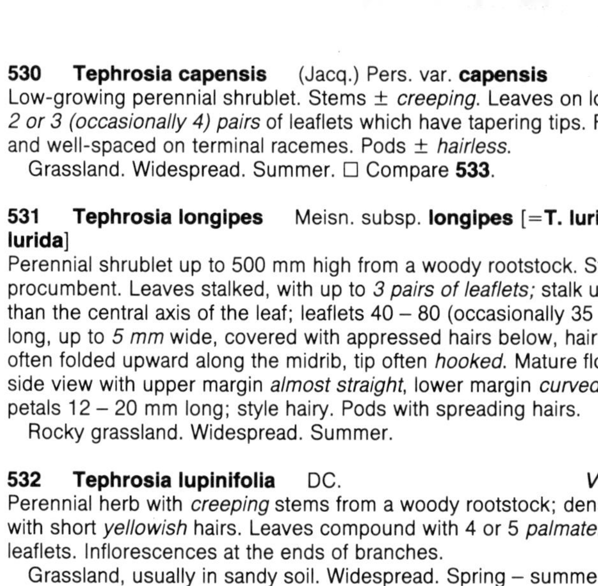

530 Tephrosia capensis (Jacq.) Pers. var. **capensis**
Low-growing perennial shrublet. Stems ± *creeping*. Leaves on long stalks with *2 or 3 (occasionally 4) pairs* of leaflets which have tapering tips. Flowers few and well-spaced on terminal racemes. Pods ± *hairless*.
Grassland. Widespread. Summer. □ Compare **533**.

531 Tephrosia longipes Meisn. subsp. **longipes** [=**T. lurida** Sond. var. **lurida**]
Perennial shrublet up to 500 mm high from a woody rootstock. Stems erect or procumbent. Leaves stalked, with up to *3 pairs of leaflets;* stalk usually longer than the central axis of the leaf; leaflets 40 – 80 (occasionally 35 – 120) mm long, up to *5 mm* wide, covered with appressed hairs below, hairless above, often folded upward along the midrib, tip often *hooked*. Mature flower bud in side view with upper margin *almost straight*, lower margin *curved*. Flowers with petals 12 – 20 mm long; style hairy. Pods with spreading hairs.
Rocky grassland. Widespread. Summer.

532 Tephrosia lupinifolia DC. *Vingerblaarertjie*
Perennial herb with *creeping* stems from a woody rootstock; densely covered with short *yellowish* hairs. Leaves compound with 4 or 5 *palmately* arranged leaflets. Inflorescences at the ends of branches.
Grassland, usually in sandy soil. Widespread. Spring – summer.

533 Tephrosia multijuga R.G.N.Young
Erect perennial shrublet from a woody rootstock. Stems slender, stiff and *much-branched*. Leaves on short stalks to almost stalkless; leaflets *6 – 8 (rarely 9) pairs*, 10 – 20 (sometimes 25) mm long and *tapering to a fine point*. Flowers 3 – 6 mm long, pink or white. Pods covered with short appressed hairs.
Rocky grassland. Pretoria/Magaliesberg region. Summer. □ Compare **530**.

534 Tephrosia rhodesica Bak.f.
Much-branched perennial *shrublet* up to ± 1,5 m high. Stems *densely covered* with short spreading yellowish hairs. Leaves with *6 – 12 pairs* of leaflets, each 15 – 20 mm long, 5 – 10 mm wide, lower surface covered with *appressed hairs*. Flowers well-spaced in terminal racemes; petals up to 10 mm long; style twisted. Pods *densely covered* with spreading yellowish or rust-coloured hairs.
Bushveld, on rocky ridges. Pretoria/Magaliesberg region. Spring – summer.

535

535 Trifolium africanum Ser. *Wild clover/Wildeklawer*
Delicate spreading perennial herb with *ribbed* stems. Leaves on *long stalks*, trifoliolate, subtended by 2 stipules, each up to 20 mm long and ending in a *thread-like* point, 4 – 8 mm long; leaflets with side veins ending in minute *marginal teeth*. Flowers in a compact, *dome-shaped* head; inflorescence stalk up to 60 mm long.
A weed of damp and disturbed areas. Widespread. Summer.

536

536 *Trifolium pratense L. *Red clover/Rooiklawer*
Perennial herb with spreading or *creeping* stems. Leaves palmately compound; leaflets hairless, side veins ending in minute *marginal teeth;* stipules pointed but *not thread-like*. Flowers crowded in *round heads subtended by 2 leaves*.
A weed of damp and disturbed areas. Widespread. Spring – summer.

537

537 Vigna vexillata (L.) A. Rich.
Herb with ± slender twining or trailing stems from a tuberous rootstock. Leaves trifoliolate and sparsely covered with hairs; terminal leaflet *much larger* than the other 2. Inflorescence stalk erect, up to 300 mm long, with usually *1 or 2* flowers at the end. Flowers with the *keel twisted* and style ± *cylindrical*. Pods covered with coarse hairs.
Grassland. Widespread. Spring – summer.

530 *Tephrosia capensis*

531 *Tephrosia longipes*

532 *Tephrosia lupinifolia*

533 *Tephrosia multijuga*

534 *Tephrosia rhodesica*

535 *Trifolium africanum*

536 *Trifolium pratense*

537 *Vigna vexillata*

GENTIANACEAE (See page 20)

538 Chironia palustris Burch. subsp. **transvaalensis** (Gilg) Verdoorn *Bitterwortel*

538

Erect bushy perennial herb up to 700 mm high. Leaves *blue-green;* those higher on the stem up to 7 mm wide and not obviously 3-veined. Inflorescence with *well-spaced flowers.* Flowers *rose-pink;* calyx ± *as long as* corolla tube; anthers *slightly twisted;* buds with calyx lobes and bracts *not tapering* into a long slender point.

Marshy places, often forming clumps. Widespread. Spring – summer. Compare **539**.

539 Chironia purpurascens (E. Mey.) Benth. & Hook.f. subsp. **humilis** (Gilg) Verdoorn

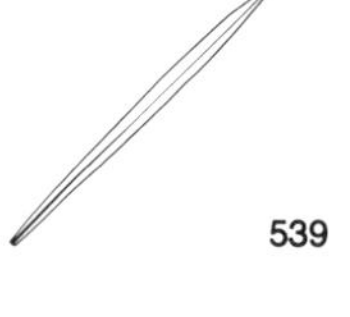
539

Erect perennial herb up to 500 mm high but generally much smaller. Stems usually 4-angled. Inflorescence with *flowers often in 3s*, the central one *almost stalkless* or with a stalk up to 6 mm long. Flowers *deep magenta-pink;* calyx *longer* than the corolla tube; anthers *strongly twisted;* buds with calyx lobes and bracts *tapering* to a long point.

Damp or marshy places, often in large colonies. Widespread. Spring – summer. ☐ Compare **538**.

GERANIACEAE (See page 21) See also **90**.

540 Monsonia angustifolia E. Mey. ex A. Rich. *Crane's bill/Angelbossie*

540

Annual herb. Stems erect or decumbent, hairy, with a *reddish or purplish tinge.* Leaves with margin slightly *uneven and toothed;* stipules often ± spiny. Petals *9 – 12 (occasionally 15) mm* long with *5 dark blue or greyish main veins;* hairless; rarely white. Fruits erect, up to 50 mm long, tipped with a long slender beak (remains of dried style) which often becomes twisted after the dried nutlets have broken up.

Grassland and bushveld, often in disturbed places. Widespread. Summer – autumn.

541 Monsonia burkeana Planch. ex Harv. [=**M. biflora** DC.] *Naaldebossie*

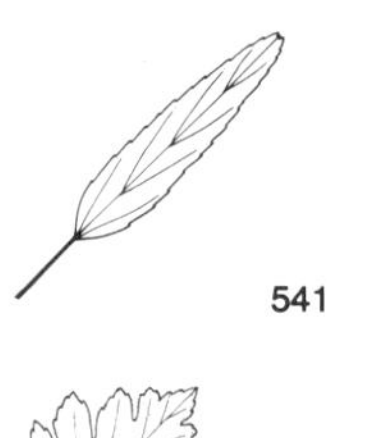
541

Perennial herb with several slender, erect and sparsely branched shoots from a woody rootstock. Leaves with margin ± regularly toothed; stipules rarely ± spiny. Petals *14 – 24 (rarely 11) mm* long, with *5 conspicuous veins* from the base; hairless, except for a few *long crinkled hairs* on the inner surface below the middle; white to pale pink, mauve or blue. Fruits tipped with a long thin beak which often becomes twisted after the dried nutlets have broken up.

Grassland, often in sandy soil and on rocky ridges. Widespread. Spring. For white-flowered form see **89**.

542 Pelargonium luridum (Andr.) Sweet

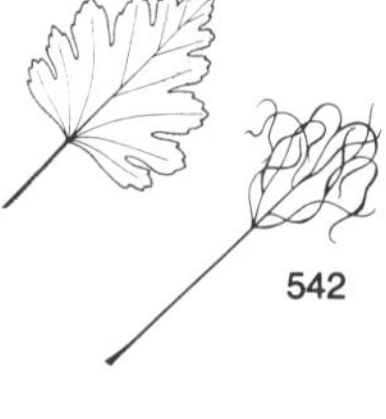
542

Rosette plant with an underground tuber; covered with long hairs and minute stalkless glands throughout. Leaves very variable (even on the same plant) from *shallowly lobed* to *strongly dissected*, with the segments thread-like in some forms. Inflorescence erect, up to *1 m* high. Flowers grouped in umbels; petals in various shades of pink to pale cream or whitish.

Grassland, often in moist places. Widespread. Spring – summer.

543 Pelargonium pseudofumarioides Knuth

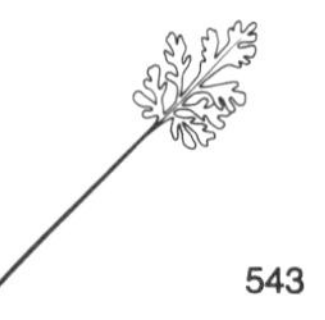
543

Lax herb with a woody perennial taproot; branches long and ± *prostrate.* Leaves stalked, deeply bipinnately *dissected* into *narrow segments.* Inflorescence stalk erect, 25 – 80 mm long, with clusters of 7 – 13 flowers at the end. Calyx with a mixture of long and short non-glandular hairs; corolla tube *elongated* (up to 18 mm long), lobes pinkish, 2 with dark pink markings.

Grassland, usually in sandy places; rare. Mainly Suikerbosrand/ Witwatersrand region. Summer.

538 *Chironia palustris*

539 *Chironia purpurascens*

540 *Monsonia angustifolia*

541 *Monsonia burkeana*

542 *Pelargonium luridum*

543 *Pelargonium pseudofumarioides*

IRIDACEAE (See page 21) See also **646**.

544 Anomatheca grandiflora Bak.
Herb with up to 6 *soft*, sword-shaped leaves. Flowers irregular, subtended by paired bracts; perianth segments lance-shaped and form a cup which is *more than half* the length of the perianth tube; lower 3 segments with a *dark red blotch* near the base; style with *6 branches*. Seeds *scarlet*.
Fairly rare in usually moist, shady places. Widespread. Summer. Compare **549**.

545 Anomatheca laxa (Thunb.) Goldbl.
In habit very similar to the previous species. Flowers with the perianth segments *broadly egg-shaped*, held at *right angles* to and *less than half* the length of the tube; lower 3 segments marked with a *blotch of dark red* near the base.
Moist shady places. Widespread but not common. Spring – summer.

546 Dierama medium N.E.Br. var. **mossii** N.E.Br. *Hair-bell/Grasklokkie*
Erect perennial. Leaves *2 – 4 mm* wide and finely ribbed. Flowering spikes well-spaced and *pendulous*, with *very slender* axes. Flowers bell-shaped, *pendulous* and subtended by *whitish* membranous bracts.
Moist places, often along streams. Mainly Magaliesberg. Spring – summer.

547 Gladiolus crassifolius Bak.
Erect herb up to 1 m high, with globose corms covered with matted fibres. Leaves arranged in a fan, stiff and leathery, with *raised yellow* margins and ribs. Inflorescence often borne *at an angle* to the leaves. Flowers arranged in 2 rows, all turned in the *same direction;* perianth bell-shaped, the lower side-lobes bearing a *dark blotch* in the centre; pink, purplish to almost white.
Grassland. Widespread. Summer – autumn.

548 Gladiolus elliotii Bak.
Erect perennial herb up to 800 mm high. Leaves ± 7, *bluish green*, ± 20 mm broad; margin yellowish. Flowers up to ± 25 in an erect spike, arranged in *2 rows* pointing in *opposite* directions when open; perianth with white or milky blue background densely *speckled* with pink to maroon spots, the latter concentrated to form a *dark line* in the middle of the lobes; 3 lower lobes with a *yellow blotch*.
Grassland. Widespread. Summer. □ For white-flowered form see **94**.

549 Schizostylis coccinea Backh. & Harv. *Kaffir lily/Kafferlelie*
Herbaceous perennial with several *sword-shaped* leaves arranged in 2 ranks. Inflorescence a rather *stout* terminal spike. Flowers 5 – 10, well-spaced, *regular*, pink or scarlet, *without* dark blotches; bracts large, becoming brown and membranous at the tip.
Moist places, usually in semi-shade along streams; uncommon. Widespread. Summer. □ Compare **544**.

550 Tritonia nelsonii Bak.
Herbaceous perennial ± 500 mm high. Leaves 4 – 8, spreading like a fan in 1 plane, *bluish green*, prominently *ribbed.* Inflorescence many-flowered. Flowers funnel-shaped, orange-red; lower perianth segments each with a green, *upward-pointing outgrowth* on inner surface near base.
Grassland, on rocky ridges. Widespread. Summer. □ Also **715**.

544 *Anomatheca grandiflora*

545 *Anomatheca laxa*

546 *Dierama medium*

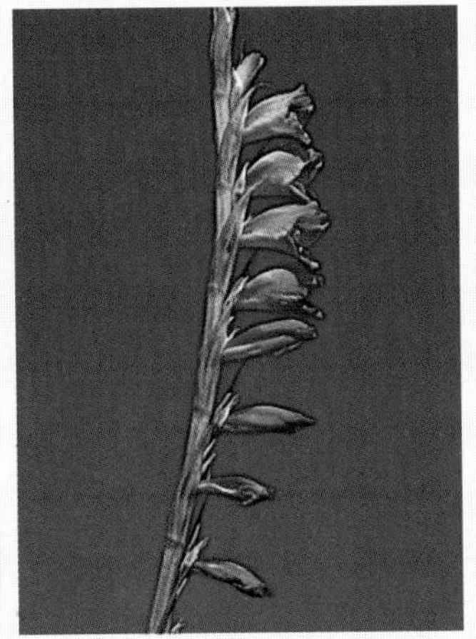

547 *Gladiolus crassifolius*

547 *G. crassifolius* (whitish variant)

548 *Gladiolus elliotii*

549 *Schizostylis coccinea*

550 *Tritonia nelsonii*

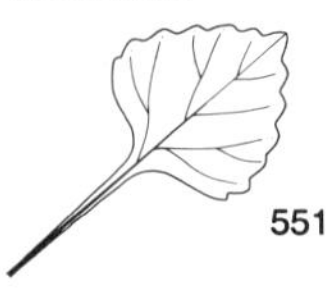
551

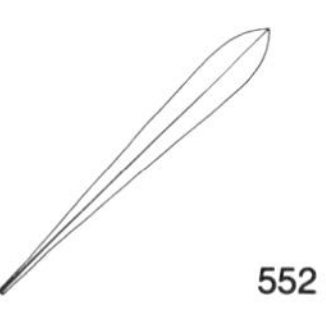
552

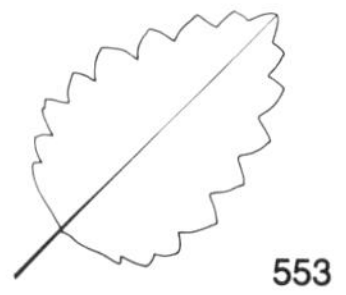
553

LAMIACEAE (See page 22) See also **98**.

551 Aeollanthus buchnerianus Briq. [=**A. canescens** Guerke]
Perennial, *semi-succulent* and ± *hairy* shrublet up to 500 mm high. Leaves stalked, egg-shaped, with *scallop-toothed* margin. Inflorescence with numerous *overlapping*, broadly egg-shaped and hairy bracts. Flowers pale mauve to rosy pink.

Rocky places, often in semi-shade. Widespread. Summer – autumn.

552 Stachys hyssopoides Burch. ex Benth. *Pienksalie*
Perennial herb with a *creeping* rootstock; usually *hairless*. Stems erect, *simple or sparsely branched*. Leaves stalkless, *leathery*. Inflorescence a spike with widely spaced, ± *2-flowered* clusters. Calyx lobes usually with a *fringe of white hairs* along the margin. Corolla pink or mauve-purple.

Grassland, often in moist, heavy soils. Witwatersrand/Suikerbosrand region. Spring – summer.

553 Tetradenia brevispicata (N.E.Br.) Codd [=**Iboza brevispicata** N.E.Br.]
Deciduous *shrub* with twiggy stems and greyish black bark; usually *leafless* at flowering stage. Leaves with fine *velvety* hairs on lower surface; margin *scalloped* to almost toothed. Male and female flowers on separate plants. Flowers minute, *bell-shaped*.

Dry rocky slopes. Magaliesberg. Winter – spring.

LILIACEAE (See page 22) See also **105**, **356**, **357**, **364**, **657 – 660**.

554 Aloe davyana Schonl. var. **davyana**
Succulent with leaves in a *basal rosette*. Leaves with upper surface green and dotted with many *whitish spots*, lower surface whitish green and *without spots;* margin armed with sharp brown prickles. Racemes *conical* with ± *densely congested* buds. Flowers pale pink.

Grassland and bushveld, often forming extensive stands in overgrazed areas. Widespread. Winter.

Sometimes treated as **A. greatheadii** Schonl. var. **davyana** (Schonl.) Glen & Hardy.

555 Aloe pretoriensis Pole Evans
Unbranched *succulent;* stemless or with stout erect stem up to 500 mm high. Leaves in a dense rosette, *greyish green* with a whitish powdery covering, *without spots;* margin armed with reddish spines. Inflorescence up to 2 m high, with 5 – 8 flowering branches. Flowers with the perianth ± cylindrical to 3-angled, and *without* a basal constriction.

Rocky ridges, in grassland or bushveld; rare and localized. Pretoria region. Winter.

556 Aloe transvaalensis Kuntze
Succulent with leaves in a *basal rosette*. Leaves dull green above, with many oval *whitish spots* arranged in transverse bands; lower surface pale milky green, ± *spotted* or without spots; margin armed with sharp brown prickles. Racemes bearing *well-spaced flowers*.

Grassland, often in stony places. Widespread. Summer.

Sometimes considered a synonym of **A. zebrina** Bak.

557 Aloe verecunda Pole Evans
Erect perennial *succulent* with short stems. Leaves *long and narrow*, arranged in 2 ranks or rarely in a basal rosette, dying back in winter; upper surface grooved; lower surface with *white raised spots at the base;* margin with *small white teeth*. Inflorescence *unbranched*, densely flowered. Flowers deep pink to scarlet.

Grassland, on rocky ridges. Widespread. Summer.

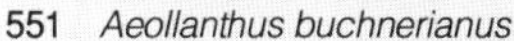

551 *Aeollanthus buchnerianus*

552 *Stachys hyssopoides*

553 *Tetradenia brevispicata* (male left, female right)

554 *Aloe davyana*

555 *Aloe pretoriensis*

556 *Aloe transvaalensis*

557 *Aloe verecunda*

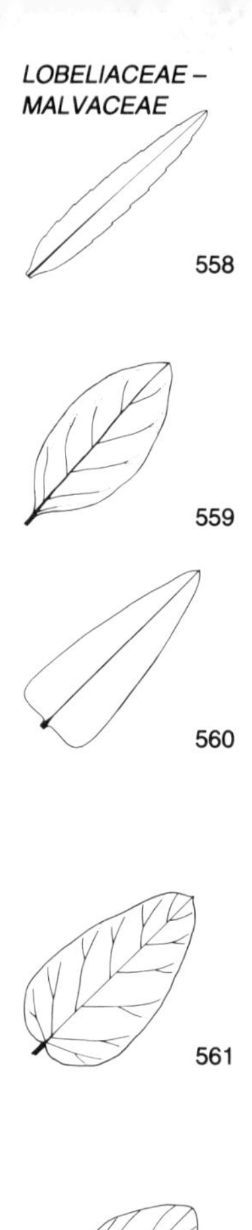

LOBELIACEAE (See page 22)

558 Cyphia stenopetala Diels *Baroe*

Perennial herb with slender, sparsely branched, *twining* stems from a tuberous rootstock; usually growing ± erect with grass stems for support. Leaves *stalkless*, margin *toothed*. Flowers in axils of upper leaves; corolla *2-lipped* and tubular towards the base, *11 – 21 mm* long.

Grassland, often in rocky places. Widespread. Summer. ☐ Compare **126**.

LORANTHACEAE (See page 22)

559 Tapinanthus rubromarginatus (Engl.) Danser *Lighted matches/Vuurhoutjies*

Deciduous hemiparasite growing as a shrublet on the host. Leaves *in tufts*, with a thin, usually *dark reddish margin*. Berries reddish.

Parasitic on a number of hosts, but particularly common on **Protea caffra** (**587**). Widespread. Spring.

LYTHRACEAE (See page 22)

560 Nesaea schinzii Koehne var. **rehmannii** Koehne

Erect or decumbent, much-branched herbaceous shrublet; *hairless*. Leaves stalkless, long and narrow, *broadened at the base;* margin *rolled under*. Inflorescences usually *3-flowered*.

Damp places. Widespread. Summer.

MALPIGHIACEAE (See page 23)

561 Triaspis hypericoides (DC.) Burch. subsp. **nelsonii** (Oliv.) Immelman *Klapperbossie*

Semi-woody climbing *shrublet* with annual *twining* shoots from a perennial rootstock. Leaves stalked, egg-shaped; base ± rounded or slightly heart-shaped; ± hairless when mature. Flowers in axillary racemes; 1 of the 5 petals with a *fringe of long hairs* along whole margin; pink, fading to white. Fruit comprises *3 saucer-shaped* (winged) carpels.

Rocky grassland. Pretoria/Magaliesberg region. Spring.

MALVACEAE (See page 23)

562 Hibiscus aethiopicus L. var. **ovatus** Harv.

Low-growing perennial herb from a woody rootstock; stems and leaves with *bristly, star-shaped* hairs. Leaves *oval*, with a *blunt tip;* margin usually smooth. Flowers solitary, with a lower calyx whorl (epicalyx) of 7 – 9 *very narrow*, pointed segments, ± 5 mm long; petals usually pale yellow, rarely pinkish red; stigmas *bright red*.

Grassland. Widespread. Spring – summer.

For yellow-flowered form see **370**.

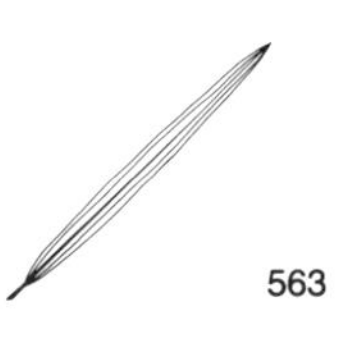

563 Hibiscus microcarpus Garcke

Low-growing herb from a woody perennial rootstock; covered with *rough hairs* throughout. Leaves *unlobed*, *long* and relatively *narrow* (1 – 15 mm); margin with star-shaped hairs, smooth or with a few coarse teeth. Flowers yellow or pink; maroon centre absent or present; epicalyx comprises 7 or 8 segments.

Grassland and disturbed places. Widespread. Summer.

For yellow-flowered form see **374**.

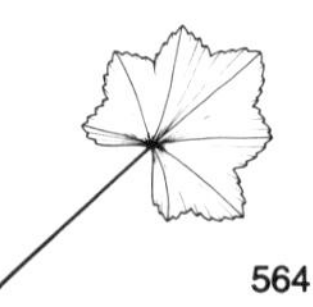

564 *Malva verticillata L.

Bushy biennial herb up to 1 m high. Leaves on long stalks; margin toothed. Flowers in clusters; calyx ± inflated, with triangular lobes; petals ± *twice as long as the calyx*, pale pinkish with *darker veins*.

A native of Asia. Naturalized in disturbed places, often along streams. Widespread. Spring – summer.

***M. parviflora** L. (Small mallow/Kiesieblaar) is usually *decumbent*, with the *petals barely longer than the calyx and usually white*.

558 *Cyphia stenopetala*

559 *Tapinanthus rubromarginatus*

560 *Nesaea schinzii*

561 *Triaspis hypericoides*

562 *Hibiscus aethiopicus*

563 *Hibiscus microcarpus*

564 *Malva verticillata*

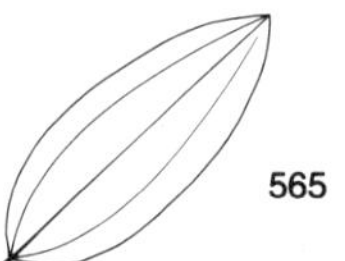

565

MELASTOMATACEAE (See page 23)

565 Dissotis debilis (Sond.) Triana var. **debilis** forma **debilis**

Slender annual herb with sparsely branched erect shoots; internodes below floral leaves up to 300 mm long. Stems *hairy* and often tinged with pink. Leaves with scattered long hairs on upper surface and 3 prominent, ± *parallel veins.* Flowers in dense, many-flowered heads subtended by *2 pairs of leaves.*

Wet places in grassland. Mainly Pretoria/Magaliesberg region. Summer.

MESEMBRYANTHEMACEAE (See page 23)

566 Frithia pulchra N.E.Br. *Fairy elephant's foot/Olifantsvoet*

Small, stemless, perennial leaf succulents; subterranean, with only the *tips of leaves protruding above ground level.* Leaves ± 5 – 7, erect, slightly concave on the inner surface, rounded on the outer surface; tip *flattened* and *translucent.* Flowers stalkless, borne among the leaves; pink or red with a whitish centre, rarely white.

Confined to the summit of the Magaliesberg range, growing in areas of white quartz pebbles and difficult to locate if not in flower. Summer.

567 Khadia acutipetala (N.E.Br.) N.E.Br. *Khadivygie*

Low-growing, *tufted* perennial *succulent* from a fleshy rootstock; aerial stems up to ± 60 mm high. Leaves distinctly *3-angled*, tapering to a ± sharp point; both surfaces covered with numerous *transparent dots.* Flowers solitary, on short, ± flattened stalks.

Summit grassland on rocky ridges, often in white quartz gravel. Widespread. Spring.

MIMOSACEAE (See page 23)

568 Dichrostachys cinerea (L.) Wight & Arn. subsp. **africana** Brenan & Brumm. *Sickle bush/Sekelbos*

Much-branched deciduous *shrub* or small tree; often *flat-topped;* armed with *unpaired spinescent branchlets*, the latter often with leaves. Leaves feathery, bipinnate. Inflorescence a *pendulous spike*, the upper part with *pink sterile flowers*, the lower part with *yellow fertile flowers.* Pods *curly and twisted*, densely clustered in heads.

Bushveld. Mainly Pretoria/Magaliesberg area. Summer. □ Also **395**.

568

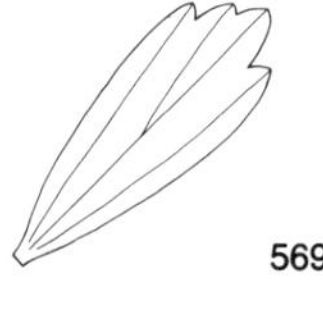

569

MYROTHAMNACEAE (See page 24)

569 Myrothamnus flabellifolia (Sond.) Welw. *Resurrection plant/Opstandingsplant*

Small erect shrublet. Leaves in pairs, each folded *like a fan;* tip broad, with a *wavy edge.* Male and female flowers on different plants. Flowers inconspicuous, reddish, clustered in *terminal spikes.* During periods of drought the whole plant dries out and appears to die, but *revives* within hours after rain.

In shallow soil over sheets of rock. Mainly Pretoria/Magaliesberg region and Suikerbosrand. Spring – summer.

MYRTACEAE (See page 24)

570 *Eucalyptus sideroxylon A. Cunn. ex Woolls *Black ironbark/Swartbasbloekom*

Large evergreen tree up to 25 m high; bark *black, thick and hard*, rough, deeply furrowed, adhering to the main trunk and *not exfoliating in large pieces.* Leaves stalked, pendulous, *grey-green.* Inflorescences comprise solitary axillary umbels bearing up to 7 flowers. Buds with a *cone-shaped* lid. Flowers when open *without perianth* but with numerous white, pink or red stamens. Capsules stalked.

A native of Australia. Not naturalized but often grown in plantations and for shelter on farms, and thus a conspicuous feature of the Highveld landscape. Widespread. Spring – summer.

570

565 *Dissotis debilis*

566 *Frithia pulchra*

567 *Khadia acutipetala*

568 *Dichrostachys cinerea*

569 *Myrothamnus flabellifolia*

570 *Eucalyptus sideroxylon*

NYCTAGINACEAE (See page 24)

571 *Mirabilis jalapa L. *Four o'clock/Vieruurtji*

571

Erect shrubby herb with annual aerial parts from a tuberous perennial taproot; *hairless*. Stems ± *square* in cross-section, brittle. Leaves stalked, ± *heart-shaped*. Flowers clustered at *branch tips;* calyx *tubular* with a spreading 5-lobe limb, white, yellow, red or variegated; surrounded by *5 calyx-like green bracts.*
A native of South America. Cultivated as a garden ornamental and now naturalized in disturbed and often moist places. Widespread. Spring – summer. For yellow-flowered form see **398**.

OCHNACEAE (See page 24)

572 Ochna pretoriensis Phill. *Bergpruim*

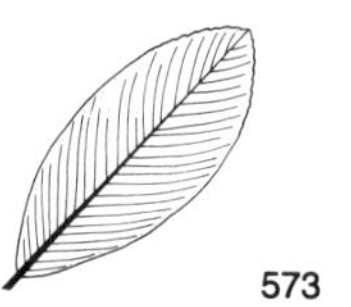

572

Deciduous or ± evergreen *shrub* up to ± 2 m high; much-branched, rather spreading; bark *rough*, brownish. Leaves on very short stalks, *10 – 15 mm* wide; margin *shallowly toothed*. Flowers appear before the leaves, usually *solitary* on short shoots; petals yellow, *stalked*, anthers opening with *pores;* calyx becomes ± reflexed and pinkish green to *bright red* at fruiting stage. Fruit elliptic-globose, ± fleshy, shiny black.
Bushveld, on rocky, often north-facing hillsides. Mainly Pretoria/Magaliesberg region. Spring. ☐ For flowers see **399**.

573 Ochna pulchra Hook. *Peeling plane/Lekkerbreek*

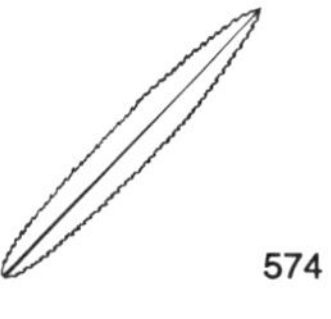

573

Deciduous shrub or small tree; sometimes dwarfed, with numerous erect shoots from underground stems; branches brittle; bark grey, *flaking* in membranous pieces to expose *smooth, creamy white patches*. Leaves on short stalks, ± elliptic, 20 – 40 mm wide, shiny green (bronze or red in spring); margin *shallowly toothed in upper half*. Inflorescences terminate short branches, *many-flowered*, *pendulous*, appear with the young leaves. Flowers fragrant; calyx becomes ± reflexed and turns *bright pinkish red* in fruit. Seed kidney-shaped, ± fleshy, shiny black.
Bushveld, on rocky hillsides and in sandy soils. Mainly Pretoria/Magaliesberg region. Spring. ☐ For flowers see **400**.

ONAGRACEAE (See page 24)

574 Epilobium hirsutum L.

574

Erect, *sparsely branched* perennial herb up to ± 2 m high; densely *covered with spreading whitish hairs*. Leaves mostly opposite but become alternate towards the tip of the stem, stalkless, *stem-clasping* at the base; margin *coarsely* toothed. Flowers with petals bright purplish pink and *deeply notched* at the tips; stigma deeply divided into *4 lobes*. Capsules narrow, *30 – 80 mm* long.
Moist grassland, usually in vleis. Widespread. Summer.

575 *Oenothera rosea L'Herit. ex Ait.
Rose evening primrose/Pienkaandblom

575

Erect or decumbent, much-branched perennial or annual herb. Leaves *alternate*, with stalks up to 10 mm long. Flowers solitary, axillary, *open near sunrise;* sepals open with a single slit and become *deflexed to 1 side* as they do so. Fruit a club-shaped capsule with *4 narrow winged angles*.
Mainly moist disturbed places, often in the shade. A weed from South America. Widespread. Spring – summer.

571 *Mirabilis jalapa*

572 *Ochna pretoriensis*

573 *Ochna pulchra*

574 *Epilobium hirsutum*

575 *Oenothera rosea*

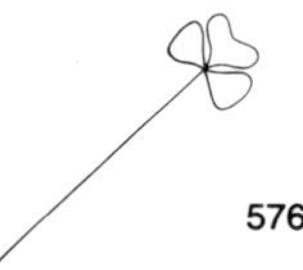

576

577

OXALIDACEAE (See page 25)

576 Oxalis depressa Eckl. & Zeyh. *Sorrel/Suring*

Small perennial herb; ± *hairless*. Leaves on slender stalks, *trifoliolate;* leaflets often flushed with *purple below*. Flowers *solitary* on erect stalks which are much longer than the leaves; subtended by 2 minute *hair-like* bracts; corolla pink or white with a *yellow centre*, *less than 15 mm* long, hairless.

Grassland; uncommon. Widespread. Summer. □ Compare **577**.

577 Oxalis obliquifolia Steud. ex Rich. *Sorrel/Suring*

Perennial herb with long, slender, underground rhizomes which bear small bulbs. Leaflets *3 on slender stalks*, ± *hairy*. Flowers *solitary* on a long stalk, pinkish violet with a *yellow centre*. Capsule ± as long as calyx.

Grassland and rock crevices, often in moist places. Widespread. Summer. Compare **576**.

O. semiloba Sond. has an inflorescence stalk which terminates in *several* flowers. Widespread in grassland, often in moist or disturbed places. Summer.

578

PEDALIACEAE (See page 25)

578 Ceratotheca triloba (Bernh.) Hook.f. *Wild foxglove/Vingerhoedblom*

Erect *annual* up to ± 2 m high; most parts covered with fine hairs; emits an *unpleasant smell* when crushed. Leaves ± deeply divided into 3 lobes; margin bluntly toothed. Flowers *pendulous;* corolla has lower lip with conspicuous *purplish stripes*. Fruit a *hairy* capsule with 2 prominent *horns* at the tip.

Grassland, particularly along roadsides and in disturbed places. Mainly Pretoria/Magaliesberg region. Summer.

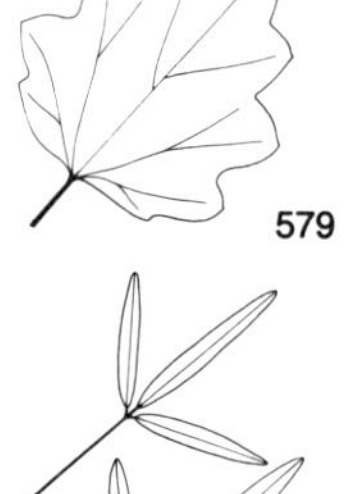

579

579 Dicerocaryum eriocarpum (Decne) Abels [=**D. zanguebarium** (Lour.) Merr. subsp. **eriocarpum** (Decne) Ihlenf.] *Devil's thorn/Elandsdoring*

Mat-forming perennial herb with long trailing shoots from a woody rootstock; plants crushed in water yield a mucilaginous mass formerly used as soap substitute. Leaves *deeply lobed*, upper surface grey-green, *lower surface whitish*. Fruit a *flattened*, elliptic and *very hard disc* lying flat on the ground, with 2 very sharp vertical *spines* from near the centre of the upper side.

Grassland, particularly trampled areas and abandoned fields; usually in sandy soil. Mainly Pretoria/Magaliesberg region. Summer – autumn.

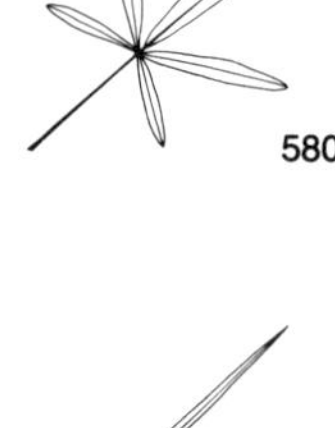

580

580 Sesamum triphyllum Welw. ex Aschers. var. **triphyllum** *Wild sesame/Wildesesam*

Erect, sparsely branched perennial herb up to ± 1 m high; emits a *strong smell* when crushed; ± hairless. Leaves vary from *simple to deeply palmately divided;* margin faintly toothed. Flowers solitary, axillary, brownish pink, subtended by *small black glands*. Fruit a cylindrical capsule with a pointed tip, *splitting in half* when ripe.

Grassland and bushveld, often in disturbed places, particularly along roadsides. Mainly Pretoria/Magaliesberg region. Spring – summer.

581

POLYGALACEAE (See page 26)

581 Polygala hottentotta Presl.

Slender, erect, *sparsely branched* herb with rigid annual stems from a perennial rootstock. Leaves *few*, 2 mm or less wide. Inflorescence a *many-flowered, elongated* (up to 200 mm long) terminal raceme. Flowers *pendulous;* sepals petal-like, *conspicuously veined; 2 front sepals separate*.

Common in grassland, often in damp places. Widespread. Summer – autumn. □ Compare **667** and **668**.

576 *Oxalis depressa*

577 *Oxalis obliquifolia*

578 *Ceratotheca triloba*

579 *Dicerocaryum eriocarpum*

580 *Sesamum triphyllum*

581 *Polygala hottentotta*

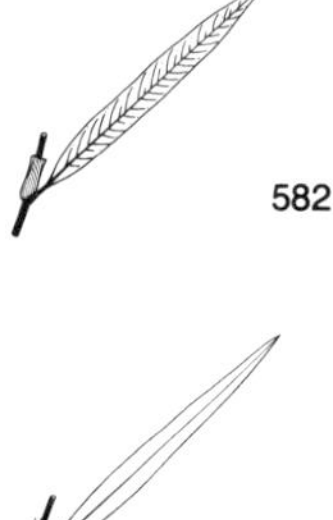

582

583

POLYGONACEAE (See page 26)

582 *Polygonum lapathifolium L. subsp. **maculatum** (S.F.Gray) T.-Dyer & Trim. *Spotted knotweed/Hanekam*

Robust, erect *annual* herb up to 3 m high. Stems often *reddish*. Leaves on short stalks; *midrib and lateral veins conspicuous;* stipular sheaths (ocreae) at base of leaves tubular, *brownish and hairless*. Inflorescences often *drooping*.

Naturalized from Europe. Wet places, particularly riverbanks and shores of dams. Widespread. Summer.

583 Polygonum salicifolium Willd. *Snake root/Slangwortel*

Slender erect or basally decumbent *annual* herb up to ± 500 mm high. Stems green, becoming brown below. Leaves stalkless, *tapering to both ends;* stipular sheaths (ocreae) with upward-pointing *bristly hairs*, terminally *fringed with stiff bristles*. Inflorescence branches ± *erect*, with densely flowered spikes.

Moist and swampy places, but also waste land and roadsides. Widespread. Summer.

P. senegalense Meisn. subsp. **senegalense** is a robust, erect *perennial* herb up to 3 m high. Leaves on short stalks with conspicuous midrib and lateral veins; sheaths *hairless* or with a fringe of short hairs at the rim. Inflorescence stalks covered with minute *orange* stalkless *glands*. Mainly Pretoria/Magaliesberg region. Summer.

P. limbatum Meisn. is a *perennial* herb with the basal shoots sometimes decumbent and rooting at the lower nodes. Stipular sheaths with spreading upper rim, *green and leaf-like* with a fringe of hairs. Wet places. Summer.

583.1

583.1 P. pulchrum Blume is a stout erect annual or perennial herb up to 2 m high; stems *brownish* and densely covered with *appressed brown hairs*. Leaf margin edged with *short bristly hairs;* stipular sheaths with terminal *fringe of bristles*. Wet places. Summer.

PORTULACACEAE (See page 26)

584 Anacampseros subnuda V. Poelln. *Haaskos*

Perennial *succulent* from a thick rootstock. Leaves often tinged with *purple-brown;* covered with *fine whitish hairs when young*, becoming *hairless with age;* stipules *longer* than the leaves, *curled*. Flowers with sepals ± 9 mm long; petals ± 10 mm long; stamens 15 – 20.

Rocky ridges, usually in shallow soil. Widespread. Summer.

Two other species are claimed to occur in the field guide region:

A. filamentosa (Haw.) Sims is similar to the previous species but has more or less *straight* stipules, sepals ± 12 mm long, petals ± 14 mm long and up to 25 whitish stamens; **A. lanigera** Burch. has *young and old leaves* covered with *soft white hairs*, *curled* stipules, sepals relatively short (up to 7 mm), with the upper surface covered with *minute projections* (papillae), and petals ± 9 mm long. Both species are rare and confined mainly to the Magaliesberg.

585

585 Portulaca kermesina N.E.Br.

Annual or perennial *succulent* with *erect* or ± *erect* stems. Leaves ± *alternate*, long, narrow and *cylindrical*, subtended by *whitish stipular hairs*. Petals bright carmine.

Grassland, usually in sandy soils. Widespread. Spring – summer.

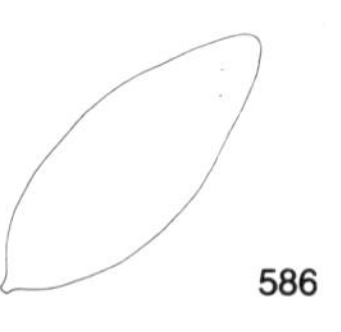

586

586 *Portulaca quadrifida L.

Prostrate *annual succulent* with ± swollen taproot. Stems often *reddish* and rooting at the nodes. Leaves *opposite* and *flattened*. Flowers 1 – 4 at the ends of branches, surrounded by 4 leaves and numerous *long hairs;* corolla yellow or pink.

Cosmopolitan as a weed, mainly in disturbed places. Probably exotic. Widespread. Summer. ☐ Compare **416**.

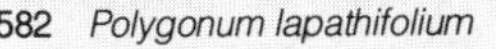

582 *Polygonum lapathifolium*

583 *Polygonum salicifolium*

584 *Anacampseros subnuda*

585 *Portulaca kermesina*

586 *Portulaca quadrifida*

PROTEACEAE (See page 26)

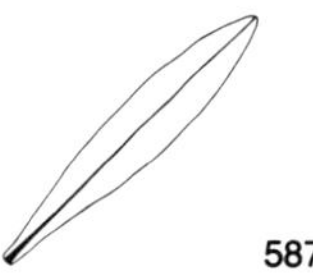

587

587 Protea caffra Meisn. *Sugarbush/Suikerbos*

Evergreen tree up to ± 4 m high, usually with a distinct main stem; bark thick, *rough* and *blackish*, with a network of fissures. Leaves ± stalkless, thick and leathery, *dull grey-green, hairless.* Flower heads ± sweetly scented, surrounded by pink or creamy green bracts; lower bracts often covered with *very short silvery hairs.*

Grassland, usually in pure stands on mainly south-facing slopes of rocky hillsides. Widespread. Summer.

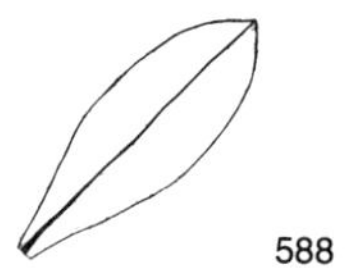

588

588 Protea roupelliae Meisn. subsp. **roupelliae** *Transvaal silverleaf/Silwerblaarsuikerbos*

Evergreen tree up to ± 6 m high, with a short main stem; bark thick and fissured, blackish. Leaves stalkless, *grey-green,* ± covered with *silvery hairs,* leathery. Flower heads goblet-shaped; outer involucral bracts with the tips *brown, recurved, with splitting margins;* inner bracts *spoon-shaped,* pink to creamy yellow.

Grassland, at high altitudes on rocky ridges; growing in pure stands, or in association with **P. caffra** (**587**). Mainly Suikerbosrand/Witwatersrand region. Summer.

RANUNCULACEAE (See page 26)

589

589 Clematopsis scabiosifolia (DC.) Hutch. *Pluimbossie*

Shrublet up to 1 m high, with annual shoots from a woody rootstock; covered with *silvery hairs* throughout. Leaves ± bipinnate with the ultimate leaflets ± pinnately lobed. Flowers *drooping;* sepals petal-like, densely covered with *hairs;* anthers yellow. Fruiting heads *upright,* with numerous conspicuous persistent and *feathery styles.*

Grassland, particularly in sandy soil on rocky ridges. Widespread. Summer.

Putative hybrids with **Clematis brachiata** (**147**) have been reported.

ROSACEAE (See page 27)

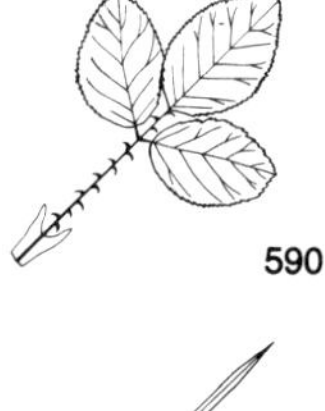

590

590 Rubus rigidus J.E.Sm. *Bramble/Braam*

Perennial shrub or scrambler with *recurved prickles.* Leaves compound, *densely covered with white hairs on lower surface,* terminal leaflet on a short stalk; margin *toothed;* midrib often with minute prickles. Inflorescences terminal and axillary, many-flowered. Flowers with petals *slightly shorter* than the sepals. Fruits globose, fleshy, hairy, red ripening to black.

Bushveld, along streams and in ravines. Mainly Pretoria/Magaliesberg region. Spring – summer.

RUBIACEAE (See page 27)

591

591 Kohoutia virgata (Willd.) Brem.

Slender erect herb from a woody perennial rootstock. Stems much-branched, *4-angled.* Leaves *well-spaced,* 1 – 4 mm wide; stipules long, *hair-like.* Flowers in branched inflorescences at the ends of stems, pinkish red or white.

Grassland and bushveld. Widespread. Spring – summer.

RUTACEAE (See page 27)

592

592 Calodendrum capense (L.f.) Thunb. *Cape chestnut/Wildekastaiing*

Deciduous to semi-deciduous tree; bark *smooth.* Leaves *opposite,* simple, with *gland dots* which resemble pinpricks when the leaf is held up to the light. Flowers in large clusters at the ends of branches; sterile stamens petal-like and marked with prominent *pinkish red glands.* Fruit a 5-angled capsule, warty.

Wooded ridges and kloofs. Mainly Magaliesberg. Spring.

587 *Protea caffra*

588 *Protea roupelliae*

589 *Clematopsis scabiosifolia*

590 *Rubus rigidus*

591 *Kohoutia virgata*

592 *Calodendrum capense*

SCROPHULARIACEAE (See page 28) See also **163** and **168**.

593

593 Craterostigma wilmsii Engl. ex Diels

Perennial herb with a *flat basal rosette* of leaves. Leaves and inflorescence covered with *whitish hairs*. Flowers with the stamens in 2 pairs: the upper pair attached to the upper lip, filaments of the lower pair attached to a large *yellow cushion* on the *3-lobed* lower lip and *strongly deflexed*.

Marshy grassland, often among rocks; localized. Mainly Pretoria/Magaliesberg region. Spring – summer.

594

594 Graderia subintegra Mast. *Wild penstemon*

Perennial herb with erect or usually *trailing* shoots from a woody rootstock. Stems square in cross-section. Leaves *alternate*, stalkless and covered with short hairs; margin toothless or with 1 or 2 lobes on each side of the midrib. Flowers pink with the lower surface whitish, rarely white; corolla with the outer surface covered with *short hairs;* filaments hairy.

Common in grassland. Widespread. Spring – summer.

For white-flowered form see **165**.

595

595 Nemesia fruticans (Thunb.) Benth. *Wildeleeubekkie*

Herb with few to numerous *slender* erect stems from a woody taproot. Leaves with smooth or *toothed* margins. Corolla with a *spur;* upper lip 4-lobed; lower lip 2-lobed; pink, mauve, purple or white, with *2 yellowish areas* in the throat. Capsules laterally compressed and 2-chambered.

Grassland, particularly in rocky places. Widespread. Spring.

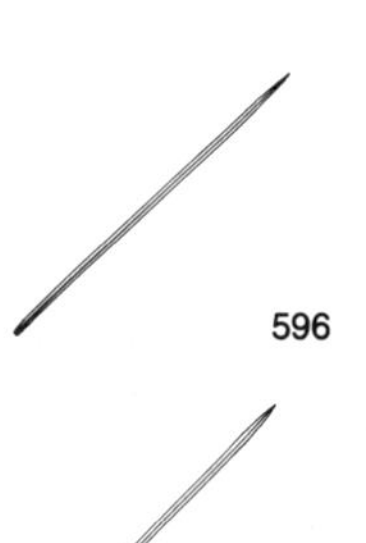

596

596 Sopubia cana Harv.

Erect perennial herb from a woody rootstock. Leaves *very narrow*, densely covered with *grey hairs*. Flowers solitary in axils of bracts near ends of shoots; calyx densely covered with grey hairs; corolla with 5 *rounded* lobes; stamens *protruding* from corolla.

Parasite in grassland, often on ridges or in moist places; uncommon. Mainly Pretoria/Magaliesberg region. Summer.

597

597 Sopubia simplex (Hochst.) Hochst.

Erect perennial herb from a woody rootstock. Leaves essentially *hairless*. Flowers similar to the previous species but with the calyx *hairless* on the outer surface, and the inner surface of the lobes densely covered with whitish hairs.

Parasitic in grassland, often on rocky ridges and in moist places; uncommon. Mainly Suikerbosrand and Magaliesberg. Summer.

593 *Craterostigma wilmsii*

594 *Graderia subintegra*

596 *Sopubia cana*

595 *Nemesia fruticans*

597 *Sopubia simplex*

598

598 Striga asiatica (L.) Kuntze *Witchweed/Rooiblom*
Upright, *sparsely branched* herb, often more bushy when growing in maize fields. Leaves ± *spreading* and *harsh* to the touch owing to a covering of minute hairs with *prominent bulbous swellings* at the base. Flowers ± *12 mm* long; corolla with upper lip *much shorter* than the lower, red or rarely bright yellow; calyx with ± *10* prominent veins.

Parasitic on grasses; very often found as a parasite on maize. Widespread. Summer – autumn.

599

599 Striga bilabiata (Thunb.) Kuntze
Slender erect herb, occasionally sparsely branched. Stems sometimes *purplish* at the base. Leaves covered with *rough* hairs. Flowers with corolla distinctly *2-lipped;* calyx with *5 prominent veins.*

Parasitic on grasses. Widespread. Spring.

S. gesnerioides (Willd.) Vatke has leaves that are *scale-like* and covered with *soft hairs.* The stems are often tinged with *purple.* Parasitic, sometimes on tobacco. Summer – autumn.

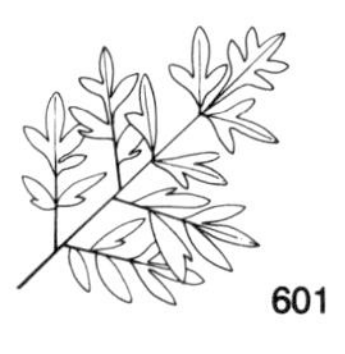

600

600 Striga elegans Benth. *Large witchweed/Grootrooiblom*
Slender erect herb. Stems simple or rarely slightly branched. Leaves stiff and *erect*, with a *rough* texture owing to the presence of minute hairs which are slightly inflated at the base. Flowers *12 – 20 mm* long; corolla bright scarlet on inner and orange-yellow on outer surface, upper lip *not much* shorter than the lower; calyx with ± 10 prominent veins.

Parasitic on grasses, rarely on maize. Widespread. Summer – autumn.

A pink-flowered plant which is very common at Suikerbosrand and is also found in the Magaliesberg may be a colour variant of this species. Summer.

601

601 Sutera aurantiaca (Burch.) Hiern. *Cape saffron/Saffraanbossie*
Small, bushy, *aromatic* herb from a woody rootstock. Shoots slender, covered with glandular hairs. Leaves in *tufts*, finely bipinnately *dissected*, covered with short *glandular hairs.* Flower colour variable: orange, red, pink or brownish.

Grassland. Widespread, the pink form mainly in the Pretoria/Magaliesberg region. Spring – summer. □ For orange-flowered form see **728**.

STERCULIACEAE (See page 28) See also **686** and **731**.

602

602 Hermannia boraginiflora Hook. *Gombossie*
Perennial herb with *erect*, sparsely branched shoots; plants often yellowish green. Leaves stalked, dotted with minute, *star-shaped* hairs; margin toothed; tip often *broad, 3-toothed;* stipules small, leaf-like, undivided. Flowers axillary on long, *single-flowered* stalks towards tips of shoots, *drooping;* corolla *shorter than sepals*, with lobes lacking pouches, pale mauve or pinkish to almost white; anthers protruding, *dark purple.* Capsules with 5 *spreading horns* on top.

Bushveld. Pretoria/Magaliesberg region. Spring – summer.

603

603 Hermannia resedifolia (Burch.) R.A. Dyer
Slender perennial herb; hairless. Shoots ± *prostrate* with erect tips. Leaves ± stalked, *deeply dissected; stipules dissected.* Inflorescences towards ends of shoots, erect, usually *2-flowered.* Flowers *drooping*, dark red.

Grassland, usually in vleis. Witwatersrand/Suikerbosrand region. Spring – summer.

604

604 Hermannia tomentosa (Turcz.) Schinz ex Engl.
Herb with perennial taproot and outer (sometimes also inner) branchlets *decumbent and trailing.* Leaves stalked, usually *greyish green* and all *directed to the same side, densely covered* with minute, star-shaped hairs; margin barely to distinctly toothed, except in lower third. Flowers bell-shaped, with the petals *shorter than the calyx.*

Grassland, often on rocky ridges. Mainly Magaliesberg. Spring – summer.

598 *Striga asiatica*

599 *Striga bilabiata*

600 *Striga elegans*

600 ? *S. elegans* (pink variant)

601 *Sutera aurantiaca*

602 *Hermannia boraginiflora*

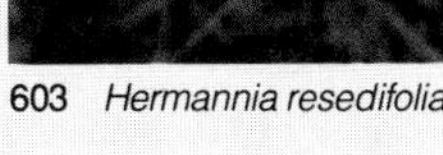

603 *Hermannia resedifolia*

604 *Hermannia tomentosa*

THYMELAEACEAE (See page 28)

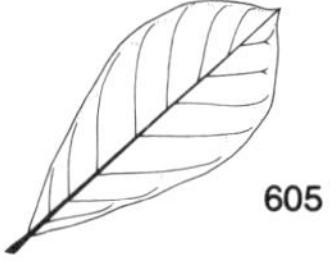

605

605 Dais cotinifolia L. *Pompon tree/Kannabas*

Small, ± deciduous tree up to ± 4 m high; bark smooth, grey-brown. Leaves stalked, opposite or alternate. Flowers borne in dense *globose heads*, subtended by ± 4 broad, *brownish bracts.*

Wooded kloofs; very rare. Mainly Witwatersrand/Suikerbosrand region. Late spring.

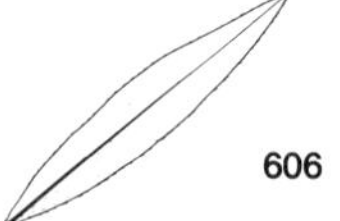

606

606 Gnidia gymnostachya (Meisn.) Gilg

Erect shrublet with a woody rootstock; covered with *silky hairs* throughout. Leaves almost stalkless. Flowers in an *elongated terminal spike*, stalkless, *tubular* with *brownish red lobes*, *hairy* on the outer surface.

Grassland. Mainly Witwatersrand/Suikerbosrand region. Summer.

TILIACEAE (See page 28)

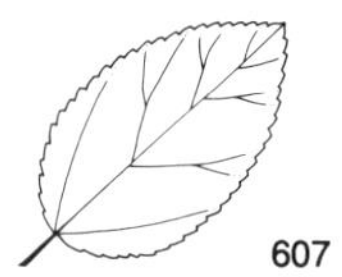

607

607 Grewia occidentalis L. *Crossberry/Kruisbessie*

Deciduous shrub or small tree up to 3 m high; older stems *4-angled.* Leaves light green, stalked, blade *3-veined* from the base; margin *finely toothed.* Petals with a *greyish green* outer surface. Fruit a reddish brown berry, usually with *4 lobes.*

Clumps of bush and rocky places, often in the shade of trees. Mainly Pretoria/Magaliesberg region. Spring – summer.

VELLOZIACEAE (See page 29)

608 Xerophyta viscosa Bak.

Perennial herb with *basal* tuft of leaves. Leaves with *stiff, sharp* hairs along the margin and keel. Flowers solitary on long stalks; white with yellow anthers, usually with outer surface of perianth tinged with pale mauve; stalks and bases of outer perianth segments with *dark glands.*

Rocky slopes, often in dense colonies on rock sheets. Mainly Pretoria/Magaliesberg region. Summer. □ Also **177**.

VERBENACEAE (See page 29)

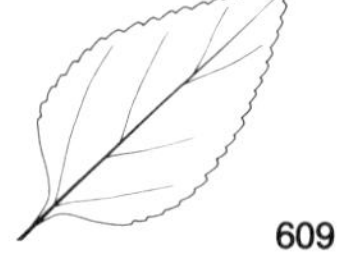

609

609 *Lantana camara L. *Lantana*

Much-branched shrub. Stems *4-angled* with *scattered recurved prickles.* Leaves covered with *rough hairs; foul-smelling* when crushed. Inflorescences *flat-topped.* Flowers in the centre open first and usually *change colour* as they fade; colour very variable: pink, yellow, orange or orange-brown. Fruits blackish, *fleshy*, shiny and globose.

A weed from tropical America, usually growing under and among trees. Widespread. Summer – winter. □ For orange-brown form see **734**.

605 *Dais cotinifolia*

606 *Gnidia gymnostachya*

607 *Grewia occidentalis*

608 *Xerophyta viscosa*

609 *Lantana camara*

BLUE OR BLUE-PURPLE FLOWERS

(See also **166, 474, 602, 731**)

Blue flowers can be distinguished easily but are relatively rare. Blue-purple (violet) ones are more common, but these grade into red-purple, so it is sometimes difficult to decide to which purple group a flower belongs. A few red-purple flowers are included in this section in order to keep purplish-coloured species of the same genus together. An additional problem in separating these colours is that blue and blue-purple flowers are probably the most difficult to record on film, the colours often showing up in tones of pink and mauve. If a purple flower is not found in this section, consult the chapter Pink to red or red-purple flowers (page 186).

Anthocyanins dissolved in the cell sap are responsible for the blue and blue-purple colouring of the flower petals. The colour they produce varies according to the pH of the sap, being red in an acid solution and blue in a more alkaline one.

Bees visit blue flowers more frequently than any other insect group, and irregular blue flowers in particular are nearly always bee-pollinated. The nymphalid group of butterflies also shows a strong preference for blues, purples and yellows. Some fly species, too, have been recorded as pollinators for this colour group, although such instances are uncommon. To bees blue and blue-purple probably represent one single colour and may be perceived as green. Through the eyes of insects the green foliage of plants is believed to be a dull yellow-grey, a neutral background against which the insect-green flowers would contrast vividly.

GUIDE TO THE FAMILIES WHICH INCLUDE BLUE OR BLUE-PURPLE FLOWERS

BLUE OR BLUE-PURPLE FLOWERS

- PETALS 3 OR 6 (MONOCOTYLEDONS)
  - OVARY SUPERIOR
    - Alliaceae
    - Aponogetonaceae
    - Liliaceae
    - Pontederiaceae
  - OVARY INFERIOR
    - Iridaceae
    - Orchidaceae
    - Velloziaceae
- PETALS 4 OR 5 (DICOTYLEDONS)
  - PETALS ± FREE
    - FLOWERS REGULAR
      - Campanulaceae
      - Meliaceae
      - Sterculiaceae
    - FLOWERS ± IRREGULAR
      - Fabaceae
      - Polygalaceae
  - PETALS CLEARLY UNITED
    - FLOWERS REGULAR
      - LEAVES OPPOSITE
        - Buddlejaceae
        - (L) Periplocaceae
        - Rubiaceae
      - LEAVES ALTERNATE/ROSULATE
        - (L) Asteraceae
        - Boraginaceae
        - (L) Campanulaceae
        - (L) Convolvulaceae
        - Ehretiaceae
        - (T) Solanaceae
    - FLOWERS ± IRREGULAR
      - Acanthaceae
      - Lamiaceae
      - Lentibulariaceae
      - (L) Lobeliaceae
      - Scrophulariaceae
      - Selaginaceae
      - Verbenaceae

(L) At least some members with *milky latex*
(T) At least some members with *thorns/spines*

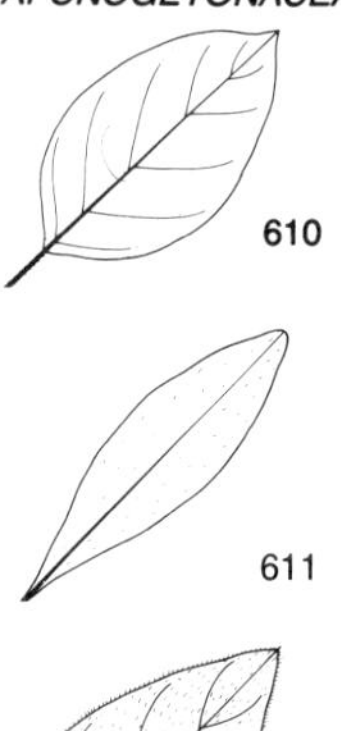

ACANTHACEAE (See page 16)

610 Barleria obtusa Nees

Scrambling perennial shrublet; irregularly branched and covered with *silky hairs* throughout. Leaves on short stalks, *oval*. Flowers in axillary *clusters* towards the ends of branchlets. Seeds hairy.

Grassland and bushveld, on rocky ridges. Mainly Pretoria/Magaliesberg region. Autumn.

611 Blepharis integrifolia (L.f.) E. Mey. ex Schinz ***Rankklits***

Herb with *trailing* stems from a perennial rootstock. Stems with *spreading hairs*. Leaves on very short stalks, lance-shaped; *whitish spreading hairs* occurring sparsely, mainly on the upper surface. Inflorescence *stalkless*, *congested*, bracts prominently *spiny* at the tips. Corolla *3-lobed*, blue, mauve or white.

Grassland and bushveld, often in sandy soil. Widespread. Summer.

612 Ruellia cordata Thunb.

Herbaceous shrublet from a woody rootstock. Leaves with stalk less than 5 mm long, *broadly egg-shaped* with slightly tapering, heart-shaped or rounded base and tapering tips; covered with minute, tightly *appressed white hairs*. Sepals 5, with *3 joined together* for ± half their length.

Grassland. Widespread. Spring – summer.

ALLIACEAE (See page 16)

613 Agapanthus campanulatus Leighton subsp. **patens** (Leighton) Leighton ***Bloulelie***

Deciduous perennial with a short thick rhizome. Leaves *strap-shaped*, arranged in a basal cluster. Flowers borne in a terminal *umbel*, completely enclosed by *2 large bracts* when in bud; perianth segments *spreading or recurved* above.

Grassland, usually in rocky places. Mainly Suikerbosrand. Summer.

A. inapertus Beav. subsp. **intermedius** Leighton has *tubular* flowers with the perianth segments joined for ± half their length, and *only slightly recurved* above. Rarely recorded from rocky ridges on the Witwatersrand.

APONOGETONACEAE (See page 17)

614 Aponogeton junceus Lehm. ex Schlechtd. subsp. **junceus** ***Wateruintjie***

Aquatic herb with a tuberous rhizome. Leaves basal, erect, long, *narrow* and ± *cylindrical*, sometimes with an expanded floating blade. Flowers densely crowded in *forked spikes*, white, pink or mauve, becoming green with age.

Marshy places, ponds and rivers. Widespread. Spring – summer.

For white-flowered form see **20**.

610 *Barleria obtusa*

611 *Blepharis integrifolia*

612 *Ruellia cordata*

613 *Agapanthus campanulatus*

614 *Aponogeton junceus*

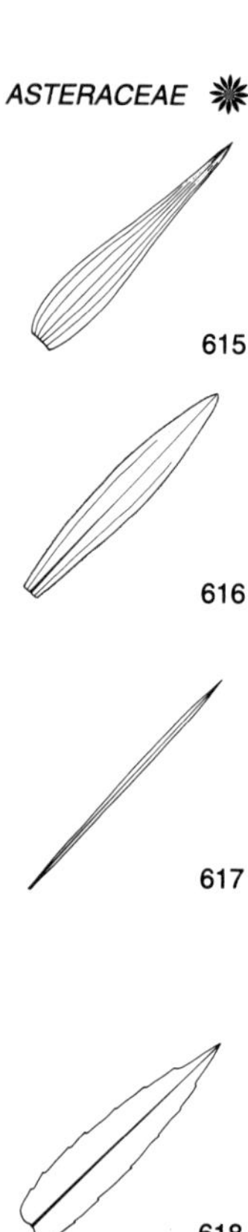

ASTERACEAE (See page 17)
Group A

615 Aster harveyanus Kuntze *Bloublommetjie*
Erect, sparsely branched herb from a woody rootstock. Stems *hairless*. Stem leaves half-clasping at base, with *3 – 5 prominent*, ± *longitudinal veins;* margin fringed with *rough hairs*. Flower heads with ray flowers mauve, disc flowers yellow; involucral bracts hairless.
Grassland. Widespread. Spring.

616 Castalis spectabilis (Schltr.) T. Norl. *Bloubietou*
Herb with several *erect* stems from a woody perennial rootstock. Leaves *stalkless*, lance-shaped; upper surface with *sunken glands;* lower surface with glandular hairs. Flower heads solitary on long stalks; ray flowers white with a purple tinge; disc flowers *dark purple*.
Grassland. Widespread. Spring.

617 Felicia filifolia (Vent.) Burtt Davy subsp. **filifolia** *Draaibos*
Much-branched perennial shrublet up to ± 1 m high; twigs *hairless*, with a *creamy* colour. Leaves alternate or in tufts, *needle-like* and ± *grooved*. Flower heads borne in profusion, each solitary from leaf tufts *along the length* of the stems; ray flowers mauve to white, disc flowers yellow; flowers ± aromatic.
Grassland, on rocky ridges. Mainly Witwatersrand/Suikerbosrand region. Spring. □ Compare **34**.

ASTERACEAE (See page 17)
Group B See also **474**.

618 Denekia capensis Thunb.
Perennial or annual herb; usually *glandular*. Leaves stalkless, *long and narrow*, often lobed at the base; green and hairy above, *white-felted* below. Flower heads ± 3 mm in diameter, in terminal clusters of up to ± 20, white or blue fading to white.
Moist places, sometimes in shallow water. Widespread. Spring – autumn. For white-flowered form see **41**.

619 Sphaeranthus incisus Robyns
Short-lived perennial herb with *prostrate and erect* shoots; plants low-growing; *sticky and aromatic*. Leaves alternate, stalkless, forming *narrow wings* where they join the stem; margin ± toothed. Flower heads *pointed-globose* (actually an aggregate of many small heads), stalked and borne *opposite the leaves* along the length of the shoots, purple; subtending bracts with *pointed* tips.
Damp places, mainly along streams; rare. Pretoria/Magaliesberg region. Spring – summer.

615 *Aster harveyanus*

616 *Castalis spectabilis*

617 *Felicia filifolia*

618 *Denekia capensis*

619 *Sphaeranthus incisus*

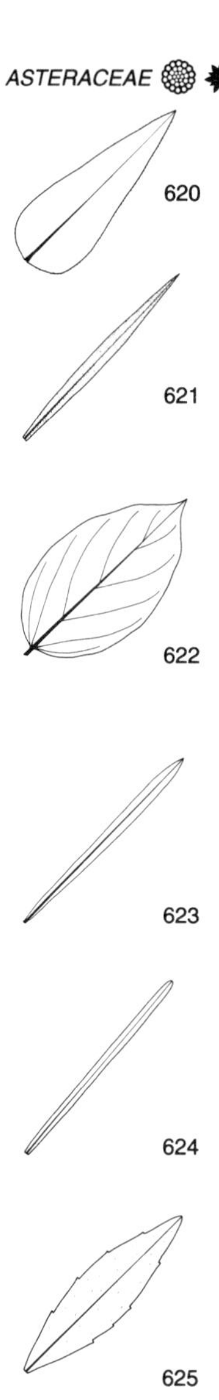

620 Vernonia galpinii Klatt *Perskwasbossie*
Perennial herb up to 500 mm high, with several to many *erect* stems from a woody rootstock; most parts covered with rough hairs. Leaves stalkless, green. Stems terminated by a *large, solitary flower head*, up to 25 mm across.
Grassland, usually in rocky places. Widespread. Spring.

621 Vernonia natalensis Sch. Bip.
Perennial herb up to 1 m high; most parts *densely covered with silvery hairs.* Leaves stalkless, *long and narrow;* base *tapering;* both surfaces covered with *silvery silky hairs.* Flower heads in a *cluster* at end of each stem; bracts around head with *long curved tips.*
Grassland. Widespread. Spring. □ Compare **622**.

622 Vernonia oligocephala (DC.) Sch. Bip. ex Walp. *Bitterbossie*
Perennial herb up to 1 m high, producing many erect stems from a woody rootstock. Leaves almost stalkless, *oval to egg-shaped;* base *rounded; dull green* and ± hairless above, covered with *silvery silky hairs* below; often coming abruptly to a rather long point. Flower heads numerous, clustered together in ± flat-topped groups at the ends of the flowering shoots; bracts with purple tips.
Common in grassland. Widespread. Spring. □ Compare **621**.

623 Vernonia poskeana Vatke & Hildebr.
Slender, erect annual or short-lived perennial herb, usually *much-branched* and with a *single stem;* stem and leaves with *indistinct gland dots;* very thinly covered with down throughout. Leaves stalkless, *long and narrow.* Flower heads with stalks *up to 50 mm* long, often paired; involucral bracts in several series, with *sharp, hair-like* tips.
Bushveld, often a weed in disturbed places, particularly along roadsides. Mainly Pretoria/Magaliesberg region. Spring – summer. □ Compare **624**.

624 Vernonia staehelinoides Harv. *Blouteebossie*
Multi-stemmed perennial shrublet, woody at base; stems and leaves covered with numerous *short* hairs, giving a *greyish* appearance. Stems ± *wiry.* Leaves very narrow; margins *rolled under.* Flower heads numerous on ± long flexuous stalks, rarely white; involucral bracts *woolly* at the margins.
Rocky ridges in summit grassland. Widespread. Summer – autumn. Compare **623**.

625 Vernonia sutherlandii Harv.
Perennial herb up to 600 mm high, from a woody rootstock. Stems rough, with *forked hairs.* Leaves ± large (up to 60 mm long) and concentrated mainly *towards the base* of stems; both surfaces *green* and with *scattered rough* hairs; margin often *toothed.* Flower heads several, on long flowering shoots which are ± *leafless* towards the ends; bracts with long tips.
Grassland, often on rocky ridges. Widespread. Spring.

ASTERACEAE (See page 17)
Group C

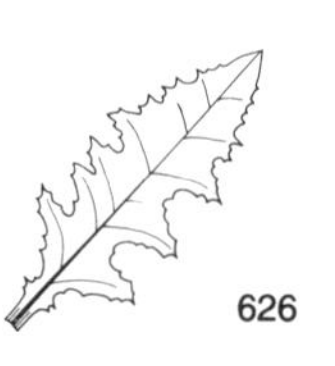

626 *Cichorium intybus L. *Chicory/Sigorei*
Erect perennial herb up to ± 1 m high; taproot fleshy; milky latex present. Basal leaves large, with the margin *irregularly toothed and lobed.* Flower heads on *well-branched,* ± leafless stems; comprise only strap-like ray flowers; tip of each ray corolla divided into 5 teeth.
A weed introduced from Asia and Europe. Moist places, usually near areas of human habitation. Widespread. Summer.

620 *Vernonia galpinii*

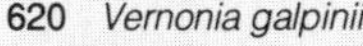

621 *Vernonia natalensis*

622 *Vernonia oligocephala*

623 *Vernonia poskeana*

624 *Vernonia staehelinoides*

625 *Vernonia sutherlandii*

626 *Cichorium intybus*

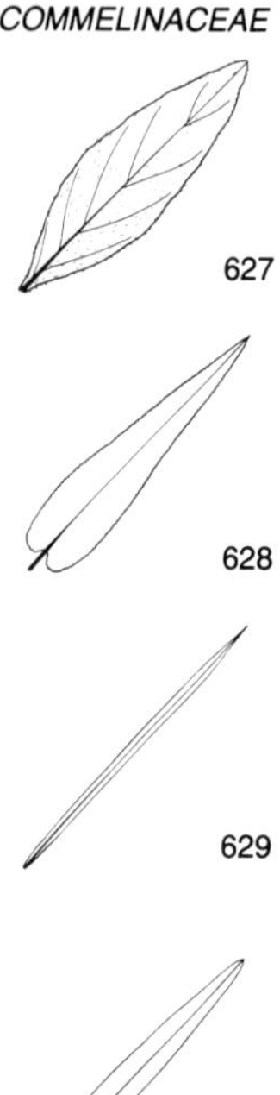

BORAGINACEAE (Excluding Ehretiaceae; see page 17)

627 *Heliotropium amplexicaule Vahl *Blue heliotrope*

Low-growing perennial herb; hairy throughout. Stems *prostrate*, with the tips curving upwards. Leaves on short stalks. Inflorescence terminal, usually forked into 2 – 4 spikes which are ± *coiling.* Flowers pointing *upwards*, mauve or blue, with a *yellow* centre.

A native of South America and now naturalized in grassland and disturbed places, particularly in and around Pretoria. Spring – summer.

BUDDLEJACEAE (See page 18)

628 Buddleja salviifolia (L.) Lam. *Sagewood/Saliehout*

Evergreen or semi-deciduous shrub with *4-angled* stems. Leaves dull *greyish green;* lower surface densely covered with minute *star-shaped* hairs, upper surface *rough and wrinkled.* Flowers sweetly scented.

Mainly along streams. Widespread. Winter.

CAMPANULACEAE (See page 18)

629 Lightfootia denticulata (Burch.) Sond. var. **transvaalensis** Adamson *Muistepelkaroo*

Perennial shrublet with many decumbent or erect stems; old stems with *persistent* leaf bases. Leaf margin usually distinctly *toothed.* Petals ± *free.*

Grassland, often in moist or rocky places. Widespread. Summer – autumn.

630 Wahlenbergia caledonica Sond.

Slender erect perennial herb. Leaves *well-spaced*, mainly on lower part of stem (but not in a rosette); margin *not wavy.* Flowers with corolla 8 – 16 mm long, blue or white; style *3-lobed*, with 3 *minute glands* present between their bases.

Grassland, often in rocky or seasonally moist places. Widespread. Summer.

Very similar to **W. undulata** DC. which has a *conspicuously wavy* leaf margin. ☐ Compare **58**.

COMMELINACEAE (See page 19)

631 Commelina diffusa Burm.f.

Herb with *decumbent trailing* stems. Leaves up to 90 mm long, ± 10 mm wide. Flowering spathes *distinctly stalked*, folded, with margins *free* at the base; upper flower(s) protruding; *dry* inside.

Grassland, in moist places. Mainly Magaliesberg. Summer.

632 Commelina erecta L.

Perennial herb with *decumbent, spreading*, branched stems from a small rootstock. Leaves usually *folded upward* along the midrib, greyish green, *lobed* (eared) before narrowing abruptly into the sheath. Flowering spathes *almost stalkless* and clustered at the tips of the stems; folded, with margins *joined* at the base; *mucilaginous* (wet) inside.

Grassland. Widespread. Summer.

633 Commelina livingstonii C.B.Cl.

Perennial herb with spreading branched stems from a woody crown. Stems covered with *short hairs*. Leaves ± 10 mm wide, *folded* along midrib, *greyish green*. Flowering spathes *clustered* at tips of stems, ± *stalkless*, folded, with margins *joined* at the base; inner surface *wet* at the time of flowering, outer surface covered with *bristly hairs*. Capsule *triangular*.

Grassland. Widespread. Spring.

C. modesta Oberm. is a more slender bush from rocky habitats. The spathes are *solitary* at the tips of stems and the leaves are *flat*, ± *4 mm* wide, gradually tapering into the basal sheath. Mainly Pretoria/Magaliesberg region.

C. benghalensis L. (Benghal wandering Jew/Blouselblommetjie) usually has *long, reddish brown hairs* at the mouth of the leaf sheaths. It is a common, probably indigenous weed of disturbed places. Summer.

627 *Heliotropium amplexicaule*

628 *Buddleja salviifolia*

629 *Lightfootia denticulata*

630 *Wahlenbergia caledonica*

631 *Commelina diffusa*

632 *Commelina erecta*

633 *Commelina livingstonii*

634 Cyanotis speciosa (L.f.) Hassk.

Doll's powderpuff/Bloupoeierkwassie

Herb forming *basal* leaf clusters annually from a short perennial rootstock. Leaves with *lower* surface covered with *short*, ± *erect* (not appressed) hairs. Flowers on *erect* shoots; stamens *very hairy*.

Grassland. Widespread. Spring – summer.

C. lapidosa Phill. has leaves with *appressed* hairs on *both* surfaces, and *decumbent* flowering shoots. It forms spreading colonies on rocks, mainly in the Magaliesberg and Suikerbosrand.

635 Floscopa glomerata (Willd. ex Schult. & Schult. f.) Hassk.

Perennial herb with *sparsely branched*, decumbent stems; *rooting freely* from the lower nodes. Flowers small, sepals *densely covered with glandular hairs;* open only for a short period in the mornings.

Moist areas along streams, often in the water. Mainly Pretoria/Magaliesberg region. Summer.

CONVOLVULACEAE (See page 19)

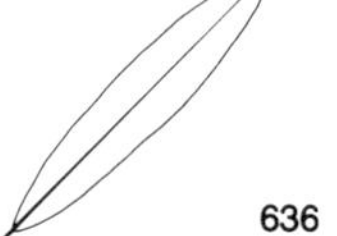

636

636 Evolvulus alsinoides (L.) L. var. **linifolius** (L.) Bak.

Slender, erect or ± *trailing* herb with a perennial taproot; covered with *silky hairs* throughout. Leaves ± *stalkless*. Flowers 6 – 8 mm in diameter, with *2* styles.

Bushveld and grassland, usually in sandy soil. Mainly Pretoria/Magaliesberg region. Summer.

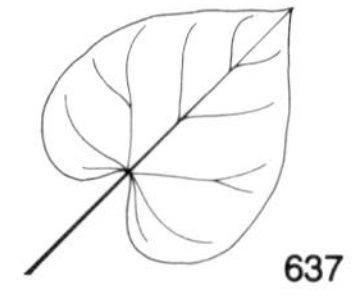

637

637 *Ipomoea purpurea (L.) Roth *Morning glory/Purperwinde*

Twining annual herb. Stems *hairy*. Leaves stalked; blade *broadly heart-shaped* with pointed tip; both surfaces sparsely covered with hairs. Inflorescences axillary, bearing 1 to a few flowers. Calyx with *bristly hairs* at the base. Corolla variable in colour: purplish blue with *reddish midpetaline areas*, pale purple, pink to white.

A native of tropical and subtropical America. Cultivated in gardens and now naturalized as a weed in disturbed places. Widespread. Summer – autumn. For pink-flowered form see **493**.

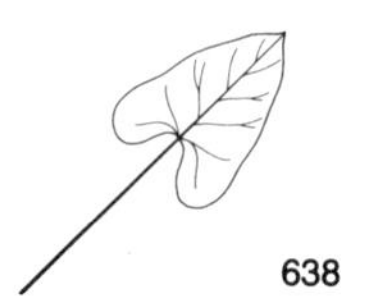

638

638 Ipomoea sinensis (Desr.) Choisy subsp. **blepharocephala** (Hochst. ex A. Rich.) Verdc.

Annual herb with trailing or twining stems. Leaves stalked, *distinctly heart-shaped* at the base. Flowers stalked, in *clusters* of up to 5 on the tips of slender inflorescence stalks *more than 10 mm* long; corolla ± 15 – 20 mm in diameter, ± twice as long as the calyx, pale mauve, often with darker mauve to magenta inside the tube; stigma *pale mauve*.

Bushveld. Pretoria/Magaliesberg region. Summer.

634 *Cyanotis speciosa*

635 *Floscopa glomerata*

636 *Evolvulus alsinoides*

637 *Ipomoea purpurea*

638 *Ipomoea sinensis*

EHRETIACEAE (See page 20)

639 Ehretia rigida (Thunb.) Druce *Puzzle-bush/Deurmekaarbo*

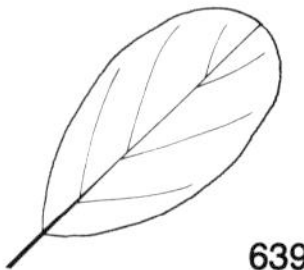

639

Irregularly branched, deciduous shrub or small tree; branches often *drooping*. Leaves sometimes clustered on *shortened* lateral shoots; often with *minute swellings* (domatia) in the axils of the lower pair of main side veins; margin closely fringed with minute *rough hairs* (use hand lens). Berries turn yellow as they ripen, then red and eventually black.

Bushveld, on ridges, and in bush clumps in grassland. Widespread. Spring.

FABACEAE (See page 20)

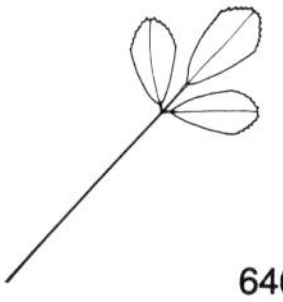

640 *Medicago sativa L. *Lucerne/Luser*

640

Herbaceous perennial *shrublet* with numerous erect branches arising at the crown of a woody taproot; ± *hairless*. Leaves trifoliolate; stalk with 2 lance-shaped stipules at the base; leaflets with margin smooth, or *finely toothed* towards the tip. Flowers congested in *cylindrical clusters* up to 40 mm long. Pods *coiled* 2 – 3 times into a spiral, smooth.

An escape from cultivation, often found along roadsides. A native of Europe and Asia. Widespread. Spring – autumn.

641 Mundulea sericea (Willd.) A. Chev. *Cork bush/Visgi*

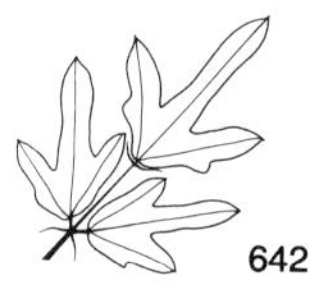

641

Shrub or *small tree* up to 5 m high; bark *thick*, light grey, furrowed and *very corky;* branchlets striate. Leaves *silver-grey* to light green; leaflets covered with *silky silver* hairs. Corolla with minute hairs covering back of standard. Pods flattened, densely covered with *golden brown* hairs.

Grassland and bushveld, usually associated with rocky outcrops or sandy soils. Widespread. Spring – summer.

642 Neorautanenia ficifolius (Benth.) C.A. Sm. *Blou-ertjie*

642

Perennial herb with *long creeping* branches from a large tuberous rootstock; most parts with spreading hairs; young growth covered with *silky hairs*. Leaves stalked, trifoliolate, with terminal leaflet *distinctly stalked;* leaflets ± *3-lobed*, subtended by conspicuous, *stipule-like outgrowths;* margins densely fringed with hairs. Flowers many, in axillary spikes; style with a *small bulge* at its junction with the ovary. Pods velvety.

Grassland, often in deep sandy soil. Mainly Pretoria/Magaliesberg region. Spring.

643 Otholobium polystictum (Benth. ex Harv.) C.H. Stirton [=**Psoralea polysticta** Benth. ex Harv.] *Vlieëbos*

643

Perennial *shrub* up to ± 1,5 m high. Stems covered with very *short white hairs*. Leaves ± *stalkless*, trifoliolate; leaflets with broad *rounded* tips, and conspicuous *gland dots* when viewed against the light (also visible as small pits, particularly on the lower surface); midrib ending in a short protuberance. Flowers ± stalkless, *clustered in axils* of upper leaves, pale blue. Pods almost *spherical*, ± 5 mm long, hairy.

Grassland, on rocky hillsides. Widespread. Spring – summer.

IRIDACEAE (See page 21)

644 Aristea woodii N.E.Br. *Blousuurkanol*

Herbaceous *evergreen* perennial with underground rhizome. Leaves in a basal *rosette*. Flowers in *dense clusters* along an erect flowering stem; bright blue, opening in the morning, fading soon afterwards.

Grassland, often on rocky ridges. Mainly Suikerbosrand. Summer.

645 Babiana hypogea Burch. var. **hypogea** *Bobbejaanuintjie*

Perennial herb with a corm which lies deep underground and has a long *fibrous* neck. Leaves dull green, *hairy*, distinctly *ribbed and pleated*. Flowers sweetly scented, produced *at ground level*.

Grassland, usually in sandy soil. Widespread. Summer – autumn.

639 *Ehretia rigida*

639 *E. rigida* (berries)

640 *Medicago sativa*

641 *Mundulea sericea*

642 *Neorautanenia ficifolius*

643 *Otholobium polystictum*

644 *Aristea woodii*

645 *Babiana hypogea*

646 Gladiolus pretoriensis Kuntze
Slender perennial herb; *hairless;* with a *single* basal leaf up to 500 mm long, *1 – 2 mm* wide. Leaf broadly H-shaped in cross-section. Inflorescence slender, *wiry*, bearing 4 – 9 flowers. Flowers dull purple or pink; lower side lobes with a *yellow blotch* outlined in *purple;* other lobes with a dark midrib.
Grassland, on stony hills; rare. Mainly Pretoria area. Summer.

647 Lapeirousia sandersonii Bak. *Autumn painted petals/Blou-angelie*
Erect perennial with corm which has a brown membranous covering. Leaves ± 4, the lowest up to 1 m long, the higher ones becoming progressively shorter. Inflorescence *much-branched*. Flowers have perianth lobes ± equal in size, with a *violet streak* on each of the lower 3 lobes; style branches *deeply* forked.
Rocky grassland. Mainly Pretoria/Magaliesberg region. Summer – autumn.

648 Moraea thomsonii Bak. [=**M. stricta** Bak.] *Bloutulp*
Herb with underground corm which has a covering of medium to coarse fibres. Leaf *single*, up to ± 600 mm long and 1,5 mm thick, *cylindrical*, usually absent at the time of flowering. Flowers open in the afternoon; similar to **648.1** but *not spotted in appearance*.
Grassland, often in moist places; sometimes a garden weed. Widespread. Winter – spring.
648.1 Gynandriris simulans (Bak.) R.C.Fost. (Vleibloutulp) is superficially very similar to the previous species. It has an underground corm with a covering of coarse fibres. Leaves 1 or 2, long, narrow (2 – 4 mm), *grooved*. Flowers open mid-afternoon and fade by evening; perianth segments mauve with *darker spots* and a *yellow spot;* style branches *flattened* with paired crests. Grassland, usually in vleis. Mainly Witwatersrand/Suikerbosrand region. Spring.

LAMIACEAE (See page 22)
649 Ajuga ophrydis Burch. ex Benth.
Small herb with several erect annual stems from a short perennial rhizome. Leaves usually in a *basal rosette;* blade ± *thick;* margin with a *few coarse teeth*, tip *blunt or rounded*. Flowers pale blue or rarely white.
Grassland, often in colonies. Mainly Witwatersrand/Suikerbosrand region. Spring – summer.

649

650 Becium obovatum (E. Mey. ex Benth.) N.E.Br. var. **obovatum**
Small shrublet with several herbaceous stems arising annually from a woody rootstock. Leaves almost smooth to densely covered with hairs. Inflorescence with flowers crowded near the tip. Corolla *10 – 16 mm* long, upper lip usually with longitudinal *violet lines*, rarely pure white.
Common in grassland. Widespread. Spring.
For white-flowered form see **97**.

650

651 Hemizygia canescens (Guerke) Ashby
Erect herbaceous shrublet with most parts aromatic and covered with unbranched hairs. Leaves with blade *densely covered* with *greyish* hairs on both surfaces. Flowers white, pale mauve to purplish; stamens *protruding* beyond the lower lip, filaments of the lower pair *united* for most of their length; stigma *club-shaped*.
Rocky grassland. Widespread. Summer – autumn.

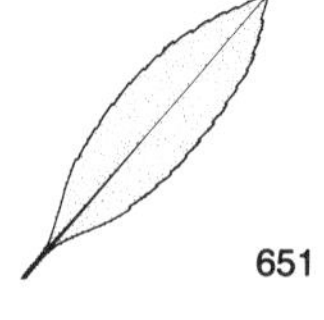
651

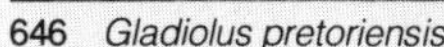

646 *Gladiolus pretoriensis*

647 *Lapeirousia sandersonii*

648 *Moraea thomsonii*

648.1 *Gynandriris simulans*

649 *Ajuga ophrydis*

650 *Becium obovatum*

651 *Hemizygia canescens*

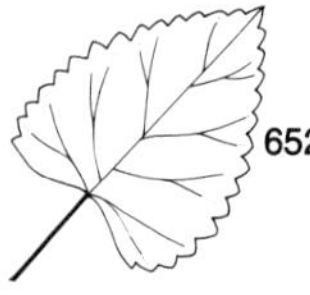
652

652 Plectranthus hereroensis Engl.
Herbaceous shrublet up to 1 m high; stem usually solitary, branching above. Leaves distinctly stalked; blade egg-shaped with minute *reddish to brownish glands* on the lower surface; margin toothed. Corolla with lower lip forming a *deep boat-shape;* pale to deep blue, rarely white.
Rocky and usually wooded hillsides. Widespread. Summer – autumn.

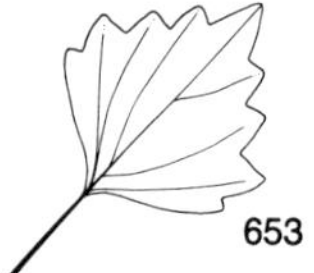
653

653 Plectranthus madagascariensis (Pers.) Benth. var. **ramosior** Benth.
Semi-succulent perennial shrublet; *aromatic*. Leaves 20 – 40 mm long with *scallop-toothed* margin; stippled with minute reddish brown glands on the lowe surface. Flowers with upper sepal of the mature calyx *much broader* than other sepals; corolla white or pale mauve with purplish markings on the upper lip.
Rocky grassland, often on dolomite. Widespread. Summer – autumn. Also **99**.

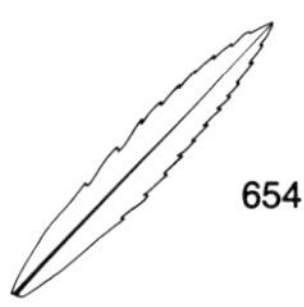
654

654 Pycnostachys reticulata (E. Mey.) Benth.
Erect, *sparsely* branched shrublet. Leaves not distinctly stalked; margin *toothed*. Flowers in *dense*, terminal, *spike-like* inflorescences; subtended by 5 *rigid*, *spine-like* sepals.
Moist places in grassland. Widespread. Summer – autumn.

655

655 Salvia runcinata L.f. *Wildesali*
Erect perennial herb with stems and leaves minutely *gland-dotted*. Stems *hairy* Leaves usually *deeply incised*, covered with *rough* hairs and *aromatic* when crushed. Flowers with corolla pale blue to white, 7 – 14 mm long.
Grassland and under trees, often in vleis, disturbed places or overgrazed veld. Widespread. Spring – summer.
Very similar to **S. repens** Burch. ex Benth. (Kruipsalie) which usually has a more pronounced *creeping* rootstock, and to **S. stenophylla** Burch. ex Benth. which has almost *smooth* stems and sometimes *undivided* leaves.

LENTIBULARIACEAE (See page 22)

656

656 Genlisea hispidula Stapf subsp. **hispidula**
Herb usually with both foliage leaves and *pitcher leaves;* rootless, but with root-like stalks of pitcher leaves. Foliage leaves in a *rosette* at the base. Pitche leaves densely congested on lower part of the stem, stalked, descending into the substrate, colourless, slender, tubular, with 2 ribbon-like, *spirally-twisted arms* at the tip; tube with transverse bands of inwardly directed hairs. Flowers blue, with a greenish or yellowish *spur*.
Marshy places. Mainly Magaliesberg. Summer.

LILIACEAE (Excluding Alliaceae; see page 22)

657 Drimiopsis burkei Bak.
Small bulbous plants. Leaves 2 – 4, ± *flat* on the ground, semi-succulent, *narrowed* at the base, often *mottled* above (particularly towards the base) and *purplish* below. Flowers on short stalks, crowded on a short raceme; inner 3 perianth segments *erect* with *incurled* tips; purple, pale mauve or greenish white.
Grassland, usually in stony places. Widespread. Spring.

652 *Plectranthus hereroensis*

653 *Plectranthus madagascariensis*

654 *Pycnostachys reticulata*

655 *Salvia runcinata*

656 *Genlisea hispidula*

657 *Drimiopsis burkei*

658 Ledebouria cooperi (Hook.f.) Jessop
Bulbous herb. Leaves 1 – 4, *erect* and *clasping at the base;* with brownish purple markings; margin often reddish. Perianth segments often *uniformly coloured* (usually pink, but also mauve, greenish or white).
Grassland, often in moist places. Widespread. Spring.

659 Ledebouria ovatifolia (Bak.) Jessop
Bulbous plant. Leaves *oval*, with a stalk-like base, *firmly appressed* to the soil surface; usually with *purple spots* above and purplish below; sometimes absent at the time of flowering. Inflorescence usually *curved outwards* (lower part of stalk often flat on the ground with the upper part erect); perianth segments purplish green.
Grassland. Widespread. Spring.

660 Ledebouria revoluta (L.f.) Jessop
Bulbous herb. Leaves ± erect, *more than 15 mm* wide, ± *soft in texture; drop* soon after drying out; *with or without* purple spots. Inflorescence up to 200 mm long. Flowers mauve or greenish.
Grassland. Widespread. Spring.
L. marginata (Bak.) Jessop is similar but has ± *firm* leaves which *persist for a long time* after drying out; the tips are often *twisted* in the upper half.

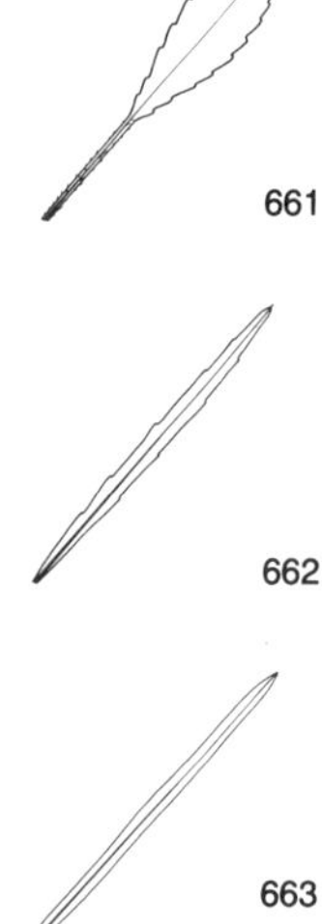
661 662 663 664

LOBELIACEAE (See page 22)
661 Lobelia erinus L. [=**L. nuda** Hemsl.] *Wild lobelia*
Small, *slender*, erect *annual* herb. Leaves towards base sometimes ± forming a *rosette;* blade usually 4 – 20 mm wide, narrowing into a stalk-like base or with stalks up to 15 mm long. Stigma lobes *short and broad*, surrounded by a ring of pollen-collecting hairs.
Seasonally wet places in grassland, often forming extensive stands. Widespread. Spring.

662 Lobelia flaccida (Presl.) A.DC. subsp. **flaccida**
Slender, erect annual or short-lived perennial herb up to ± 500 mm high. Stems often *narrowly winged*. Leaves *well-spaced*, stalkless, narrow; margin *toothed*. Flowers widely spaced on elongated terminal axes; corolla with *2 bumps* at the mouth of the tube, lower lip 3-lobed and much larger than the upper.
Grassland, usually in moist places. Widespread. Summer.

663 Monopsis decipiens (Sond.) Thulin [=**Lobelia decipiens** Sond.]
Erect, sparsely branched herb. Leaves ± numerous and densely set, linear (0,8 – 2 mm wide), with *sharp, coarse hairs* mainly along the margin and the midrib of the lower surface. Stigma lobes *linear*, with a ring of pollen-collecting hairs *well below* them.
Grassland, usually in seasonally wet places. Widespread. Spring – summer.

MELIACEAE (See page 23)
664 *Melia azedarach L. *Syringa/Sering*
Medium-sized *deciduous* tree. Leaves bipinnately compound; leaflets with *deeply toothed* margins, *unpleasantly scented* when crushed. Flowers borne in large, showy, axillary panicles, often before the new leaves are fully expanded; petals *pale lilac;* stamen tube *dark purple*. Drupes globose, pale yellow.
Native to a large area extending from India to Australia. Naturalized in disturbed places and along streams. Widespread. Spring.

658 *Ledebouria cooperi*

659 *Ledebouria ovatifolia*

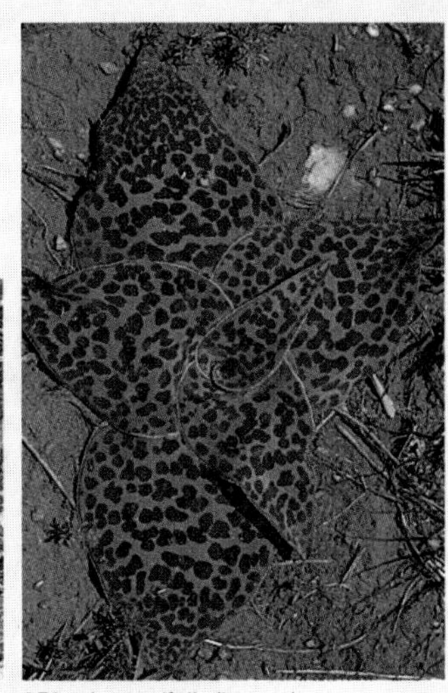

659 *L. ovatifolia* (leaves)

660 *Ledebouria revoluta*

661 *Lobelia erinus*

662 *Lobelia flaccida*

663 *Monopsis decipiens*

664 *Melia azedarach*

ORCHIDACEAE (See page 24)
665 Eulophia clavicornis Lindl. var. **clavicornis**
Perennial herb with a rhizome resembling a *string of beads*. Leaves *absent or partly developed* at the time of flowering. Flowers with a *cylindrical* spur and the petals broader than the sepals.
Grassland, often in rocky places. Widespread. Spring.
Var. **inaequalis** (Schltr.) A.V. Hall has *bright yellow* flowers (see **405**).

PERIPLOCACEAE (See page 25)
666 Raphionacme hirsuta (E. Mey.) R.A. Dyer ex Phill.
Khadi-root/Khadiworte
Decumbent perennial herb, sprouting annual shoots from a continuation of a large, often flattened and ± round, *underground tuber*. Leaves on short stalks, *broadly elliptic* to almost *rounded*, ending in a sharp point; venation lighter than main colour and *clearly visible; almost hairless* above, but with short spreading hairs below. Flowers on new growth, often before the appearance of leaves; corolla lobes blunt.
Grassland. Widespread. Spring.

666

POLYGALACEAE (See page 26)
667 Polygala amatymbica Eckl. & Zeyh.
Small, tufted herb from a woody taproot. Leaves *oval or elliptic* with a sharp point, almost stalkless. Flowers borne between the leaves, solitary or in few-flowered racemes; 2 of the 5 sepals enlarged and *not distinctly* veined.
Common in grassland. Widespread. Spring.

667

668 Polygala uncinata E. Mey. ex Meisn. *Wild violet/Wildeviooltjie*
Perennial herb with semi-erect, *sparsely branched* annual stems from a woody rootstock. Leaves with the tip usually *rounded and sharply hooked*. Flowers in *terminal*, few-flowered racemes; the 2 petal-like sepals with dark *purple veins on the outer surface* (conspicuous in bud), deep violet on the inner surface; 2 front sepals united.
Grassland, particularly on rocky ridges. Widespread. Spring – summer. Compare **581**.

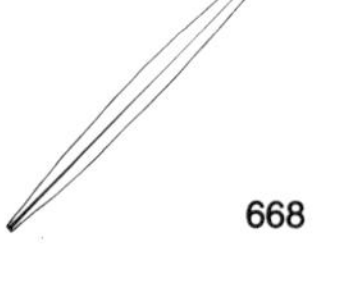

668

PONTEDERIACEAE (See page 26)
669 *Eichornia crassipes (Mart.) Solms-Laub.
Water hyacinth/Waterhiasint
Evergreen perennial aquatic herb with *long feathery* roots; free-floating or rooting in shallow water; multiplies rapidly by means of runners. Leaves with lower portion of stalk *conspicuously swollen;* blade ± *rounded*. Flowers borne on an erect axis; perianth with uppermost lobe displaying a *dark blue and yellow* patch.
A weed of aquatic habitats, often floating in masses on dams and streams. Native to South America. Widespread. Summer.

RUBIACEAE (See page 27)
670 Pentanisia angustifolia (Hochst.) Hochst.
Trailing to erect shrublet from a fleshy rootstock; usually *hairless*. Leaves stalkless, long and *narrow* (3 – 10 mm). Flowers borne in compact heads at tips of long stalks; corolla thinly covered with down.
Grassland. Widespread. Spring – summer. ☐ Compare **671**.

671 Pentanisia prunelloides (Eckl. & Zeyh.) Walp.
Wild verbena/Sooibrandbossie
Trailing to erect shrublet from a fleshy rootstock; most parts with *downy hairs*. Leaves stalkless, usually *broadly oval* (10 – 30 mm wide). Inflorescence a many-flowered head on a long stalk.
Grassland. Widespread. Spring – summer. ☐ Compare **670**.

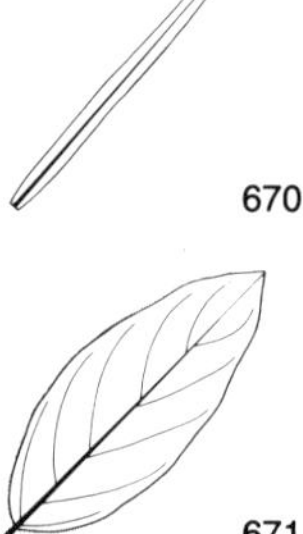

670

671

665 *Eulophia clavicornis* var. *clavicornis*

666 *Raphionacme hirsuta*

667 *Polygala amatymbica*

668 *Polygala uncinata*

669 *Eichornia crassipes*

670 *Pentanisia angustifolia*

671 *Pentanisia prunelloides*

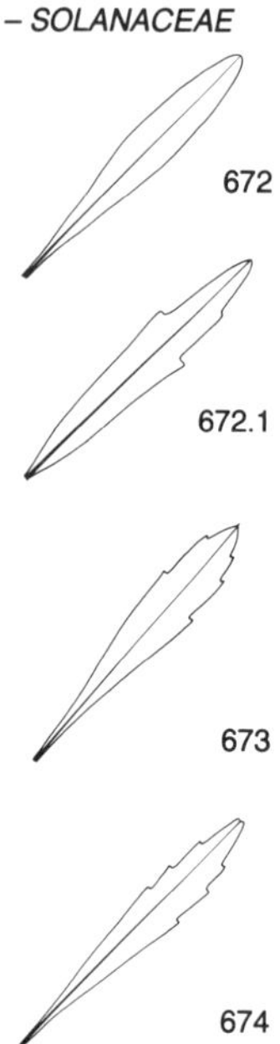

SCROPHULARIACEAE (See page 28) See also **166**.

672 Buchnera longespicata Schinz

Small bushy herb with several erect stems. Leaves stalkless, narrow, ± fleshy, *rough* to the touch, particularly on the lower surface. Inflorescence terminal. Flowers *stalkless* in *opposite* pairs; corolla tube cylindrical, *slightly curved*, lobes ± *equal* in size. Capsule ± ellipsoid, straight, enclosed by the calyx tube.

Marshy grassland. Mainly Pretoria/Magaliesberg region. Spring.

672.1 B. reducta Hiern is an erect *unbranched* herb up to 300 mm high. Leaves at base ± 15 mm wide; margin smooth or slightly toothed. Flowers *smaller* than in the previous species, *deep blue;* calyx tube with rough hairs on the outer surface. A hemi-rootparasite; marshy grassland. Widespread. Summer – autumn.

673 Sutera caerulea (L.f.) Hiern *Ruikbossie*

Bushy perennial herb; *strongly aromatic* when crushed. Stems ± *erect*. Leaves stalkless, gradually tapering to the base; margin with a few *widely spaced* teeth. Flower-bearing stems *not zigzag*. Corolla pale blue or pinkish with a *bright yellow* centre.

Grassland, mainly on ridges and often wedged between rocks. Widespread. Summer. □ Compare **674**.

674 Sutera palustris Hiern

Bushy *aromatic* herb. Stems usually forming *tangled clumps*. Leaves simple and narrow with untoothed or toothed margins. Flower-bearing stems *zigzag*. Flowers mauve or whitish with a yellow centre.

Grassland, particularly rocky places. Widespread. Summer. Compare **673**.

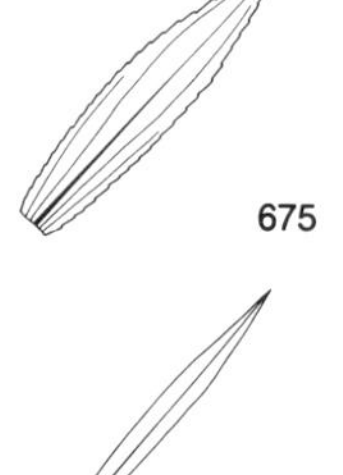

675 Veronica anagallis-aquatica L.

Annual or short-lived perennial herb, often rooting at the lower nodes. Stems ± fleshy, *hollow*, often with a reddish tinge. Leaves stalkless, *stem-clasping* at the base. Flowers in *long axillary racemes* towards the ends of stems; corolla pale blue with *purplish stripes*. Capsules surrounded by the persistent calyx.

Moist and often shady places, mainly along streams. Widespread. Spring – autumn.

SELAGINACEAE (See page 28)

676 Selago capitellata Schltr. *Blou-aarbossie*

Shrublet with erect and decumbent branches from a woody rootstock. Leaves numerous, *densely crowded*, often in tufts; stalkless. Flowers clustered in *small heads*, pale blue to white.

Grassland, particularly on rocky ridges. Widespread. Summer.

SOLANACEAE (See page 28)

677 *Datura stramonium L. *Thorn apple/Olieboom*

Robust herbaceous annual up to ± 1 m high. Leaves stalked, egg-shaped; margin *coarsely and distantly* toothed or ± lobed; give off an *unpleasant smell* when crushed. Flowers solitary, axillary; calyx up to 40 mm long; corolla funnel-shaped with *5 prominent teeth* on the rim; white to mauve-purple. Capsules covered with *relatively short* spreading spines up to *10 mm* long.

A weed of disturbed places and cultivated land. A native of North America. Widespread. Summer. □ For white-flowered form see **171**.

672 *Buchnera longespicata*

672.1 *B. reducta*

673 *Sutera caerulea*

674 *Sutera palustris*

675 *Veronica anagallis-aquatica*

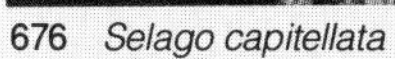

676 *Selago capitellata*

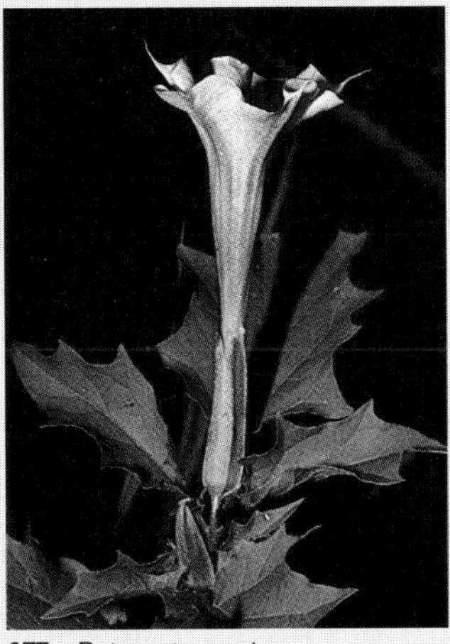

677 *Datura stramonium*

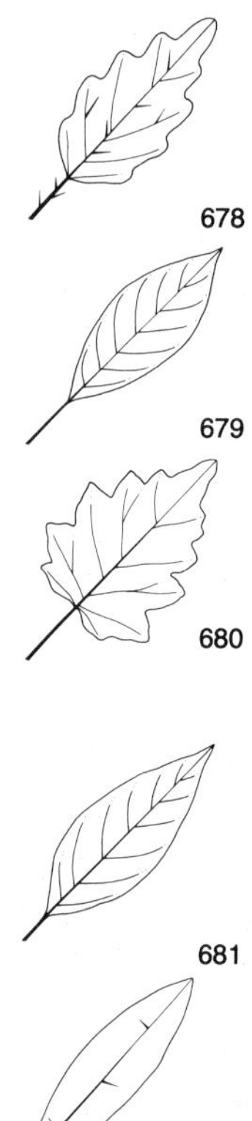

678 *Solanum elaeagnifolium Cav. *Silverleaf bitter apple/Satansbos*
Much-branched perennial shrublet from a woody rootstock; generally up to ± 300 mm high; armed with *numerous reddish prickles* on the stems and on the stalk and midrib of leaves. Leaves stalked, densely covered with *whitish or silvery felt* on lower surface; margin smooth or slightly wavy. Flowers borne on short woolly stalks towards the tips of branches. Berries globose, *yellow*.
A native of North America, now a troublesome weed. Widespread. Spring – summer. □ Compare **682**.

679 Solanum giganteum Jacq. *Goat bitter apple/Geneesblaarboom*
Soft-wooded shrub up to 2 m high, with *prickles* on branches. Leaves *thinly covered with downy hairs* above, densely covered with *white velvety hairs* below; margin smooth. Inflorescences terminal. Berries *bright red* when ripe.
Rocky areas. Mainly Pretoria/Magaliesberg region. Summer.

680 Solanum incanum L. *Bitter apple/Bitterappel*
Perennial shrublet with *prickles* on branches and leaves. Leaves *dark green* above, covered with *greyish white felt* below; margin *deeply lobed*. Flowers few in *axillary* clusters. Fruit yellow when ripe, resembling a small tomato.
Grassland. Widespread. Spring – autumn.

681 *Solanum mauritianum Scop. *Bugweed/Luisboom*
Soft-wooded perennial *shrub or small tree* up to ± 4 m high; most parts with *greyish velvety*, star-shaped hairs; *unarmed*. Leaves stalked, lower surface densely covered with whitish felt; margin *smooth;* stalks subtended by conspicuous *egg-shaped lobes*. Flowers in dense *terminal* clusters. Berries globose, densely covered with *star-shaped hairs*, *yellow* when ripe.
A native of South America, now a weed, particularly of disturbed wooded areas and along streams. Widespread. Autumn – winter.

682 Solanum panduriforme E. Mey. *Poison apple/Gifappel*
Perennial shrublet from a rootstock deep underground; usually *unarmed*. Leaves hairy, particularly below; both surfaces ± *alike in colour;* blade lance-shaped; margin smooth. Fruit ± 20 mm across, fleshy and *yellow* when ripe.
Grassland. Widespread. Spring – summer. □ Compare **678**.

683 Solanum rigescens Jacq. *Wildelemoentjie*
Shrublet with *straight long yellow spines* on stems and leaves, including the midrib and main side veins. Leaves *hairy on both* surfaces, with the margin *lobed*. Flowers often *clustered* together on the flowering stalk. Berries *scarlet*.
Grassland. Widespread. Summer.

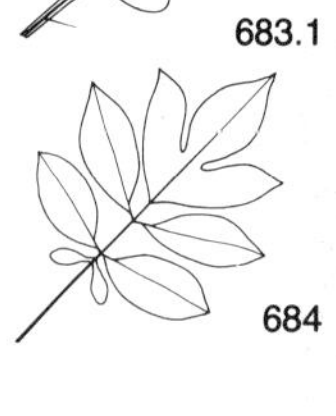

683.1 S. supinum Dun. has the leaves smaller, less spiny and often more *deeply lobed*. Flowers *solitary*. Berries *yellow* with the persistent calyx lobes *very spiny*, relatively *wide* and *joined* towards the base.

684 *Solanum seaforthianum Andr. *Potato creeper*
Herbaceous *creeper*. Leaves *deeply dissected*, often *unevenly compound* with 2 – 4 pairs of *opposite* leaflets at the base. Inflorescence *terminal*, comprising many well-spaced flowers. Fruits bright *red*.
Clumps of bush. Mainly Pretoria/Magaliesberg region. Summer.

685 *Solanum sisymbrifolium Lam. *Wild tomato/Doringbitterappel*
Perennial *bushy shrublet* up to 1,5 m high. Stems densely covered with thin, *straight, reddish brown spines* up to 30 mm long. Leaves deeply *pinnately lobed*, with star-shaped hairs and *straight, red-brown spines*, particularly on the midrib and stalk. Corolla white to pale bluish. Berries *bright red*, subtended by the enlarged spiny calyx (which enclosed the very young fruit).
A weed of disturbed places. Native to South America. Widespread. Summer – autumn. □ For white-flowered form see **174**.

678 *Solanum elaeagnifolium*

679 *Solanum giganteum*

680 *Solanum incanum*

681 *Solanum mauritianum*

682 *Solanum panduriforme*

683 *Solanum rigescens*

684 *Solanum seaforthianum*

685 *Solanum sisymbrifolium*

686

STERCULIACEAE (See page 28) See also **731** and **602**.

686 Hermannia coccocarpa (Eckl. & Zeyh.) Kuntze *Moederkappie*
Sprawling twiggy shrublet from a woody perennial taproot; covered with short *glandular hairs* throughout. Leaves on short stalks; margin *coarsely toothed*, often reddish. Inflorescences on long slender stalks near the ends of shoots, *2-flowered*. Flowers *pendulous*, purple-mauve, pinkish, red or rarely white. Capsules *oblong*, relatively large.
Grassland. Widespread. Spring – autumn.

VELLOZIACEAE (See page 29)

687 Xerophyta retinervis Bak. *Monkey's tail/Bobbejaanstert*
Perennial with stout, sometimes sparsely branched, erect stems which are densely covered with a thick mantle of fire-charred, *closely packed persistent leaf bases*, and have inside numerous densely packed roots (the basal part of the true stem dies off at an early stage and is replaced by the roots). Flowers usually blue or mauve, rarely white. Capsules covered with rough *hairs*.
Rocky ridges. Widespread. Spring. □ For white-flowered form see **176**.

VERBENACEAE (See page 29)

688

688 Clerodendrum triphyllum (Harv.) H. Pearson var. **triphyllum**
Herbaceous shrublet from a perennial rootstock; almost hairless to densely covered with hairs. Leaves mostly in *whorls of 3*, stalkless and ± fleshy. Flowers in slender, few-flowered inflorescences in axils of most leaves; distinctly *2-lipped*.
Grassland. Widespread. Spring.

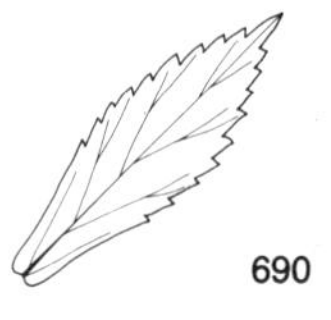
689

689 Lantana rugosa Thunb. *Bird's brandy*
Much-branched perennial shrublet up to ± 1 m high, covered with *rough hairs*. Leaves with veins sunken in upper surface but prominent on lower. Flowers in *dense heads*. Fruits fleshy and *purple*.
Common in clumps of bush and on rocky ridges, usually in shady places. Widespread. Summer.

690

690 *Verbena bonariensis L. *Wild verbena/Blouwaterbossie*
Erect, *sparsely branched* herb up to ± 2 m high; covered with *rough hairs*. Leaves *stalkless* and ± clasping at the base; margin toothed. Inflorescences terminal, *congested*, *more robust* in appearance than those of **V. brasiliensis**.
A common weed of disturbed and often moist places; native to South America. Widespread. Summer. □ Compare **691**.

691

691 *Verbena brasiliensis Vell.
Erect, *sparsely branched* herb up to ± 1,5 m high; covered with *rough hairs*. Leaves *distinctly stalked* or with the base narrowly tapering; margin sharply *toothed*. Inflorescences *slender and smaller* than in **V. bonariensis**.
A native of South America and now a common weed of disturbed and moist places. Widespread. Summer. □ Compare **690**.
***V. officinalis** L. (European verbena/Europese verbena), a common weed of European origin, is similar but has *deeply lobed* or *pinnately divided* lower leaves. The flowers are ± well-spaced on *long*, narrow, terminal spikes. Widespread in disturbed places.

692

692 *Verbena tenuisecta Briq. *Fine-leaved verbena/Fynblaarverbena*
Prostrate to ± erect herb from a perennial rootstock. Leaves *deeply bipinnate or tripinnate;* both surfaces hairy, especially along the midrib of the lower surface; clasping at the base. Flowers in dense terminal spikes which lengthen during the fruiting stage; bright mauve, fading to blue or often white.
A weed from South America. Common in disturbed places, particularly along roadsides. Widespread. Spring – summer.

686 *Hermannia coccocarpa*

687 *Xerophyta retinervis*

688 *Clerodendrum triphyllum*

689 *Lantana rugosa*

690 *Verbena bonariensis*

691 *Verbena brasiliensis*

692 *Verbena tenuisecta*

ORANGE TO BROWN OR RED-BROWN FLOWERS

(See also **150, 192, 315, 344, 365, 381 – 384, 439, 472, 508, 606, 760**)

This group comprises an assemblage of species with relatively uncommon floral colours. Some of the paler orange flowers grade into yellow, and if an orange flower is not in this part of the book it is likely to be found in the section on Yellow or cream flowers (page 92), particularly among the Malvaceae entries. Species with a true orange colouring are rare. Also in this section are brown flowers, some of which grade into white or green, and red-brown (maroon) to almost black flowers.

Orange colours are often due to the presence of carotenoid pigments in the cells of the petals. The darker brownish and maroon colours may be the result of several pigments such as the carotenoids, anthocyanins and chlorophyll occurring together in the same cell or in different cell layers lying on top of one another.

Flowers in this colour group are visited by a large variety of insects, including bees and wasps. Moths may pollinate some of the tubular brownish flowers (**720** and **721**), and flies are attracted to the carrion smell of the brownish red members of the Asclepiadaceae family (**694 – 697**), the colours of which are probably similar to those of rotting meat. Birds' sensitivity to red flowers is not exclusive, and some of the tubular and nectar-rich orange flowers are very popular with sunbirds (**716 – 718** and **726**). To insects orange may appear red to purple. Brownish colours are not particularly attractive to them and many such flowers appear to rely on scent to attract pollinators, especially moths at night. Members of the Cyperaceae and Typhaceae are pollinated by wind rather than by insects.

GUIDE TO THE FAMILIES WHICH INCLUDE ORANGE TO BROWN OR RED-BROWN FLOWERS

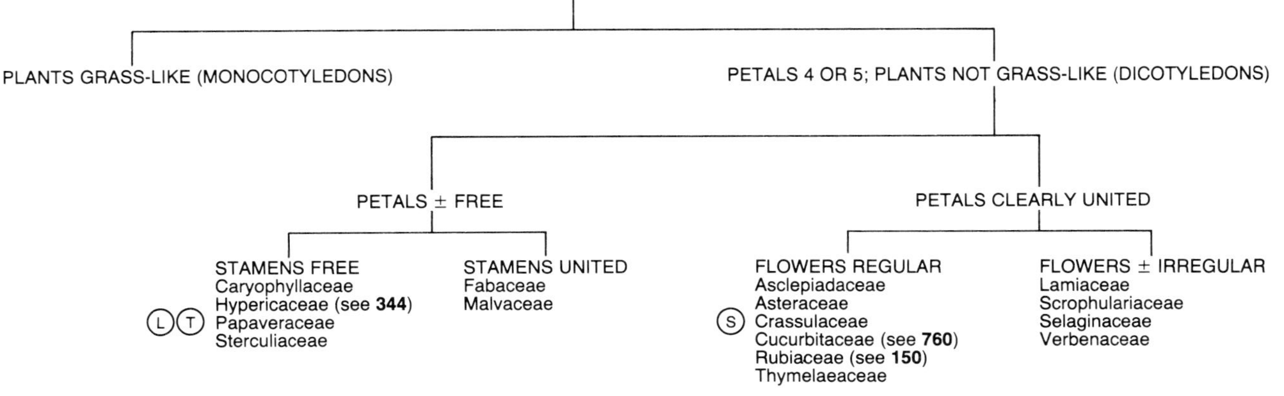

(L) At least some members with *milky latex*
(S) At least some members *succulent*
(T) At least some members with *thorns/spines*

ALLIACEAE (See page 16)

693 Tulbaghia acutiloba Harv. *Wild garlic/Wildeknoffel*

Perennial herb from an underground bulb-like corm, sometimes with a *faint* smell of garlic. Leaves long, narrow (2 – 5 mm), folded and ± V-shaped in cross-section, often produced *after* flowering. Flowers pendulous, with perianth segments *strongly reflexed;* corona *very indistinctly* 3-lobed, orange, light brown to purplish.

Grassland. Widespread. Early spring.

T. leucantha Bak. is barely distinguishable from the previous species. Leaves narrow (up to 2 mm), produced at the same time as the flowers. Flowers with perianth segments *not strongly* reflexed; corona ± *3-lobed*, orange. Grassland, usually in moist places.

ASCLEPIADACEAE (See page 17) See also **192**.

694 Brachystelma barberiae Harv. ex Hook.f. *Platvoetaasblom*

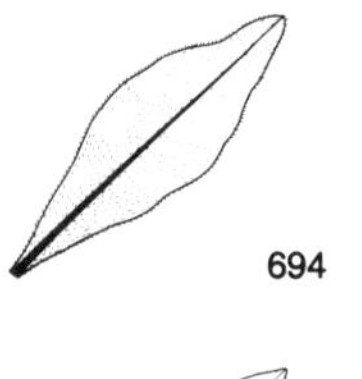

694

Perennial herb with short annual shoots from a ± *disc-shaped* underground tuber; covered with *coarse* hairs; sap *watery*. Leaves on short stalks, up to 100 x 25 mm. Flowers up to 50 in 1 large, stalkless, *spherical mass* on the ground, unpleasantly scented, sometimes appearing before the leaves; corolla tube bell-shaped, inner surface with crimson-brown bands on a yellowish background; lobes slender, *united at the tips* into a cage-like structure, greenish outside, maroon to crimson-brown on the inner face.

Grassland; rare. Widespread. Spring.

695 Brachystelma foetidum Schltr. *Hottentot's bread/Hottentotsbrood*

695

Perennial herb with 1 to several annual stems from a large, disc-shaped underground tuber; *hairy; watery* sap present. Leaves on short stalks; blade usually ± *folded upwards* along the midrib; margin often ± *wavy*. Flowers purple-brown to nearly black, with a *putrid* smell.

Grassland; rare. Widespread. Spring – summer.

696 Huernia hystrix (Hook.f.) N.E.Br. var. **hystrix** *Porcupine huernia/Ystervark-huernia*

Tufted *succulent*. Stems erect, leafless, with *4 – 5 angles*, hairless; ridges with sharply *pointed teeth*. Flowers few, appearing towards the base of stems and opening consecutively; corolla tube *bowl-shaped;* lobes 5, broadly triangular, alternating with 5 distinct *short points*, spotted dull reddish brown, densely covered with short, tapering, *erect bristles*.

Rocky ridges, growing in dense clusters. Widespread. Summer.

697 Stapelia leendertziae N.E.Br. *Bell stapelia/Aasklok*

Tufted *succulent*. Stems erect, leafless, covered with *velvety hairs, 4-angled;* ridges with soft teeth. Flowers large, with a prominent *bell-shaped* tube (about 80 mm long); corolla smooth on the outer surface, wrinkled and velvety inside, deep maroon or blackish purple, foul-smelling.

Rocky places, growing in large patches, often beneath woody vegetation; rare. Suikerbosrand. Summer.

693 *Tulbaghia acutiloba*

694 *Brachystelma barberiae*

695 *Brachystelma foetidum*

696 *Huernia hystrix*

697 *Stapelia leendertziae*

ASTERACEAE (See page 17)
Group A ✱ See also **472**.

698 *Tithonia rotundifolia (Mill.) Blake *Red sunflower*

698

Robust annual herb up to ± 2 m high, with well-spaced branches. Leaves stalked, ± egg-shaped, covered with rough hairs; margin smooth or deeply 3-lobed. Flower heads terminate branches; inflorescence stalk *distinctly swollen* and *hollow* just below the heads; corolla of ray flowers bright orange-red above, golden yellow below.

A weed native to South America. Disturbed and waste places, usually near habitation. Widespread. Autumn – winter.

ASTERACEAE (See page 17)
Group B

699 Dicoma macrocephala DC.

699

Perennial herb with *prostrate* or spreading stems from a woody rootstock. Leaves ± stalked, *elliptic;* ± hairless and *greyish green* above, *white-felted* below. Flower heads solitary at the ends of branches, stalkless, elongated and tapering, *open at night;* involucral bracts often with a purplish tinge, tips bristly, separated from disc flowers by a dense whorl of long brownish bristles; disc flowers much shorter than the involucral bracts. Seeds with tufts of long, stiff, straight hairs.

Grassland. Widespread. Spring – summer.

700 Stoebe vulgaris Levyns *Bankrupt bush/Bankrotbos*

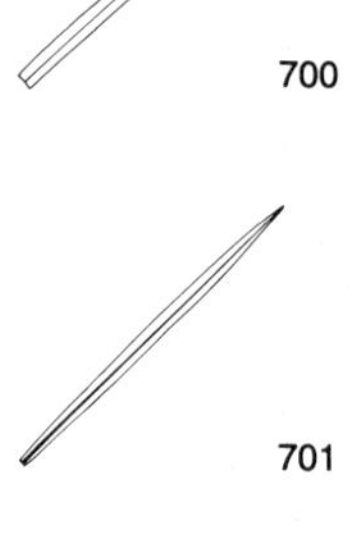

700

701

Intricately branched, greyish perennial shrublet; branches slender and wiry, with numerous tufts of *small, heath-like* leaves (up to 4 x 0,5 mm). Leaves with upper surfaces covered with *white woolly hairs.* Flower heads minute, surrounded by *brownish yellow* inner involucral bracts; arranged in large panicles. Flowers inconspicuous, purple-tipped. Characteristic *globose galls covered with white woolly hairs* are usually present and frequently mistaken for the flower heads.

Grassland, proliferating in overgrazed areas. Widespread. Spring – autumn. For flower-like galls see **49**.

CARYOPHYLLACEAE (See page 18)

701 Polycarpaea corymbosa (L.) Lam.

Erect annual herb. Stems *wiry* and very sparsely branched, usually with *whitish* hairs. Leaves appear to be in *whorls* at well-spaced nodes, with numerous *thin, membranous* basal scales; silvery green. Inflorescence many-flowered, ± *flat-topped.*

Grassland, mainly in shallow soil on rocky ridges. Widespread. Summer.

CRASSULACEAE (See page 19)

702 Kalanchoe rotundifolia (Haw.) Haw. *Nentabos*

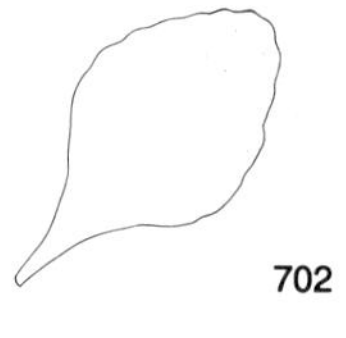

702

Erect and sparsely branched *succulent* herb. Leaves elliptical to rounded, sometimes slightly lobed; *blue-green* with a *whitish bloom.* Flowers borne in a ± flat-topped inflorescence on a long erect stalk; *4* of each floral part; corolla tubular, *twisting* with age, orange-red.

Grassland and bushveld; shady positions, often forming dense stands among rocks or under trees or shrubs. Widespread. Autumn. □ Also **501**.

698 *Tithonia rotundifolia*

699 *Dicoma macrocephala*

700 *Stoebe vulgaris*

701 *Polycarpaea corymbosa*

702 *Kalanchoe rotundifolia*

CYPERACEAE (See page 19)

703 Bulbostylis burchellii (Fical. & Hiern) C.B.Cl.
Tufted, grass-like perennial herb. Leaves all arising from near base of stems, *very numerous*, erect, *thread-like*, hairless except for whitish hairs at the base; old leaves dry to yellowish brown. Inflorescence stalks slender, erect; spikelets pale brown, *cylindrical*, with *spirally overlapping* bracts, arranged terminally in ± congested clusters on slender branching stalks.
Grassland, very common on rocky ridges. Spring – summer.

704 Coleochloa setifera (Ridley) Gilly
Densely tufted perennial herb. Leaves mainly basal, slender and *very tough*. Inflorescences ± sparse, borne near tips of stems, comprise small but dense clusters of few spikelets on stalks.
Rocky ridges, often in seepage areas. Mainly Pretoria/Magaliesberg region. Summer.

705 *Cyperus esculentus L. *Yellow nutsedge/Geeluintjie*
Erect hairless herb; rhizomes producing ± globose tubers at the tips. Stems *3-angled*. Leaves grass-like, *shiny*. Inflorescence a terminal compound umbel subtended by 3 – 5 *leaf-like* bracts; spikelets arranged along axis up to 20 mm long, compressed, light brown or yellowish brown.
A troublesome weed of disturbed places; probably exotic. Widespread. Summer.
***C. rotundus** L. (Purple nutsedge/Rooiuintjie) is a closely allied species characterized by stems *thickened* at the base and *red-brown* inflorescences.

706 Cyperus rupestris Kunth var. **rupestris**
Densely tufted, dwarf perennial herb; hairless; roots fibrous, very numerous. Leaves basal, erect, *thread-like* (1 mm wide), ± cylindrical, tapering to a sharp point. Spikelets clustered in *solitary* heads at tips of ± cylindrical erect stems, *flattened*, dark rusty brown, subtended by up to 3 *thread-like* bracts.
Rock sheets, usually in shallow soil at the edges of rain pools. Widespread. Summer.

707 Mariscus congestus (Vahl) C.B.Cl.
Erect *unbranched* perennial herb up to ± 1,3 m high. Stems robust, *3-angled*, hairless. Leaves few, basal, 6 – 10 mm wide, with a *narrow groove* on upper surface. Inflorescence terminal, subtended by up to 10 *unequal* leaf-like bracts; spikelets very numerous, densely congested in ± *globose* to short *cylindrical* spikes, *flattened*, ± 2 mm wide, dark brown or rusty-coloured, often with a narrow greenish margin.
Grassland, moist or marshy places. Widespread. Summer.

708 Schoenoplectus corymbosus (Roth. ex Roem. & Schult.) J. Raynal
Perennial with several robust erect stems from a rhizome. Stems green and *leafless, cylindrical*, filled with a *white spongy* tissue. Inflorescences borne *terminally* at the base of an erect, sharply pointed bract; comprise several clusters of brown spikelets.
Marshy grassland, usually forming dense stands. Widespread. Spring – summer.

703 *Bulbostylis burchellii*

704 *Coleochloa setifera*

705 *Cyperus esculentus*

706 *Cyperus rupestris*

707 *Mariscus congestus*

708 *Schoenoplectus corymbosus*

FABACEAE (See page 20) See also **315** and **508**.

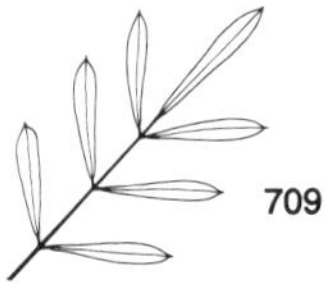

709

709 Indigofera burkeana Benth. ex Harv.
Perennial shrublet up to 400 mm high with a woody taproot; branched mainly from the base. Leaves compound with ± 7 leaflets, the side ones usually *opposite*. Inflorescence with stalk *longer* than the leaves. Petals 7 – 10 mm long, *hairless*. Pods pointing *downward*.
Grassland, particularly rocky areas. Widespread. Spring.

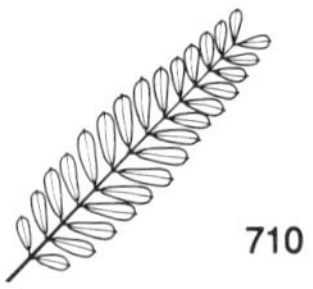

710

710 *Sesbania punicea (Cav.) Benth. *Sesbania*
Deciduous shrub or small tree up to 3 m high. Leaves compound with *10 – 14 pairs* of leaflets, drooping, hairless. Flowers borne in showy axillary clusters; calyx *scarcely lobed*. Pods *4-angled*, with short wings on the angles; tip *sharply* pointed.
A native of South America. Naturalized as a weed in moist, disturbed places, particularly along streams. Widespread. Spring – summer.

711

711 Tephrosia acaciifolia Bak.
Erect shrublet with long slender stems. Leaves well-spaced, *simple*, *stalkless*, ± 60 – 120 mm long; side veins *ending in the margin;* lower surface covered with appressed hairs. Flowers orange, salmon-pink, purple or mauve; in well-spaced groups (usually pairs) along an elongated axis.
Grassland, often in moist places. Mainly Pretoria/Magaliesberg region. Summer. □ Compare **712**.

712

712 Tephrosia elongata E. Mey. var. **elongata**
Slender, semi-erect herb from a woody rootstock; stems, fruits and lower (sometimes also upper) surface of leaves covered with short spreading hairs. Leaves on *very short stalks;* comprising 1 or 2 pairs of leaflets (rarely simple); leaflets 40 – 90 (rarely 30 – 150) mm long, with *numerous ascending* side veins which merge into a marginal vein. Inflorescences at the ends of shoots, *long and slender*, with few, well-spaced flowers towards tip. Sepals and petals *densely covered with hairs* on outer surface; style hairless. Pods flat and hairy.
Grassland, particularly rocky outcrops. Widespread. Spring – summer. Compare **711**.

IRIDACEAE (See page 21)

713 Gladiolus dalenii Van Geel *Wild gladiolus/Wildeswaardlelie*
Erect perennial up to 1,5 m high; corm covered with soft brown fibres. Leaves 10 – 30 mm wide, hairless, with *prominent ribs*, pointing upward, arranged in a *fan*. Flowers orange-yellow, densely covered with minute orange dots.
Grassland, often in vleis or rocky places; usually in groups. Widespread. Spring – summer.

714 Gladiolus woodii Bak.
Perennial herb with an underground corm. Leaves that are well developed *absent* at the time of flowering (a *single*, ± hairy leaf appears after flowering). Inflorescence erect, with 2 – 4 reduced, closely sheathing leaves towards the base; bearing 4 – 12 flowers spaced or close together. Flowers small, 2-lipped, *deep purple-maroon or dark brown* (mainly Witwatersrand) to greenish yellow (mainly Pretoria).
Grassland, usually among rocks. Mainly Pretoria/Witwatersrand region. Spring. □ For yellow-flowered form see **353**.

715 Tritonia nelsonii Bak.
Herbaceous perennial ± 500 mm high. Leaves 4 – 8, spreading like a fan in 1 plane, *bluish green*, prominently *ribbed*. Inflorescence many-flowered. Flowers funnel-shaped, orange-red; lower perianth segments each with a green, *upward-pointing outgrowth* on inner surface near base.
Grassland, on rocky ridges. Widespread. Summer. □ Also **550**.

709 *Indigofera burkeana*

710 *Sesbania punicea*

711 *Tephrosia acaciifolia*

712 *Tephrosia elongata*

713 *Gladiolus dalenii*

714 *Gladiolus woodii*

715 *Tritonia nelsonii*

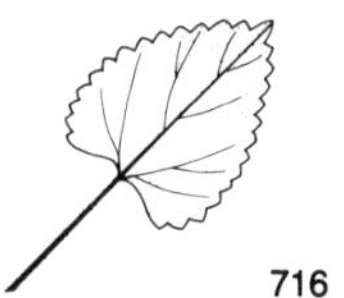

716

717

LAMIACEAE (See page 22)

716 Leonotis dysophylla Benth. *Wild dagga/Wildedagga*

Robust perennial shrub up to ± 2 m high. Stems erect, sparsely branched. Leaves stalked, usually *longer* than 50 mm and covered with velvety hairs. Flowers in widely spaced whorls towards ends of branches; corolla densely covered with *orange hairs.*

Grassland and bushveld, often in disturbed places. Mainly Pretoria/ Magaliesberg region. Spring – summer. □ Compare **717**.

This species is treated by some authors as **L. ocymifolia** (Burm.f.) Iwarsson var. **raineriana** (Visiani) Iwarsson.

717 Leonotis microphylla Skan *Rock dagga/Klipdagga*

Low-growing perennial shrublet with ± slender stems and a thick woody rootstock. Leaves stalked, *less* than 20 mm long, often *folded* along midrib, ± hairy. Flowers on shoots up to 1,5 m high; corolla densely covered with *orange hairs.*

Rocky grassland. Widespread. Summer. □ Compare **716**.

This species is treated by some authors as **L. ocymifolia** (Burm.f.) Iwarsson var. **schinzii** (Guerke) Iwarsson.

LILIACEAE (Excluding Alliaceae; see page 22) See also **365**.

718 Aloe marlothii Berger var. **marlothii** *Mountain aloe/Bergaalwyn*

Succulent with *single erect* stem usually 2 – 3 m high; densely covered with remains of the old dry leaves. Leaves with *margin* and *both surfaces* covered with scattered spines. Inflorescence a many-branched panicle comprising *horizontally* to *obliquely* arranged racemes.

Usually on rocky ridges and hillsides. Mainly Pretoria/Magaliesberg region and Suikerbosrand. Autumn – winter.

719 Chortolirion angolense (Bak.) Berger [=**Haworthia angolensis** Bak.]

Small, succulent perennial with a *bulb* formed by the persistent bases of the old leaves; roots fleshy. Leaves *basal*, long and narrow, forming a sheath at the base; margin with *small teeth*. Inflorescence erect, bearing few flowers, often appearing *before* the new leaves. Flowers tubular, *2-lipped*, ± erect; perianth segments with a *green-brown* stripe down the centre.

Grassland. Widespread. Spring.

720 Dipcadi cf. **ciliare** (Zeyh. ex Harv.) Bak. *Slanguintjie*

Bulbous plant. Leaves *absent* at the time of flowering; later up to 6 leaves present, with strongly *crinkled* margins and long *yellowish* hairs. Inflorescence ± 250 mm high. Flowers green or brown, ± 12 mm long, perianth segments ± *equal*, spreading somewhat near the apex, *without* 'tails'.

Grassland. Widespread. Spring. □ For green-flowered form see **770**.

721 Dipcadi viride (L.) Moench *Grootslymuintjie*

Bulbous plant, hairless. Leaves 1 – 4, *long and straight*, ± 20 mm wide, tapering towards the tip; *bluish green*, soft-textured, ± folded lengthwise down the middle, indistinctly veined. Inflorescence an erect raceme up to ± 1 m high, open flowers pointing in *1 direction*. Flowers with perianth ± 12 mm long (excluding 'tails'), the outer segments with *long, tail-like appendages.*

Grassland, often in vleis. Widespread. Spring – summer.

722 Urginea multisetosa Bak.

Perennial herb with scaly bulb; bulb scales disintegrate into *stiff bristles* at apex. Leaves usually appear *after* the flowers. Inflorescence an elongated raceme. Flowers *well-spaced;* bracts of the lower flowers (best seen in the young inflorescences) with an *outgrowth* near the base; perianth segments just joined at the base, brownish cream, with a darker *stripe* on the back.

Grassland. Widespread. Spring.

716 *Leonotis dysophylla*

717 *Leonotis microphylla*

718 *Aloe marlothii*

719 *Chortolirion angolense*

720 *Dipcadi* cf. *ciliare*

721 *Dipcadi viride*

722 *Urginea multisetosa*

MALVACEAE (See page 23) See also **381 – 384**.

723 Hibiscus subreniformis Burtt Davy

Erect, sparsely branched shrublet up to ± 1,5 m high; most parts *densely covered* with glistening, star-shaped hairs (often sticky to the touch). Leaves *broadly egg-shaped;* base ± heart-shaped; margin toothed. Flowers pale orange; corolla *10 – 15 mm* long, outer surface with star-shaped hairs; anthers and stigmas orange; epicalyx bracts (leafy whorl below calyx) *8 – 10, narrow,* ± half the length of the sepals.

Bushveld, on rocky ridges. Pretoria/Magaliesberg region. Spring – summer.

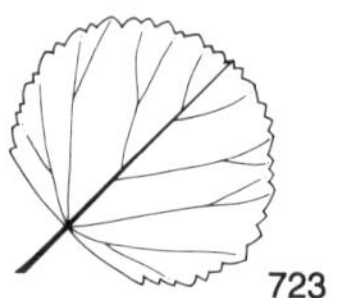

723

724 Pavonia burchellii (DC.) R.A. Dyer

Somewhat herbaceous shrublet up to 1 m high; young growth *hairy.* Leaves thin, with *3 – 5 lobes* or angles; margin *toothed.* Flowers with 5 (sometimes 8) epicalyx bracts ± the *same length as* the sepals; pale orange.

Usually in light shade under trees or among rocks. Widespread. Spring – summer.

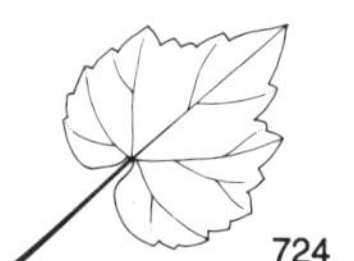

724

PAPAVERACEAE (See page 25)

725 Papaver aculeatum Thunb. *Wild poppy/Wildepapawer*

Erect annual herb covered with long, *stiff, yellowish* hairs and *spines.* Leaves in the basal rosette stalked, those on the stems stalkless; margin shallowly to deeply *pinnately lobed.* Flowers on long stalks, *drooping* in bud. Capsules without spines, opening by means of *pores* below the flattened top.

Grassland and disturbed places; rare. Widespread. Summer.

725

SCROPHULARIACEAE (See page 28)

726 Halleria lucida L. *Tree fuchsia/Notsung*

Deciduous or semi-deciduous *shrub or small tree;* bark light-coloured, peeling in longitudinal sections; branchlets often reddish brown. Leaves on stalks which are often reddish; blade egg-shaped, shiny green turning bronze in autumn; margin *finely* toothed. Flowers *tubular,* in leaf axils or in tufts directly *from trunks and branches,* with abundant nectar. Berries round, red or purplish black and tipped with the long, dried-out, *persistent* style.

Along streams and in kloofs. Widespread. All year.

727 Manulea parvifolia Benth.

Annual or short-lived perennial herb up to 1 m high, covered with *fine hairs* throughout. Leaves in a basal *rosette, strap-shaped.* Inflorescence terminal, *much-branched,* many-flowered. Flowers ± regular with a *very slender* tube.

Grassland and bushveld. Widespread. Spring – summer.

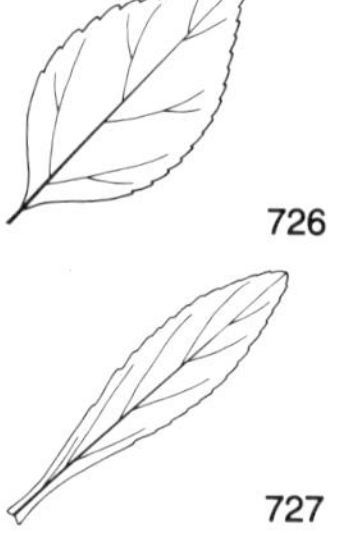

726

727

728 Sutera aurantiaca (Burch.) Hiern *Cape saffron/Saffraanbossie*

Small bushy *aromatic* herb from a woody rootstock. Shoots slender, covered with short glandular hairs. Leaves in *tufts,* finely bipinnately *dissected,* covered with short *glandular hairs.* Flower colour very variable: orange, brownish, red or pink.

Grassland, particularly vleis. Widespread, the orange form mainly in the Witwatersrand/Suikerbosrand region. Spring – summer.

For pink-flowered form see **601**.

729 Sutera burkeana (Benth.) Hiern *Bruinblommetjie*

Erect perennial *shrublet* up to 1 m high. Leaves in *tufts,* minute, with the blade usually *deeply dissected* or sharply toothed. Flowers terminal, tubular.

Grassland, particularly rocky places. Widespread. Summer.

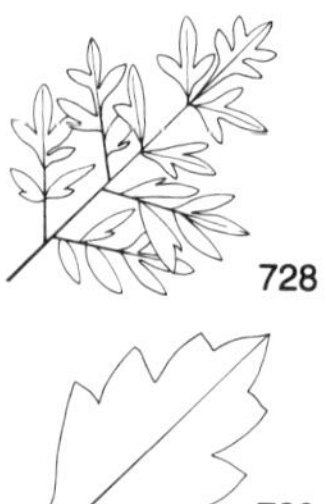

728

729

723 *Hibiscus subreniformis*

724 *Pavonia burchellii*

725 *Papaver aculeatum*

726 *Halleria lucida*

727 *Manulea parvifolia*

728 *Sutera aurantiaca*

729 *Sutera burkeana*

SELAGINACEAE (See page 28)

730 Hebenstretia angolensis Rolfe *Katster*

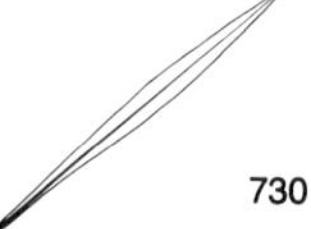

730

Much-branched perennial shrublet up to ± 1,5 m high. Leaves stalkless, *long and narrow;* margin usually smooth. Flowers numerous, in elongated terminal spikes; corolla *orange* or yellow, with a *red-brown* or red blotch, distinctly *4-lobed.*

Grassland, usually on rocky ridges. Widespread. Summer. □ Compare **431**.

STERCULIACEAE (See page 28)

731 Hermannia depressa N.E.Br. *Rooi-opslag*

731

Herb with stems and leaves *flat on the ground* and spreading from a woody perennial taproot; often growing in patches; very sparsely covered with hairs. Leaves on short stalks, ± oval, usually with a *purplish red to reddish brown* tinge; margin *bluntly toothed.* Flowers *drooping* from ± erect stalks; colour very variable: orange, copper, pinkish, mauve, yellow, purple or creamy white.

Grassland, particularly trampled areas, often on pavements. Widespread. Spring – autumn.

THYMELAEACEAE (See page 28) See also **439** and **606**.

732 Gnidia microcephala Meisn. *Besembossie*

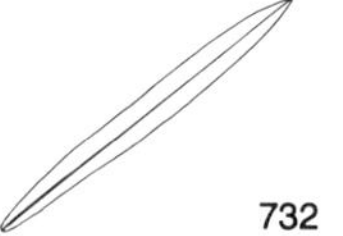

732

Erect herbaceous perennial from a woody rootstock. Stems numerous, *slender and wiry*, with *well-spaced* branches, hairless. Leaves stalkless, 0,5 – 3 mm wide, *hairless.* Flowers up to 20 in terminal heads surrounded by overlapping *broad brown* bracts.

Grassland. Widespread. Spring.

TYPHACEAE (See page 28)

733 Typha capensis (Rohrb.) N.E.Br. *Bulrush/Papkuil*

Erect *aquatic* herb up to ± 2,5 m high with a creeping rhizome; hairless throughout. Leaves ± basal, strap-shaped, leathery, *blue-green*, rising above the water. Flowering stems tall, erect, *unbranched.* Inflorescence terminal, comprising a *slender upper zone* with light brown male flowers and below it a *thicker zone* with numerous minute female flowers; the male part is shed soon after flowering, but the female part becomes a deep *velvety brown.*

Marshy areas and along watercourses, forming large colonies. Widespread. Summer.

VERBENACEAE (See page 29)

734 *Lantana camara L. *Lantana*

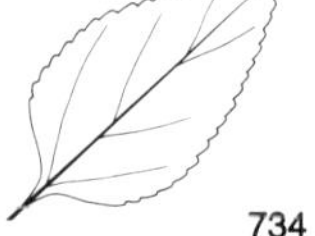

734

Much-branched shrub. Stems *4-angled*, with *scattered recurved prickles.* Leaves covered with *rough hairs*, *foul-smelling* when crushed. Inflorescences flat-topped. Flowers in the centre open first and usually change colour as they fade; colour very variable: pink, yellow, orange or orange-brown. Fruit blackish, *fleshy*, shiny and globose.

A weed from tropical America, usually growing under and among trees. Widespread. Summer – winter. □ For yellow-pink form see **609**.

730 *Hebenstretia angolensis*

731 *Hermannia depressa*

732 *Gnidia microcephala*

734 *Lantana camara*

733 *Typha capensis*

GREEN OR GREENISH FLOWERS

(See also **27, 57, 93, 103, 118, 185, 189, 191, 300, 326, 364, 366, 413, 414, 418, 441, 446, 452, 487, 569, 657, 660, 693**)

Pure green colours are rare, and most of the flowers included in this colour group are yellowish, whitish or brownish green. Flowers that are greenish are often small and inconspicuous. A few species whose greenish fruits could be mistaken for flowers are included in this section.

Green floral colours are usually produced by chlorophyll, the pigment also responsible for the green colouring of leaves. Insoluble in water, chlorophyll occurs with other substances in roundish green bodies called chloroplasts which are distributed throughout the green parts of the plant. Photosynthesis takes place in the chloroplasts, and in this process the chlorophyll is of paramount importance in trapping a portion of the light energy radiated from the sun.

Pollinators that visit green flowers include bees, moths (**770 – 772**) and flies (**793** and **794**). Some of the smaller, inconspicuous flowers, for example those of members of the Cyperaceae and Urticaceae, are wind-pollinated. Although some pure green flowers are not easily seen by insects and depend on odour to attract pollinators, others may be scentless and rendered conspicuous by the presence of pigments reflecting ultraviolet rays. In the absence of ultraviolet effects, green flowers are probably perceived by insects as a dull yellow-grey, thus blending with the similarly coloured background of foliage.

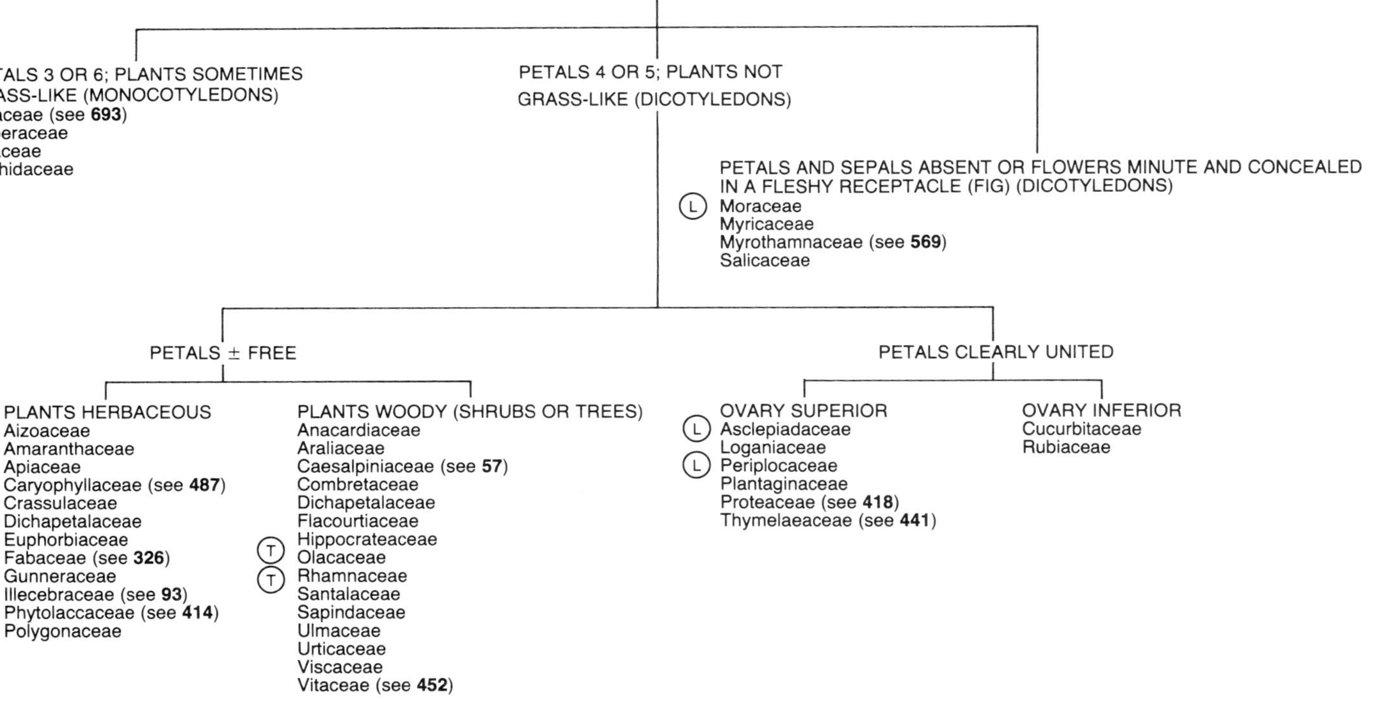

GUIDE TO THE FAMILIES WHICH INCLUDE GREEN OR GREENISH FLOWERS
GREEN OR GREENISH FLOWERS
PETALS 3 OR 6; PLANTS SOMETIMES GRASS-LIKE (MONOCOTYLEDONS)
Alliaceae (see 693)
Cyperaceae
Liliaceae
Orchidaceae
PETALS 4 OR 5; PLANTS NOT GRASS-LIKE (DICOTYLEDONS)
PETALS AND SEPALS ABSENT OR FLOWERS MINUTE AND CONCEALED IN A FLESHY RECEPTACLE (FIG) (DICOTYLEDONS)
(L) Moraceae
Myricaceae
Myrothamnaceae (see 569)
Salicaceae
PETALS ± FREE
PLANTS HERBACEOUS
Aizoaceae
Amaranthaceae
Apiaceae
Caryophyllaceae (see 487)
(S) Crassulaceae
Dichapetalaceae
(L) Euphorbiaceae
Fabaceae (see 326)
Gunneraceae
Illecebraceae (see 93)
Phytolaccaceae (see 414)
Polygonaceae
PLANTS WOODY (SHRUBS OR TREES)
Anacardiaceae
Araliaceae
Caesalpiniaceae (see 57)
Combretaceae
Dichapetalaceae
Flacourtiaceae
Hippocrateaceae
(T) Olacaceae
(T) Rhamnaceae
Santalaceae
Sapindaceae
Ulmaceae
Urticaceae
Viscaceae
Vitaceae (see 452)
PETALS CLEARLY UNITED
OVARY SUPERIOR
(L) Asclepiadaceae
Loganiaceae
(L) Periplocaceae
Plantaginaceae
Proteaceae (see 418)
Thymelaeaceae (see 441)
OVARY INFERIOR
Cucurbitaceae
Rubiaceae
(L) At least some members with milky latex
(S) At least some members succulent
(T) At least some members with thorns/spines

AIZOACEAE (See page 16)

735

735 Psammotropha myriantha Sond.

Low-growing, tufted, perennial herb. Stems thick, short, erect and persistent; concealed by a *rosette* of *densely crowded* leaves at the base. Leaves long and narrow, with a distinct midrib and *terminal bristle*. Flowering stem annual, simple or *much-branched*, bearing *whorls* of leaves and flowers at the nodes. Flowers with petal-like segments *incurved* and greenish, with a wide *membranous margin*.

Grassland, on rocky outcrops, often in crevices. Widespread. Spring.

AMARANTHACEAE (See page 16)

736

736 *Amaranthus hybridus L. *Pigweed/Misbredie*

Erect annual herb. Stems strongly *ribbed*, often tinged with red. Leaves stalked, broadly lance- to egg-shaped. Flowers small, greenish, *densely clustered* in long terminal and axillary spikes.

Native to the New World and now a common weed of disturbed places. Widespread. Summer – autumn.

ANACARDIACEAE (See page 16)

737

737 Rhus dentata Thunb. *Nana-berry/Nanabessie*

Bushy deciduous shrub or small tree. Stems often reddish and hairy when young. Leaves trifoliolate; leaflets *egg-shaped*, smooth or slightly hairy, *strongly toothed* in the upper half. Flowers small, in drooping axillary or terminal clusters. Fruits ± globose, yellow, turning brown or reddish when mature.

A component of woody vegetation in kloofs, on rocky ridges and particularly along streams. Widespread. Spring. □ Compare **743**.

738

738 Rhus discolor E. Mey. ex Sond.

Sparsely branched *shrublet* up to ± 500 mm high; with an underground rootstock. Leaves with the upper surface green and the lower *white-felted;* tip often *sharply* pointed. Flowers very small, in dense terminal and axillary inflorescences.

Grassland; uncommon, except in the Suikerbosrand. Widespread. Spring – summer.

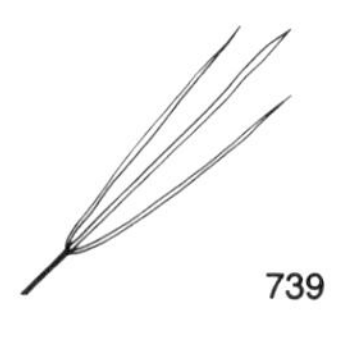
739

739 Rhus gracillima Engl.

Slender, *very sparsely branched* perennial shrublet up to ± 1 m high; sprouting from a perennial rootstock; hairless or covered with short hairs. Leaves stalked, trifoliolate; leaflets long and *very narrow* (± 1 mm). Male and female flowers on different plants. Flowers many, *well-spaced* in terminal sprays, greenish yellow.

Grassland, usually on rocky ridges. Mainly Pretoria/Magaliesberg region. Spring.

740 Rhus lancea L.f. *Karee*

Evergreen tree with a dense, rounded crown; bark dark brown, rough and fissured; branchlets with tiny *raised brownish* spots. Leaves stalked, trifoliolate, dark green; leaflets narrowly lance-shaped, hairless, with the margin *smooth*. Male and female flowers on separate plants. Flowers minute, in many-flowered panicles towards the ends of branches. Fruit ± *globose*, 4 – 5 mm across, green turning yellowish brown and with a brittle shell when ripe.

Grassland and bushveld, usually in wooded areas. Widespread. Winter. Compare **741**.

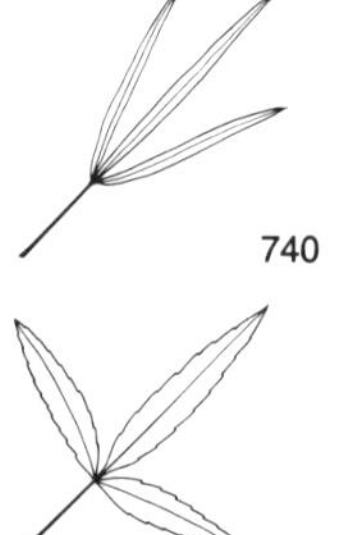
740

741

741 Rhus leptodictya Diels *Mountain karee/Bergkaree*

Rounded *evergreen* tree; branches ± drooping; bark rough, dark brown. Leaves stalked, trifoliolate, pale green; leaflets with margin ± *toothed*. Male and female flowers on separate plants. Flowers minute, borne in clusters at the ends of branches. Fruits *flattened*.

Grassland and bushveld, often in rocky places. Summer. □ Compare **740**.

735 *Psammotropha myriantha*

735 *P. myriantha* (habit, before flowering)

736 *Amaranthus hybridus*

737 *Rhus dentata*

738 *Rhus discolor*

739 *Rhus gracillima*

740 *Rhus lancea*

741 *Rhus leptodictya*

742 Rhus magalismontana Sond. *Bergtaaibos*
Dwarf, *multi-stemmed* evergreen *shrublet* up to ± 500 mm high, from a woody rootstock, *grey-green;* young growth often *bronze, coral pink or red*, with numerous brownish dots. Leaves trifoliolate, ± *erect*, rigid and leathery, with prominent venation; stalks slightly winged when young. Flowers minute, in dense sprays. Fruits ± flattened, yellowish, turning reddish when ripe.
Grassland and bushveld, on rocky ridges and often in dense stands. Widespread. Spring.

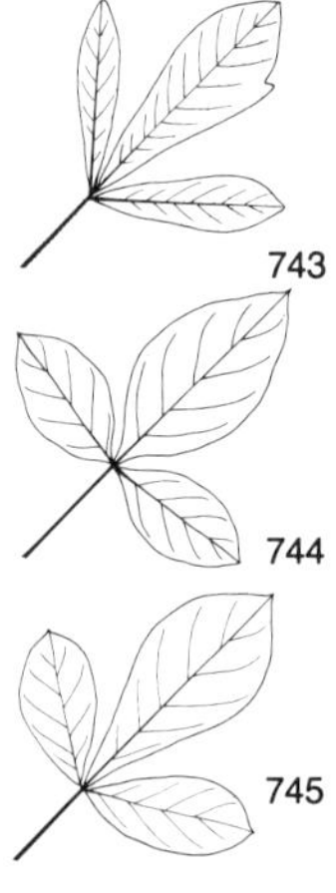

743 Rhus pyroides Burch. *Common wild currant/Taaibos*
Much-branched shrub or tree up to ± 4 m high; twigs and both surfaces of leaves usually *densely covered with hairs; spinescent shoots* sometimes present. Leaflets ± egg-shaped. Flowers minute, borne in panicles towards ends of branchlets.
Grassland and bushveld; common, particularly in disturbed areas. Widespread. Spring – summer. □ Compare **737**.

744 Rhus rigida Mill. [=**R. eckloniana** Sond.] *Kliptaaibos*
Shrub up to 1,5 m high. Leaflets hairless or sparsely covered with hairs and *folded upward* along the midrib; margin sometimes *wavy*. Flowers minute, greenish yellow, borne in axillary panicles.
Often growing between rocks. Widespread. Spring – summer.

745 Rhus zeyheri Sond. *Blue currant/Bloutaaibos*
Attractive deciduous *shrub* or small tree. Leaves *hairless* and conspicuously *bluish green*. Flowers minute, borne mainly in axillary groups. Fruits *reddish*.
Fairly common in the Magaliesberg and around Pretoria. Spring – summer.

APIACEAE (See page 16) See also **185**.

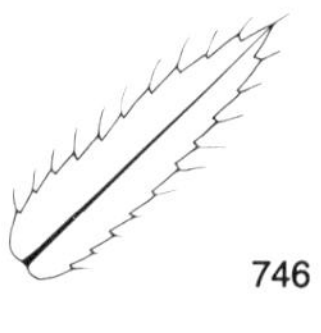

746 Alepidea setifera N.E.Br. *Kalmoes*
Erect herbaceous perennial with fleshy roots, up to 500 mm high. Leaves at base in a *rosette*, stalked, oval, fringed with numerous *long bristles;* stem leaves stalkless, *overlapping* and closely covering the stem, fringed with *long bristles*. Flowers 13 – 15 in each dense terminal head, which looks like a flower and is surrounded by 8 – 10 rigid and sharply pointed, equal or unequal *bracts;* bracts greenish white, *resembling petals*.
Moist and swampy grassland. Magaliesberg. Summer.

747 Heteromorpha trifoliata (Wendl.) Eckl. & Zeyh. [=**H. arborescens** (Spreng.) Cham. & Schlechtd.] *Parsley tree/Wildepietersieliebos*
Deciduous shrub or small tree; bark *smooth*, shiny, *peels off horizontally in papery pieces*. Leaves borne on stalks, the bases of which are *stem-clasping;* blade simple to pinnately compound, varying even on the same branch. Flowers borne in *compound spherical umbels* at the ends of branches.
Wooded areas, particularly rocky hillsides, clumps of bush and along streams. Widespread. Spring.

ARALIACEAE (See page 17)

748 Cussonia paniculata Eckl. & Zeyh.
Highveld cabbage tree/Hoëveldse kiepersol
Deciduous tree with erect stems terminating in a *rosette* of leaves. Stems simple or sparsely branched. Leaves large, once *palmately compound*, long-stalked, *grey-green;* leaflets with coarsely dissected margins. Flowers densely clustered in *long loose sprays*, greenish yellow.
Grassland and wooded areas, often on rocky ridges. Widespread. Spring.
C. transvaalensis Reyneke also has *grey-green* leaves, but it can easily be distinguished from the previous species because the primary leaflets are *redivided* into smaller leaflets, and the inflorescence is a *compound umbel* of dense *spikes*. Bushveld. Magaliesberg.

742 *Rhus magalismontana*

742 *R. magalismontana* (fruit)

743 *Rhus pyroides*

744 *Rhus rigida*

745 *Rhus zeyheri*

746 *Alepidea setifera*

747 *Heteromorpha trifoliata*

748 *Cussonia paniculata*

ASCLEPIADACEAE (See page 17) See also **27, 189** and **191**.

749

749 Asclepias affinis (Schltr.) Schltr. *Cartwhee*

Perennial herb with rather stout, erect or leaning stems from a tuberous rootstock; ± covered with *bristly hairs* throughout. Leaves on short stalks, egg-shaped; base ± *square*. Inflorescence comprises numerous flowers clustered into a terminal, *flat-topped head* which is turned *sideways*. Flowers with a *distinct* stalk; corolla lobes reflexed; corona lobes opening upwards, greenish or yellowish.

Grassland. Widespread. Spring.

750

750 Asclepias burchellii Schltr.

Erect, sparsely branched, perennial shrub up to ± 1 m high; young (and sometimes older) stems *densely covered with short, whitish hairs*. Leaves long and narrow with margins *rolled downward*, greyish green. Flowers 3 – 10 in ea drooping, axillary umbel; corolla reflexed, covered with short hairs on the lower surface; corona *broadly D-shaped* in side view, *without* a distinct tooth or horn in the cavity, often *brownish*. Fruit inflated, tapering into a narrow tip, covered with numerous bristle-like protuberances and whitish hairs.

Grassland and bushveld, often along roadsides. Widespread. Spring – summer. □ Compare **189**.

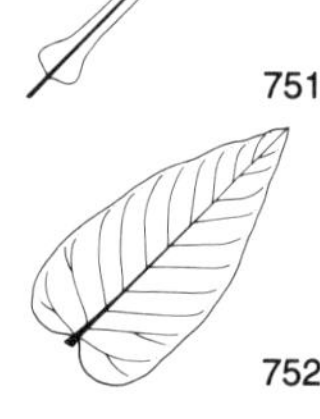

751

751 Asclepias eminens (Harv.) Schltr.

Perennial herb with tuberous roots. Stems *semi-erect to prostrate*, with linear leaves. Flowers with petals strongly reflexed and sometimes purplish brown; corona lobes *longer* than the central column (stigmatic area).

Grassland. Widespread. Spring – summer.

Very similar to **A. gibba** (E. Mey.) Schltr., which has the corona lobes ± *leve* with the tip of the central column.

752

752 Asclepias glaucophylla (Schltr.) Schltr. *Bloumelkbo*

Perennial herb up to 500 mm high, with clusters of erect shoots from a tuberous rootstock. Leaves with a *bluish grey bloom* and *heart-shaped* base. Flowers with sepals and petals green; corona *brownish*.

Rare in grassland. Mainly Pretoria/Magaliesberg region. Spring – summer.

753

753 Pentarrhinum insipidum E. Mey. *Donkieperske*

Slender *twining* herb from a woody perennial rootstock; sparsely covered with hairs throughout. Leaves pointing downward, stalked, *heart-shaped*, with a pointed tip. Inflorescences axillary, ± umbel-like. Flowers greenish yellow tinged with *purple-brown;* corolla lobes reflexed, margin fringed with minute hairs; corona lobes with a *central cavity* formed by infolded margins, and with an *inward-directed horn*. Follicles solitary, ± inflated, knobbly.

Grassland and clumps of bush, often twining in fences. Widespread. Summer.

749 *Asclepias affinis*

750 *Asclepias burchellii*

751 *Asclepias eminens*

752 *Asclepias glaucophylla*

753 *Pentarrhinum insipidum*

COMBRETACEAE (See page 18)

754

754 Combretum apiculatum Sond. subsp. **apiculatum**

Red bushwillow/Rooibos

Small, ± deciduous tree; bark fissured and ± scaly; *hairless*. Leaves stalked; tip *sharply* pointed and *twisted;* often covered with a *shiny*, ± sticky secretion, particularly on the young growth. Inflorescences comprise axillary spikes, 30 – 70 mm long. Flowers greenish yellow. Fruit with 4 papery wings.

Bushveld. Pretoria/Magaliesberg region. Spring.

755 Combretum erythrophyllum (Burch.) Sond.

River bushwillow/Vaderlandswilg

Large deciduous tree; bark ± *smooth*, creamy brown; often with reddish autumn colours. Leaves both opposite and alternate on the same tree; stalked; first leaves in spring often *mottled with whitish patches;* lower, and sometimes also upper, surface sparsely covered with hairs. Flowers creamy green, densely clustered in stalked, *globose*, axillary flower heads. Fruits golden brown, with 4 papery wings.

Grassland and bushveld; usually alongside rivers and streams. Widespread. Spring.

755

756 Combretum molle R.Br. ex G. Don

Velvet bushwillow/Basterrooibos

Deciduous tree up to ± 5 m high; bark light brown, rough and flaking. Leaves stalked; lower surface with *prominently raised* veins and often a *reddish* tinge; both surfaces *densely covered with velvety hairs*. Flowers in sweet-scented axillary spikes which appear before the leaves. Fruits 4-winged, up to 15 mm in diameter, papery, turning reddish then brown.

Wooded hillsides, usually in rocky places. Widespread. Spring.

756

757 Combretum zeyheri Sond. *Large-fruited bushwillow/Raasblaar*

Deciduous tree with a round, leafy crown; bark greyish, ± smooth, becoming rough and mottled with age. Leaves stalked, sometimes ± folded upward along the midrib, ± *hairless* when mature, turning yellow in winter. Flowers in dense axillary spikes, ± *50 mm* long, scented. Fruits 4-winged, up to *60 mm* in diameter, green turning light brown.

Bushveld, often on rocky hillsides. Pretoria/Magaliesberg region. Spring.

757

CRASSULACEAE (See page 19)

758 Crassula lanceolata (Eckl. & Zeyh.) Endl. ex Walp. subsp. **transvaalensis** (Kuntze) Toelken [=**C. schimperi** Fischer & C.A. Mey. var. **schimperi**]

Small erect succulent producing new shoots annually from fleshy (carrot-like) perennial roots; branches *not rooting* at the nodes. Leaves stalkless, flattened, lance-shaped, lower ones ± *longer* than the upper ones, terminating in a *colourless* tip. Flowers clustered on short *axillary* branchlets; sepals almost as long as petals, sharply pointed; corolla turning *brown* with age.

Grassland. Widespread. Summer.

Subsp. **lanceolata** has the branches often *rooting* at nodes (plants often mat-forming) and all leaves ± *equal* in length (rarely longer than 6 mm), *without* a pronounced terminal tip. Rocky places, often in the shade. Widespread.

758

754 *Combretum apiculatum*

755 *Combretum erythrophyllum*

756 *Combretum molle*

757 *Combretum zeyheri*

758 *Crassula lanceolata* subsp. *transvaalensis*

CUCURBITACEAE (See page 19)

759

759 Kedrostis africana (L.) Cogn.
Herbaceous *climber* with unforked tendrils and a woody rootstock. Leaves ± stalkless, *deeply* cut into *narrow* lobes. Male and female flowers on the same plant. Flowers few, in axillary clusters with short *stalks;* petals 1 – 2 mm long. Fruit ± globose, with a short point, red.
Clumps of bush. Widespread. Summer.

760

760 Trochomeria macrocarpa (Sond.) Hook.f. *Bobbejaankomkommer*
Herb with annual trailing or climbing stems from a tuberous rootstock; tendrils unforked; covered with short, rough hairs throughout. Leaves stalked, deeply divided into 3 – 5 lobes, with the segments often irregularly lobed. Male and female flowers on different plants. Flowers solitary, axillary, often appearing *before* the leaves; corolla with a *long tube*, lobes *up to 10 times as long as they are wide*, spreading or twisted; yellowish or brownish green, often tinged with maroon. Fruit egg-shaped, bright orange-red.
Grassland and bushveld. Widespread. Spring.

CYPERACEAE (See page 19)

761 Carex cernua Boott. var. **austro-africana** Kuekenth.
Tufted, grass-like perennial herb. Stems with *distinct angles*. Leaves mostly basal, uppermost stem leaves *longer than* the inflorescence. Inflorescence comprises *3 or 4* erect or *drooping female spikes*, 30 – 50 mm long, ± 4 mm wide, and a *single erect male spike;* female flowers surrounded by a *closed, sac-like structure* (utricle).
Grassland, marshy places. Widespread. Spring.

762 Fuirena pubescens (Poir.) Kunth
Slender erect perennial herb; aerial stems with leaves *along their length*. Leaves forming a sheath at the base, with a small *outgrowth* (ligule, as in grasses) at its junction with the blade, *hairy*. Inflorescence ± crowded; spikelets with bracts *spirally* overlapping, *hairy*.
Grassland, usually in moist places. Widespread. Spring – summer.

DICHAPETALACEAE (See page 19)

763

763 Dichapetalum cymosum (Hook.) Engl. *Poison leaf/Gifblaar*
Woody *dwarf* perennial from extensively spreading rhizomes. Leaves *alternate*, with 2 minute *linear stipules* at the base of the stalk; usually covered with soft hairs. Flowers axillary, greenish white. Fruits yellowish when ripe.
Grassland, usually forming extensive colonies, particularly in sandy soils. Common in the Pretoria/Magaliesberg region. Spring. □ Compare **798**.

759 *Kedrostis africana*

760 *Trochomeria macrocarpa*

760 *T. macrocarpa* (fruit)

761 *Carex cernua*

762 *Fuirena pubescens*

763 *Dichapetalum cymosum*

EUPHORBIACEAE (See page 20) See also **300** and **307**.

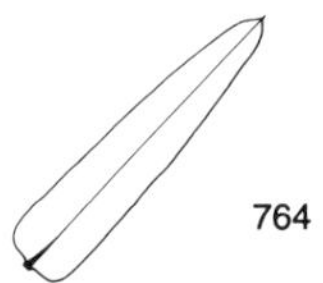
764

764 Euphorbia epicyparissias E. Mey. ex Boiss.
Shrublet with *reddish* stems; ends of branchlets *densely* covered with numerous spirally arranged leaves. Leaves *bluish green*, stalkless, linear-oblong with the apex *rounded* and *abruptly pointed*.
Grassland, often forming small clumps in seasonally moist soil. Mainly Suikerbosrand. Spring – summer.

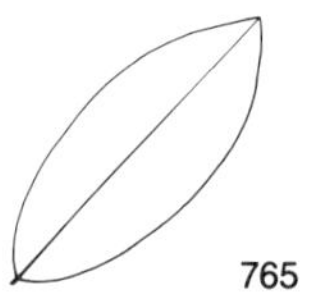
765

765 Phyllanthus parvulus Sond. *Dye bush/Kleurbossie*
Small shrublet with *slender*, ± erect stems from a woody perennial taproot; side shoots spreading. Stems often covered with minute nodules. Leaves stalkless, *egg-shaped*, arranged in *2 ranks*, ± appressed to the stem and pointing towards the end of it, often ± *overlapping*. Male and female flowers on the same plant. Flowers solitary, axillary, all pointing in the *same direction*, *pendulous;* colour variable: usually greenish or creamy, often tinged with pink. Capsules pendulous.
Grassland. Widespread. Spring – summer.

766

766 *Pointsettia geniculata (Orteg.) Small [=**Euphorbia geniculata** Orteg.] *Painted euphorbia/Gekleurde euphorbia*
Erect, *sparsely branched* annual up to 600 mm high. Leaves clustered at the ends of branches; lower surface *lighter in colour* than the upper. Flowers congested in *terminal clusters*. Capsules 3-lobed.
A native of tropical North America; a weed of disturbed places. Widespread. Summer.

FLACOURTIACEAE (See page 20)

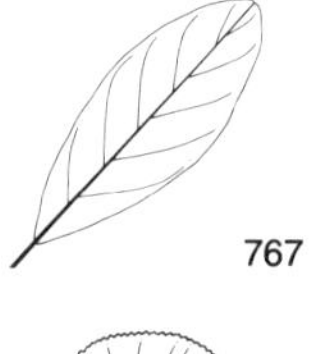
767

767 Kiggelaria africana L. *Wild peach/Wildeperske*
Evergreen to semi-deciduous tree; bark *smooth*, grey; crown usually with an occasional *bright yellow* leaf. Leaves stalked, ± elliptic, dull green above, densely covered with *white felt* below, with pockets (domatia) in the axils of side veins; margin toothed, particularly on sucker shoots, or smooth. Male and female flowers on separate trees. Male flowers in *many-flowered*, drooping, axillary inflorescences. Female flowers *solitary* in upper leaf axils. Fruit globose, ± woody, yellowish green, densely covered with hairs, knobbly; splits into 5 valves. Seed black with a *bright orange-red* covering.
Wooded kloofs and along streams. Widespread. Spring.

GUNNERACEAE (See page 21)

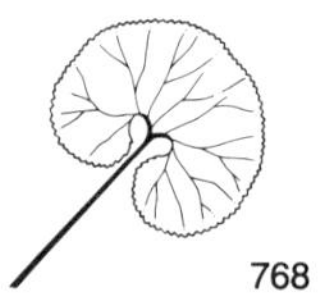
768

768 Gunnera perpensa L. *River pumpkin/Rivierpampoen*
Herbaceous perennial without aerial stems and arising from a brittle *creeping* rhizome. Leaves stalked, large (up to 300 mm wide), *like those of pumpkins*. Inflorescence erect, *up to 1 m* high, densely covered with flowers.
Marshy areas and along streams. Rare and localized. Widespread. Summer.

764 *Euphorbia epicyparissias*

765 *Phyllanthus parvulus*

766 *Pointsettia geniculata*

767 *Kiggelaria africana* (female)

767 *K. africana* (male)

768 *Gunnera perpensa*

769

HIPPOCRATEACEAE (See page 21)

769 Salacia rehmannii Schinz *Wildelemoentjie*

Sparsely branched *shrublet* from an underground rootstock; usually less than 500 mm high. Leaves leathery; margin with *shallow, well-spaced* teeth. Flowers axillary, borne ± along length of stems. Fruits bright orange, fleshy.

Grassland, usually forming dense stands. Mainly Pretoria/Magaliesberg region. Spring.

LILIACEAE (See page 22) See also **103**, **118**, **364**, **366**, **657** and **660**.

770 Dipcadi cf. **ciliare** (Zeyh. ex Harv.) Bak. *Slanguintjie*

Bulbous plant. Leaves *absent* at the time of flowering; later up to 6 leaves present, with strongly *crinkled* margin and long *yellowish* hairs. Inflorescence ± 250 mm high. Flowers green or brown, ± 12 mm long; perianth segments ± *equal*, spreading somewhat near the apex, *without 'tails'*.

Grassland. Widespread. Spring. □ For brown-flowered form see **720**.

771 Dipcadi marlothii Engl.

Bulbous plant. Leaves basal, *grass-like* and ± *spirally twisted* in the upper part, the outer ones with short white straggling hairs along the margin and at the base. Inflorescence ± *1 m* high, the floral axis *drooping sharply* in bud (as if wilted). Open flowers ± 18 mm long, all pointing in the same direction; perianth segments with tips curved slightly backward, *without 'tails'*.

Grassland, plants usually solitary. Widespread. Spring.

772 Dipcadi rigidifolium Bak. *Skaamblommetjie*

Bulbous plant, hairless. Leaves 2 or 3, *strap-shaped*, ± *25 mm* wide, dark blue-green, *hard-textured*, closely ribbed, with a prominent yellow or red margin; tip rounded, with a tiny sharp point. Inflorescence up to 500 mm high, bearing 8 – 20 well-spaced flowers. Flowers with perianth ± 15 mm long (excluding appendages), outer segments with *tail-like appendages* (5 – 14 mm long).

Bushveld, often in clayish soil. Pretoria/Magaliesberg region. Spring.

773 Drimia elata Jacq. *Jeukbol*

Bulbous herb; bulb with *reddish*, densely packed scales. Leaves appear after the flowers. Inflorescence an erect terminal raceme up to ± 1 m high. Flowers subtended by *whitish membranous* bracts which have a *small outgrowth* (spur) just below the middle; perianth lobes *fused at the base*, forming a short tube, variable in colour, usually greenish, whitish or pinkish.

Grassland and bushveld. Widespread. Summer.

774 Eucomis autumnalis (Mill.) Chitt. subsp. **clavata** (Bak.) Reyneke *Pineapple flower/Wildepynappel*

Bulbous herb with a rosette of broad, strap-shaped leaves often with *wavy* margins; hairless. Inflorescence stalk erect and ending in a *tuft of green, leaf-like bracts* above the densely packed flowers on *short stalks*.

Grassland, particularly moist places and rocky ridges. Widespread. Summer.

775 Ornithogalum tenuifolium Delaroche subsp. **tenuifolium** *Bosui*

Slender erect bulbous herb, 0,3 – 1 m high. Leaves ± 5, forming a *sheath* at the base, usually 8 – 20 mm wide, *blue-green* and hairless. Flowers with stalks up to 7 mm long, not increasing greatly in length during fruit development; petals white, with a *central* green to dark brown *longitudinal band*.

Grassland. Widespread. Spring.

769 *Salacia rehmannii*

770 *Dipcadi* cf. *ciliare*

771 *Dipcadi marlothii*

772 *Dipcadi rigidifolium*

773 *Drimia elata*

775 *Ornithogalum tenuifolium*

774 *Eucomis autumnalis*

LOGANIACEAE (See page 22)

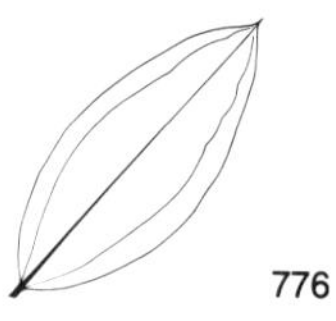

776 Strychnos pungens Soler.
Spine-leaved monkey orange/Botterklapper
Deciduous to evergreen small tree up to ± 3 m high; bark thick and fissured; branchlets thick, rough and corky, with ± *swollen* nodes. Leaves on short stalks; blade leathery and *rigid*, *spine-tipped* and with *3 – 5 distinct veins* from the base. Flowers in axillary clusters on short stalks; corolla tube with a dense *fringe of hairs* at the mouth. Fruit globose, hard, large (up to 100 mm in diameter), golden brown when ripe.
Rocky ridges. Mainly Pretoria/Magaliesberg region. Spring.

MORACEAE (See page 23)

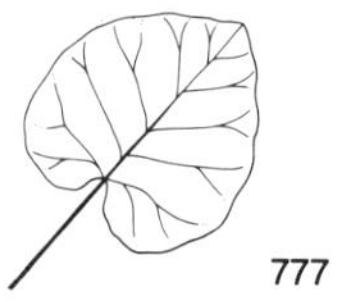

777 Ficus abutilifolia Miq. *Large-leaved rock fig/Grootblaarrotsvy*
Deciduous shrub or small tree. Leaves *roundly heart-shaped*, with yellowish venation; margin often *wavy*. Figs axillary, covered with *fine hairs*, and reddish with white specks when ripe.
Rocky hills and outcrops, the stem and roots often white and flattened against the rocks. Mainly Magaliesberg. All year.

778 Ficus ingens (Miq.) Miq. var. **ingens**
Red-leaved rock fig/Rooiblaarrotsvy
Deciduous shrub or small stunted tree. Leaves *broadly egg-shaped or triangular*, with a *heart-shaped* or *rounded* base and *5 or 6 pairs* of pale side veins; *bright red* or *reddish brown* in spring. Figs axillary, *smooth*, pinkish to red with white specks when ripe.
Rocky places, often as dense, shrubby growth covering rocks. Widespread. All year.

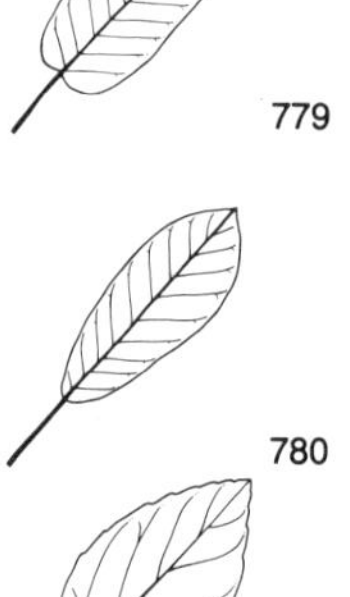

779 Ficus salicifolia Vahl. *Wonderboom fig/Wonderboomvy*
Evergreen shrub or tree, rarely reaching the considerable proportions of the Wonderboom group of specimens in northern Pretoria. Leaves *narrowly egg-shaped*, with a rounded or *weakly heart-shaped* base and *10 – 12 pairs* of side veins. Figs axillary, *smooth*, creamy pink to red with white specks when ripe.
Usually on rocky ridges. Mainly Pretoria/Magaliesberg region. All year.
This species is sometimes treated as **F. cordata** Thunb. subsp. **salicifolia** (Vahl.) C.C. Berg.

780 Ficus thonningii Blume *Common wild fig/Gewone wildevy*
Small to medium-sized *evergreen* tree. Leaves *elliptic* to *obovate-elliptic*, with a *narrowly rounded* base. Figs axillary, *densely covered with hairs*, greyish brown or yellow when ripe.
Sandy flats and stony slopes, occasionally an epiphytic strangler on other trees. Mainly Pretoria/Magaliesberg region. All year.

780.1

780.1 F. sur Forssk. (Broom cluster fig/Besemtrosvy) is the only other wild fig in the field guide region. It is a medium-sized to large deciduous tree of moist kloofs, mainly in the Magaliesberg. Leaf margin often with *widely spaced and blunt* teeth. Figs *large* (25 – 40 mm in diameter), borne in *clusters* on the main branches, trunk and even underground on the roots.

776 *Strychnos pungens*

777 *Ficus abutilifolia*

778 *Ficus ingens*

779 *Ficus salicifolia*

780 *Ficus thonningii*

MYRICACEAE (See page 23)

781 Myrica pilulifera Rendle *Broad-leaved waxberry/Breëblaarwasbessie*

Small *evergreen* tree up to 3 m high. Leaves stalked, *rounded to triangular* at the base, usually *more than 20 mm* wide. Male and female flowers usually on separate plants. Flowers small, borne in short spikes in axils of leaves. Fruits globose, covered with white wax.

Usually along streams. Mainly Magaliesberg. Spring.

781

782 Myrica serrata Lam. *Lance-leaf waxberry/Smalblaarwasbessie*

Evergreen shrub or small tree densely covered with leaves. Leaves *narrowing gradually* at the base, *5 – 20 mm* wide; margin smooth or usually toothed; lower surface *gland-dotted*. Flowering spikes often with a reddish tinge.

Along streams and in marshy vleis. Mainly Pretoria/Magaliesberg region. Summer.

782

OLACACEAE (See page 24)

783 Ximenia caffra Sond. var. **caffra** *Sourplum/Suurpruim*

783

Shrub or small, bushy tree, often armed with *short spinescent branchlets*. Leaves and young branchlets covered with *rusty, velvety hairs*. Flowers with the upper surface of the petals densely covered with *long white hairs*. Fruit fleshy and bright orange to red (sometimes with white speckles) when ripe.

Bushveld, sparsely distributed in particularly rocky terrain. A hemi-rootparasite with separate male and female plants. Mainly Pretoria/ Magaliesberg region. Spring.

ORCHIDACEAE (See page 24)

784 Bonatea porrecta (H.Bol.) Summerh.

Erect, *unbranched* perennial herb with fleshy tuberous roots. Stem leaves *withered* at flowering time; otherwise similar to the following species.

Grassland, often among shrubs. Mainly Witwatersrand/Suikerbosrand region. Winter.

785 Bonatea speciosa (L.f.) Willd. var. **antennifera** (Rolfe) Somerville *Moederkappie*

Erect, *unbranched* perennial herb with fleshy tuberous roots. Stem *leafy* at flowering time. Leaves flat, with 1 central vein; forming a *sheath* at the base; *blue-green*. Inflorescence terminal, many-flowered. Flowers with a spur *more than 30 mm* long; upper sepal green and *helmet-shaped*.

Grassland and bushveld, usually in the shade of shrubs and trees. Widespread. Autumn.

PERIPLOCACEAE (See page 25) See also **413**.

786 Raphionacme galpinii Schltr. *Melkbol*

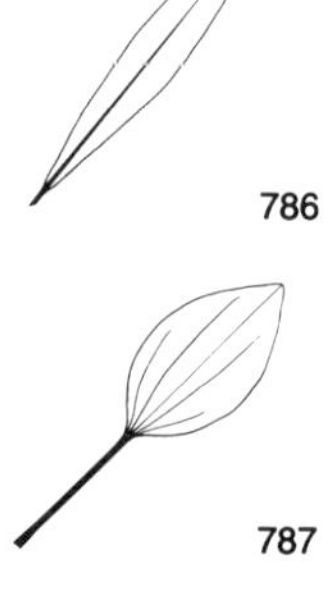

786

787

Herb with erect, branched stems from a large perennial tuber which usually has a ± tapering top and narrows into a taproot at the base. Leaves *folded upward* along the midrib, *bluish green* and usually *densely covered with hairs*. Flowers small, in axillary clusters.

Grassland. Widespread. Spring.

PLANTAGINACEAE (See page 25)

787 Plantago longissima Decne.

Herb with leaves in a *basal rosette*. Leaves narrow towards the base to form a *flattened stalk;* broad (more than 50 mm); smooth or with a few isolated hairs. Capsules with 2 – 4 seeds.

Moist areas along watercourses. Widespread. Spring – summer.

781 *Myrica pilulifera*

782 *Myrica serrata*

783 *Ximenia caffra*

783 *X. caffra* (fruit)

784 *Bonatea porrecta*

785 *Bonatea speciosa*

786 *Raphionacme galpinii*

787 *Plantago longissima*

POLYGONACEAE (See page 26)

788

788 *Rumex crispus L. *Curly dock/Wildespinasie*
Robust perennial herb. Leaves crowded towards the base, stalked, very large, hairless. Flowers in an *erect* terminal inflorescence up to ± *1,5 m* high. Fruits *3-angled*, green, turning brown as they ripen.

A native of Europe and Asia, now a weed of disturbed, and particularly moist, areas. Widespread. Spring.

789

789 Rumex lanceolatus Thunb. *Smooth dock/Gladdetongblaar*
Low-growing perennial herb. Leaves stalked, *narrowly elliptic;* margin with minute *teeth*. Flowers arranged in whorls in an erect, terminal, sparsely branched and leafless inflorescence. Fruits *3-angled*, green, turning brownish as they ripen.

Moist places along streams. Widespread. Spring.

RHAMNACEAE (See page 27)

790

790 Berchemia zeyheri (Sond.) Grubov *Red ivory/Rooi-ivoor*
Deciduous to ± evergreen tree with a dense leafy crown; young twigs often reddish purple. Leaves on short stalks, ± oval with *rounded* tips; *side veins conspicuous*, ± *sunken* in upper surface, reaching *to the margin*. Flowers solitary or clustered in leaf axils. Berries 1-seeded, red.

Bushveld, often on rocky ridges and along streams. Mainly Pretoria/ Magaliesberg region. Spring.

791

791 Helinus integrifolius (Lam.) Kuntze *Soap bush/Seepbos*
Sprawling, ± woody perennial *climber;* some shoots reduced to unbranched *coiled tendrils*. Leaves stalked; blade roundish, often ± *folded upward* along the midrib, base square to rounded, tip rounded, with a minute sharp protuberance; side veins *conspicuous*. Flowers small, in few-flowered axillary umbels. Capsules globose, *tapering at the base* into a long stalk; crowned with remains of the calyx.

Bushveld, wooded kloofs and clumps of bush, usually in rocky places. Widespread. Summer.

792

792 Rhamnus prinoides L'Herit. *Dogwood/Blinkblaar*
Evergreen shrub or small tree; sometimes ± climbing. Leaves with dark green and *very shiny* upper surface; stalks subtended by 2 long, *narrow stipules*. Flowers axillary, inconspicuous. Fruits shiny dark red to black when mature.

Often along watercourses. Widespread. All year.

793

793 Ziziphus mucronata Willd. subsp. **mucronata**
Buffalo-thorn/Blinkblaar-wag-'n-bietjie
Shrub or tree, ± deciduous, with a ± drooping crown; branches typically with 1 *hooked* and 1 *straight thorn* at each node. Leaves shiny green and *3-veined* from the base; margin usually with minute *blackish glands* near its junction with the stalk. Flowers in axillary clusters, inconspicuous. Fruits yellowish to reddish brown, with a *circular scar* where the stalk is attached at the base.

Widespread and common in various habitats. Spring – summer.

A form with few or no thorns, more hairy branchlets and relatively large fruits also occurs in the field guide region.

794

794 Ziziphus zeyheriana Sond.
Dwarf buffalo-thorn/Dwerg-blinkblaar-wag-'n-bietjie
Shrublet up to 400 mm high with many sparsely branched, upright shoots from an extensive underground rootstock. Branches with 1 *hooked* and 1 *straight* thorn at each node. Leaves shiny green, with 3 *prominent veins* from the base; margin usually with 1 – 4 *minute blackish glands* near its junction with the stalk. Flowers and fruits very similar to the previous species.

Grassland, often forming large colonies. Widespread. Spring.

788 *Rumex crispus*

789 *Rumex lanceolatus*

790 *Berchemia zeyheri*

791 *Helinus integrifolius*

792 *Rhamnus prinoides*

793 *Ziziphus mucronata*

793 *Z. mucronata* (fruit)

794 *Ziziphus zeyheriana*

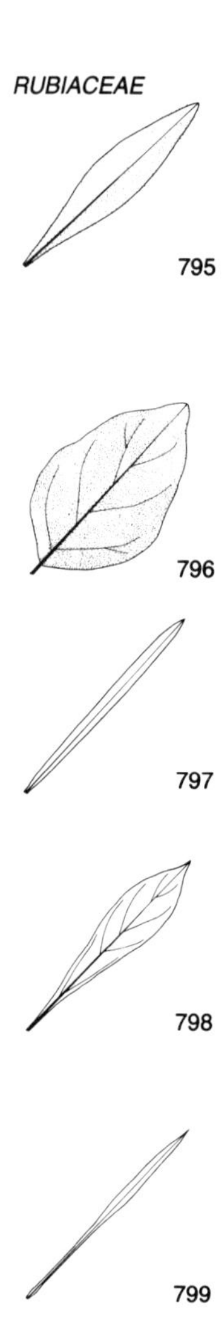

RUBIACEAE (See page 27)

795 **795 Anthospermum hispidulum** E. Mey. ex Sond.
Dwarf shrub with decumbent or erect, often *reddish brown* branches. Leaves apparently clustered in *dense whorls* on the stem; usually both surfaces densely covered with *whitish spreading hairs*. Male and female flowers usually on separate plants.
Summit grassland on rocky ridges and outcrops. Widespread. Summer.

796 **796 Canthium gilfillanii** (N.E.Br.) O.B. Miller
Velvet rock alder/Fluweelklipels
Small deciduous tree, up to ± 3 m high; bark smooth. Leaves soft, *velvety*. Flowers in branched *axillary* inflorescences; corolla lobes 5, creamy green. Fruit a drupe, black when ripe.
Rocky ridges. Widespread. Spring.
C. mundianum Cham. & Schlechtd. differs from the previous species only in that its leaves are *hairless*. The 2 species often grow together and appear to be no more than variations of the same species.

797 **797 Galium capense** Thunb. subsp. **garipense** (Sond.) Puff
Sprawling herb, often leaning on surrounding vegetation. Stems *long and slender*, with well-spaced branches. Leaves arranged in *whorls of 6 – 8; pale green*, ± *hairless*, with 1 vein.
Grassland, usually localized in wet places, particularly vleis. Widespread. Spring – summer.

798 **798 Pygmaeothamnus zeyheri** (Sond.) Robyns var. **zeyheri**
Sand apple/Goorappel
Erect, sparsely branched *dwarf shrublet* (rarely more than 200 mm high) from a woody rootstock. Leaves *opposite* or in *whorls of 3*, erect, distinctly stalked, *hairless;* tip slightly *twisted*. Fruits ± large, fleshy and yellow when ripe.
Sandy or stony grassland and bushveld, often forming bright green colonies. Mainly Pretoria/Magaliesberg region. Spring. □ Compare **763**.

799 **799 Rubia horrida** (Thunb.) Puff *Kleefgras*
Scrambling, creeping or climbing perennial herb. Stems with *minute recurved prickles* and distinctly 4-ribbed. Leaves in *whorls of 6 – 8*, up to 50 mm long, *1 – 8 mm* wide, lance-shaped, narrowing (often imperceptibly) towards the base into a slender stalk; only midrib prominent; margin and midrib with *minute recurved prickles*. Inflorescence comprises several to many flowers. Flowers with 5 petals and stamens. Fruit globose, ± fleshy, dark purple.
Wooded areas and clumps of bush. Widespread. Summer.

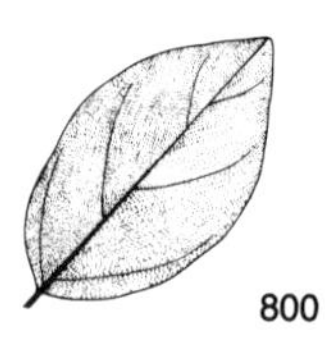

800 **800 Tapiphyllum parvifolium** (Sond.) Robyns
Mountain medlar/Bergmispel
Much-branched deciduous shrub or small tree. Leaves often *crowded* on dwarf shoots, *relatively small* (rarely more than 40 mm long), *densely covered with woolly hairs;* network of veins *not clearly visible* on lower surface. Flowers in axillary clusters, up to 5 mm in diameter. Fruit light brown when ripe.
Usually rooted between rocks on ridges and hillsides, often in exposed situations near the summit. Widespread. Spring.

801 **801 Vangueria infausta** Burch. *Wild medlar/Mispel*
Deciduous shrub or small tree; bark ± smooth. Leaves *large* (usually more than 100 mm long), *densely covered with woolly hairs*, particularly when young and on the veins of the lower surface; network of veins *conspicuous* on lower surface; sometimes with numerous *elongated* galls caused by insect activity; older leaves often twisted or curled and *rough* to the touch. Flowers in axillary clusters, up to 6 mm in diameter. Fruits yellowish to brown when ripe.
Mainly on rocky hillsides. Widespread. Spring.

795 *Anthospermum hispidulum* (female)

795 *A. hispidulum* (male)

796 *Canthium gilfillanii*

797 *Galium capense*

798 *Pygmaeothamnus zeyheri*

799 *Rubia horrida*

800 *Tapiphyllum parvifolium*

801 *Vangueria infausta*

802

SALICACEAE (See page 27)

802 *Salix babylonica L. *Weeping willow/Treurwilger*

Deciduous tree with long, *slender, drooping* branches. Leaves narrow and lance-shaped; both surfaces *bright green;* margin toothed. *Only female* trees occur in South Africa. Flowers borne in *drooping spikes*, each supported by a hairy bract.

Along streams, spreading vegetatively (usually assisted by man) in the absence of seeds. A native of China. Spring. □ Compare **425**.

803

SANTALACEAE (See page 27)

803 Osyris lanceolata Hochst. & Steud. *Transvaal sumach/Bergbas*

Sparsely branched *evergreen* shrub or small tree. Bark *blackish* with the living inner bark conspicuously pinkish red. Leaves *alternate, bluish green*, thick and leathery, with a pointed tip. Flowers axillary, greenish yellow. Berries crowned with the remains of the sepals; orange to bright red when ripe.

Usually on rocky ridges and hillsides. Sparsely distributed and apparently a hemiparasite. Spring – autumn.

804

SAPINDACEAE (See page 27)

804 Dodonaea angustifolia L.f. *Sand olive/Sandolien*

Much-branched shrub with dark grey, *stringy* bark. Leaves *shiny*, light green, covered with a *resinous secretion*. Male and female flowers usually on separate plants. Flowers with sepals 4 – 7; petals absent; filaments very short. Capsules with 2 or 3 thin *papery wings;* greenish red.

Bushveld. Mainly Pretoria/Magaliesberg region. Autumn – spring.

805

ULMACEAE (See page 28)

805 Celtis africana Burm.f. *White stinkwood/Witstinkhout*

Deciduous tree up to ± 10 m high; young shoots velvety; bark *smooth* and greyish. Leaves *3-veined* from the base; covered with ± *velvety hairs;* margin toothed in *upper half*. Flowers in axillary clusters, inconspicuous, creamy green. Drupe globose, pale yellow.

Wooded areas and clumps of bush, often on dolomite. Widespread. Spring.

806

URTICACEAE (See page 29) See also **446**.

806 Pouzolzia mixta Solms [=**P. hypoleuca** Wedd.] *Soapbush/Seepbos*

Deciduous shrub; bark *smooth*. Leaves stalked, ± egg-shaped, with long tapering tips; distinctly *3-veined* from the base; dull green and hairy above, densely covered with *white felt* below. Flowers minute, male and female on same plant, borne in axillary clusters; anthers release the pollen explosively. Capsules shiny, brown or whitish.

Bushveld, on dry rocky hillsides. Mainly Magaliesberg. Spring.

VISCACEAE (See page 29)

807 Viscum rotundifolium L.f. *Mistletoe/Voëlent*

Evergreen hemiparasite, often forming *rounded clusters* on the host. Leaves small, ± *rounded*, thick and leathery, often bluish green. Flowers very small and *inconspicuous*. Berries *bright scarlet* with a sticky pulp.

A common parasite on many hosts, notably **Ehretia rigida** (**639**) and **Ziziphus mucronata** (**793**). Widespread. Autumn – spring.

V. combreticola Engl. is a *leafless* shrub with branches that are usually yellowish green, *pendulous*, and conspicuously *flattened* when young. Fruits orange when ripe. Usually parasitic on species of **Combretum** and **Acacia**. Mainly Pretoria/Magaliesberg region.

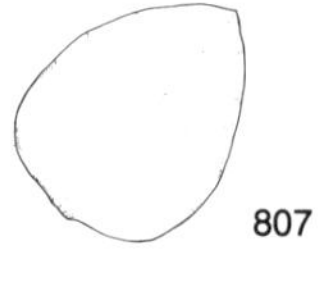

807

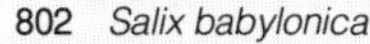

802 *Salix babylonica*

803 *Osyris lanceolata*

804 *Dodonaea angustifolia*

805 *Celtis africana*

806 *Pouzolzia mixta*

807 *Viscum rotundifolium*

807 *V. rotundifolium* (berries)

THE GRASSES

Grasses are flowering plants which, because of their adaptation to wind pollination, have flowers that are considerably reduced and lack the colourful petals so typical of many flowers. The family to which the grasses belong – Poaceae – has also acquired a peculiar terminology, and for this reason we have decided to treat this specialized group of plants in a section of its own.

The Poaceae is one of the largest of the flowering plant families. With about 500 genera, it ranks third behind the Asteraceae and Orchidaceae, and with more than 8 000 species it takes fourth place, behind the Asteraceae, Orchidaceae and Fabaceae. However, in terms of number of individual plants the Poaceae is the largest and most widely distributed family of flowering plants in the world. In the field guide area this family is not only the largest (about 240 species), but also in numbers it dominates the vegetation of both grassland and bushveld areas.

Directly as cereals, and indirectly as fodder for domestic livestock, the grasses are by far the most important food source for man. They withstand grazing better than other plants because the main growing region of each leaf is at the base of the blade, instead of throughout the leaf as in most other plants. The leaves also have the ability to continue growing for an extended time, an ability not shared by the mature leaves of other plant groups. In grasses the growth region, or intercalary meristem, allows the blade to continue growing from the base after the upper part has been grazed away.

Grasses are most frequently confused with the sedges (Cyperaceae), another family which is pollinated mainly by wind and has reduced flowers borne in bracteate clusters and lacking colourful petals. Although there are well over 100 sedge species in the field guide area, most are relatively uncommon and prefer rather specialized wet habitats. A few sedges have been included in the main colour sections (see **74 – 76**, **297**, **703 – 708**, **761** and **762**; compare also **733** of the Typhaceae family). Some conspicuous characters which distinguish Poaceae from Cyperaceae are given below.

Character	Poaceae	Cyperaceae
Stems	jointed with distinct nodes and internodes; internodes ± round in cross-section	usually not jointed and often triangular in cross-section
Leaves	in 2 ranks; sheath split open with overlapping margins; ligule usually present	in 3 ranks; sheath closed (tubular); ligule absent or poorly developed
Inflorescence	usually spikes, racemes or panicles; not subtended by leaf-like bracts	often umbellate or in heads; subtended by leaf-like bracts
Flower	each flower of the spikelet contained between 2 bracts (lemma and palea)	each flower of the spikelet in the axil of a single bract (glume)

Table 1. Selected morphological differences between POACEAE and CYPERACEAE

IDENTIFICATION OF GRASSES IN FLOWER

Vegetatively the grasses are rather similar and it is essential to recognize features of the reproductive structures (or 'flowers') in order to distinguish between genera and between species. In many grasses the highly condensed spikelets are extremely difficult to interpret and painstaking dissection under the microscope may be necessary to reveal their true construction. However, in this guide we follow a visual approach based only on details of external morphology, and although picture-matching is perhaps a not very reliable method to identify a grass, we believe that our selection of species will ensure a high rate of correct identifications. The use of a hand lens with about 10x magnification is, however, essential to compare the external morphology of the spikelets. The 74 grass species described in this section are those most likely to be seen. They have been sorted into three groups (A, B and C) according to the visual appearance of the inflorescence (Table 2). Group C has been subdivided into two (C.1 and C.2) on the basis of the presence or absence of conspicuous awns.

Group A (**808 – 830**)

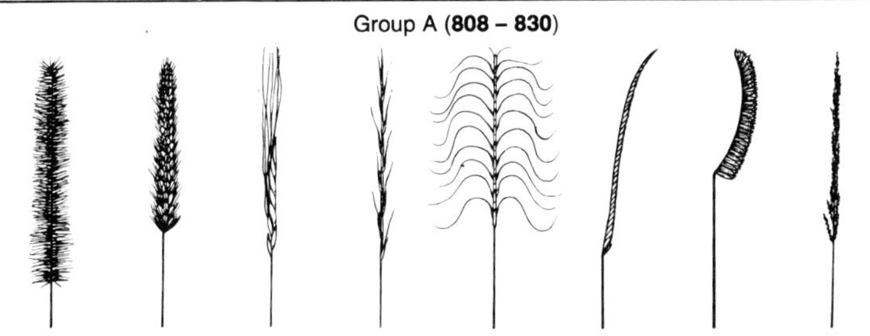

Inflorescence a single terminal spike or spike-like raceme; alternatively, a panicle with side branches contracted close to the central axis, forming a narrow, spike-like mass.

Group B (**831 – 846**)

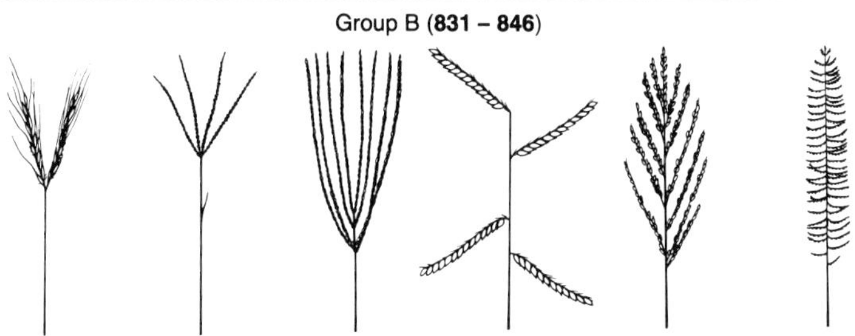

Inflorescence of 2 or more unbranched, spike-like side branches arranged digitately or ± digitately at or near the top of a central axis; alternatively, spike-like, unbranched side branches well and often regularly spaced along the central axis, and always with the spikelets densely packed along 1 side of the rhachis.

Group C

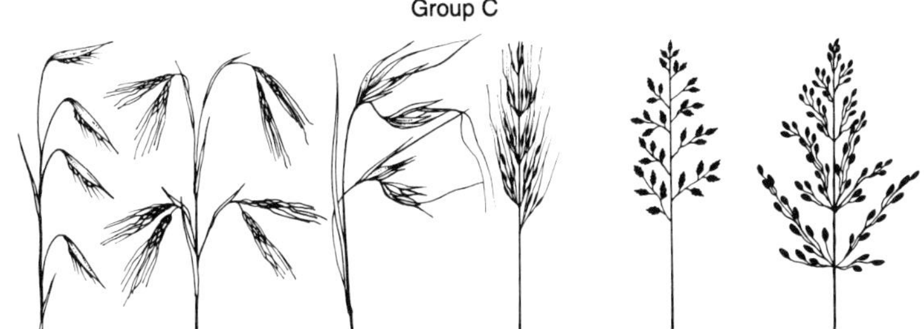

Inflorescence an open branched system with the side branches bearing solitary, paired or multiple spike-like racemes, either on short or long slender stalks often subtended by boat-shaped spathes, or digitately arranged; alternatively, an open panicle with a central axis and numerous, often branched side branches, with the spikelets not densely packed on 1 side of the rhachis.

Group C.1 (**847 – 862**)

Spikelets with awns conspicuous and more than 10 mm long.

Group C.2 (**863 – 881**)

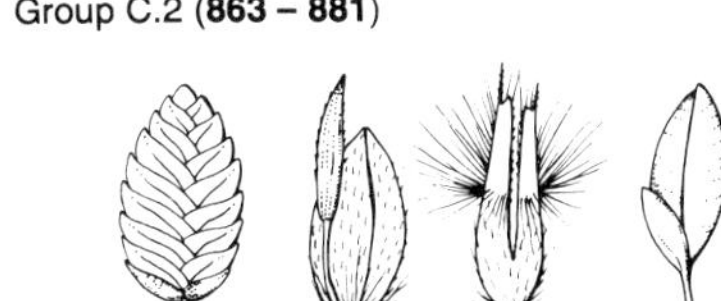

Spikelets with awns absent or less than 10 mm long.

Table 2. Guide to the grass groups

Compare the inflorescence of the grass to be identified with the illustrations in Table 2 to determine to which group it belongs. The drawings in this table depict only a few selected examples of inflorescences or spikelets and not all the possibilities included in the field guide. Although not all grasses will easily fit into one of the four groups, most of them will, thus simplifying the final identification. Proceed by comparing the grass with the photographs under the relevant group, noting also the cross references at the beginning of each group. Having matched a specimen with one of the photographs, compare it with the accompanying drawings, using a hand lens to study the spikelets if necessary. Also consult the species description for additional diagnostic features and habitat details.

Each species entry consists of a colour photograph of one or more inflorescences, line drawings, and descriptive text which has been kept very short, particularly when the photograph alone would ensure a correct identification.

The information on habitat can be useful since grasses adapted to moist or marshy sites or disturbed places are usually consistently present in such habitats. The designation of succession in some entries refers to the progressive change in composition of a plant community from initial colonization of a bare area towards a largely stable climax. Pioneer grasses are those that favour disturbed areas where they prepare the habitat for the more stable subclimax and climax species which supplant them. Climax grasses form part of the more or less established and undisturbed plant communities which are in equilibrium with existing environmental conditions. The statement on some species' palatability to grazers may be of interest to farmers. 'Sour', in terms of veld grazing, refers to the fact that the grasses are tall, wiry and tufted, rapidly losing their nutritive value after flowering and becoming fibrous, hard and unpalatable during the dry season.

When attempting to identify a grass, pay particular attention to the parts of the plant highlighted in Figure 4. These may be matched against the line drawings for each species which detail its most visible diagnostic characters. The letter at the bottom of each panel in Figure 4 corresponds to that at each species entry, and to the explanatory notes supplied on the opposite page. Figures are not drawn to the same scale.

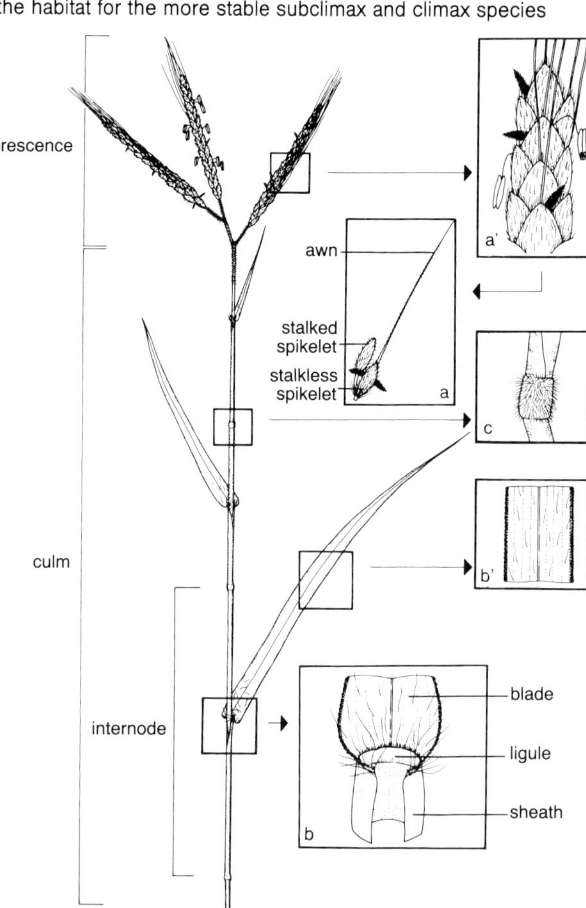

Figure 4. **Dichanthium aristatum** (Poir.) C.E.Hubb. Culm with terminal inflorescence showing those parts of the grass plant depicted in the line drawings for each species. a. Spikelet or group of spikelets. a'. Enlarged portion of inflorescence. b. Portion of leaf at junction of sheath and blade. b'. Portion of leaf blade. c. Node.

a. Spikelet or group of spikelets

The spikelet, comparable to the flower of petaloid plants, comprises one or more stalkless flowers and their attendant chaffy bracts. All are densely arranged on a slender axis (rhachilla) which is often zigzag and concealed by the overlapping bracts. At the base of the spikelet may be two bracts: the lower or first glume, and the upper or second glume. Each flower is typically tightly enclosed by two additional bracts, the lemma (resembling the glumes) and the palea (generally enfolded by and shorter than the lemma). The lemma and palea with the enclosed flower is termed a floret (see Figure 14, page 343, for a drawing of a typical grass spikelet). Some of the bracts may bear accessory structures such as hairs or bristles, or awns, which are bristle-like outgrowths of the glume or lemma (rarely the palea) and may be simple or branched. Some awns are sensitive to changes in humidity and may display coiling movements which drill the fruit into the ground.

The actual flowers of grasses are minute and very similar, and for classification purposes the bracts surrounding the flowers are far more important. Some quite unrelated grasses may look superficially very similar until the structure of the spikelets – the sex of the flower(s), the number, size and shape of the different bracts, and the number of florets – is carefully examined with the aid of a lens. Spikelet comparison also serves to check that an identification is correct. In some grasses the spikelets are borne in pairs (as in Figure 4), one member of each pair stalkless, the other on a stalk. Usually the members of a pair are quite different. The stalkless spikelet is usually awned and bisexual, and the stalked one awnless and male or sterile. In some of the drawings stamens and feathery stigmas are shown protruding from between the bracts. Their presence or absence should not be considered diagnostic, as they have been added merely because of their presence in the live material when the drawings were made.

a'. Enlarged portion of inflorescence

Supplied for a few species only, this type of drawing shows the arrangement of the spikelets on the inflorescence axis at the time of flowering. It should, however, be noted that the inflorescence of a species may change its appearance at the various stages of development (for example, **830**).

b. Portion of leaf at the junction of sheath and blade

This drawing shows the base of the leaf blade, the ligule and part of the sheath. The blade is free of the culm and usually long and narrow. Note whether the blade is flat, folded or cylindrical, and whether the base is tapering or expanded and ± heart-shaped. The ligule is an extension of the leaf sheath and occurs on the inner surface of the leaf at the junction of sheath and blade. It may be a thin, white or brownish membrane, a membrane tipped with hairs, or a fringe of hairs. Although the form of the ligule is often useful for identifying species, between individuals of the same species there may be some variation in the degree of hairiness at the sheath/blade junction. The drawings should therefore serve as a rough guide only. The leaf sheath is the split tubular portion of the leaf, usually surrounding the culm with overlapping margins. Its presence can be used to distinguish between a grass and a sedge, while its hairiness and colour may be helpful for species recognition.

b'. Portion of leaf blade

Grass leaves show no differentiation between stalk and blade (lamina), although in a few species the blade may taper at the base into a narrow, stalk-like section (for example, **878**). Part of the blade has been illustrated mainly to indicate a difference between the degree of blade expansion at the base and at a position closer to the tip.

c. Node

The jointed stem of a grass, called a culm, is made up of a series of nodes and internodes. Nodes are often swollen and are the parts of the culm from which the leaves arise. They may be hairless, or have short or long hairs which can be appressed, spreading, or backward-pointing. The hairiness of the nodes is sometimes diagnostic and has been illustrated for a few species.

IMPORTANT

Although this section covers 74 of the most common grass species in the field guide area, this number represents less than half the number of species that occur here. The selection of species has been based not only on the frequency with which they occur, but also on the ease with which they may be recognized. We have, for example, given little attention to the genera *Eragrostis* and *Aristida*, both of which are represented by many species in the field guide area, but most of these are difficult to recognize, particularly from photographs.

POACEAE (See page 26)

Group A (See also **837**, **869**, **876, 878**)

808 Aristida adscensionis L. subsp. **adscensionis**
[=**A. curvata** (Nees) Dur. & Schinz.]
Annual bristle grass/Eenjarige steekgras

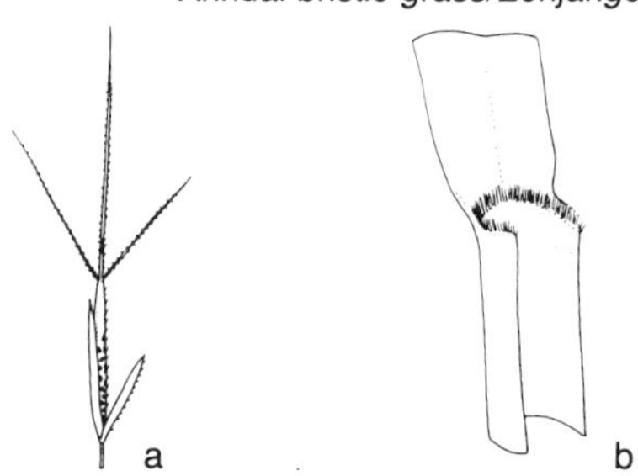

Annual growing in tufts; often tinged with purple. Disturbed places. Indicative of veld deterioration.

809 Aristida congesta Roem. & Schult. subsp. **congesta**
White stick grass/Witsteekgras

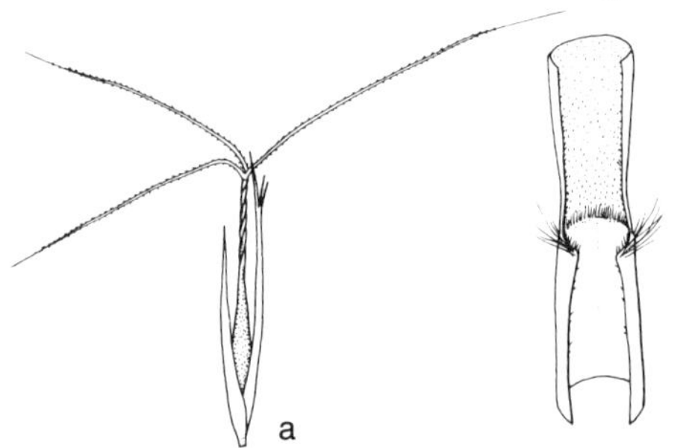

Annual or perennial growing in tufts; inflorescence sometimes with 1 or 2 branches at the base. Disturbed places. Indicative of veld deterioration.

810 Aristida transvaalensis Henr. *Klipgras*

Perennial growing in tufts; culms usually profusely branched; 2 awns much shorter than the third. Rocky ridges, often wedged in rock fissures.

811 Cenchrus ciliaris L. *Blue buffalo grass/Bloubuffelsgras*

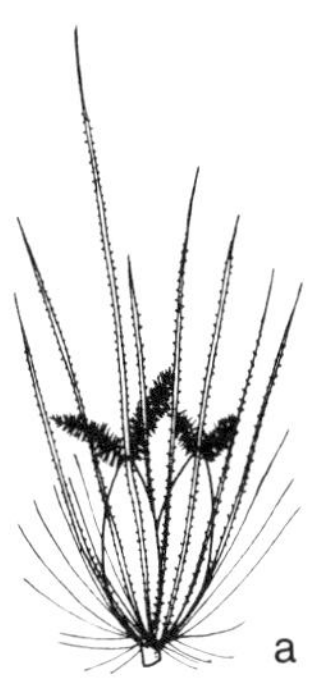
a

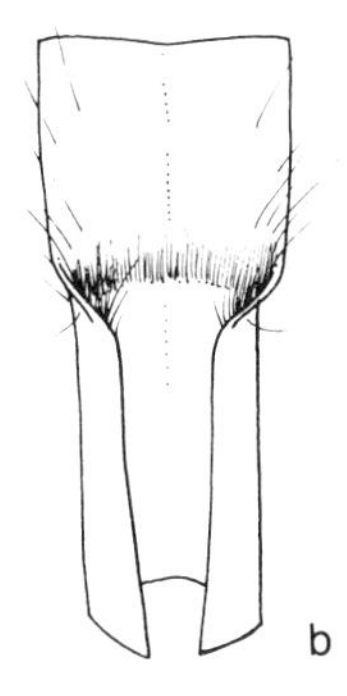
b

Perennial growing in tufts or spreading by means of stolons. Disturbed places, often along roadsides. A valuable pasture grass.

812 Elionurus muticus (Spreng.) Kunth
[=**E. argenteus** Nees] *Sour grass/Suurgras*

a

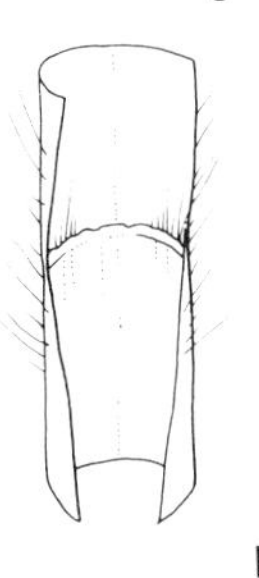
b

Perennial growing in tufts; spikes curling back at maturity. Open grassland, often on stony hillsides. Unpalatable climax or subclimax grass. Indicative of sourveld.

813 Enneapogon cenchroides (Roem. & Schult.) C.E. Hubb.
Grey sour grass/Vaalsuurgras

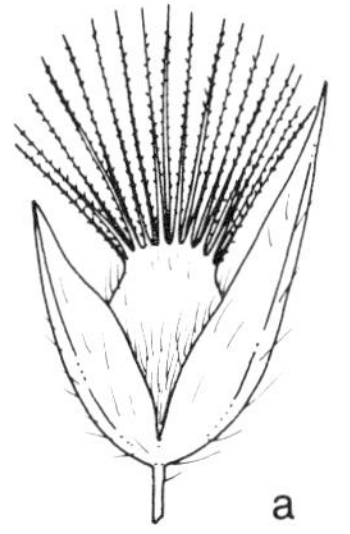
a

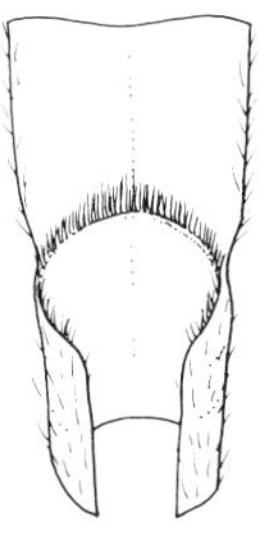
b

Annual growing in tufts. Disturbed places. Relatively unpalatable pioneer grass.

814 Harpochloa falx (L.f.) Kuntze
Caterpillar grass/Ruspergras

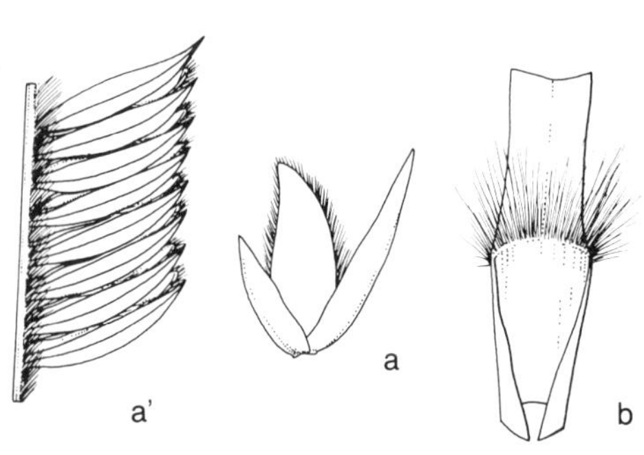

Perennial growing in tufts. Open grassland, often on stony hillsides. Highly palatable climax grass.

815 Heteropogon contortus (L.) Roem. & Schult.
Spear grass/Assegaaigras

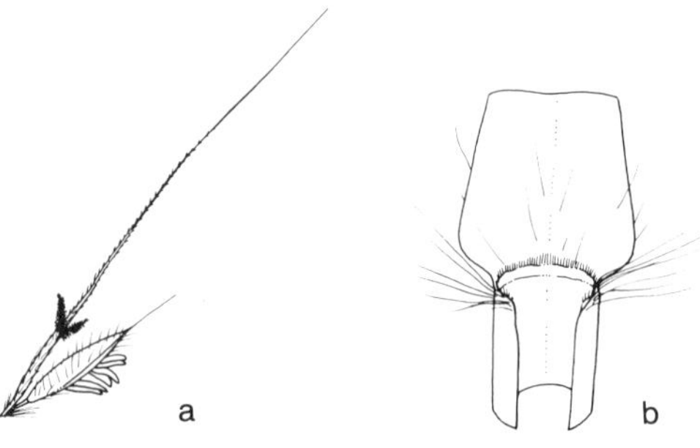

Perennial growing in tufts. Open grassland and stony hillsides. Palatable.

816 Imperata cylindrica (L.) Raeuschel
Cottonwool grass/Donsgras

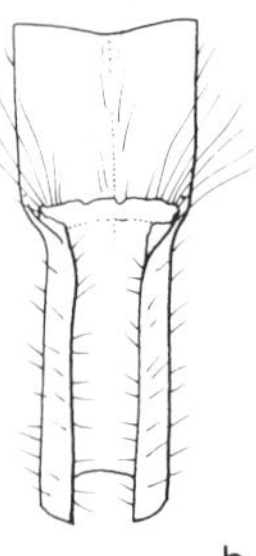

Perennial with spreading rhizomes. Moist places and along streams, often forming pure stands in vleis. Unpalatable climax grass.

817 Microchloa caffra Nees *Pincushion grass/Elsgras*

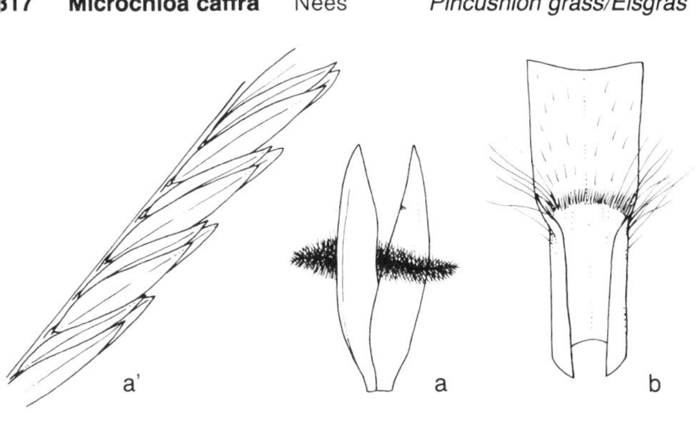

Perennial growing in short tufts. Often in shallow soil overlying sheets of rock. Unpalatable pioneer grass.

818 *Pennisetum setaceum (Forssk.) Chiov.
Fountain grass/Pronkgras

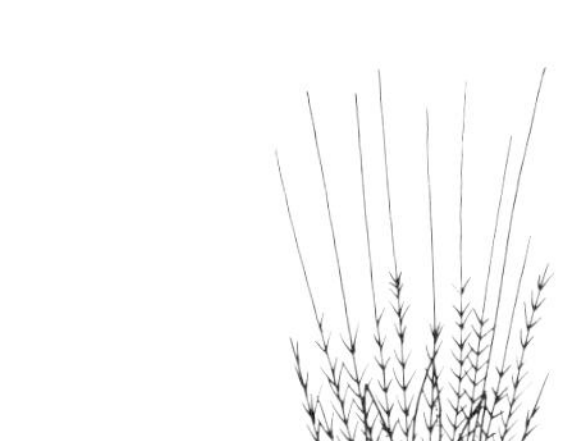

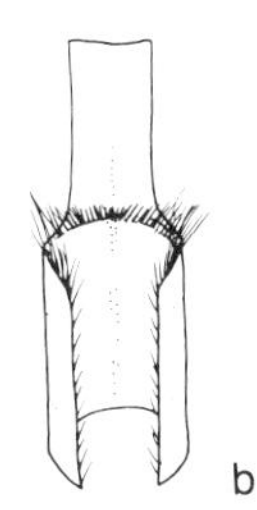

Perennial growing in tufts. Disturbed places, often along roadsides; an escape from cultivation; native to tropical Africa. Unpalatable.

819 Pennisetum thunbergii Kunth *Kleinmannagras*

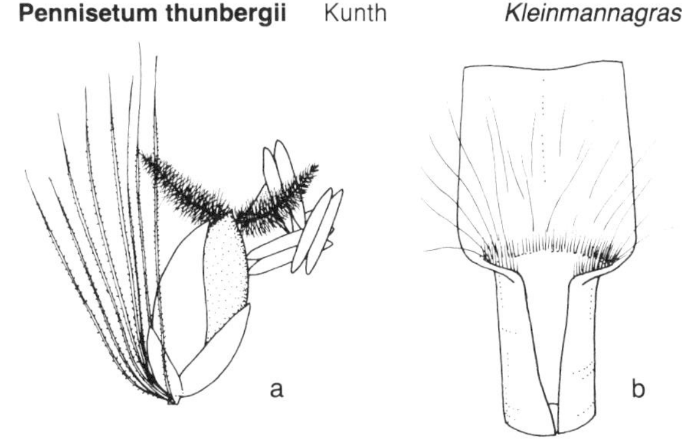

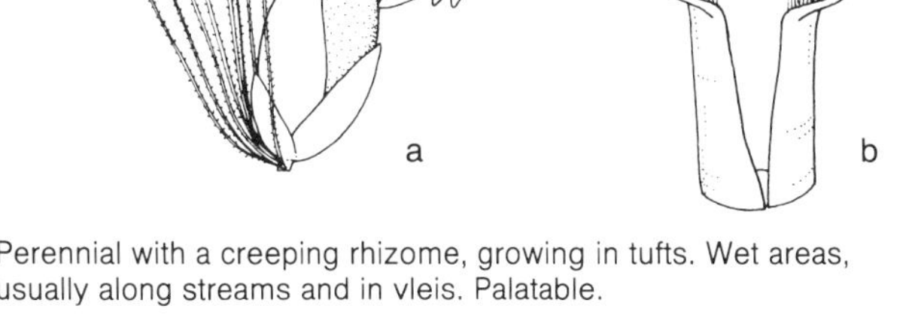

Perennial with a creeping rhizome, growing in tufts. Wet areas, usually along streams and in vleis. Palatable.

820 Perotis patens Gand. *Bottle-brush grass/Katstertgras*

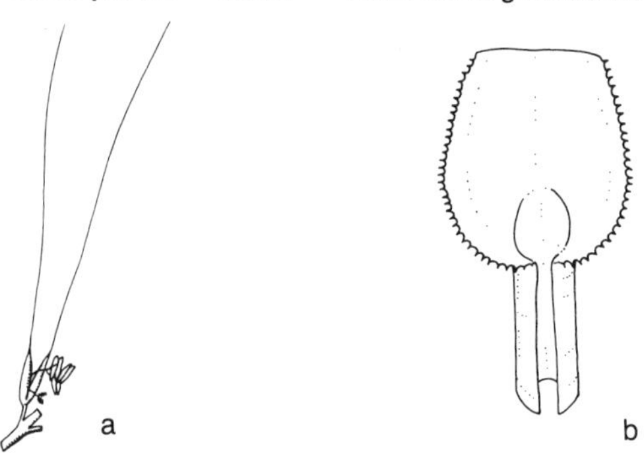

Annual growing in short tufts. Disturbed places. A pioneer grass, often in sandy soil; increases under conditions of poor veld management.

821 Schizachyrium sanguineum (Retz.) Alst.
[=**S. semiberbe** Nees] *Red autumn grass/Rooiherfsgras*

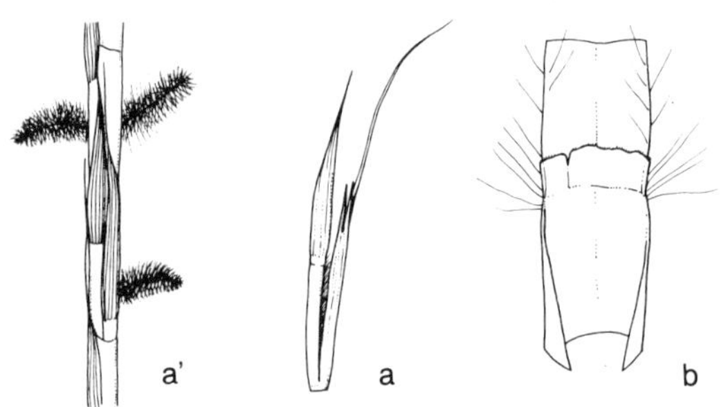

Perennial growing in tufts; turns reddish in autumn. Open grassland, often on stony hillsides. Moderately palatable climax grass.

822 Setaria nigrirostris (Nees) Dur. & Schinz
Black seed setaria/Swartsaadmannagras

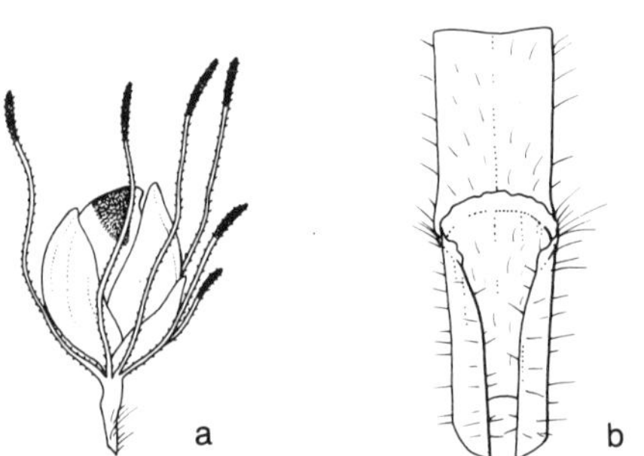

Perennial growing in tufts; spikelets usually with dark purple tips. Open grassland, often in black clay soil. Palatable climax grass.

823 Setaria pallide-fusca (Schumach.) Stapf & C.E. Hubb.
Garden setaria/Tuin-setaria

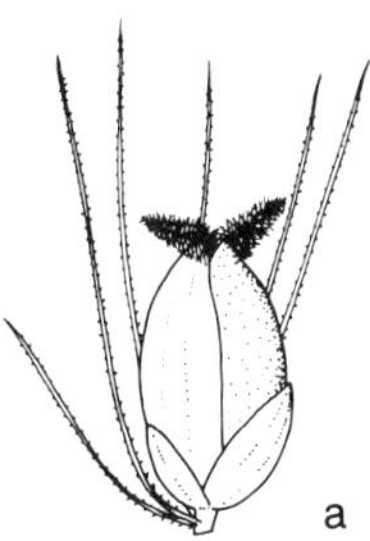
a

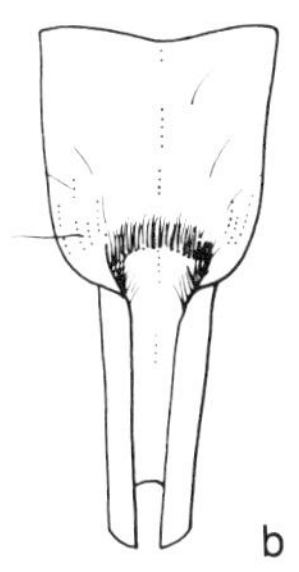
b

Annual growing in loose tufts; low-growing; leaves yellowish green; old inflorescences often orange-yellow. Disturbed places. Palatable pioneer grass. Sometimes treated as **S. pumila** (Poir.) Roem. & Schult.

824 Setaria sphacelata (Schumach.) Moss var. **sericea** (Stapf) Clayton
Golden setaria/Katstertmannagras

a

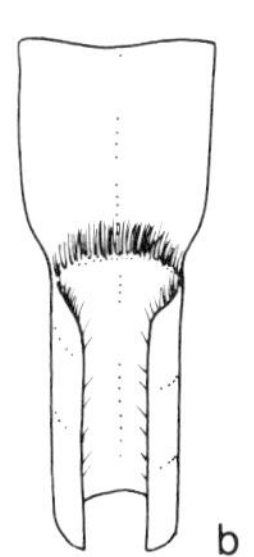
b

Perennial growing in tufts usually more than 1 m high. Open grassland, often in moist places. Flowering in summer and autumn. Highly palatable.

825 Setaria sphacelata (Schumach.) Moss var. **sphacelata** [=**S. perennis** Hack.]

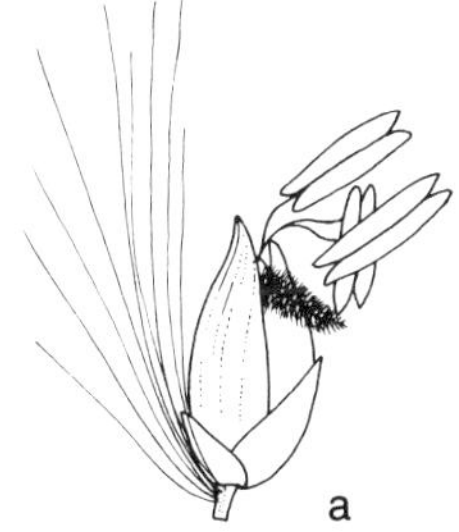
a

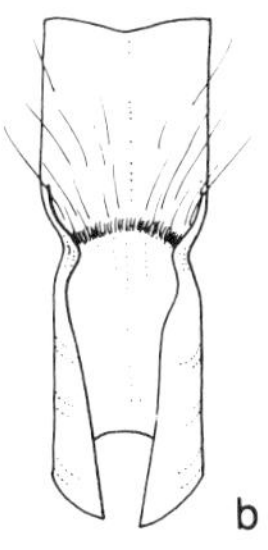
b

Perennial growing in tufts rarely more than 400 mm high. Open grassland, often on rocky hillsides. Flowering in spring and early summer. Palatable.

826 Setaria verticillata (L.) Beauv.
Sticky bristle grass/Klitsgras

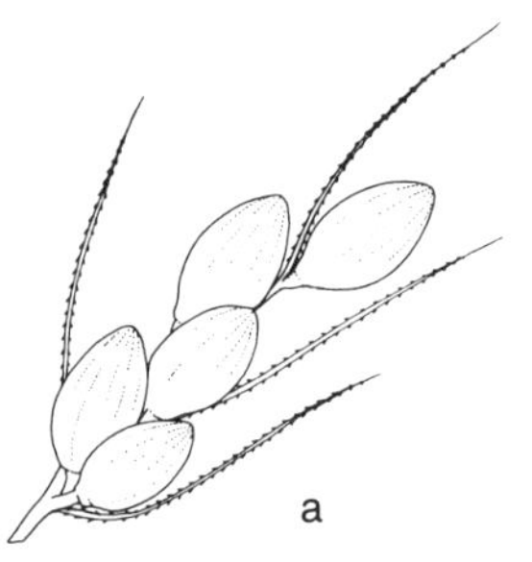

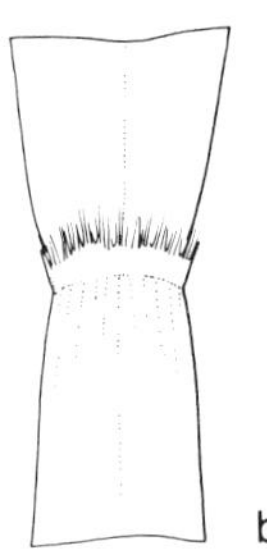

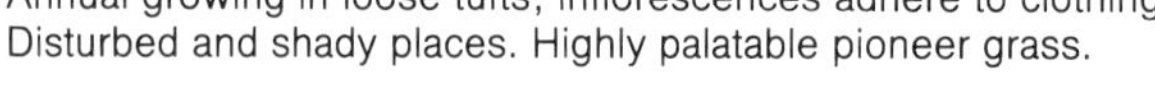

Annual growing in loose tufts; inflorescences adhere to clothing. Disturbed and shady places. Highly palatable pioneer grass.

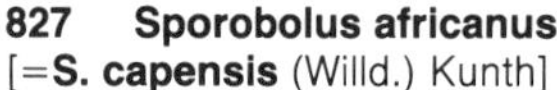

827 Sporobolus africanus (Poir.) Robyns & Tournay [=**S. capensis** (Willd.) Kunth]
Rat's-tail dropseed/Taaipol

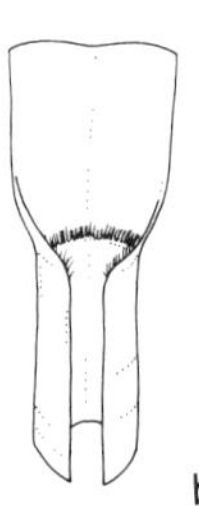

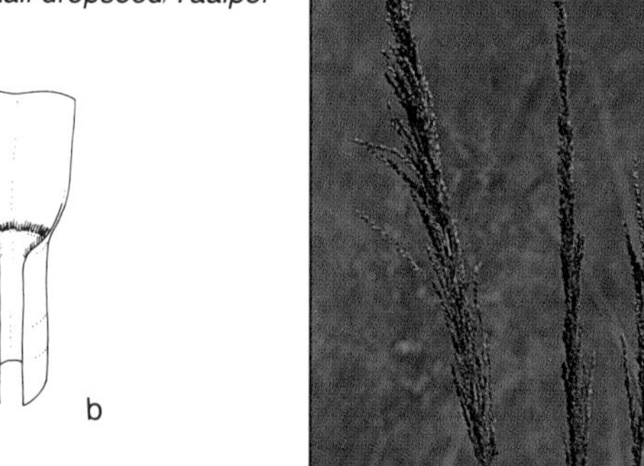

Perennial growing in tufts, very difficult to uproot. Open grassland and disturbed places. Unpalatable.

828 Trachypogon spicatus (L.f.) Kuntze [=**T. capensis** (Thunb.) Trin.]
Giant spear grass/Bokbaardgras

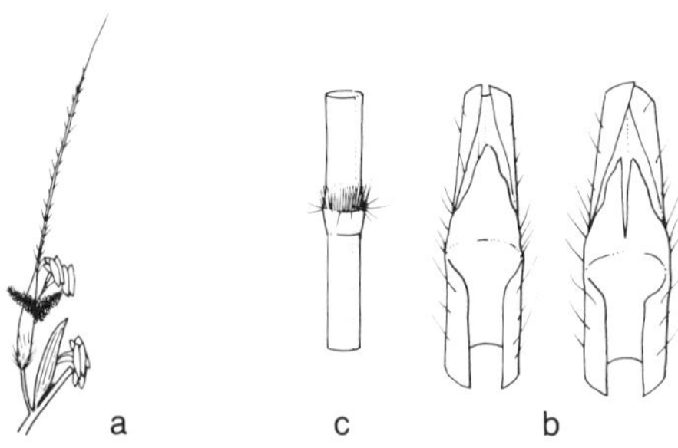

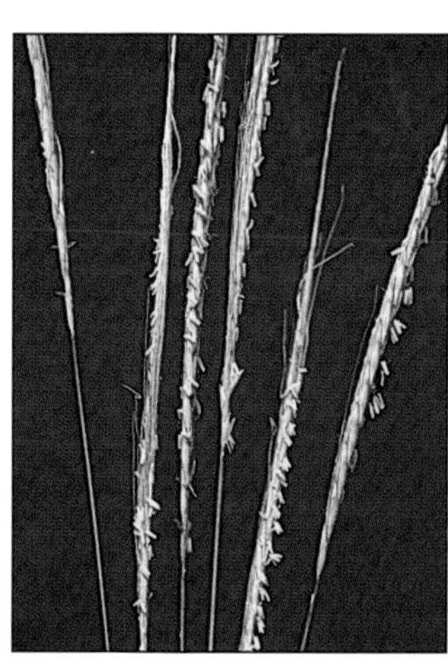

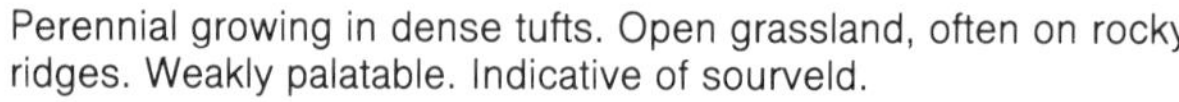

Perennial growing in dense tufts. Open grassland, often on rocky ridges. Weakly palatable. Indicative of sourveld.

829 Tragus berteronianus Schult.
Carrot seed grass/Wortelsaadgras

Low-growing annual; spikelets adhere to clothing. Disturbed places.

830 Urelytrum agropyroides (Hack.) Hack.
[=**U. squarrosum** Hack.] *Centipede grass/Varkstertgras*

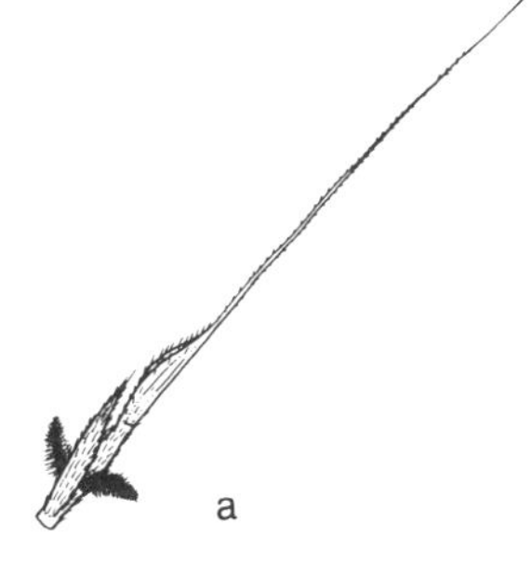

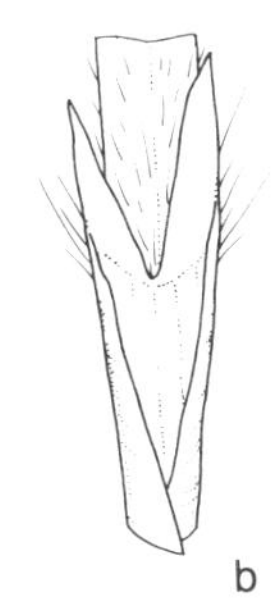

Robust perennial growing in tufts up to 1,5 m high; bitter-tasting. Open grassland, often on rocky ridges. Unpalatable climax grass.

POACEAE Group B
(See also Figure 4, **847**, **863**, **870**, **871**, **881**)
831 Alloteropsis semialata (R.Br.) Hitchc.
Blackseed grass/Swartsaadgras

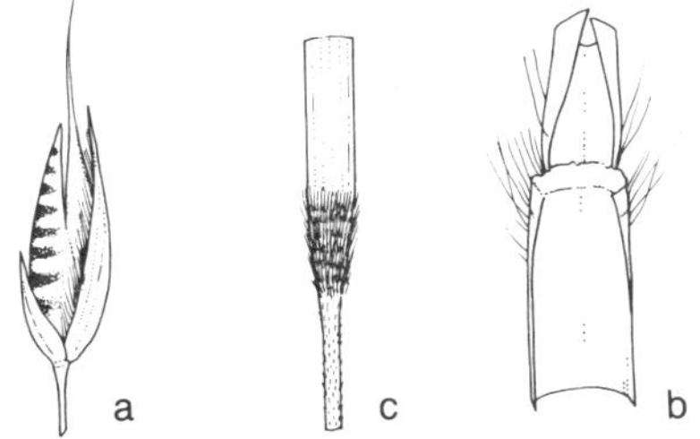

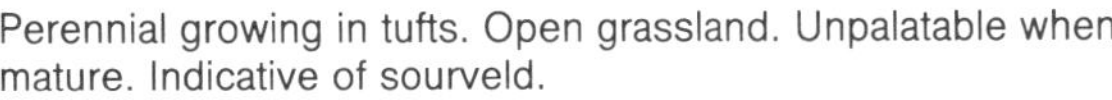
Perennial growing in tufts. Open grassland. Unpalatable when mature. Indicative of sourveld.

832 Andropogon schirensis A. Rich. *Tweevingergras*

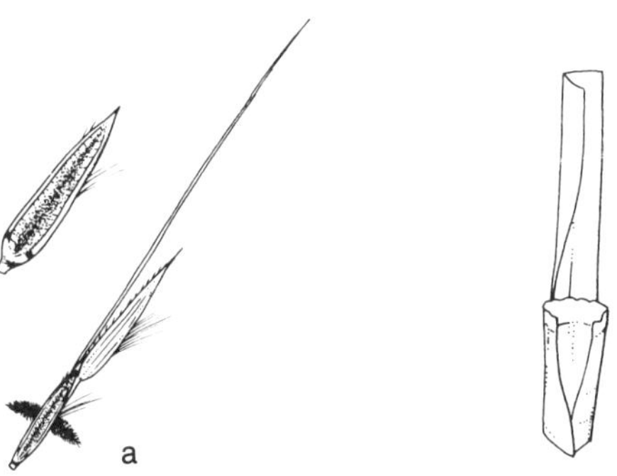

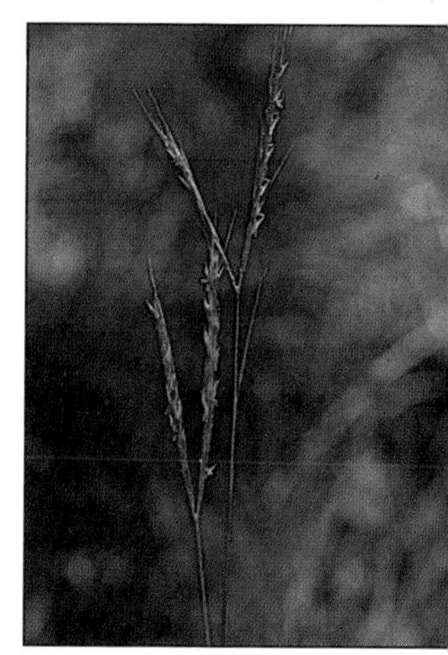

Perennial growing in tufts; leaves often with a reddish brown tinge. Usually on rocky hillsides.

833 Bothriochloa insculpta (A. Rich.) A. Camus
Pinhole grass/Stippelgras

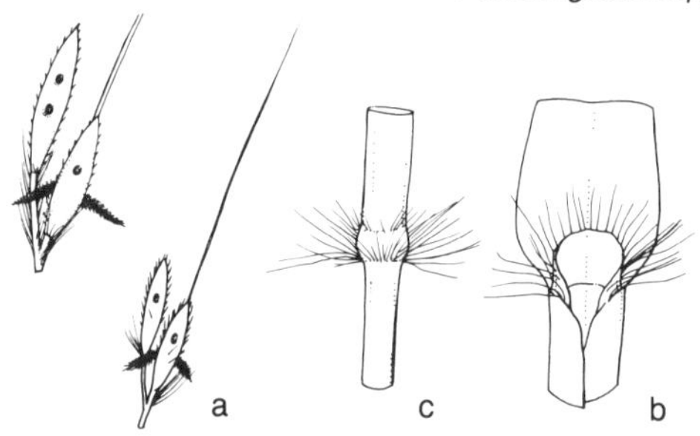

Perennial growing in tufts or by means of stolons; lower glume of some or all spikelets with 1 – 3 pits. Often in disturbed places, particularly along roadsides and pavements. Compare Figure 4.

834 Brachiaria serrata (Thunb.) Stapf
Velvet grass/Fluweelgras

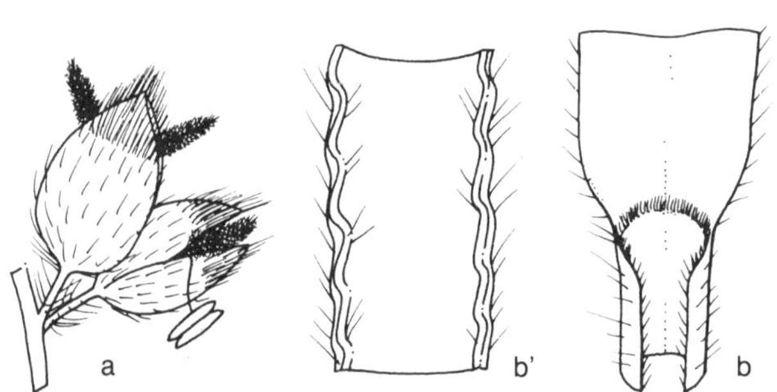

Perennial growing in tufts. Open grassland, often on rocky hillsides. Palatable. Indicative of veld in good condition.

835 Chloris gayana Kunth *Rhodes grass/Rhodes-gras*

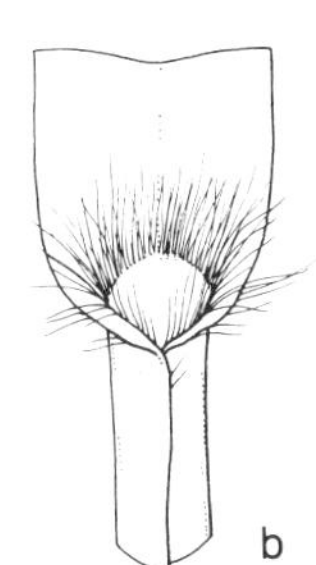

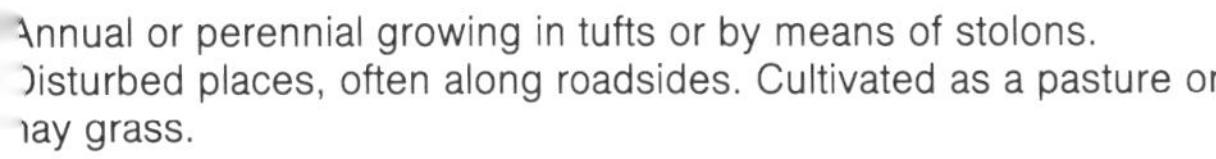

Annual or perennial growing in tufts or by means of stolons. Disturbed places, often along roadsides. Cultivated as a pasture or hay grass.

836 Chloris pycnothrix Trin. *Spiderweb grass/Spinnerakgras*

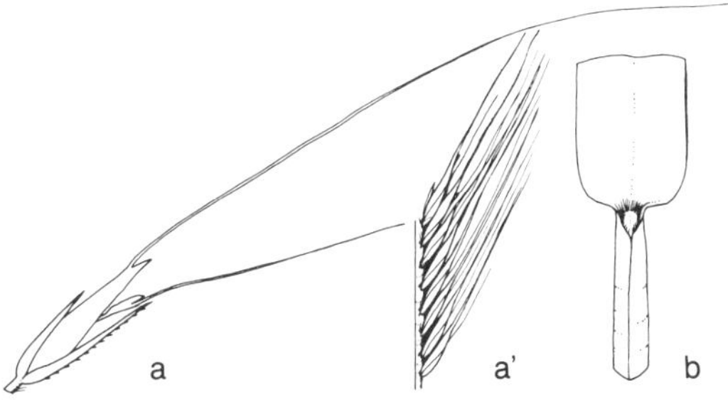

Low-growing annual, spreading by means of stolons. Disturbed places, often a weed in gardens and on pavements. Fairly palatable.

837 Chloris virgata Swartz *Feathertop grass/Witpluimgras*

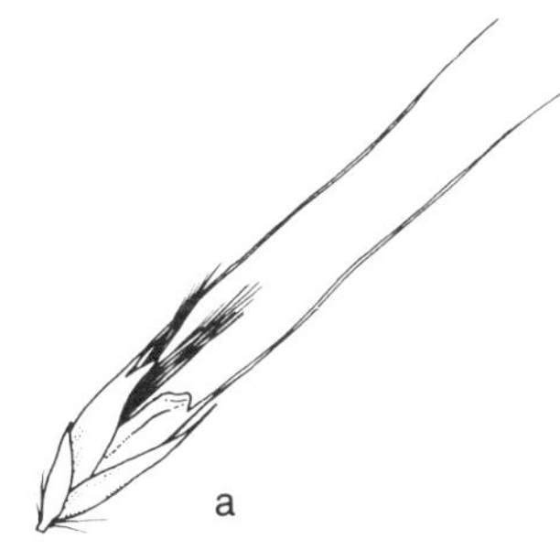

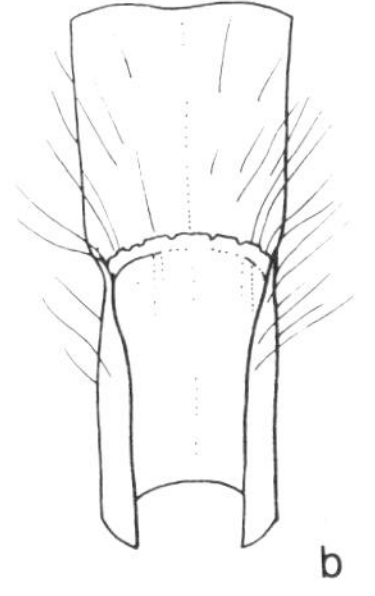

Annual or short-lived perennial growing in tufts. Disturbed places, often along roadsides. Palatable, providing good grazing and hay.

838 **Cynodon dactylon** (L.) Pers. *Couch grass/Kweek*

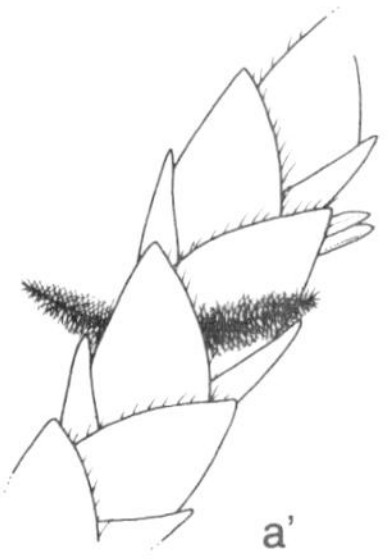

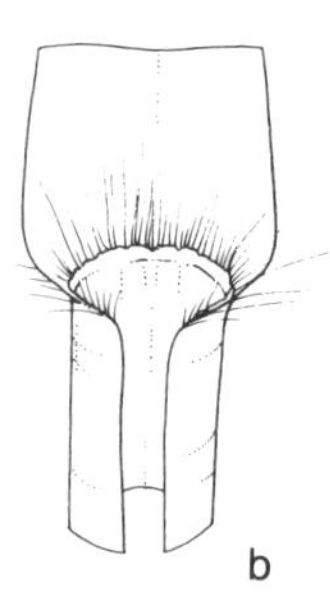

Creeping perennial. Disturbed places. Used as a lawn grass. Palatable pioneer grass.

839 **Digitaria diagonalis** (Nees) Stapf var. **diagonalis**

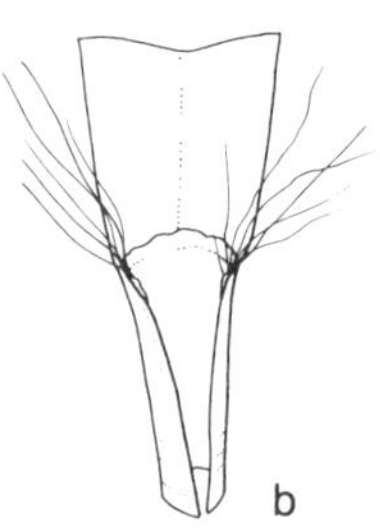

Perennial growing in tufts up to 1,5 m high; lower leaf sheaths conspicuously hairy. Sour grassland, often on hillsides. Palatable climax grass.

840 **Digitaria eriantha** Steud [=**D. smutsii** Stent]
Finger grass/Vingergras

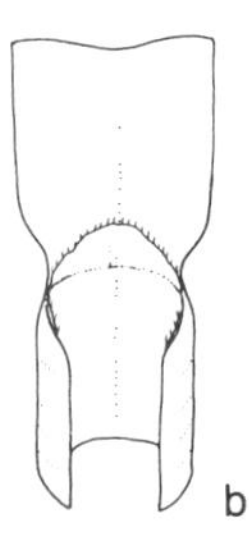

Perennial growing in tufts. Open grassland. Very palatable climax grass; cultivated as a pasture or hay grass.

841 Diheteropogon amplectens (Nees) Clayton
[=**Andropogon amplectens** Nees]
Broad-leaved blue grass/Breëblaarblougras

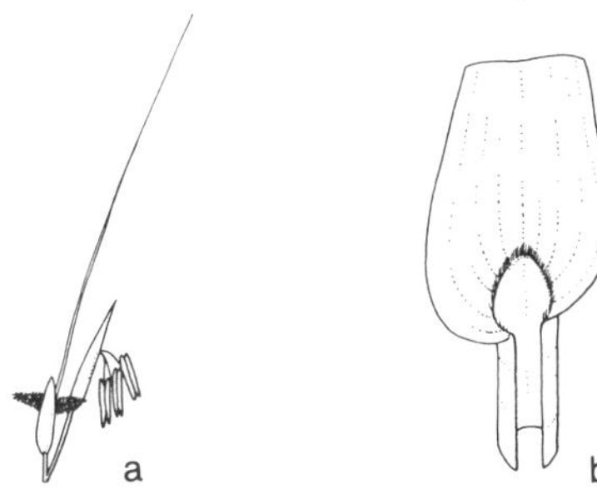

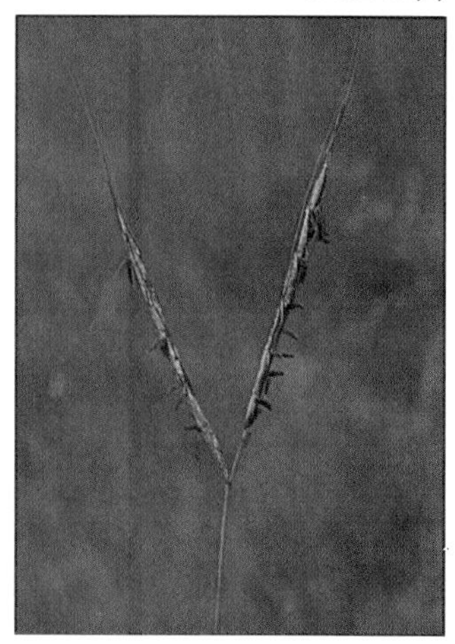

Bluish perennial growing in tufts; blade bases broad and stem-clasping. Open grassland, often on hillsides. Moderately palatable.

842 Eleusine coracana (L.) Gaertn. subsp. **africana** (K.-O'Byrne) Hilu & De Wet [=**E. africana** K.-O'Byrne]
Goose grass/Jongosgras

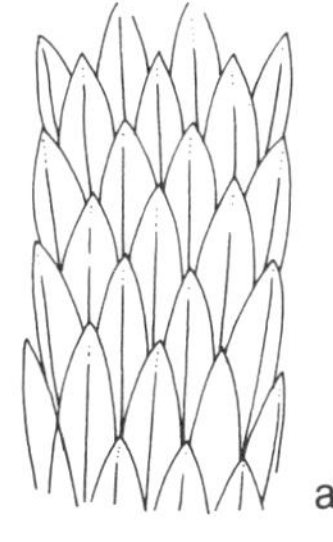

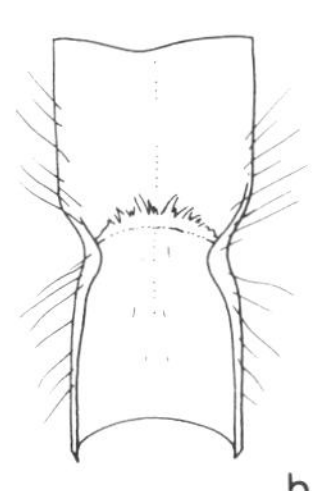

Annual or short-lived perennial growing in tufts; very difficult to uproot. A weed of disturbed places. Relatively unpalatable.

843 *Paspalum dilatatum Poir.
Common paspalum/Gewone paspalum

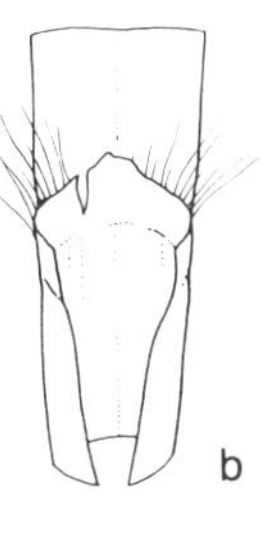

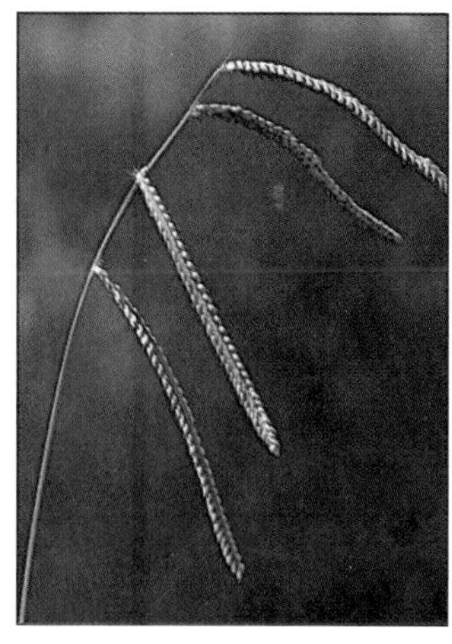

Evergreen perennial growing in tufts. Moist places, often along streams and in vleis. Palatable. A native of South America.

844 *Paspalum urvillei Steud.

Tall paspalum/Langbeenpaspalum

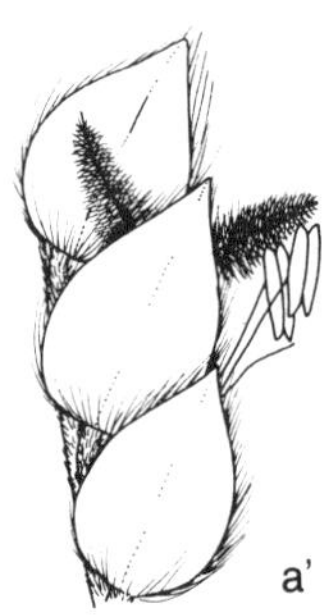

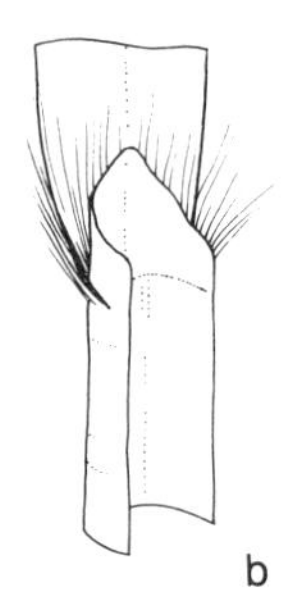

Perennial growing in tufts up to about 2 m high. Wet places, particularly along streams. Highly palatable. A native of South America.

845 Pogonarthria squarrosa (Roem. & Schult.) Pilg.

Herringbone grass/Sekelgras

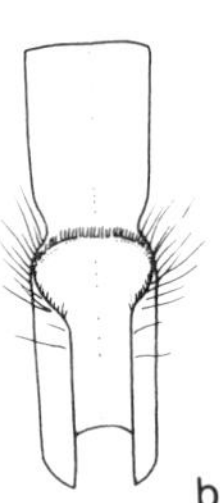

Perennial growing in tufts. Disturbed places. Relatively unpalatable pioneer or subclimax grass.

846 Urochloa mosambicensis (Hack.) Dandy

Common signal grass/Bosveldbeesgras

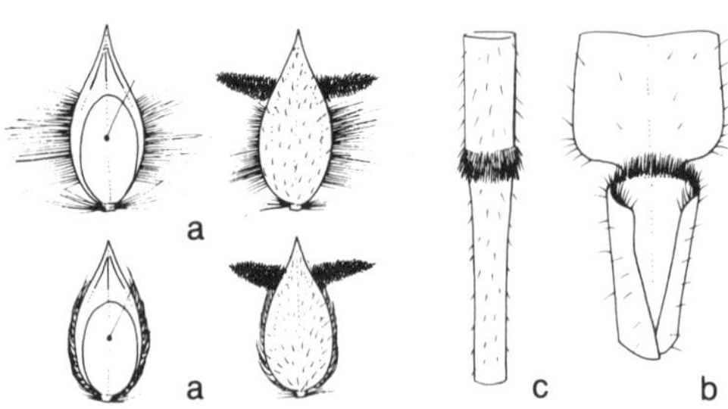

Short-lived perennial with ± creeping stems. Disturbed places. Highly palatable.

U. panicoides Beauv. and **U. trichopus** (Hochst.) Stapf are rather similar annual species.

POACEAE Group C.1

847 Andropogon eucomus Nees *Old man's beard/Veergras*

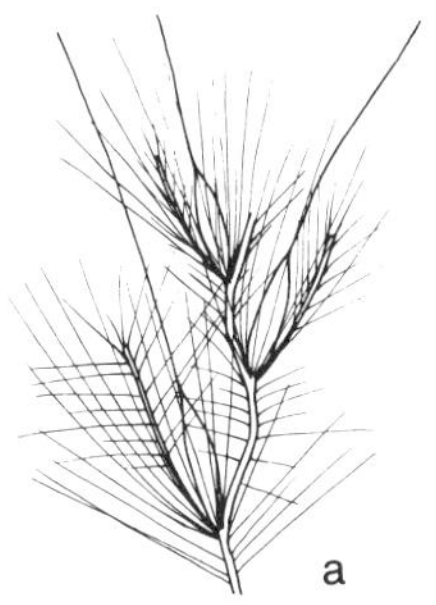

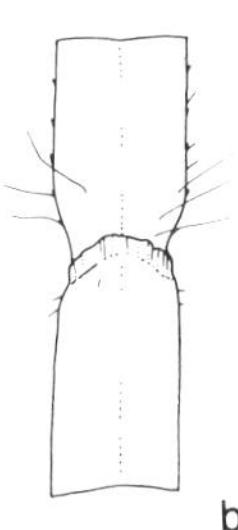

Perennial growing in tufts. Wet places, often in vleis and seepage areas; also along roads.

848 Aristida congesta Roem. & Schult. subsp. **barbicollis** (Trin. & Rupr.) De Winter [=**A. barbicollis** Trin. & Rupr.]
White stick grass/Witsteekgras

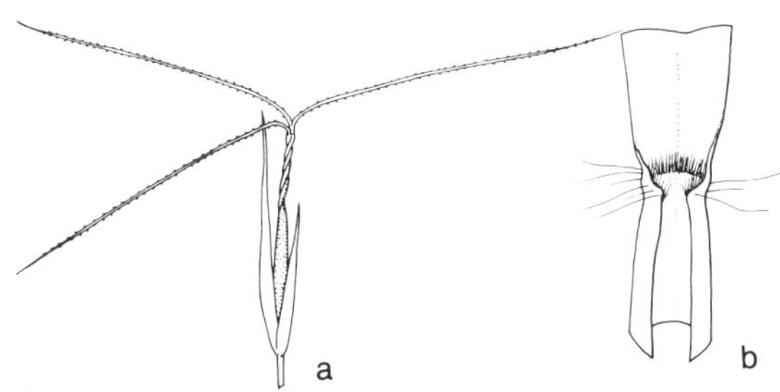

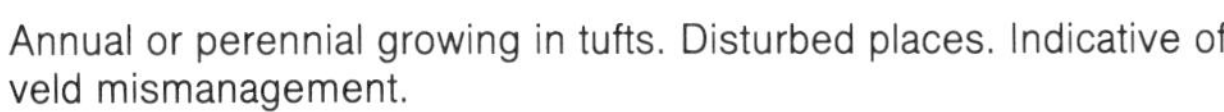

Annual or perennial growing in tufts. Disturbed places. Indicative of veld mismanagement.

849 Aristida scabrivalvis Hack.

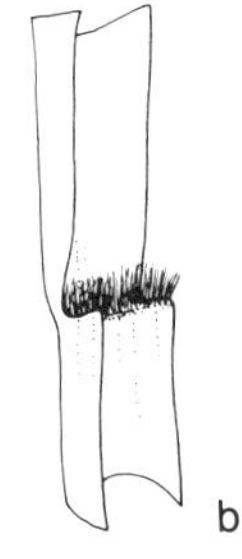

Annual growing in tufts; spikelets purple, lower glume shorter than the upper. Disturbed places.

A. bipartita (Nees) Trin. & Rupr. is a perennial with the lower glume longer than the upper.

850 Chrysopogon serrulatus Trin. [=**C. montanus** Trin. var. **tremulus** (Hack.) Stapf] *Golden beard grass/Gouebaardgras*

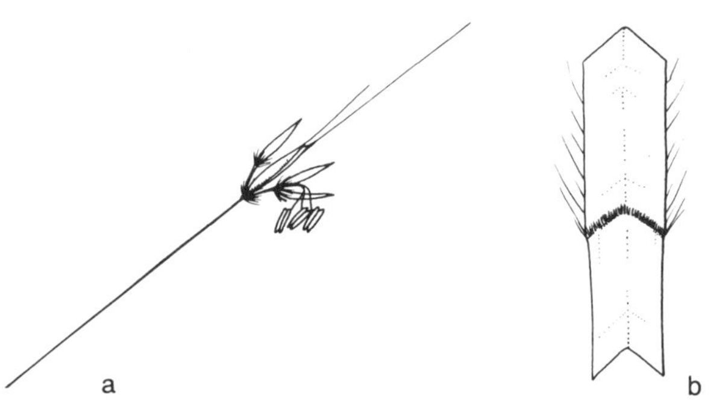

Perennial growing in tufts; spikelets with golden hairs at the base. Rocky hillsides, often on dolomite. Palatable climax grass.

851 Cymbopogon excavatus (Hochst.) Stapf ex Burtt Davy *Broad-leaved turpentine grass/Breëblaarterpentyngras*

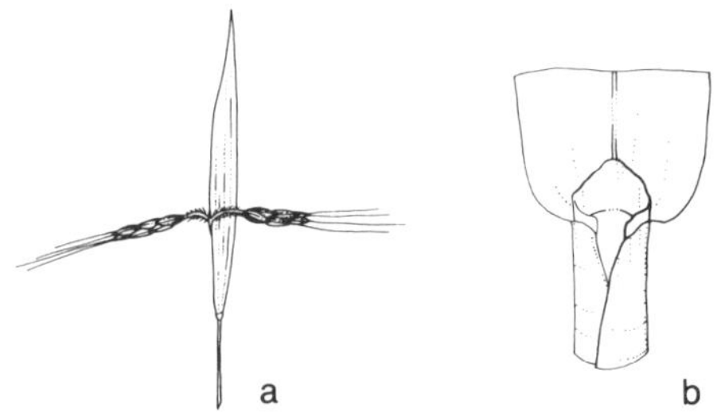

Perennial growing in tufts; leaves yellowish green, tasting strongly of turpentine; blade bases broad. Open grassland. Unpalatable.

Sometimes treated as **C. caesius** (Hook. & Arn.) Stapf.

852 Cymbopogon plurinodes (Stapf) Stapf ex Burtt Davy *Turpentine grass/Terpentyngrass*

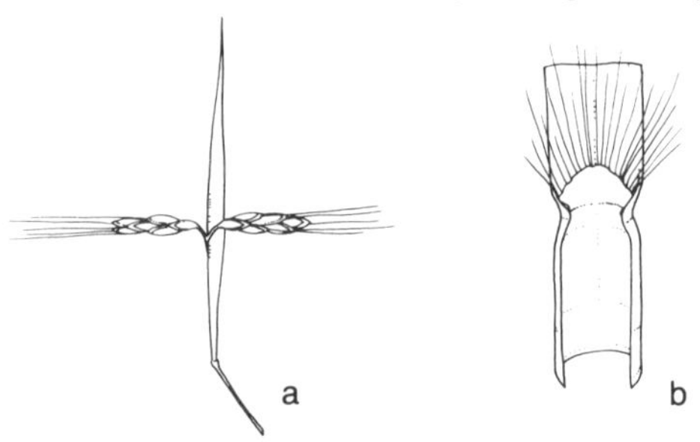

Perennial growing in tufts; leaves less than 3 mm wide, tasting of turpentine. Open grassland. Moderately palatable climax grass.

Sometimes treated as **C. pospischilii** (K. Schum.) C.E. Hubb.

853 Cymbopogon validus (Stapf) Stapf ex Burtt Davy
Giant turpentine grass/Reuseterpentyngras

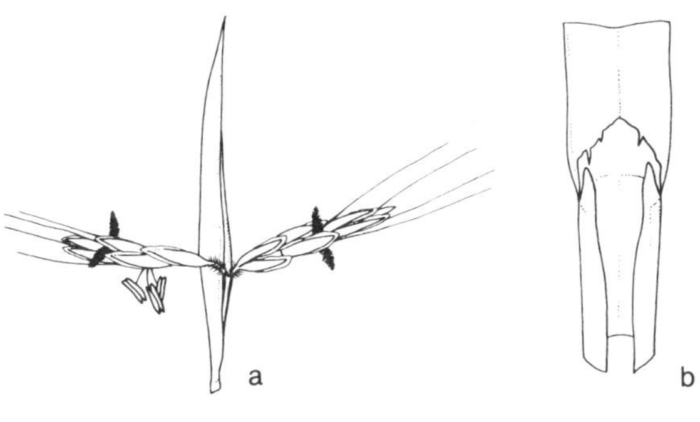

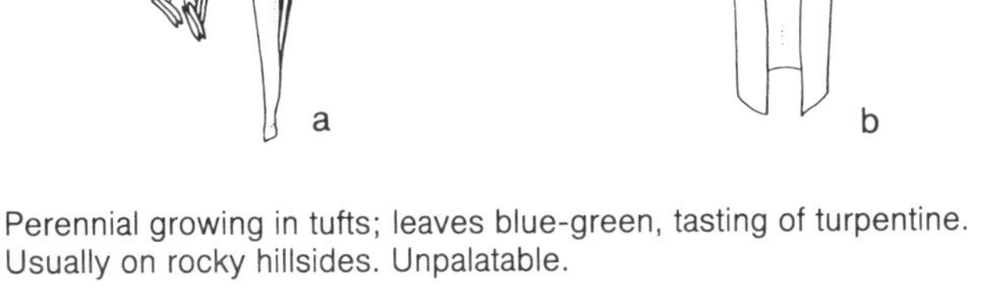

Perennial growing in tufts; leaves blue-green, tasting of turpentine. Usually on rocky hillsides. Unpalatable.

854 Hyparrhenia hirta (L.) Stapf *Thatch grass/Dekgras*

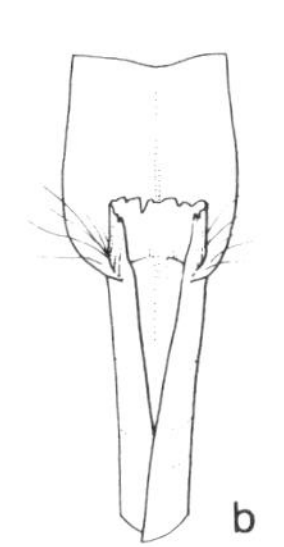

Perennial growing in tufts; racemes not deflexed. Open grassland, often dominant in old cultivated fields and along roadsides. Palatable, particularly before flowering.

H. quarrei Robyns has all or only some racemes deflexed.

855 Hyparrhenia tamba (Steud.) Stapf [=**H. glauca** Stent]
Blue thatch grass/Bloudekgras

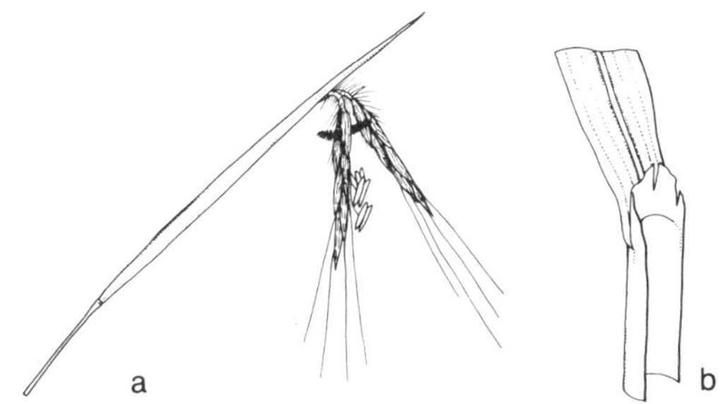

Robust perennial growing in tufts up to 2,5 m high; leaves blue-green with whitish midrib, not aromatic. Moist places, often in dense stands along streams and roadsides.

856 Loudetia simplex (Nees) C.E. Hubb.
Russet grass/Stingelgras

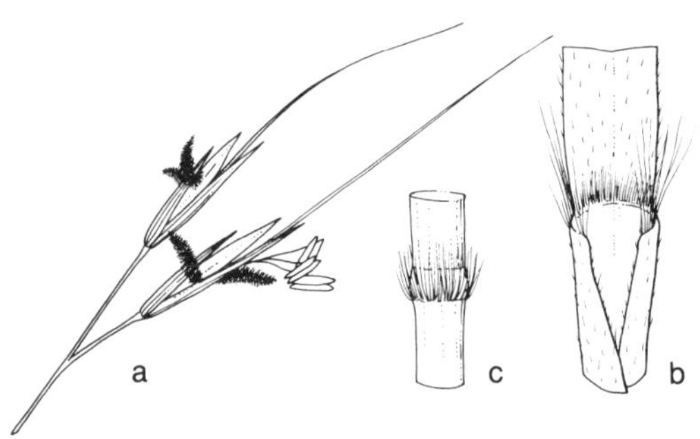

Perennial growing in tufts. Usually on rocky hillsides. Unpalatable. Indicative of sourveld.

857 Monocymbium ceresiiforme (Nees) Stapf
Wild oat grass/Wildehawergras

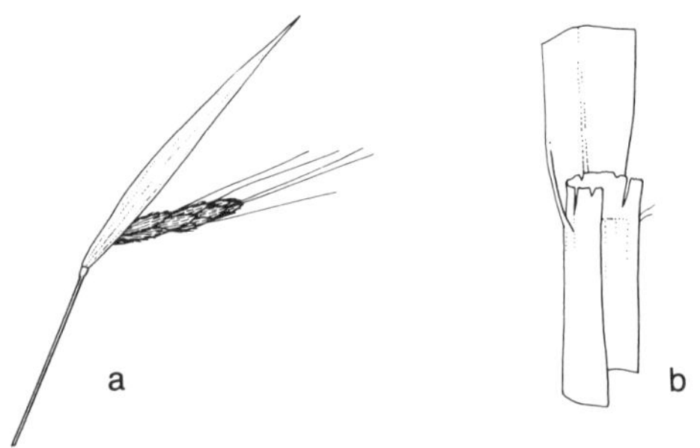

Perennial growing in tufts. Open grassland, often on rocky ridges or in vleis. Relatively palatable. Indicative of sourveld.

858 Stipagrostis uniplumis (Licht.) De Winter var. **neesii** (Trin. & Rupr.) De Winter [=**Aristida uniplumis** Licht. var. **neesii** Trin. & Rupr.] *Silky bushman grass/Blinkaarboesmansgras*

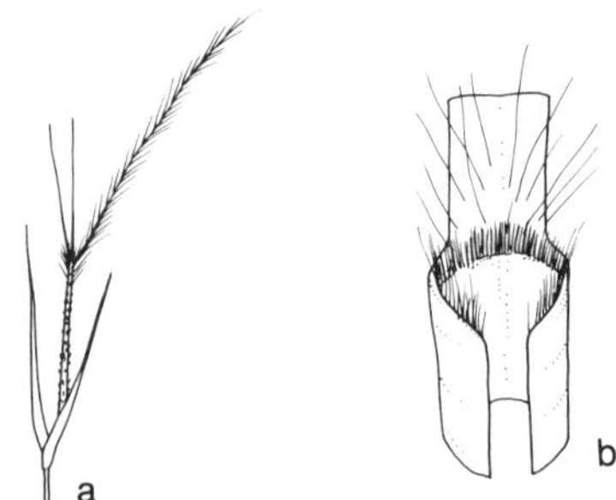

Perennial growing in tufts; central awn feathery. Open grassland, often in red sandy soil. Palatable.

859 Themeda triandra Forssk. *Red grass/Rooigras*

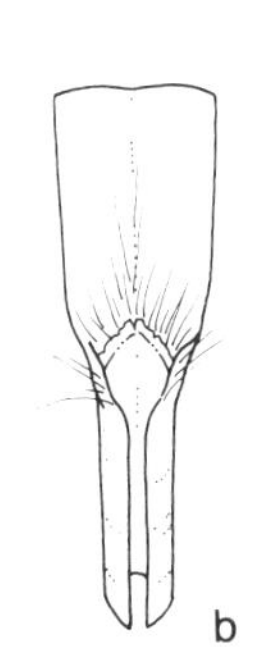

a

Perennial growing in tufts; colour and hairiness variable. Open grassland, often growing in abundance. Palatable climax grass. Indicative of good veld management.

860 Tristachya biseriata Stapf. *Trident grass/Drieblomgras*

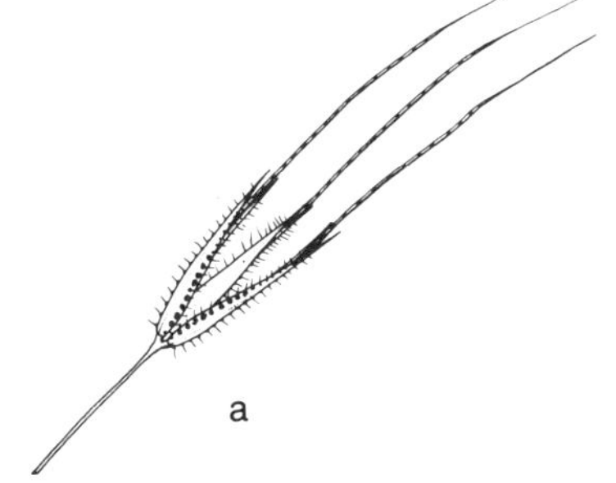

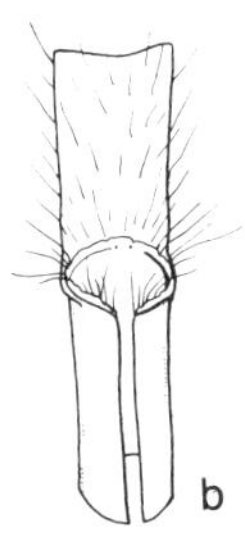

Perennial growing in tufts usually less than 500 mm high. Stony hillsides. Palatable climax grass.

861 Tristachya leucothrix Nees [=**T. hispida** (L.f.) K. Schum.] *Hairy trident grass/Harige drieblomgras*

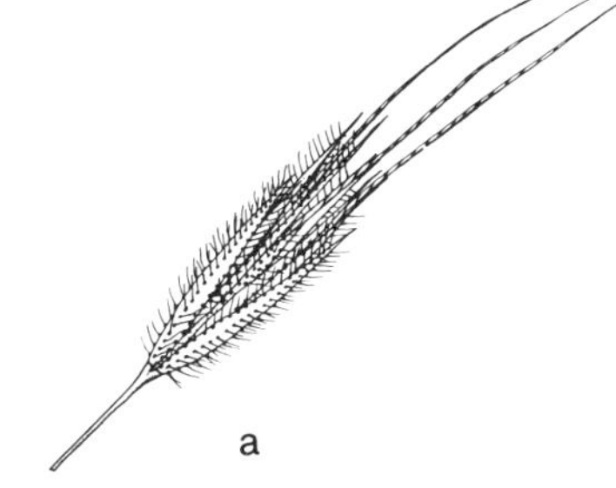

Perennial growing in tufts usually less than 500 mm high; basal leaf sheaths densely covered with golden hairs. Open grassland and rocky hillsides. Highly palatable climax grass.

862 Tristachya rehmannii Hack. *Broom grass/Besemgras*

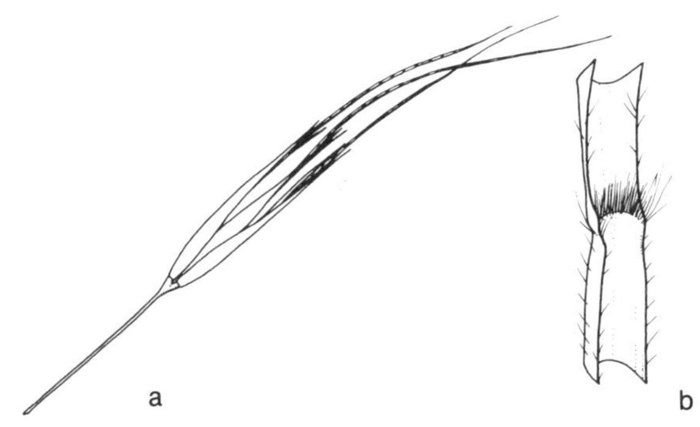

Perennial growing in tufts; blue-green; culms wiry, up to 1 m high. Open grassland, often on rocky ridges. Unpalatable climax grass.

POACEAE Group C.2 (See also **813**, **827**, **839**, **845**)
863 Bewsia biflora (Hack.) Goossens [=**Diplachne biflora** Hack. ex Schinz] *Blousaadgras*

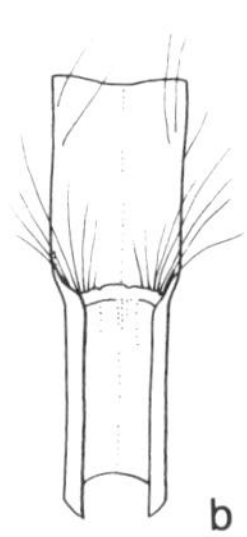

Perennial growing in tufts up to about 300 mm high. Stony hillsides and open grassland.

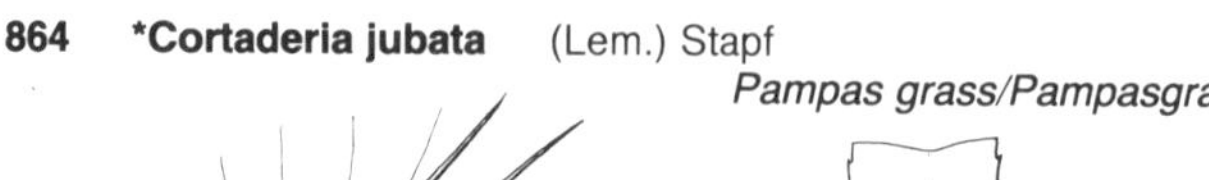

864 *Cortaderia jubata (Lem.) Stapf
Pampas grass/Pampasgras

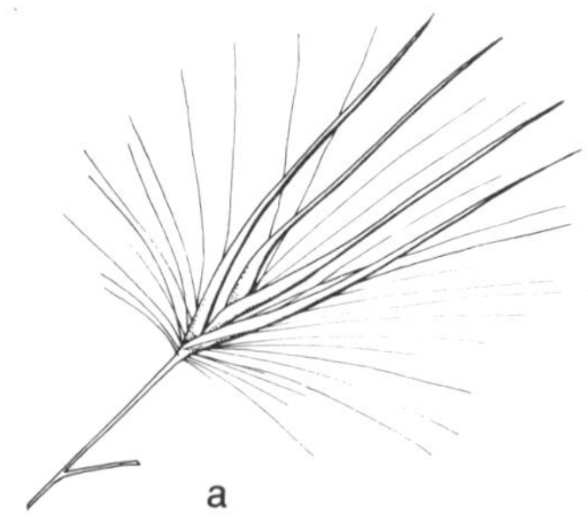

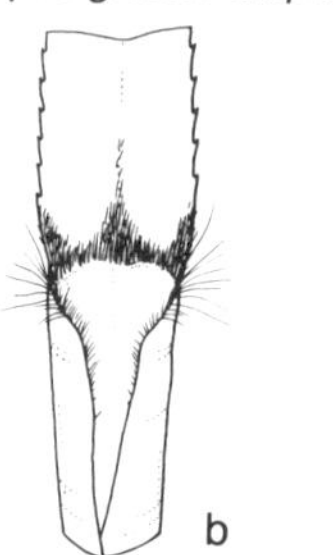

Robust perennial growing in tufts; foliage leaves less than half the length of the culms. Disturbed places. A native of South America.
***C. selloana** (J.A. & J.J. Schult.) Aschers. & Graebn. has foliage leaves almost reaching the white plumes.

865 Eragrostis capensis (Thunb.) Trin.
Heart seed love grass/Hartjiesgras

Perennial growing in tufts up to about 300 mm high. Open grassland, often on stony hillsides. Relatively palatable.

866 Eragrostis curvula (Schrad.) Nees
Weeping love grass/Oulandsgras

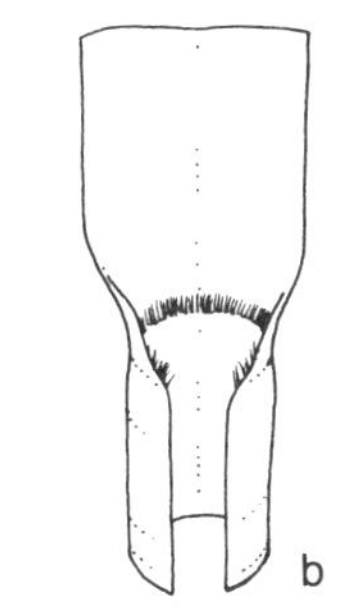

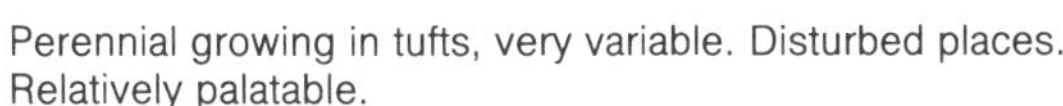

Perennial growing in tufts, very variable. Disturbed places. Relatively palatable.

867 Eragrostis gummiflua Nees *Gum grass/Kleefgras*

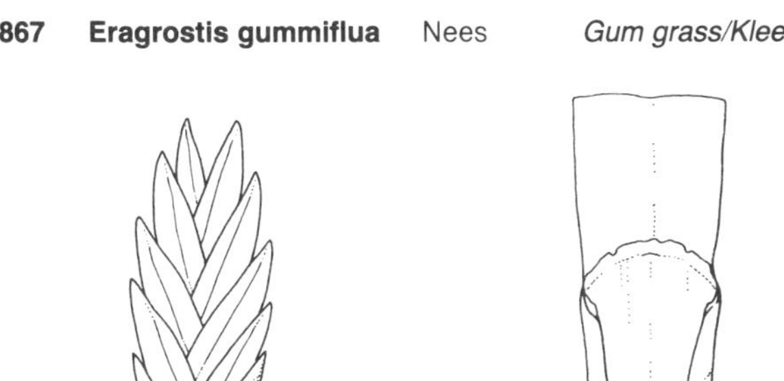

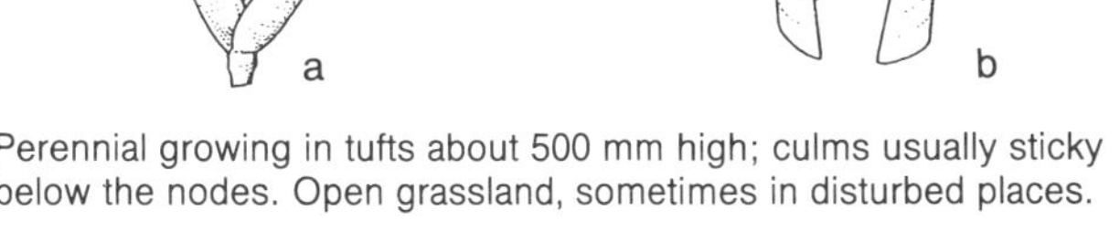

Perennial growing in tufts about 500 mm high; culms usually sticky below the nodes. Open grassland, sometimes in disturbed places.

868 Eragrostis racemosa (Thunb.) Steud.
Narrow-heart love grass/Smalhartjiesgras

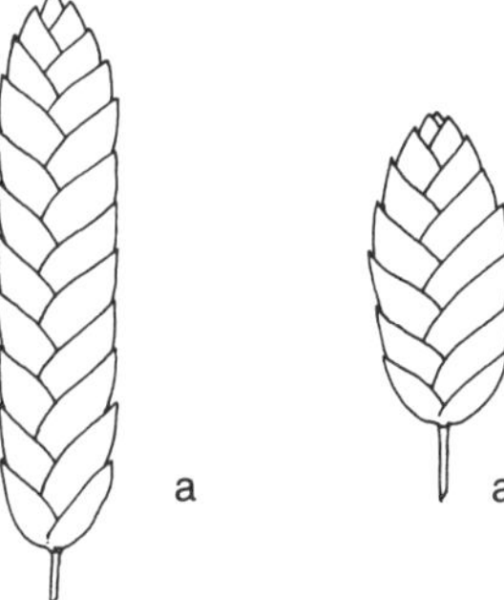

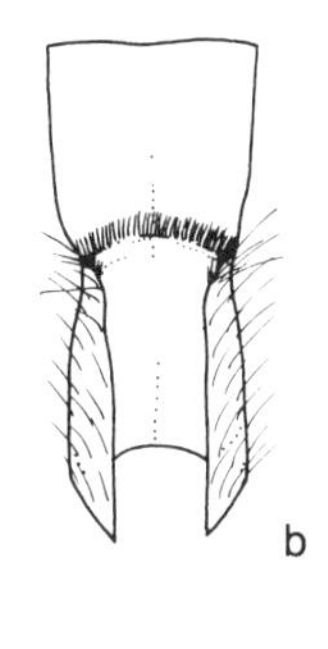

Small perennial, 150 – 300 mm high, growing in tufts. Open grassland. Palatable climax grass.

869 Eragrostis superba Peyr.
Saw-tooth love grass/Weeluisgras

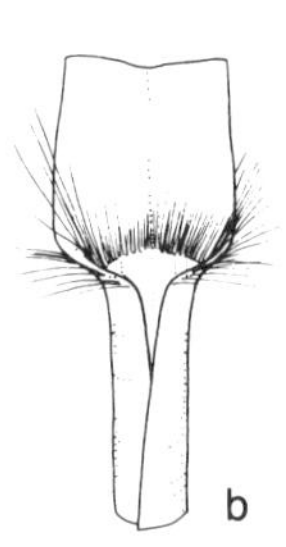

Perennial growing in tufts about 500 mm high. Open grassland and disturbed places. Palatable.

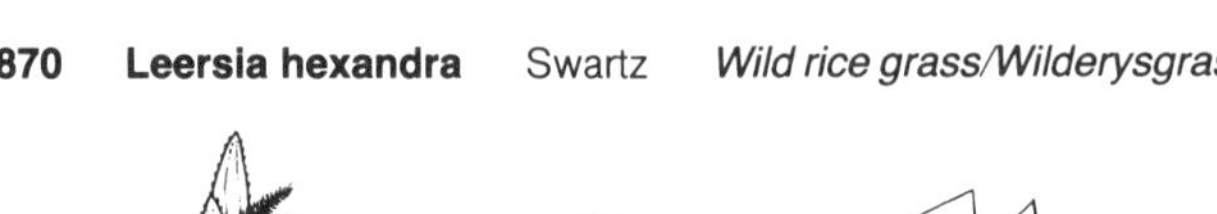

870 Leersia hexandra Swartz *Wild rice grass/Wilderysgras*

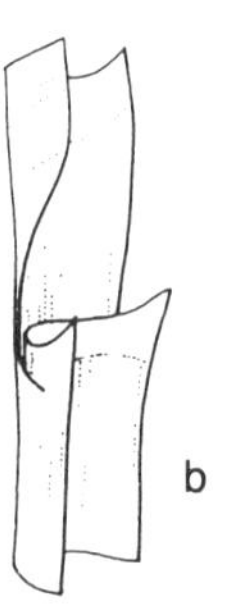

Perennial with creeping rhizomes. Moist places, growing even in water and often forming pure stands in vleis. Palatable.

871 Miscanthus junceus (Stapf) Pilg. [=**Miscanthidium junceum** (Stapf) Stapf]
Sedge-leaved broom grass/Biesieblaarruigtegras

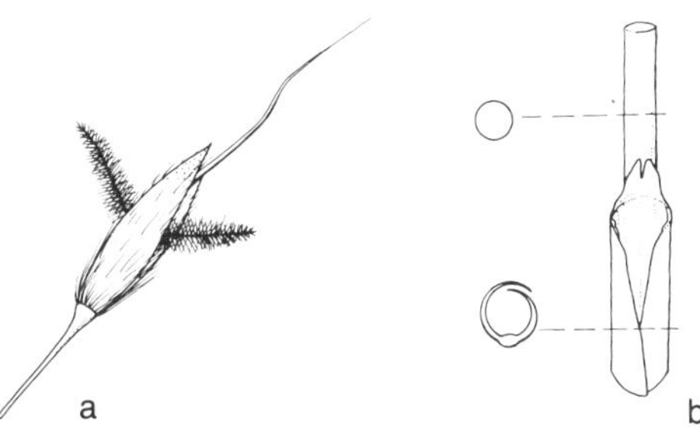

Robust perennial growing in tufts up to 2 m high; blades cylindrical. Along streams or in marshy places. Unpalatable.

872 Panicum maximum Jacq. *Guinea grass/Buffelsgras*

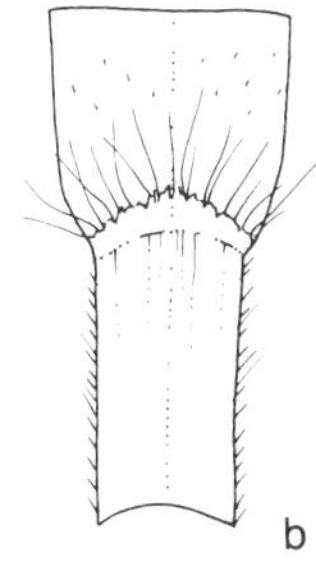

Perennial growing in tufts; spikelets usually purplish. Disturbed and shady places, often under trees. A valuable hay grass.

873 Panicum natalense Hochst.
Natal panicum/Suurbuffelsgras

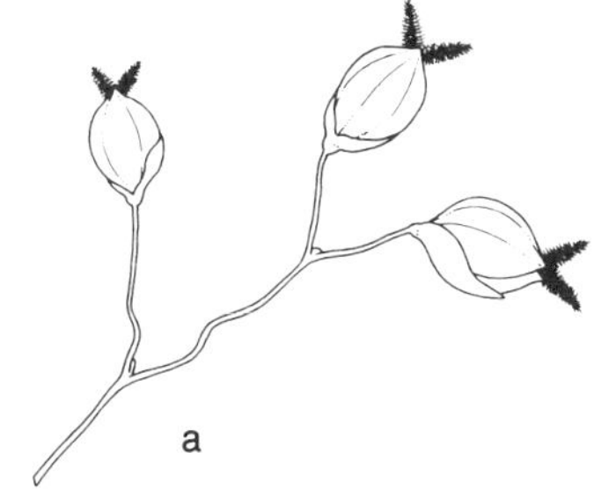

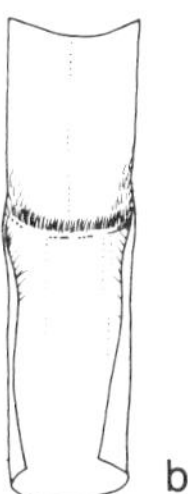

Perennial growing in tufts; spikelets usually whitish. Open grassland, often on stony hillsides. Unpalatable. Indicative of sourveld.

874 Phragmites australis (Cav.) Steud.
[=**P. communis** Trin.] *Common reed/Fluitjiesriet*

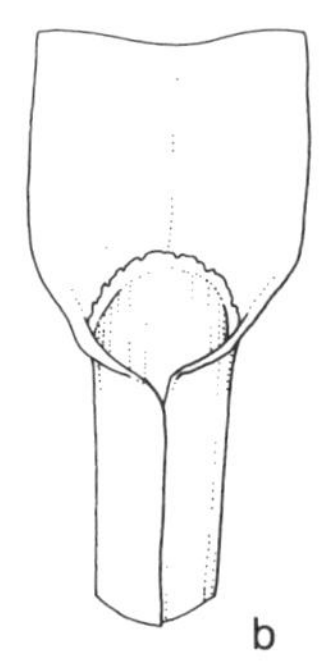

Tall perennial with creeping rhizomes. Marshy places and along streams, often in pure stands. Unpalatable.

875 *Poa annua L. *Winter grass/Wintergras*

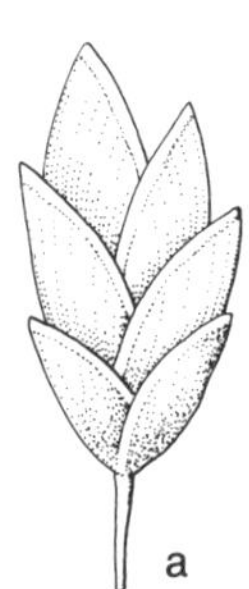

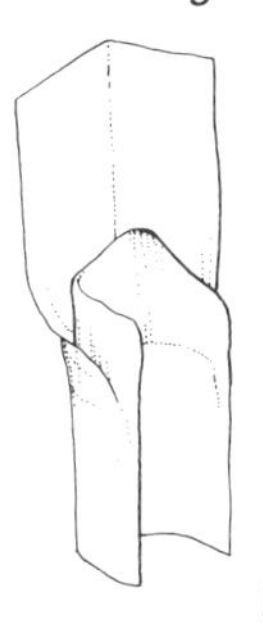

Annual growing in short tufts; leaf tips almost rounded. A weed in moist, disturbed places, particularly under shady conditions in gardens. A native of Europe and Asia.

876 Rhynchelytrum nerviglume (Franch.) Chiov.
[=**R. setifolium** (Stapf) Chiov.] *Mountain red top/Bergblinkgras*

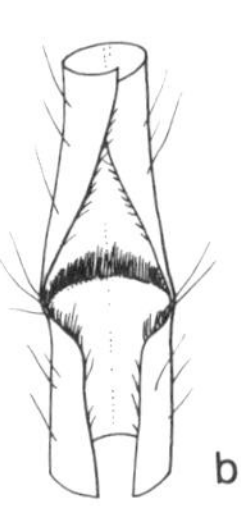

Perennial growing in tufts; leaves blue-green and thread-like; inflorescences silvery pink, fading to white. Open grassland and rocky hillsides. Relatively unpalatable climax grass.

877 **Rhynchelytrum repens** (Willd.) C.E. Hubb.
[=**R. villosum** (Parl.) Chiov.] *Natal red top/Natalse rooipluim*

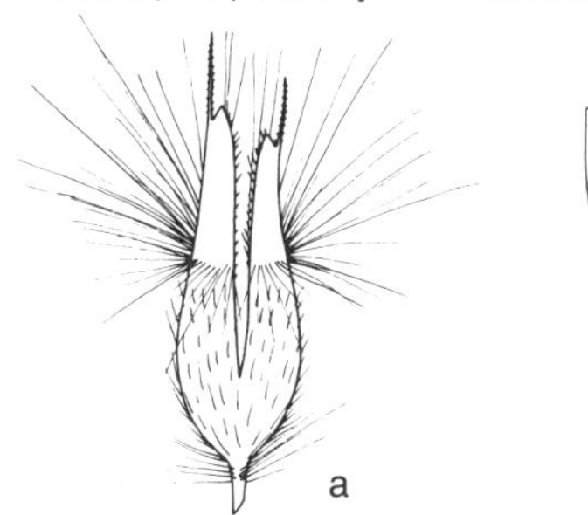

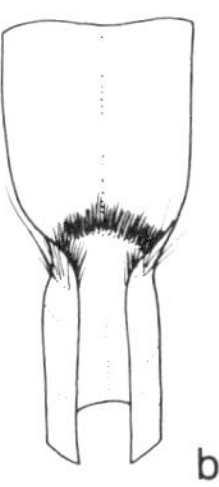

Annual or short-lived perennial growing in tufts; leaf blades bright green, expanded; inflorescences pink, fading to white. Disturbed places, common along roadsides. Palatable pioneer or subclimax grass.

878 **Setaria lindenbergiana** (Nees) Stapf
Mountain bristle grass/Randjiesgras

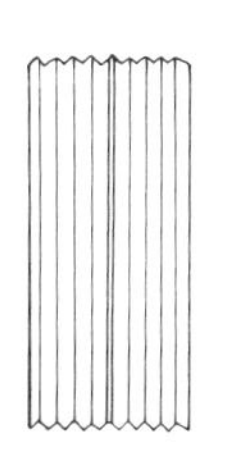

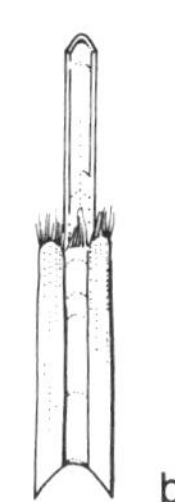

Perennial growing in tufts; blades with stalk-like base. Rocky ridges, often under trees.

S. megaphylla (Steud.) Dur. & Schinz is a shade-loving species with pleated leaves up to 50 mm wide.

879 **Sorghum bicolor** (L.) Moench. subsp. **arundinaceum** (Desv.) De Wet & Harlan [=**S. verticilliflorum** (Steud.) Stapf]
Common wild sorghum/Wildesorghum

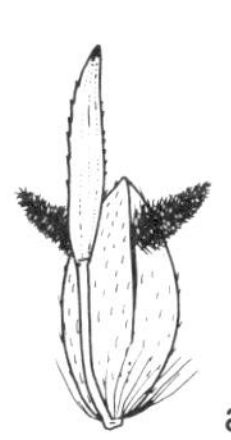

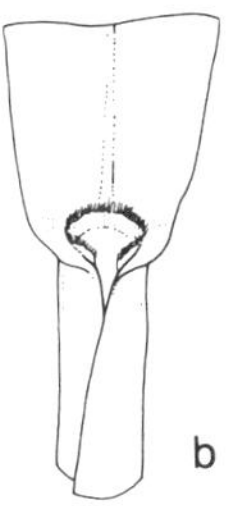

Annual or short-lived perennial growing in tufts. Disturbed places, often along streams. Relatively palatable.

***S. halepense** (L.) Pers. is a perennial with an extensive system of branched rhizomes.

880 Trichoneura grandiglumis (Nees) Ekman var. **grandiglumis**
Rolling grass/Kleinrolgras

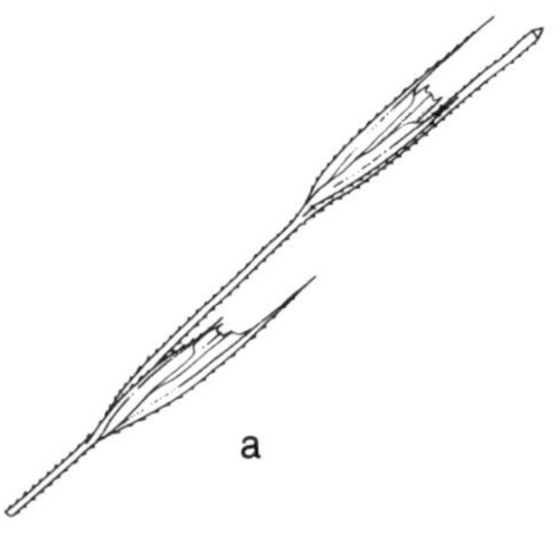

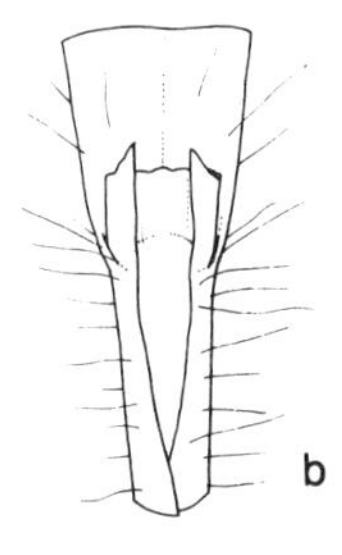

Low-growing perennial. Open grassland and disturbed areas. Unpalatable. Sometimes increasing under conditions of veld mismanagement.

881 Triraphis andropogonoides (Steud.) Phill.
Triraphis/Perdegras

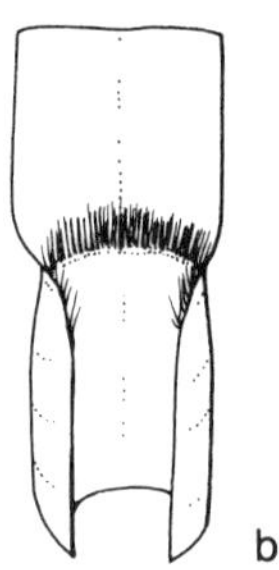

Robust perennial up to 1,5 m high. Open grassland and rocky hillsides. Unpalatable.

GLOSSARY

This glossary mainly concerns descriptive terms used in the identification sections of this book. Synonyms commonly encountered in botanical works are supplied for some terms, and are given in parenthesis at the end of the definition. With few exceptions, only the meanings actually used in the text are given. Several other technical terms are defined on first use in the introductory section.

achene a small, dry, one-seeded fruit that does not split open.
alien a plant introduced by man from elsewhere and now more or less naturalized (=exotic). Compare **indigenous, naturalized**.
alternate applied to leaves placed singly at different heights on a stem. See Figure 5. Compare **opposite, rosulate/rosette, whorled**.

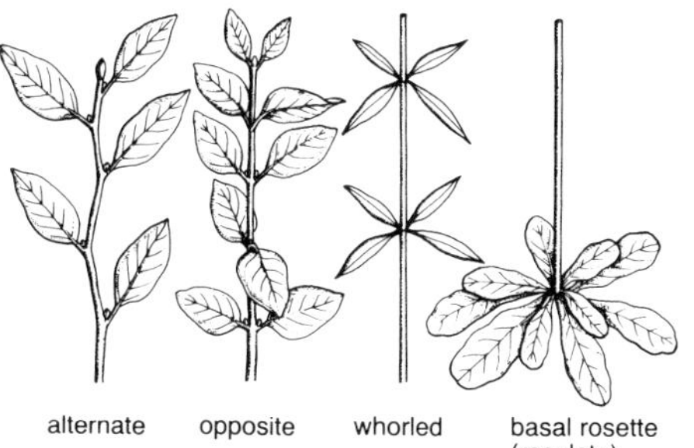

Figure 5. Leaf arrangement

annual a plant which completes its life cycle from germination to seeding and death within one year. Compare **biennial, perennial**.
anther the part of the stamen containing the pollen; usually borne on a slender stalk (filament). See Figure 8.
apex, apical the tip of an organ (plural: apices).
appressed lying close to or pressed flat against a surface or structure, as the hairs on certain leaves.
aril a fleshy outer covering or appendage that encloses the seed or part thereof, and develops from its stalk; often brightly coloured.
awn a long, stiff, bristle-like projection borne at the end or from the side of an organ; frequently present on the flowering glumes of grasses. See Figure 14.
axil the upper angle between the leaf and the stem on which it is carried (see Figure 10); **axillary** in, or arising from, an axil.
axis the main stem of a plant, or inflorescence, on which other organs are borne.
beak a long, prominent, and substantial point; applied particularly to the extension of a pistil or a fruit.
bearded with tufts of stiff hairs.
berry a many-seeded fleshy fruit with a soft outer portion and the seeds embedded in the fleshy or pulpy tissue (e.g. the tomato). Compare **drupe**.
biennial a plant which grows and develops in the first year, and fruits and seeds in the second; living for two growing seasons. Compare **annual, perennial**.
bipinnate, bipinnately compound when the first divisions (pinnae) of a leaf are further divided, i.e. with leaflets (pinnules) borne on branches of the rhachis. See Figure 6. Compare **pinnate**.
bisexual containing both male (stamens) and female (pistil) reproductive organs in a single flower. See Figure 8. Compare **unisexual**.
blade the flat, expanded part of a leaf (=lamina). See Figure 10.
bloom 1. the flower, or process of flowering. 2. a thin layer of white waxy powder on some leaves and fruits.
bract a usually small, leaf-like structure, in the axil of which arises a flower or a branch of an inflorescence; **bracteate** having bracts.
branchlet a twig or small branch.
bulb a swollen underground organ comprising a short, disc-like stem with fleshy and tightly overlapping leaf bases (e.g. the onion). Compare **corm, tuber**. **Bulbil** a small daughter bulb arising from the mother bulb (=bulblet); **bulbous** having bulbs; **bulbous hairs** hairs with an inflated base.

calyculus see **epicalyx**.
calyx collective term for all the sepals of a flower; the outer whorl of most flowers; usually green. See Figure 8. Compare **epicalyx**.
capsule a dry fruit produced by an ovary comprising two or more united carpels and usually opening by slits or pores. Compare **follicle, pod**.
carpel one of the leaf-derived, usually ovule-bearing units of a pistil or ovary; sometimes free, but usually united to form a compound pistil or ovary. The number of carpels in a compound pistil is generally difficult to establish, but often equals the number of chambers or stigmatic lobes per pistil.
chamber the cavity of an ovary which contains the ovules (=locule). See Figure 8.
cladode, cladophyll a leaf-like structure formed by a modified stem, as in the genus *Protasparagus*.
clasping used for leaf bases that partly or completely enclose the stem.
climax species a plant species forming part of a plant community at the terminal stage of ecological succession, i.e. a relatively stable (climax) community which is in dynamic equilibrium with its environment. Compare **pioneer species, succession**.
coherent similar parts or organs in close contact but not united.
coma the tuft of hairs at the ends of some seeds, as in the Asclepiadaceae.
compound consisting of several parts; e.g. a compound leaf has two or more separate leaflets. See Figure 6.

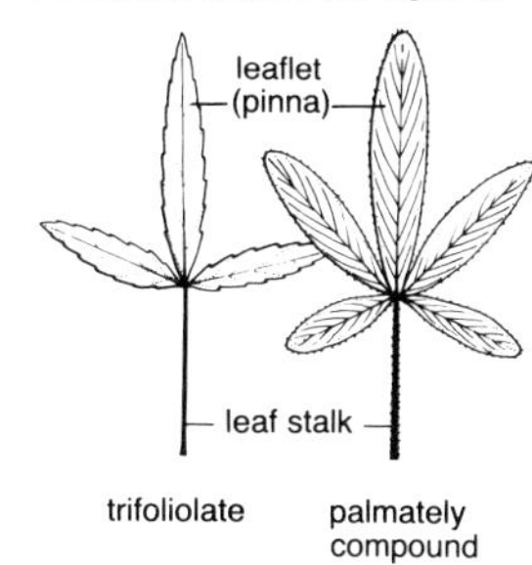

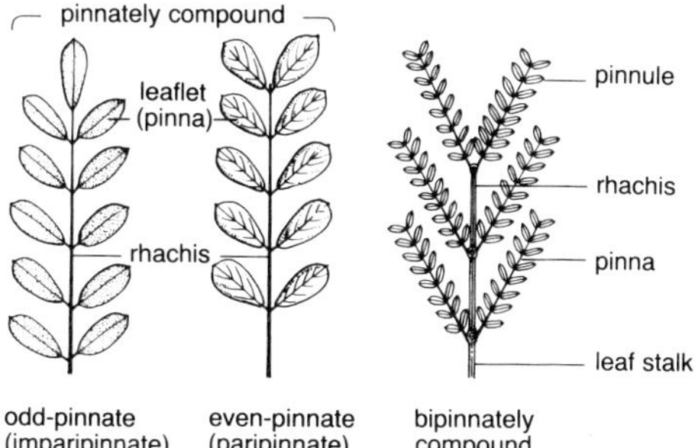

Figure 6. Compound leaves

cone a rounded or elongate structure comprising, on a central axis, many overlapping bracts which bear pollen, spores or seed; characteristic of many gymnosperms.
congested crowded.
connective the tissue between the chambers (locules) of the anther.

corm a shortened (compressed) and swollen underground stem which produces leaves at the top; enclosed by dry, fibrous leaf bases; characteristic of many Iridaceae. Compare **bulb, tuber**.
corolla collective term for all the petals of a flower; usually coloured. See Figure 8.
corona a whorl of appendages between the petals and the stamens, sometimes united to form a ring; usually borne on the petals or corolla tube, or modified from the stamens. Characteristic of the Asclepiadaceae. See Figure 7.

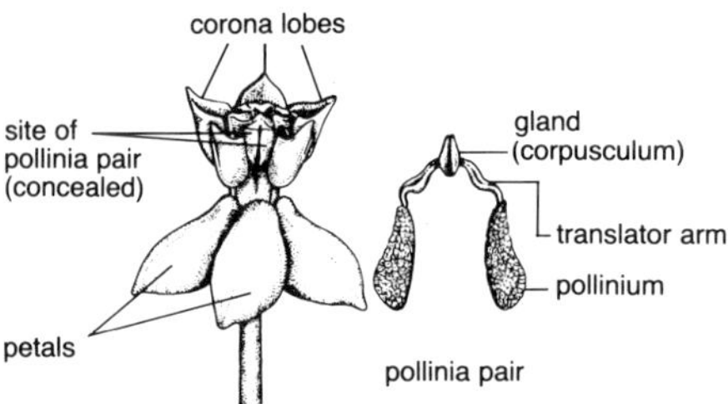

Figure 7. Floral structure in Asclepiadaceae

creeping a non-technical term referring to a trailing shoot which takes root along most of its length or at the nodes.
crown the persistent base of a herbaceous perennial.
culm the stem of grasses (Poaceae) and sedges (Cyperaceae).
cyathium a flower-like inflorescence characteristic of the genus *Euphorbia*; it consists of a central 3-chambered ovary (equivalent to a female flower) surrounded by groups of single stamens (each equivalent to a male flower), all grouped together within petal-like bracts and glands.
deciduous shedding leaves at the end of the growing season. Compare **evergreen**.
decumbent lying on the ground but with the ends growing upward.
deflexed bent abruptly downward or outward; often synonymous with **reflexed**.
dehiscent opening, as in anthers or fruit.
digitate hand-like; where the parts are attached at the same point, as the leaflets of a palmately compound leaf. See Figure 6.
disc (disk) 1. the fleshy outgrowth developed from the receptacle at the base of the ovary or from the stamens surrounding the ovary, usually in the form of a ring, cushion, or of separate gland-like parts; often secreting nectar. 2. the central part of the head-like inflorescence of the Asteraceae.
disc flowers (florets) the regular tube-like flowers at the centre of the flower heads of some members of the Asteraceae. See Figure 12. Compare **ray flowers**.
discoid having only disc flowers (e.g. some members of the Asteraceae). Compare **radiate**.
dissected deeply divided or irregularly cut into many segments.
drooping inclining downwards, but not quite pendulous. Compare **pendulous**.
drupe a fleshy, indehiscent fruit with one or more seeds, each of which is surrounded by a hard stony layer formed by the inner part of the ovary wall (e.g. stone fruit such as peaches, olives). Compare **berry**.
egg-shaped having the outline of an egg, with the narrow end above the middle (=ovate). Compare **obovate**.
elliptic, elliptical, ellipsoid oval and narrowed to rounded ends, widest at or about the middle.
entire see **smooth**.
epicalyx one or more whorls of sepal-like bracts borne on the stalk of the flower just below the whorl of true sepals (calyx), as in the Malvaceae (=calyculus). Compare **calyx**.
epiphyte a plant that grows on another plant but is not parasitic on it; usually with its roots not in the ground. Compare **parasite**.
evergreen retaining green leaves throughout the year, even during winter. Compare **deciduous**.
exfoliate to peel off in thin flakes, as the bark of certain shrubs and trees.
filament the thread-like stalk of the stamen bearing the anther. See Figure 8.

floret a small flower, usually one of a dense cluster; especially o the Asteraceae or Poaceae.
flower the structure concerned with sexual reproduction in a flowering plant (see Figure 8). Generally interpreted as a short length of stem with four sets of modified leaves attached to it. Outermost are the **sepals**, usually green, leaf-like, in the bud stage enclosing and protecting the other flower parts, and collectively known as the **calyx**. Within the sepals are the **petals** usually conspicuous and brightly coloured, collectively known as the **corolla**. Within the petals are the **stamens** which are the ma reproductive organs, each comprising a **filament** (stalk) which bears an **anther**, in which pollen grains are produced. In the centre of the flower is the female reproductive organ, the **pistil(s)**. Each pistil consists of an **ovary** (derived from modified leaves called **carpels**) at its base, a slender, ± elongated projection (more than one in some species) called a **style**, and an often enlarged tip called a **stigma** which acts as the receptive surface for pollen grains. The ovary contains a varying number c **ovules**, which after fertilization develop into **seeds**. The male an female parts may be in the same flower (**bisexual**) or in separate flowers (**unisexual**).

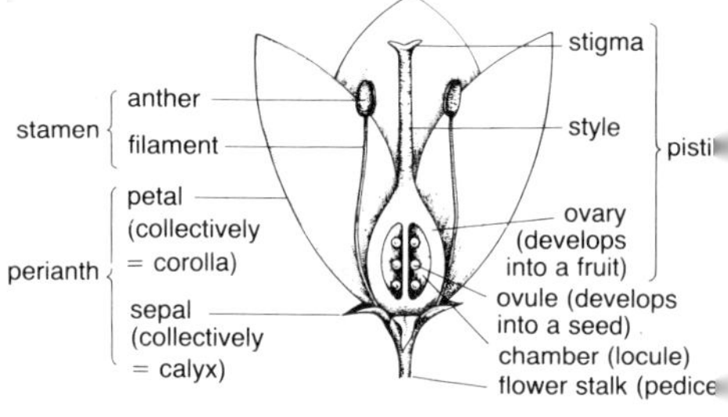

Figure 8. The parts of a flower

flower head a dense inflorescence of small, crowded and often stalkless flowers at the end of a common stalk; more or less globose or dish-shaped.
follicle a dry fruit which is derived from a single carpel and which splits open along one side only. Compare **capsule, pod**.
free not joined to each other or to any other organ (e.g. petals to petals, or stamens to petals). Compare **united**.
fruit the ripened ovary (pistil) and its attached parts; the seed-containing structure. Compare **seed**.
fused see **united**.
gland a structure that secretes one or more substances (e.g. nectar); usually found on the surface of, or within an organ (e.g. leaf, stem or flower). Compare **nectary**.
gland-dotted with translucent or coloured dots when viewed against the light, usually said of leaves with secretory cavities within its tissues (=glandular-punctate). Compare **secretory cavities**.
glandular hairs hairs terminated by minute glands, often sticky to the touch.
globose spherical, rounded.
glume one or two empty bracts at the base of a grass spikelet, usually scale-like, stiff and dry. See Figure 14. Compare **lemma, palea**.
head see **flower head**.
heart-shaped when the base of the leaf is deeply notched (=cordate). Compare **obovate**.
hemiparasite a parasitic plant which contains chlorophyll and is therefore partly self-sustaining, as in the Loranthaceae. Holoparasites lack chlorophyll and are entirely dependent on the host for nourishment, as in Cuscutaceae. Compare **epiphyte, parasite**.
herb a plant which does not develop persistent woody tissue above ground and either dies at the end of the growing season or overwinters by means of underground organs (e.g. rhizomes, bulbs, corms). Compare **woody**.

erbaceous like a herb; non-woody, soft and leafy, with a stem that dies back to the ground each year. Compare **woody**.

ypanthium the often cup-like part in some flowers between the sepal lobes and the base of the ovary, produced by the union of the bases of the sepals, petals and filaments (with or without the involvement of the receptacle); often used interchangeably with calyx tube or floral tube.

ıcised with the margin deeply cut.

ıdehiscent remaining closed and not opening when ripe or mature.

ıdigenous a plant occurring naturally in an area and not introduced from elsewhere (=native). Compare **alien, naturalized**.

ıflorescence any arrangement of more than one flower; the flowering portion of a plant, e.g. head, spike, panicle, cyathium, raceme.

ıternode the part of the stem between two successive nodes. Compare **node**.

ıterpetiolar between the leaf stalks, as an interpetiolar stipule that extends from the base of one leaf stalk across the stem to the base of the stalk of the opposite leaf (e.g. in many Rubiaceae).

ntroduced see **alien**.

nvolucral bracts one or more whorls of bracts or leafy structures (often sepal-like) that surround the base of an umbel or flower head, notably in the Asteraceae (=phyllaries). See Figure 12.

rregular flowers that can be divided into two equal halves (mirror images) along only one plane, i.e. corolla lobes unequal (=zygomorphic). See Figure 13. Compare **regular**.

keel 1. a projecting ridge running the length of an organ. 2. the two loosely united lower petals of the flowers of the Fabaceae (=carina). See Figure 9. Compare **standard, wing**.

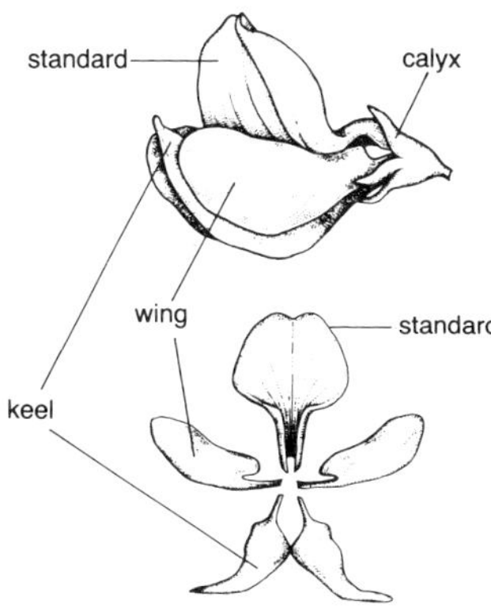

Figure 9. Floral structure in Fabaceae

lance-shaped with the shape of the end of a lance or spear, much longer than broad and tapering to the tip from a broad base (=lanceolate).

latex a liquid substance that is often white (milky) and sometimes contains rubber; found in special tubes (cells) called laticifers. Compare **sap**.

leaf an aerial outgrowth from a stem, numbers of which make up the foliage of a plant. It typically consists of a stalk (petiole) and a flattened blade (lamina), and is the principal food manufacturing (photosynthetic) organ of a green plant. See Figure 10. **Leaflet** the individual division of a compound leaf which is usually leaf-like, with a stalk of its own (=pinna, pinnule). See Figure 6.

leaf sheath the lower part of a leaf stalk which more or less completely surrounds the stem; particularly common in monocotyledons.

legume see **pod**.

lemma the small bract that encloses the palea and floret in a grass spikelet; it frequently bears an awn. See Figure 14. Compare **glume, palea**.

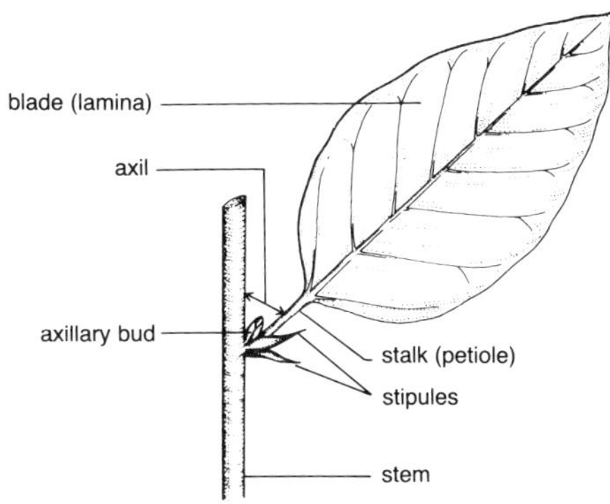

Figure 10. Parts of a simple leaf

ligule an outgrowth on the inner surface of a grass leaf at the junction between sheath and blade. Also occurs in a few sedge (Cyperaceae) species.

limb the upper, expanded portion (above the tube or throat) of a calyx or corolla with fused parts. Compare **throat, tube**.

linear long and narrow, with nearly parallel sides. Compare **oblong**.

lip 1. the large lobes, one upper and one lower, of a two-lipped corolla, as in many members of the Lamiaceae. 2. in the Orchidaceae, the lowest of the three petal-like segments (=labellum).

lobe a part or segment of an organ (e.g. leaf, petal) deeply divided from the rest of the organ but not separated; segments usually rounded.

lobed (of leaf margins) with curved or rounded edges.

margin the edge or boundary line of an organ.

mericarp a one-seeded portion of a dry dehiscent fruit which splits away as a perfect fruit, as in some members of the Geraniaceae.

midpetaline pertaining to the middle portion (often lengthwise) of a petal, as the plaits in the corolla of the Convolvulaceae.

midrib the central or largest vein or rib of a leaf or other organ.

morphology the study of form and its development.

mucilage a viscid, slimy substance, often produced in ducts in the plant; **mucilaginous** said of seeds which become slimy on contact with water, or of some leaves which produce a slimy mass when crushed in water (e.g. 579 *Dicerocaryum eriocarpum*).

native see **indigenous.**

naturalized a plant introduced from a foreign area (an alien) which has become established and is reproducing successfully in the new area. Compare **alien, indigenous**.

nectar the sugary liquid produced by flowers or other plant parts on which insects and birds feed; **nectariferous** producing nectar; **nectary** any structure which produces nectar, such as glands or special hairs.

nectar guides floral orientation cues directing a pollinator to the nectar; usually stripes or spots of a different colour on the petals.

node the point on a stem where one or more leaves arise. Compare **internode**.

nut a dry, single-seeded and indehiscent fruit with a hard outer covering, as in acorns, walnuts; **nutlet** a small nut.

ob- a prefix meaning opposite, inverse, or against.

oblong an elongated but relatively wide shape, e.g. of a leaf with more or less parallel sides (=strap-shaped). Compare **linear**.

obovate egg-shaped, with the broadest end towards the tip. Compare **egg-shaped**.

ocrea (ochrea) a stipular growth that sheaths the stem near the leaf base, as in the Polygonaceae.

odd-pinnate a pinnately compound leaf with an odd number of leaflets, and with a single terminal leaflet (=imparipinnate). See Figure 6. Compare **pinnate**.

opposite of two organs (e.g. leaves) arising at the same level on opposite sides of the stem (see Figure 5); also used for organs that arise opposite each other or when the one arises at the base of another, as a stamen opposite a petal or sepal. Compare **alternate, rosulate/rosette, whorl**.

oval broadly elliptic, the width more than half the length.

ovary the hollow basal portion of a pistil which contains the ovules within one or more chambers and which produces the fruit if pollination and fertilization take place (see Figure 8). A **superior ovary** is borne on top of the receptacle and is visible when the flower is viewed from above, as the sepals, petals and stamens are attached below its base (see Figure 11). Fruits from superior ovaries are not tipped by the remains of the perianth and stamens (e.g. oranges, grapes). An **inferior ovary** is completely enclosed by the receptacle and is usually visible as a swelling of the flower stalk below the attachment of the sepals, petals and stamens (see Figure 11). Fruits from inferior ovaries are often tipped by the remains of the perianth (or a scar if it is deciduous) (e.g. apples, guavas).

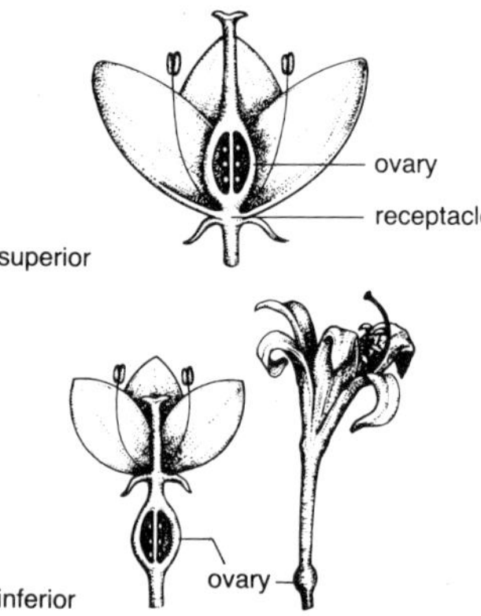

Figure 11. Ovary position

ovule the minute roundish structure(s) within the chamber of the ovary. It contains the egg cell and after fertilization develops into the seed. See Figure 8.

palea the upper of two bracts enclosing the flower in grasses. See Figure 14. Compare **glume, lemma**.

palmate with three or more parts arising from a single point and radiating outward like the fingers of an open hand; as in palmately compound leaves (see Figure 6) or palmate venation.

panicle an inflorescence with an axis that can continue to grow and does not end in a flower (i.e. the axis is indeterminate) and many branches, each of which bears two or more flowers; often loosely applied to any complex, branched inflorescence.

papilla a soft, nipple-shaped protuberance.

pappus hairs, bristles or scales which replace the calyx in some members of the Asteraceae; they often facilitate fruit dispersal. See Figure 12.

parasite a plant which obtains its food from another living plant (the host) to which it is attached. Compare **hemiparasite**.

pendulous hanging downward (=pendent). Compare **drooping**.

perennial living for three or more years. Compare **annual, biennial**.

perianth the outer sterile whorls of a flower, made up of sepals or petals or both. See Figure 8. Compare **perigone**.

perianth segments in this book, used for the parts of a perianth which are not, or scarcely, differentiated into calyx and corolla; segments either sepal- or petal-like (=tepals). Compare **perigone**.

perigone a perianth with the parts not, or scarcely, differentiated into sepals and petals; the parts then termed tepals. Compare **perianth**.

persistent remaining attached and not falling off.

petal one of the units of the inner whorl(s) of sterile appendages in flowers that together are called the corolla; often brightly coloured. See Figure 8. Applied to flowers with a differentiated perianth (compare **perianth segments**).

pinna 1. the primary division of a pinnate leaf (=leaflet). 2. the first series of branches within a bipinnate leaf which bears the pinnules. See Figure 6.

pinnate, pinnately compound when a compound leaf has its leaflets arranged in two rows along an extension (the rhachis) of the leaf stalk. See Figure 6. Compare **bipinnate, odd-pinnate**.

pioneer species refers to the first plant species which colonize bare or disturbed areas; often considered weeds. Compare **climax species, succession**.

pistil the female organ of a flower which contains the ovules and will produce the fruit with seeds; comprises the ovary, style and stigma (see Figure 8). A flower may have one pistil or many.

pitcher leaves tubular modified leaves used by insectivorous plants to trap their prey.

pod a general term applied to any dry and many-seeded dehiscent fruit, formed from one unit or carpel. In this book usually applied to a legume which is the product of a single pistil (carpel) and splits open along the two opposite sutures or seams (characteristic of many Mimosaceae, Caesalpiniaceae and Fabaceae). Compare **capsule, follicle**.

pollen a collective term for the pollen grains.

pollen grains the minute spores or grains produced in the anthers of flowering plants; each grain contains the male gametes.

pollinium a mass of cohering pollen grains transported as a single unit during pollination, as in the Asclepiadaceae (see Figure 7) and Orchidaceae.

pore a small, usually rounded opening.

procumbent with stems trailing or lying flat on the ground, but not rooting (=prostrate).

pseudobulb the thickened stem or stem base in many of the Orchidaceae.

pseudostem a false stem formed by sheathing leaf bases which overlap closely and are appressed to each other.

raceme an inflorescence in which the flowers are borne consecutively along a single (unbranched) axis, the lowest on the axis being the oldest. Each flower has a stalk. Compare **spike**.

radiate the flower heads of the Asteraceae which possess ray flowers. See Figure 12. Compare **discoid**.

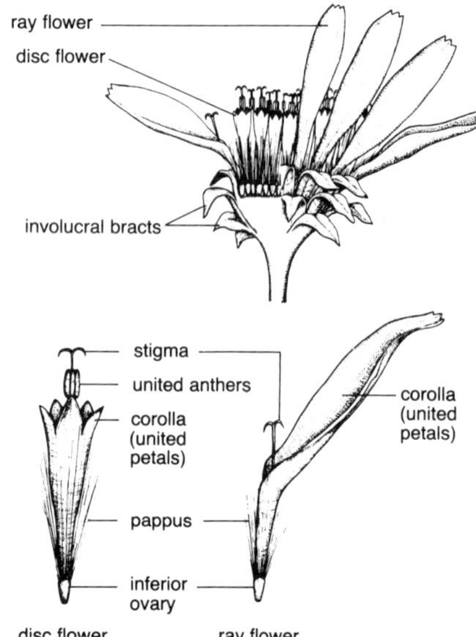

Figure 12. Structure of a radiate flower head in Asteraceae

rank a vertical row; leaves arranged in two ranks are in two vertical rows when viewed from the tip of the shoot.
ray flowers (florets) the outer flowers on the margin of an Asteraceae flower head, when two different types of flowers occur within the head; usually with a single, strap-shaped corolla (apparently a single petal). See Figure 12. Compare **disc flowers**.
receptacle the uppermost part of the flower stalk on which the floral parts are borne. See Figure 11.
recurved curved downward or backward.
reduced undeveloped or not properly developed.
reflexed bent abruptly downward or backward.
regular radially symmetrical, as in a flower that can be divided into two identical halves (mirror images) along more than one plane, i.e. the corolla lobes are equal (=actinomorphic). See Figure 13. Compare **irregular**.

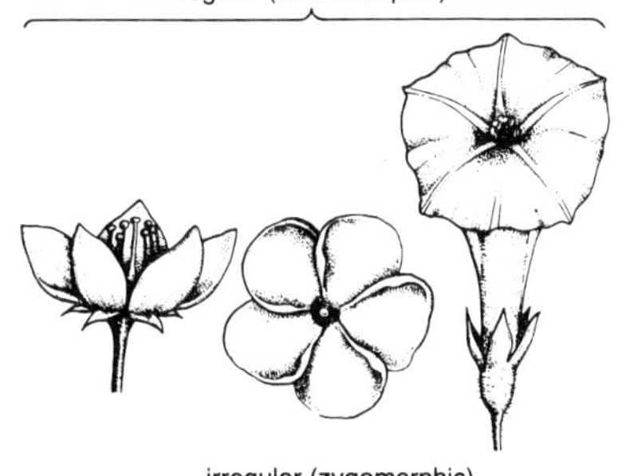

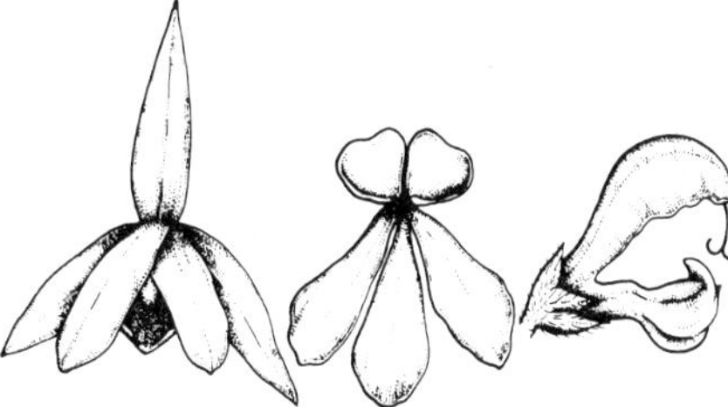

Figure 13. Flower symmetry

resin a group of substances produced by a plant from special canals or ducts found within it; not soluble in water and often sticky and aromatic. Often applied rather loosely to any shiny or sticky surface secretions. **Resinous** producing or containing resin.
rhachilla (rachilla) a small axis or rhachis; the central axis of the spikelet in the grasses (see Figure 14) and sedges (Cyperaceae).
rhachis (rachis) 1. the axis of a compound leaf (see Figure 6); 2. the axis of an inflorescence.
rhizome a creeping (more or less horizontal) underground stem which sends up new leaves and stems each season. Compare **rootstock, stolon**.
rootstock strictly a short erect underground stem. In this book used rather loosely for perennial underground organs. Compare **bulb, corm, rhizome, tuber**.
rosulate/rosette an arrangement of leaves radiating from a crown or centre, usually at ground level (see Figure 5). Compare **alternate, opposite, whorl**.
runner see **stolon**.
sap the juice of a plant; used in this book for any fluid oozing from broken-off plant organs. Compare **latex**.
scalloped the margin notched with rounded or broad and blunt teeth or projections (=crenate, crenulate). See **toothed**.
secretory cavities roundish cavities within the leaf blade that contain secretions such as resin, mucilage and oil. Compare **gland-dotted**.

seed the ripened ovule containing an embryo. Compare **fruit**.
sepal one of the outer set of usually green organs of a flower which normally encloses the other floral parts in the bud; the sepals collectively are called the calyx. See Figure 8.
sheath a tubular structure that encloses an organ or part, as in the lower portion of a grass leaf which encloses the stem.
shrub a perennial woody plant with usually two or more stems arising from or near the ground; differs from a tree in that it is smaller and does not possess a trunk or bole. Compare **tree**.
shrublet a low-growing perennial with stems that are woody mainly towards the base; usually less than 1 m high, and often more or less prostrate (=subshrub, undershrub).
silky having a covering of soft, appressed, fine hairs (=sericeous).
simple leaf with only a single blade (see Figure 10); the opposite of a compound leaf.
smooth with an even and continuous margin; lacking teeth, lobes or indentations (=entire). Compare **toothed**.
solitary (of flowers) occurring singly in each axil.
spathe a large bract that is sometimes leaf- or petal-like and encloses the young flower or inflorescence; boat-shaped in some grasses.
spike an inflorescence with stalkless flowers arranged along an elongated, unbranched axis. Compare **raceme**.
spikelet a small spike in which the flowers are subtended by and enclosed in bracts; the unit of the grass inflorescence (see Figure 14), occurring also in the sedges (Cyperaceae).

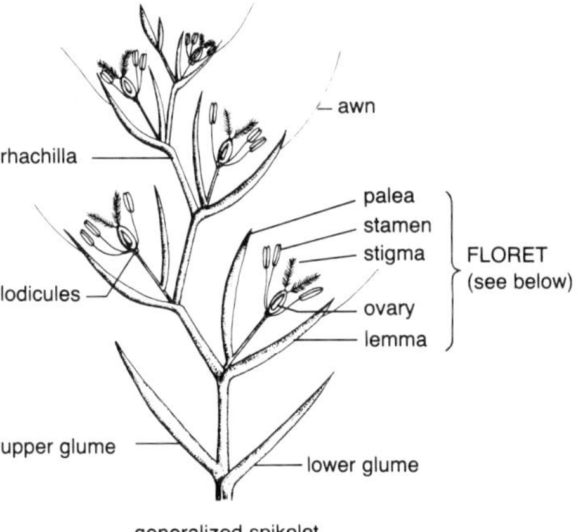

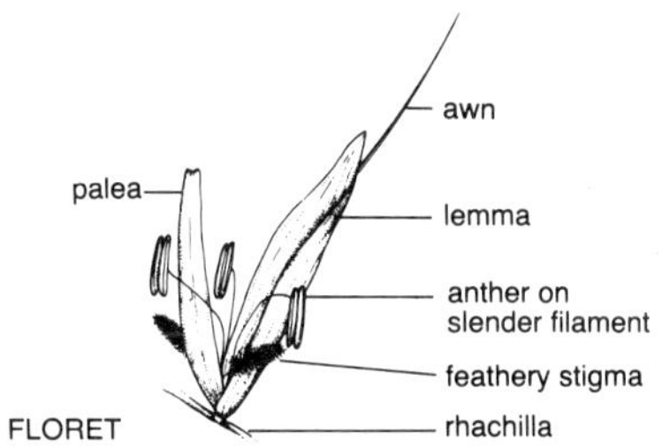

Figure 14. Structure of a grass spikelet

spine a hard, straight and sharply pointed structure, often long and narrow. Usually a modified leaf or stipule. Compare **thorn**.
spinescent ending in a spine or in a very sharp hard point, as in a spinescent shoot (=thorn).
spreading having a gradually outward direction.
spur a tubular or sac-like projection of a flower, as from the base petal or sepal; it usually contains nectar-secreting glands.

stamen one of the male reproductive organs of the flower, usually made up of a narrow stalk (filament), and an anther in which the pollen is produced. See Figure 8.

standard the large upper petal of a flower of the Fabaceae (=banner, vexillum). See Figure 9. Compare **keel, wing**.

stem the main axis of the plant or a branch of the main axis that produces leaves and buds at the nodes. Usually above ground, but sometimes modified and underground (e.g. corms, rhizomes).

stem-clasping see **clasping**.

sterile lacking functional sex organs; a sterile flower produces neither pollen nor functional ovules.

stigma the part of the pistil on which the pollen grains germinate, normally situated at the top of the style and covered with a sticky secretion. See Figure 8.

stipule a scale- or leaf-like appendage at the base of the leaf stalk in some plants; usually paired (see Figure 10). Sometimes modified as spines.

stolon a stem which grows along the ground and roots from the nodes (=runner). Compare **rhizome**.

strap-shaped see **oblong**.

striate marked with longitudinal parallel ridges, grooves, lines or streaks.

style a more or less elongated projection of the ovary which bears the stigma. See Figure 8.

subtending to stand below and close to, e.g. a bract bearing a flower in its axil.

succession the orderly change in composition of vegetation (over time) from the initial colonization of a bare area by pioneer species to the establishment of a climax series. Compare **climax species, pioneer species**.

succulent plant with fleshy and juicy organs (leaves, stems) which contain reserves of water.

taproot the stout, tapering main root of a plant which arises as a direct continuation of the embryonic root (radicle); usually pointing vertically downwards and bearing smaller side roots.

tendril a slender, usually coiling part of the leaf or stem that serves to support the stem; a climbing organ.

terminal at the tip (=apical, or distal end). Compare **ultimate**.

thorn a sharply pointed branch, or curved spine. Often used synonymously with spine.

throat the opening or orifice of a tubular or funnel-shaped corolla. Compare **limb, tube**.

toothed used in a generalized sense in this book to refer to leaf margins which are toothed in various ways, including dentate (with coarse, sharp teeth perpendicular to the margin), serrate (with sharp, forward-pointing teeth) and crenate (with shallow, rounded teeth). Compare **smooth**.

trailing lying flat on the ground, but not rooting.

tree a perennial woody plant with a single (usually) main stem and a distinct upper crown. Compare **shrub**.

trifoliolate referring to a compound leaf with three leaflets. See Figure 6.

trigonous three-angled.

tube the fused lower part of the corolla or calyx in some flowers; shaped like a hollow cylinder. Compare **limb, throat**.

tuber an underground swollen part of a stem or root which stores food; capable of producing new shoots from buds on its surface Compare **bulb, corm**.

ultimate used in this book to refer to the highest degree of branching in woody plants; the final divisions towards the extremity.

umbel an umbrella-shaped inflorescence in which the stalks of the flowers all arise from the top of the main stem; the umbels themselves may be arranged in an umbel and this inflorescence is called a compound umbel. **Umbellate** like an umbel or with umbels.

undulate with a wavy margin.

unisexual of one sex; of flowers which have functional stamens or pistils, but not both.

united joined together (=fused). Compare **free**.

valve(s) 1. a flap-like lid; 2. the segments into which some dry fruits separate when splitting open.

veld a general term for countryside and natural vegetation, usually implying a strong grassy component.

venation the arrangement of veins in an organ.

vlei a low-lying, poorly drained area into which water drains during the wet season when the soil may become waterlogged or submerged; characterized by moisture-loving, usually herbaceous, vegetation.

white-felted closely matted with a felt-like layer of white, intertwined hairs.

whorl 1. the arrangement of three or more leaves or flowers at the same node of the axis so as to form an encircling ring (=verticel). See Figure 5. Compare **alternate, opposite, rosulate/rosette**. 2. more than two of any other organs (e.g. sepals, petals, stamens) arising at the same level.

wing 1. any thin, flat extension of an organ, as in winged fruit or seed. 2. Each of the two side (lateral) petals of a Fabaceae flower (see Figure 9); compare **keel, standard**.

woody approaching the nature of wood; usually applied to perennial plants whose stems do not die back at the end of the growing season. Compare **herbaceous**.

woolly with long, soft, rather tangled hairs.

REFERENCES AND SUGGESTED READING

The following floras were freely consulted during the preparation of this field guide:

Flora Capensis, 1859 – 1925. Although now largely outdated, this is the only complete flora for southern Africa and the only source available for the identification of many groups of plants.

Flora of Southern Africa, 1963 –. This work is to succeed the *Flora Capensis*. Although a number of volumes have already been published, it will probably be completed only during the next century.

Flora of Swaziland, 1976. This, the only complete flora published recently for an area in southern Africa, is a carefully prepared work which includes descriptions for many plant species also occurring in the field guide area.

Flora of the Witwatersrand, 1987 –. Volume 1, which deals with the monocotyledons, has recently been published. It contains keys to the species and is a most useful work for the identification of those monocotyledons not treated in this field guide.

Flora Zambesiaca, 1960 –. This flora, also not yet complete, covers the plants of Mozambique, Malawi, Zambia, Zimbabwe and Botswana. As we share many species with these regions, it is a useful work to consult, particularly for some of the groups not yet treated in the *Flora of Southern Africa*.

Many other publications have been consulted in addition to these floras. Of these, a few selected references are given below. Non-technical wild flower publications which may be helpful for identifying plants in the field guide area are preceded by an asterisk.

Acocks, J.P.H. 1953. Veld types of South Africa. *Memoirs of the Botanical Survey of South Africa* 28: 1 – 192 (2nd edition with updated names and illustrations published in 1975 as *Memoirs of the Botanical Survey of South Africa* 40: 1 – 128; 3rd edition in press). With accompanying veld type map.

Bredenkamp, G.J. & Theron, G.K. 1976. Vegetation units for management of the grasslands of the Suikerbosrand Nature Reserve. *South African Journal of Wildlife Research* 6: 113 – 122.

Bredenkamp, G.J. & Theron, G.K. 1978. A synecological account of the Suikerbosrand Nature Reserve. 1. The phytosociology of the Witwatersrand Geological System. *Bothalia* 12: 513 – 529.

Bredenkamp, G.J. & Theron, G.K. 1980. A synecological account of the Suikerbosrand Nature Reserve. 2. The phytosociology of the Ventersdorp Geological System. *Bothalia* 13: 199 – 216.

Burtt Davy, J. 1926 & 1932. *A manual of the flowering plants and ferns of the Transvaal with Swaziland.* Parts 1 & 2. Longmans, London.

*Carr, J.D. 1976. *The South African Acacias.* Conservation Press, Johannesburg.

Carr, J.D. 1988. *Combretaceae in southern Africa*. Tree Society of Southern Africa, Johannesburg.
Carruthers, V. (editor) 1982. *The Sandton field book – a guide to the natural history of the northern Witwatersrand*. Sandton Nature Conservation Society, Sandton.
Chippindall, L.K.A. 1955. A guide to the identification of grasses in South Africa. *The grasses and pastures of South Africa*, Meredith, D. (editor), Part 1. Central News Agency, Johannesburg.
Coates Palgrave, K. 1983. *Trees of southern Africa*, 2nd edition. C. Struik, Cape Town.
*Coates Palgrave, K., P. & M. 1987. *Everyone's guide to trees of South Africa*, 2nd edition. Central News Agency, Johannesburg.
Codd, L.E.W. 1968. The South African species of *Kniphofia*. *Bothalia* 9: 363 – 513.
Coetzee, B.J. 1975. A phytosociological classification of the Rustenburg Nature Reserve. *Bothalia* 11: 561 – 580.
Compton, R.H. 1976. The Flora of Swaziland. *Journal of South African Botany* Suppl. vol. 11. National Botanic Gardens of South Africa, Cape Town.
Cronquist, A. 1981. *An integrated system of classification of flowering plants*. Columbia University Press, New York.
Dahlgren, R.M.T., Clifford, H.T. & Yeo, P.F. 1985. *The families of the monocotyledons*. Springer-Verlag, Berlin.
*Davidson, L. & Jeppe, B. 1981. *Acacias – a field guide to the identification of the species of southern Africa*. Centaur Publishers, Johannesburg.
Davis, P.H. & Cullen, J. 1979. *The identification of flowering plant families*. Cambridge University Press, Cambridge.
Dyer, R.A. 1975 & 1976. *The genera of southern African flowering plants*, Vols. 1 & 2. Dept. of Agricultural Technical Services, Pretoria.
*Dyer, R.A. 1983. Ceropegia, Brachystelma *and* Riocreuxia *in southern Africa*. A.A. Balkema, Rotterdam.
*Fabian, A. (text by Germishuizen, G.) 1982. *Transvaal wild flowers*. Macmillan, Johannesburg.
Faegri, K. & Van der Pijl, L. 1979. *The principles of pollination ecology*. Pergamon Press, Oxford.
Gibbs Russell, G.E., Reid, C., Van Rooy, J. & Smook, L. 1985. List of species of southern African plants, ed. 2, Part 1: Cryptogams, gymnosperms and monocotyledons. *Memoirs of the Botanical Survey of South Africa* 51: 1 – 152.
Gibbs Russell, G.E., Welman, W.G., Retief, E., Immelman, K.L., Germishuizen, G., Pienaar, B.J., Van Wyk, M. & Nicholas, A. 1987. List of species of southern African plants, ed. 2, Part 2: Dicotyledons. *Memoirs of the Botanical Survey of South Africa* 56: 1 – 270.
*Henderson, M. & Anderson, J.G. 1966. Common weeds of South Africa. *Memoirs of the Botanical Survey of South Africa* 37: 1 – 440.
*Henderson, M., Fourie, D.M.C., Wells, M.J. & Henderson, L. 1987. *Declared weeds and alien invader plants in southern Africa*. Bulletin 413, Dept. of Agriculture and Water Supply, Pretoria.
Heywood, V.H. 1976. *Plant taxonomy*. Edward Arnold, London.
Heywood, V.H. (consultant editor) 1978. *Flowering plants of the world*. Oxford University Press, Oxford.
*Hilliard, O.M. 1977. *Compositae of Natal*. University of Natal Press, Pietermaritzburg.
Jackson, B.D. 1928. *A glossary of botanical terms*. Gerald Duckworth, London.
Jeffrey, C. 1977. *Biological nomenclature*. Edward Arnold, London.
Jeffrey, C. 1982. *An introduction to plant taxonomy*. Cambridge University Press, Cambridge.
*Jeppe, B. 1974. *South African aloes*. Purnell, Cape Town.
Jones, C.E. & Little, R.J. 1983. *Handbook of pollination biology*. Van Nostrand Reinhold, New York.
Jones, S.B. & Luchsinger, A.E. 1986. *Plant systematics*. McGraw Hill, New York.
Kormondy, E.J. 1969. *Concepts of ecology*. Prentice-Hall, Englewood Cliffs, USA.
*Letty, C. (text by Dyer, R.A., Verdoorn, I.C. & Codd, L.E.) 1962. *Wild flowers of the Transvaal*. Trustees of the Wild Flowers of the Transvaal Book Fund, Pretoria.
Lewis, G.J. & Obermeyer, A.A. 1972. *Gladiolus* – a revision of the South African species. *Journal of South African Botany* Suppl. Vol. 10. Purnell, Cape Town.
Little, R.J. & Jones, C.E. 1980. *A dictionary of botany*. Van Nostrand Reinhold, New York.
*Lowrey, T.K. & Wright, S. (editors) 1987. *The flora of the Witwatersrand*, Vol. 1: The Monocotyledonae. Witwatersrand University Press, Johannesburg.
*Lucas, A. & Pike, B. 1971. *Wild flowers of the Witwatersrand*. Purnell, Cape Town.
Meadows, M.E. 1985. *Biogeography and ecosystems of South Africa*. Juta & Co., Cape Town.
Meeuse, A.D.J. 1957. The South African Convolvulaceae. *Bothalia* 6: 641 – 792.
Meeuse, A.D.J. 1962. The Cucurbitaceae of southern Africa. *Bothalia* 8: 1 – 111.
Meeuse, B.J.D. 1961. *The story of pollination*. Ronald Press, New York.
Obermeyer, A.A. 1962. A revision of the South African species of *Anthericum*, *Chlorophytum* and *Trachyandra*. *Bothalia* 7: 669 – 767.
Odum, E.P. 1971. *Fundamentals of ecology*. W.B. Saunders & Co., Philadelphia.
*Onderstall, J. 1984. *Transvaal Lowveld and escarpment*. South African wild flower guide No. 4. Botanical Society of South Africa, Cape Town.
*Palmer, E. & Pitman, N. 1972. *Trees of southern Africa*. 3 Vols. A.A. Balkema, Cape Town.
Real, L. (editor) 1983. *Pollination biology*. Academic Press, Orlando, USA.
Richards, A.J. (editor) 1978. *The pollination of flowers by insects*. Academic Press, London.
*Roberts, B.R. 1973. *Common grasses of the Orange Free State*. OFS Provincial Administration, Nature Conserv. Misc. Publ. 3: 1 – 127.
Ross, J.H. 1979. A conspectus of the African *Acacia* species. *Memoirs of the Botanical Survey of South Africa* 44: 1 – 155.
*Rourke, J.P. 1982. *The proteas of southern Africa*. Centaur Publishers, Johannesburg.
Roux, E. 1969. *Grass – a story of Frankenwald*. Oxford University Press, Cape Town.
Rutherford, M.C. & Westfall, R.H. 1986. Biomes of southern Africa – an objective categorization. *Memoirs of the Botanical Survey of South Africa* 54: 1 – 98.
Smith, C.A. 1966. Common names of South African plants. *Memoirs of the Botanical Survey of South Africa* 35: 1 – 642.
Stace, C.A. 1984. *Plant taxonomy and biosystematics*. Edward Arnold, London.
*Steward, J., Linder, H.P., Schelpe, E.A. & Hall, A.V. 1982. *Wild orchids of southern Africa*. Macmillan, Johannesburg.
*Tainton, N.M., Bransby, D.I. & Booysen, P. de V. 1976. *Common veld and pasture grasses of Natal*. Shuter & Shooter, Pietermaritzburg.
*Tree Society of Southern Africa 1974. *Trees of the Witwatersrand*. Witwatersrand University Press, Johannesburg.
*Van Gogh, J. & Anderson, J. 1988. *Trees and shrubs of the Witwatersrand, Magaliesberg and Pilanesberg*. C. Struik, Cape Town.
*Van Wyk, P. 1984. *Field guide to the trees of the Kruger National Park*. C. Struik, Cape Town.
Vogel, S. 1954. *Blütenbiologische Typen als Elemente der Sippengliederung – dargestellt anhand der Flora Südafrikas*. Gustav Fisher, Jena.
*Von Breitenbach, F. 1984. *National list of introduced trees*. Dendrological Foundation, Pretoria.
*Von Breitenbach, F. 1986. *National list of indigenous trees*. Dendrological Foundation, Pretoria.
*Von Breitenbach, J. 1974. *The wild figs of southern Africa*. Monograph No. 2. Tree Society of Southern Africa, Johannesburg.
Wells, M.J., Balsinhas, A.A., Joffe, H., Engelbrecht, V.M., Harding, G. & Stirton, C.H. 1986. A catalogue of problem plants in southern Africa. *Memoirs of the Botanical Survey of South Africa* 53: 1 – 658.

The *Flora of Southern Africa*, *Bothalia*, *Memoirs of the Botanical Survey of South Africa* and other publications of the Botanical Research Institute can be obtained from the Division of Agricultural Information, Department of Agriculture and Water Supply, Private Bag X144, Pretoria 0001.

INDEX TO SCIENTIFIC NAMES

Current scientific names are printed in bold type and synonyms in italic; page numbers in bold type refer to main entries with an illustration, and those in light type to passing references. Names preceded by * signify a protected plant (Ordinance 12, 1983).

Acacia ataxacantha 162
A. baileyana 162
A. caffra 12, 13, 14, 162
A. dealbata 14, 162
A. decurrens 162
A. karroo 13, 14, 162
A. mearnsii 14, 162
A. podalyriifolia 164
A. robusta subsp. robusta 164
A. tortilis subsp. heteracantha 13
Acalypha angustata var. glabra 130, 204
A. caperonioides 130, 204
A. petiolaris 204
Acanthaceae 9, 16, 32 – 34, 94, 188, 242
Achyranthes aspera 188
A. sicula 188
Acokanthera oppositifolia 36
Acrotome angustifolia 64
A. hispida 64
A. inflata 64
Adenia digitata 170
A. glauca 170
Adenostemma caffrum 42
Adromischus umbraticola subsp. umbraticola 202
Aeollanthus buchnerianus 220
A. canescens 220
Aerva leucura 36
*Agapanthus campanulatus subsp. patens 242
*A. inapertus subsp. intermedius 242
Agrimonia odorata 174
Aizoaceae 16, 286
Ajuga ophrydis 254
Albuca sp. 66
A. glauca 66
A. pachychlamys 66
A. setosa 66
A. shawii 150
Alectra orobanchoides 176
A. sessiliflora 176
Alepidea setifera 288
Alisma plantago-aquatica 34
Alismataceae 16, 34
Alliaceae 9, 16, 22, 34, 242, 270
Alloteropsis semialata 321
Aloe arborescens 150
A. davyana 7
A. davyana var. davyana 220
A. greatheadii var. *davyana* 220
A. marlothii var. marlothii 278
*A. mutabilis 150
*A. peglerae 12, 150
*A. pretoriensis 220
A. transvaalensis 7, 220
*A. verecunda 220
A. zebrina 220
Alysicarpus rugosus subsp. perennirufus 206
A. rugosus subsp. rugosus 206
Amaranthaceae 9, 16, 36, 188, 286
Amaranthus hybridus 286
Amaryllidaceae 16, 94, 188 – 190
*Ammocharis coranica 188
Anacampseros filamentosa 230
A. lanigera 230
A. subnuda 230
Anacardiaceae 16, 36, 94, 286 – 288
Androcymbium melanthioides var. melanthioides 66
Andropogon amplectens 325
A. eucomus 327
A. schirensis 322
Anomatheca grandiflora 218
A. laxa 218
Anthericaceae 9
Anthericum cooperi 7, 68
A. fasciculatum 68
A. longistylum 68
A. transvaalense 68
A. trichophlebium 7, 68
Anthospermum hispidulum 306
Apiaceae 9, 16, 94, 288
Apocynaceae 17, 36
Apodytes dimidiata subsp. dimidiata 62
Aponogeton junceus subsp. junceus 36, 242
Aponogetonaceae 17, 36, 242
Aquifoliaceae 17, 36
Araliaceae 17, 288
Araujia sericifera 38
Arctotis arctotoides 98
Arecaceae 9
Argemone subfusiformis 78
Argyrolobium cf. velutinum 134
A. pauciflorum var. pauciflorum 134
A. tuberosum 206
Aristea woodii 252
Aristida adscensionis subsp. adscensionis 314
A. barbicollis 327
A. bipartita 327
A. congesta subsp. barbicollis 327
A. congesta subsp. congesta 314
A. curvata 314
A. scabrivalvis 327
A. transvaalensis 314
A. uniplumis var. *neesii* 330
Asclepiadaceae 9, 17, 38, 96, 192, 268, 270, 290
Asclepias adscendens 38, 192
A. affinis 290
A. aurea 96
A. brevipes 192
A. burchellii 290
A. eminens 290
A. fallax 96
A. fruticosa 96
A. gibba 290
A. glaucophylla 290
A. meliodora 38
A. physocarpa 38
A. stellifera 192
Ascolepis capensis 54
Asparagaceae 9
Asparagus krebsianus 70
Asphodelaceae 9
Aster harveyanus 244
A. peglerae 40
Asteraceae 9, 17, 40 – 46, 98 – 120, 192 – 196, 244 – 246, 272, 310
Athrixia elata 192

*Babiana hypogea var. hypogea 252
Barleria obtusa 242
B. pretoriensis 32
Becium angustifolium 64
B. obovatum var. obovatum 64, 254
Bequaertiodendron magalismontanum 12, 176
Berchemia zeyheri 304
Bergia decumbens 56
Berkheya carlinopsis subsp. magalismontana 98
B. insignis 98
B. radula 98
B. seminivea 98
B. setifera 98
B. zeyheri subsp. zeyheri 98
Berula erecta 94
Bewsia biflora 332
Bidens bipinnata 100
B. biternata 100
B. formosa 40, 192
B. pilosa 40, 108
Blepharis integrifolia 242
Blumea mollis 194
*Bonatea porrecta 302
*B. speciosa var. antennifera 302
Boophane disticha 188
Boraginaceae 17, 20, 46, 198, 248
Bothriochloa insculpta 322
Brachiaria serrata 322
Brachylaena rotundata 108
Brachymeris athanasioides 114
*Brachystelma barberiae 270
*B. foetidum 270
Brassicaceae 9, 18, 46, 122
Bryophyllum delagoense 202
Buchnera longespicata 262
B. reducta 262
Buddleja saligna 48
B. salviifolia 248
Buddlejaceae 18, 48, 248
Bulbine abyssinica 152
B. angustifolia 152
B. capitata 152
B. narcissifolia 152
B. stenophylla 152
B. tortifolium 152
Bulbostylis burchellii 274
Burkea africana 13, 48

Caesalpiniaceae 18, 48, 122 – 124
Callilepis leptophylla 40
Calodendrum capense 12, 232
Calpurnia villosa var. intrusa 134
Campanulaceae 18, 48, 248
Canthium gilfillanii 306
C. huillense 174
C. mundianum 306
Capparaceae 18, 48, 198
Carex cernua var. austro-africana 294
Caryophyllaceae 18, 50, 198, 272
Cassia comosa var. capricornia 122
C. didymobotrya 122
C. italica subsp. arachoides 122
C. mimosoides 122
Castalis spectabilis 244
Celastraceae 18, 50, 124
Celtis africana 14, 308
Cenchrus ciliaris 315
Cephalaria zeyheriana 56
Ceratotheca triloba 228
*Ceropegia rendalii 38
Chaetacanthus cf. setiger 32
C. costatus 32
Chascanum hederaceum 182
Chironia palustris subsp. transvaalensis 216
C. purpurascens subsp. humilis 216
Chloris gayana 323
C. pycnothrix 323
C. virgata 323
Chlorophytum bowkeri 68
Chortolirion angolense 278
Chrysanthemoides monilifera subsp. canescens 100
Chrysobalanaceae 18, 124
Chrysopogon montanus var. *tremulus* 328
C. serrulatus 328
Cichorium intybus 246
Cirsium vulgare 194
Citrullus lanatus 128
Clematis brachiata 80, 232
C. oweniae 80
Clematopsis scabiosifolia 232
Cleome gynandra 48
C. maculata 198
C. monophylla 198
C. rubella 198
Clerodendrum glabrum var. glabrum 90
C. triphyllum var. triphyllum 266
Clusiaceae 9, 21
Clutia pulchella 130
Coccinia adoensis 128
C. sessilifolia 128
Colchicaceae 9
Coleochloa setifera 274
Combretaceae 18, 292
Combretum apiculatum 13
C. apiculatum subsp. apiculatum 292
C. erythrophyllum 292
C. molle 292
C. zeyheri 292
Commelina africana 124
C. africana var. africana 124
C. africana var. barberae 124
C. africana var. krebsiana 124
C. africana var. lancispatha 124
C. benghalensis 248
C. diffusa 248
C. erecta 248
C. livingstonii 248

C. modesta 248
C. subulata 124
Commelinaceae 19, 124, 248 – 250
Compositae see Asteraceae
Convolvulaceae 9, 19, 19, 52, 126, 200 – 202, 250
Convolvulus sagittatus subsp. sagittatus var. hirtellus 52
C. sagittatus subsp. sagittatus var. phyllosepalus 52
C. sagittatus var. aschersonii 52
C. sagittatus var. ulosepalus 52
Conyza bonariensis 42
C. canadensis 42
C. floribunda 42
C. podocephala 108
Corchorus asplenifolius 180
C. confusus 180
Cordylogyne globosa 38
Cortaderia jubata 332
C. selloana 332
Cotula anthemoides 108
Cotyledon barbeyi 202
C. orbiculata var. oblonga 202
Crabbea acaulis 32
C. angustifolia 32
C. hirsuta 32
C. ovalifolia 32
Crassula alba var. alba 202
C. capitella subsp. nodulosa 54
C. lanceolata subsp. lanceolata 292
C. lanceolata subsp. transvaalensis 292
C. schimperi var. *schimperi* 292
C. setulosa var. setulosa 54
C. swaziensis 54
Crassulaceae 19, 54, 126, 202, 272, 292
Craterostigma wilmsii 234
Crepis hypochoeridea 118
*Crinum bulbispermum 190
*C. graminicola 190
*C. lugardiae 190
*C. macowanii 190
Crossandra greenstockii 188
Crotalaria agatiflora 136
C. brachycarpa 136
C. eremicola 136
C. lotoides 136
C. orientalis subsp. orientalis 136
C. sphaerocarpa 136
Croton gratissimus var. subgratissimus 130
Cruciferae see Brassicaceae
Cryptolepis oblongifolia 170
C. transvaalensis 170
Cucumus hirsutus 128
C. zeyheri 128
Cucurbitaceae 19, 128, 294
Cuscuta campestris 54
Cuscutaceae 19, 19, 54
*Cussonia paniculata 14, 288
*C. transvaalensis 288
Cyanotis lapidosa 250
C. speciosa 250
Cycnium adonense 86
C. tubulosum 86
Cymbopogon caesius 328
C. excavatus 328
C. plurinodes 14, 328
C. pospischilii 328
C. validus 329
Cynodon dactylon 324
Cynoglossum hispidum 198
C. lanceolatum 198
Cyperaceae 7, 9, 19, 26, 30, 54, 130, 268, 274, 284, 294, 310
Cyperus esculentus 274
C. margaritaceus 54
C. obtusiflorus var. flavissimus 54, 130
C. obtusiflorus var. obtusiflorus 54, 130
C. rotundus 274
C. rupestris var. rupestris 274
Cyphia assimilis 74
C. stenopetala 222
Cyphostemma lanigerum 184
*Cyrtanthus breviflorus 94
*C. tuckii var. transvaalensis 190

Dais cotinifolia 238
Dalechampia capensis 130
Datura ferox 88
D. stramonium 88, 262
Delosperma herbeum 76
D. leendertziae 160
Denekia capensis 42, 244
Dianthus mooiensis subsp. kirkii 50
D. mooiensis subsp. mooiensis 50
Dicerocaryum eriocarpum 228
D. zanguebarium subsp. *eriocarpum* 228
Dichanthium aristatum 312
Dichapetalaceae 19, 294
Dichapetalum cymosum 294
Dichrostachys cinerea 13
D. cinerea subsp. africana 164, 224
Dicliptera eenii 188
Diclis reptans 86
Dicoma anomala subsp. anomala 194
D. anomala subsp. circioides 194
D. macrocephala 272
D. zeyheri 42
*Dierama medium var. mossii 218
Digitaria diagonalis var. diagonalis 324
D. eriantha 324
D. smutsii 324
Diheteropogon amplectens 325
Diospyros austro-africana var. microphylla 56
D. lycioides 14
D. lycioides subsp. guerkei 130
D. lycioides subsp. lycioides 130
D. whyteana 56
Dipcadi cf. ciliare 278, 298
D. marlothii 298
D. rigidifolium 298
D. viride 278
Diplachne biflora 332
Dipsacaceae 19, 56
*Disa woodii 168
Dissotis debilis var. debilis forma debilis 224
Dodonaea angustifolia 308
Dolichos angustifolius 206
Dombeya rotundifolia var. rotundifolia 90
Dovyalis zeyheri 144
Dracaenaceae 9
Drimia elata 298
Drimiopsis burkei 256
Drosera madagascariensis 204
Droseraceae 20, 204
Duchesnea indica 174

Ebenaceae 20, 56, 130
Ehretia rigida 14, 252, 308
Ehretiaceae 17, 20, 252
Eichornia crassipes 260
Elatinaceae 20, 56
Elephantorrhiza burkei 164
E. elephantina 164
Eleusine africana 325
E. coracana subsp. africana 325
Elionurus argenteus 315
E. muticus 315
Enneapogon cenchroides 315
Epaltes gariepina 194
Epilobium hirsutum 226
Eragrostis capensis 333
E. curvula 333
E. gummiflua 333
E. racemosa 334
E. superba 334
Erica woodii 204
Ericaceae 20, 204
Eriosema burkei 138
E. cordatum 138
E. salignum 138
Eriospermaceae 9
Eriospermum abyssinicum 152
E. cooperi 68
E. luteo-rubrum 152
E. tenellum 152
Erythrina lysistemon 206
E. zeyheri 206
Eucalyptus camaldulensis 76
E. sideroxylon 224
Euclea crispa 14
E. crispa subsp. crispa 56
*Eucomis autumnalis subsp. clavata 298
*Eulophia clavicornis var. clavicornis 168, 260
*E. clavicornis var. inaequalis 168, 260
*E. ovalis subsp. bainesii 78, 168
*E. ovalis subsp. ovalis 78, 168
*E. streptopetala 168
*E. tuberculata 168
*E. welwitschii 168
Eupatorium macrocephalum 194
Euphorbia clavaroides var. truncata 132
E. cooperi 132
E. epicyparissias 296
E. geniculata 296
E. ingens 132
E. schinzii 132
E. striata var. striata 132
E. trichadenia 204
Euphorbiaceae 9, 20, 130 – 134, 204, 296
Euryops laxus 100
Evolvulus alsinoides var. linifolius 250

Fabaceae 9, 20, 58, 134 – 144, 206 – 214, 252, 276, 310
Fadogia homblei 174
F. monticola 174
Falkia oblonga 52
Faurea saligna 12, 172
Felicia filifolia subsp. filifolia 244
F. mossamedensis 100
F. muricata subsp. muricata 40
Ficus abutilifolia 300
F. cordata subsp. *salicifolia* 300
F. ingens var. ingens 300
F. salicifolia 300
F. sur 300
F. thonningii 300
Flacourtiaceae 20, 144, 296
Flaveria bidentis 108
Floscopa glomerata 250
*Frithia pulchra 12, 224
Fuirena pubescens 294

Galinsoga parviflora 100
Galium capense subsp. garipense 306
Gardenia volkensii subsp. volkensii var. volkensii 82
Garuleum woodii 40
Gazania krebsiana subsp. serrulata 40, 100
Geigeria burkei subsp. burkei var. intermedia 102
Genlisea hispidula subsp. hispidula 256
Gentianaceae 20, 146, 216
Geraniaceae 21, 60, 216
Gerbera ambigua 102
G. piloselloides 42
G. viridifolia subsp. viridifolia 42, 192
Gesneriaceae 21, 60
*Gladiolus crassifolius 218
*G. dalenii 276
*G. elliotii 62, 218
*G. permeabilis subsp. edulis 150
*G. pretoriensis 254
*G. woodii 150, 276
Gnaphalium luteo-album 114
Gnidia caffra 180
G. capitata 180
G. gymnostachya 238
G. kraussiana var. kraussiana 180
G. microcephala 282
G. sericocephala 180
Gomphostigma virgatum 48
Gomphrena celosioides 36
Graderia subintegra 86, 234
Gramineae see Poaceae
Grewia flava 180
G. occidentalis 238
Gunnera perpensa 296
Gunneraceae 21, 296
Guttiferae see Clusiaceae
Gynandriris simulans 7, 254

*Haemanthus humilis subsp. hirsutus 190
Halleria lucida 12, 280
Haplocarpha lyrata 102
H. scaposa 102
Harpochloa falx 316
Harveya pumila 176
Haworthia angolensis 278
Hebenstretia angolensis 282
H. comosa 176

Helichrysum acutatum 110
H. argyrosphaerum 44, 196
H. aureonitens 110
H. caespititium 44, 196
H. candolleanum 196
H. cephaloideum 110
H. cerastioides var. cerastioides 44
H. chionosphaerum 44
H. coriaceum 110
H. dasymallum 110
H. epapposum 110
H. harveyanum 110
H. kraussii 112
H. kuntzei 112
H. melanacme 112
H. nudifolium 112
H. pilosellum 112
H. rugulosum 112
H. setosum 112
Helinus integrifolius 304
Heliophila rigidiuscula 46
Heliotropium amplexicaule 248
H. ciliatum 46
Hemizygia canescens 254
H. pretoriae subsp. pretoriae 64
Hermannia boraginiflora 236
H. coccocarpa 266
H. depressa 282
H. floribunda 178
H. grandistipula 178
H. lancifolia 178
H. resedifolia 236
H. tomentosa 236
H. transvaalensis 178
Hermbstaedtia odorata var. odorata 188
Heteromorpha arborescens 288
H. trifoliata 288
Heteropogon contortus 316
Hibiscus aethiopicus var. ovatus 156, 222
H. calyphyllus 156, 158
H. engleri 156
H. lunarifolius 156
H. microcarpus 156, 222
H. pusillus 156
H. subreniformis 280
H. trionum 74, 156
Hippocrateaceae 21, 298
*Holothrix randii 78
Homeria pallida 150
*Huernia hystrix var. hystrix 270
Hyacinthaceae 9
Hyparrhenia glauca 329
H. hirta 329
H. quarrei 329
H. tamba 329
Hypericaceae 21, 146
Hypericum aethiopicum subsp. sonderi 146
H. lalandii 146
Hypochoeris radicata 118
Hypoestes forskaolii 32
Hypoxidaceae 21, 148
Hypoxis acuminata 148
H. argentea 148
H. filiformis 148
H. hemerocallidea 148
H. interjecta 148
H. multiceps 148
H. obtusa 148
H. rigidula 148
H. rooperi 148

Iboza brevispicata 220
Icacinaceae 21, 62
Ilex mitis 12, 36
Illecebraceae 21, 62
Imperata cylindrica 316
Indigofera acutisepala 58, 208
I. adenoides 208
I. burkeana 276
I. comosa 208
I. confusa 210
I. cryptantha 208
I. daleoides var. daleoides 208
I. filipes 208
I. hedyantha 208
I. hilaris 210
I. melanadenia 210
I. newbrowniana 210
I. oxalidea 210
I. oxytropis 210
I. pretoriana 210
I. setiflora 210
I. sordida 210
I. spicata 210
I. zeyheri 58, 208
Ipomoea bathycolpos var. bathycolpos 200
I. bolusiana subsp. bolusiana 200
I. crassipes 200
I. magnusiana var. eenii 200
I. magnusiana var. magnusiana 200
I. obscura var. fragilis 126
I. ommaneyi 200
I. purpurea 200, 250
I. simplex 126
I. sinensis subsp. blepharocephala 250
I. transvaalensis 200
Iridaceae 9, 21, 62, 150, 218, 252 – 254, 276
Isoglossa grantii 32

Jatropha lagarinthoides 134
Justicia anagalloides 34
J. betonica 34
J. flava 94
J. pallidior 34

Kalanchoe paniculata 126
K. rotundifolia 202, 272
K. thyrsiflora 126
Kedrostis africana 294
Khadia acutipetala 224
Kiggelaria africana 296
*Kniphofia ensifolia subsp. ensifolia 154
*K. porphyrantha 154
Kohoutia amatymbica 82
K. cynanchica 82
K. lasiocarpa 82
K. virgata 232
Kyllinga alba 54

Labiatae see Lamiaceae
Lablab purpureus subsp. uncinatus 212
Lactuca capensis 46
Lamiaceae 9, 22, 64, 220, 254 – 256, 278
Landolphia capensis 36
Lannea discolor 94
L. edulis 94
Lantana camara 238, 282
L. rugosa 266
*Lapeirousia sandersonii 254
Launaea rarifolia 118
Ledebouria cooperi 258
L. marginata 258
L. ovatifolia 258
L. revoluta 258
Leersia hexandra 334
Leguminosae see Caesalpiniaceae, Fabaceae, Mimosaceae
Lentibulariaceae 22, 66, 256
Leonotis dysophylla 278
L. microphylla 278
L. ocymifolia var. *raineriana* 278
L. ocymifolia var. *schinzii* 278
Lessertia stricta 212
Leucosidea sericea 174
Lightfootia denticulata var. transvaalensis 248
Liliaceae 9, 16, 22, 66 – 72, 150 – 154, 220, 256 – 258, 278, 298
Limeum viscosum subsp. viscosum var. glomeratum 76
Limosella maior 86
Linaceae 22, 154
Linum thunbergii 154
Lippia javanica 182
L. rehmannii 182
L. scaberrima 182
Listia heterophylla 140
*Lithops lesliei 160
Lobelia angolensis 74
L. decipiens 258
L. depressa 74
L. erinus 258
L. flaccida subsp. flaccida 258
L. nuda 258
Lobeliaceae 22, 74, 222, 258
Loganiaceae 22, 74, 300
Lopholaena coriifolia 44
Loranthaceae 22, 74, 222
Lotononis calycina var. calycina 138
L. calycina var. hirsutissima 138
L. eriantha var. eriantha 138
L. foliosa 138
L. lanceolata 138
L. laxa var. laxa 140
L. laxa var. multiflora 140
L. listii 140
Loudetia simplex 330
Lythraceae 22, 222

Macrotyloma axillare 140
Maerua cafra 48
Malpighiaceae 23, 154, 222
Malva parviflora 222
M. verticillata 222
Malvaceae 9, 23, 74, 156 – 160, 222, 268, 280
Malvastrum coromandelianum 158
Manulea parvifolia 280
Mariscus congestus 274
Maytenus heterophylla 14, 50
M. polyacantha 50
M. tenuispina 124
Medicago sativa 252
Melasma scabrum 176
Melastomataceae 23, 224
Melhania prostrata 158
Melia azedarach 12, 258
Meliaceae 23, 74, 258
Melilotus alba 58
M. indica 140
Melolobium wilmsii 140
Menodora africana 166
Merremia palmata 126
M. tridentata subsp. angustifolia 126
Mesembryanthemaceae 23, 76, 160, 224
Microchloa caffra 317
Mimosaceae 23, 162 – 164, 224
Mimulus gracilis 86
Mimusops zeyheri 12, 84
Mirabilis jalapa 164, 226
Miscanthidium junceum 335
Miscanthus junceus 335
Molluginaceae 23, 76
Momordica balsamina 128
Monocymbium ceresiiforme 330
Monopsis decipiens 258
Monsonia angustifolia 216
M. attenuata 60
M. biflora 60, 216
M. burkeana 60, 216
Moraceae 23, 300
Moraea stricta 254
M. thomsonii 254
Mundulea sericea 252
Myrica pilulifera 302
M. serrata 302
Myricaceae 23, 302
Myrothamnaceae 24, 224
Myrothamnus flabellifolia 224
Myrsinaceae 24, 76
Myrsine africana 76
Myrtaceae 24, 76, 224

Nemesia fruticans 234
Neorautanenia ficifolius 252
Nesaea schinzii var. rehmannii 222
Nidorella anomala 112
N. hottentotica 112
Nolletia rarifolia 114
Nothoscordum inodorum 34
Nuxia congesta 74
Nyctaginaceae 24, 164, 226

Obetia tenax 182
Ochna pretoriensis 166, 226
O. pulchra 12, 166, 226
Ochnaceae 24, 166, 226
Oenothera indecora 166
O. rosea 226
O. stricta 166
O. tetraptera 78
Olacaceae 24, 302
Oldenlandia herbacea var. herbacea 82
O. tenella 82
Olea europaea subsp. africana 76
Oleaceae 24, 76, 166
Onagraceae 24, 78, 166, 226
Ophrestia oblongifolia var. oblongifolia 212
*Orbeopsis lutea subsp. lutea 96
Orchidaceae 9, 24, 78, 168, 260, 302, 310
Ornithogalum tenuifolium subsp. tenuifolium 298
Orthanthera jasminiflora 38
Osteospermum muricatum subsp. muricatum 102

O. scariosum var. scariosum 102
Osyris lanceolata 308
Otholobium polystictum 252
Otiophora calycophylla subsp. calycophylla 82
Oxalidaceae 25, 170, 228
Oxalis corniculata 170
O. depressa 228
O. obliquifolia 228
O. semiloba 228
Oxygonum dregeanum var. canescens 80
O. sinuatum 80
Ozoroa paniculosa 36

Pachycarpus schinzianus 38
Palmae see Arecaceae
Panicum maximum 335
P. natalense 335
Papaver aculeatum 280
Papaveraceae 25, 78, 280
Papilionaceae see Fabaceae
Parinari capensis subsp. capensis 124
Paspalum dilatatum 325
P. urvillei 326
Passifloraceae 25, 170
Pavetta gardeniifolia var. gardeniifolia 82
Pavonia burchellii 280
P. senegalensis 158
P. transvaalensis 158
Pearsonia cajanifolia subsp. cajanifolia 140
P. sessilifolia subsp. sessilifolia 140
Pedaliaceae 25, 228
Pelargonium dolomiticum 60
P. luridum 216
P. pseudofumarioides 216
Peltophorum africanum 13, 124
Pennisetum setaceum 317
P. thunbergii 317
Pentanisia angustifolia 260
P. prunelloides 260
Pentarrhinum insipidum 290
Pentzia pilulifera 114
Periplocaceae 25, 170, 260, 302
Perotis patens 318
Peucedanum magalismontanum 94
Phragmites australis 336
P. communis 336
Phylica paniculata 80
Phyllanthus parvulus 296
Phymaspermum athanasioides 114
Physalis viscosa 178
Phytolacca octandra 170
Phytolaccaceae 25, 170
Piriqueta capensis 182
Pittosporaceae 25, 172
Pittosporum viridiflorum 12, 172
Plantaginaceae 25, 78, 302
Plantago lanceolata 78
P. longissima 302
Plectranthus hereroensis 256
P. madagascariensis var. ramosior 64, 256
Plexipus adenostachyus 182
P. hederaceus 182
Plumbaginaceae 26, 78
Plumbago zeylanica 78
Poa annua 336
Poaceae 7, 9, 26, 310, 314 – 338
Pogonarthria squarrosa 326
Pointsettia geniculata 296
Pollichia campestris 62
Polycarpaea corymbosa 272
Polygala amatymbica 260
P. hottentotta 228
P. uncinata 260
Polygalaceae 26, 228, 260
Polygonaceae 9, 26, 80, 230, 304
Polygonum lapathifolium subsp. maculatum 230
P. limbatum 230
P. pulchrum 230
P. salicifolium 230
P. senegalense subsp. senegalense 230
Pontederiaceae 26, 260
Portulaca kermesina 230
P. oleracea 172
P. quadrifida 230
Portulacaceae 26, 172, 230
Pouzolzia hypoleuca 308
P. mixta 308
Priva cordifolia var. abyssinica 90
Protasparagus cooperi 70
P. laricinus 70
P. setaceus 70
P. suaveolens 70
P. transvaalensis 70
P. virgatus 154
*Protea caffra 12, 14, 222, 232
*P. gaguedi 80
*P. roupelliae subsp. roupelliae 232
*P. welwitschii 80
Proteaceae 26, 80, 172, 232
Psammotropha myriantha 286
Pseudognaphalium luteo-album 114
Psiadia punctulata 114
Psoralea polysticta 252
Psydrax livida 174
Pycnostachys reticulata 256
Pygmaeothamnus zeyheri var. zeyheri 306

Ranunculaceae 26, 80, 172, 232
Ranunculus meyeri 172
R. multifidus 172
Raphanus raphanistrum 122
Raphionacme galpinii 302
R. hirsuta 260
Rhamnaceae 27, 80, 304
Rhamnus prinoides 304
Rhamphicarpa tubulosa 86
Rhoicissus tridentata subsp. cuneifolia 184
Rhus dentata 286
R. discolor 286
R. eckloniana 288
R. gracillima 286
R. lancea 14, 286
R. leptodictya 286
R. magalismontana 288
R. pyroides 14, 288
R. rigida 288
R. zeyheri 288
Rhynchelytrum nerviglume 336
R. repens 337
R. setifolium 336
R. villosum 337
Rhynchosia adenodes 142
R. caribaea 142
R. minima var. prostrata 142
R. monophylla 142
R. nitens 142
R. totta 142
Richardia brasiliensis 84
Robinia pseudo-acacia 58
Rorippa nasturtium-aquaticum 46
R. nudiuscula 122
Rosaceae 27, 174, 232
Rothmannia capensis 84
Rubia horrida 306
Rubiaceae 9, 27, 82 – 84, 174, 232, 260, 306
Rubus rigidus 232
Ruellia cf. patula 34
R. cordata 242
Rumex crispus 304
R. lanceolatus 304
Rutaceae 27, 84, 232

Salacia rehmannii 298
Salicaceae 27, 174, 308
Salix babylonica 308
S. mucronata subsp. woodii 174
S. woodii 174
Salvia repens 256
S. runcinata 256
S. stenophylla 256
Sansevieria aethiopica 70
Santalaceae 27, 84, 308
Sapindaceae 27, 308
Sapotaceae 27, 84, 176
Sarcostemma viminale 96
Scabiosa columbaria 56
*Scadoxus puniceus 190
Schistostephium crataegifolium 114
S. heptalobum 114
Schizachyrium sanguineum 318
S. semiberbe 318
Schizobasis intricata 70
*Schizostylis coccinea 218
Schoenoplectus corymbosus 274
Scilla nervosa 72
Scrophulariaceae 9, 28, 86, 176, 234 – 236, 262, 280
Sebaea grandis 146
S. leiostyla 146
Seddera capensis 52
Selaginaceae 28, 88, 176, 262, 282
Selago capitellata 262
Senecio achilleifolius 104
S. affinis 104
S. anomalochrous 196
S. barbertonicus 116
S. breyeri 44
S. burchellii 104
S. consanguineus 104
S. coronatus 104
S. erubescens var. crepidifolius 196
S. glanduloso-pilosus 116
S. harveianus 104
S. inaequidens 104
S. inornatus 106
S. isatideus 116
S. longiflorus 116
S. lydenburgensis 106
S. orbicularis 116
S. othonniflorus 116
S. oxyriifolius 116
S. pentactinus 106
S. polyodon var. polyodon 44
S. scitus 106
S. serratuloides var. gracilis 106
S. venosus 106, 116
Sesamum triphyllum var. triphyllum 228
Sesbania punicea 276
Setaria lindenbergiana 337
S. megaphylla 337
S. nigrirostris 318
S. pallide-fusca 319
S. perennis 319
S. sphacelata var. sericea 319
S. sphacelata var. sphacelata 319
S. verticillata 320
Sida alba 160
S. cordifolia 160
S. dregei 160
S. rhombifolia 160
S. ternata 74
Silene bellidioides 50
S. burchellii var. angustifolia 198
S. burchellii var. burchellii 198
Sisymbrium thellungii 122
Sium repandum 94
Solanaceae 9, 28, 88, 178, 262 – 264
Solanum elaeagnifolium 264
S. giganteum 264
S. incanum 264
S. mauritianum 264
S. nigrum 88
S. panduriforme 264
S. pseudocapsicum 88
S. retroflexum 88
S. rigescens 264
S. seaforthianum 264
S. sisymbrifolium 88, 264
S. supinum 264
Sonchus dregeanus 120
S. nanus 120
S. oleraceus 120
S. wilmsii 120
Sopubia cana 234
S. simplex 234
Sorghum bicolor subsp. arundinaceum 337
S. halepense 337
S. verticilliflorum 337
Sphaeranthus incisus 244
Sphedamnocarpus galphimiifolius 154
S. pruriens var. *galphimiifolius* 154
S. pruriens var. pruriens 154
Sphenostylis angustifolia 58, 212
Sporobolus africanus 320
S. capensis 320
Stachys hyssopoides 220
S. natalensis var. natalensis 64
*Stapelia gigantea 96
*S. leendertziae 270
Sterculiaceae 28, 90, 178, 236, 266, 282
Stipagrostis uniplumis var. neesii 330

Stoebe vulgaris 44, 272
*Streptocarpus vandeleurii 60
Striga asiatica 236
S. bilabiata 236
S. elegans 236
S. gesnerioides 236
Strychnos pungens 12, 300
Stylosanthes fruticosa 144
Sutera aurantiaca 236, 280
S. burkeana 280
S. caerulea 262
S. palustris 262

Tagetes minuta 108
Talinum caffrum 7, 172
Tapinanthus natalitius subsp. zeyheri 74
T. rubromarginatus 222
Tapiphyllum parvifolium 306
Taraxacum officinale 120
Tephrosia acaciifolia 276
T. capensis var. capensis 214
T. elongata var. elongata 276
T. longipes subsp. longipes 214
T. lupinifolia 214
T. lurida var. *lurida* 214
T. multijuga 214
T. rhodesica 214
Tetradenia brevispicata 220
Teucrium capense 64
T. trifidum 64
Themeda triandra 14, 331
Thesium cf. costatum 84
T. magalismontanum 84
T. utile 84
Thunbergia atriplicifolia 34
T. neglecta 34
Thymelaeaceae 28, 180, 238, 282
Tiliaceae 9, 28, 180, 238
Tithonia rotundifolia 272
Tolpis capensis 120
Trachyandra asperata var. basutoensis 72
T. asperata var. nataglencoensis 72
T. erythrorrhiza 72
T. saltii var. saltii 72
Trachypogon capensis 320
T. spicatus 320
Tragopogon dubius 120
Tragus berteronianus 321
Triaspis hypericoides subsp. nelsonii 222
Tribulus terrestris 184
Trichodesma physaloides 46
Trichoneura grandiglumis var. grandiglumis 338
Trifolium africanum 214
T. pratense 214
T. repens 58
Triraphis andropogonoides 338
Tristachya biseriata 331
T. hispida 331
T. leucothrix 331
T. rehmannii 332
Tritonia nelsonii 218, 276
Triumfetta sonderi 180
Trochomeria macrocarpa 294
Tulbaghia acutiloba 270
T. leucantha 270
Turbina oblongata 202
T. oenotheroides 202
Turneraceae 28, 182
Turraea obtusifolia 74
Tylosema fassoglense 124
Typha capensis 282
Typhaceae 28, 268, 282, 310

Ulmaceae 28, 308
Umbelliferae see Apiaceae
Urelytrum agropyroides 321
U. squarrosum 321
Urera tenax 182
Urginea depressa 72
U. multisetosa 278
Urochloa mosambicensis 326
U. panicoides 326
U. trichopus 326
Ursinia nana subsp. nana 108
Urticaceae 29, 182, 284, 308
Utricularia arenaria 66
U. livida 66

Vahlia capensis 182
Vahliaceae 29, 182
Vangueria infausta 306
Velloziaceae 29, 90, 238, 266
Verbena bonariensis 266
V. brasiliensis 266
V. officinalis 266
V. tenuisecta 266
Verbenaceae 29, 90, 182, 238, 266, 282
Vernonia galpinii 246
V. natalensis 246
V. oligocephala 246
V. poskeana 246
V. staehelinoides 246
V. sutherlandii 246
Veronica anagallis-aquatica 262
Vigna vexillata 214
Viscaceae 29, 308
Viscum combreticola 308
V. rotundifolium 308
Vitaceae 29, 184

Wahlenbergia caledonica 248
W. undulata 248
W. virgata 48
Walafrida densiflora 88
W. tenuifolia 88
Waltheria indica 178

Xanthium strumarium 118
Xerophyta humilis 90
X. retinervis 90, 266
X. viscosa 90, 238
Ximenia caffra var. caffra 302
Xyridaceae 29, 184
Xyris capensis 184
X. congensis 184
Xysmalobium brownianum 96
X. undulatum 96

Zaluzianskya katharinae 86
Zanthoxylum capense 84
Zinnia peruviana 192
Ziziphus mucronata 14, 308
Z. mucronata subsp. mucronata 304
Z. zeyheriana 304
Zornia capensis 144
Z. glochidiata 144
Z. linearis 144
Z. milneana 144
Zygophyllaceae 29, 184

INDEX TO ENGLISH AND AFRIKAANS COMMON NAMES

Page numbers printed in light type refer to passing references.

Aambeibossie 36, 208
Aambeiwortel 70
Aasklok 270
African wattle 124
Agrimony 174
Akkermonie 174
Angelbossie 216
Annual bristle grass 314
Arrowleaf sida 160
Asparagus fern 70
Assegaaigras 316
Autumn painted petals 254

Bachelor's button 36
Bailey's wattle 162
Bailey-se-wattel 162
Balbossie 38, 166
Bankrotbos 44, 272
Bankrupt bush 44, 272
Baroe 74, 220
Basboontjie 164
Basterknoffel 34
Basterolienhout 48
Basterrooibos 292
Beechwood 172
Beespatat 200
Bell stapelia 270
Benghal wandering Jew 248
Bergaalwyn 150, 278
Bergbas 308
Bergbitterbossie 40
Bergblinkgras 336
Bergbrandnetel 182
Bergdisseldoring 98
Bergkaree 286
Bergkruie 114
Bergmispel 306
Bergpruim 166, 226
Bergtaaibos 288
Bergvaalbos 108
Besembossie 84, 282
Besemgras 332
Besemtrosvy 300
Beukesbossie 182
Biesieblaarruigtegras 335
Bietou 100
Bird flower 136
Bird's brandy 266
Birdlime bush 74
Bitter apple 264
Bitterappel 264
Bitterbos 56
Bitterbossie 246
Bitterhout 96
Bitterwortel 38, 216
Blaasertjie 212
Blaasklits 90
Black ironbark 224
Black locust 58
Black nightshade 88
Black seed setaria 318
Black wattle 162
Blackjack 40, 108
Blackseed grass 321
Bladderweed 74, 156
Blinkaarboesmansgras 330
Blinkblaar 304
Blinkblaar-wag-'n-bietjie 304
Bloekom 76
Blou-aarbossie 262
Blou-angelier 254
Blou-ertjie 252
Bloubietou 244
Bloublommetjie 244
Bloubos 130
Bloubuffelsgras 315
Bloudekgras 329
Bloudissel 78
Blougifbossie 194
Bloulelie 242
Bloumelkbos 290
Bloupoeierkwassie 250
Blousaadgras 332
Blouselblommetjie 248
Blousuurkanol 252
Bloutaaibos 288
Blouteebossie 246
Bloutulp 254
Blouvleibossie 116
Blouwaterbossie 266
Blue buffalo grass 315
Blue currant 288
Blue heliotrope 248
Blue thatch grass 329
Bobbejaandruif 170
Bobbejaangif 170
Bobbejaankomkommer 294
Bobbejaanstert 90, 266
Bobbejaanuintjie 252
Boekenhout 172
Boesmansdruif 184
Boesmansgif 36
Boesmansrietjie 98
Boesmanstee 122
Bokbaardgras 320
Bokhaarklawer 58
Bokhara clover 58
Bokhoring 170
Bontplakkie 202
Bosgifappel 88
Bosui 298
Bosveldbeesgras 326
Bosveldkatjiepiering 82
Botterblom 40, 100, 172
Botterklapper 300
Bottle-brush grass 318

Bowstring hemp 70
Braam 232
Bramble 232
Breëblaarblougras 325
Breëblaarterpentyngras 328
Breëblaarwasbessie 302
Broad-leaved blue grass 325
Broad-leaved turpentine grass 328
Broad-leaved waxberry 302
Bronslaai 46
Broom cluster fig 300
Broom grass 332
Bruidsbos 82
Bruinblommetjie 280
Buffalo-thorn 304
Buffelsgras 335
Bugweed 264
Bulrush 282
Bushman's grape 184
Bushman's poison 36
Bushtick 100
Bushveld gardenia 82
Buttercup 172

Canary weed 104
Candelabra euphorbia 132
Cape chestnut 232
Cape holly 36
Cape myrtle 76
Cape saffron 236, 280
Carrot seed grass 321
Cartwheels 290
Caterpillar grass 316
Centipede grass 321
Chaff flower 188
Cheesewood 172
Chicory 246
Chocolate bells 46
Christmas bush 82
Common coral tree 206
Common dandelion 120
Common hookthorn 162
Common paspalum 325
Common reed 336
Common signal grass 326
Common wild currant 288
Common wild fig 300
Common wild sorghum 337
Copper leaf 130, 204
Cork bush 252
Cosmos 40, 192
Cottonwool grass 316
Couch grass 324
Crane's bill 216
Creeping sorrel 170
Crossberry 238
Cud weed 114
Curly dock 304

Daisy-tea bush 192
Dan's cabbage 116
Dekgras 329
Deurmekaarbos 252
Devil's thorn 228
Dikbas 94
Disseldoring 98
Dodder 54
Dogwood 304
Doll's powderpuff 250
Donkieperske 290
Donsgras 316
Doringbitterappel 88, 264
Draaibos 244
Drieblomgras 331
Drolpeer 90
Drumsticks 86
Dubbeltjie 80, 184
Dwarf buffalo-thorn 304
Dwarf mobola 124
Dwerg-blinkblaar-wag-'n-bietjie 304
Dye bush 296

Eenjarige steekgras 314
Eland's pea 122
Elandsdoring 228
Elandsertjie 122
Elephant's root 164
Elsgras 317
Enkeldoring 164
European verbena 266
Europese verbena 266

Fairy elephant's foot 224
False marula 94
False nasturtium 116
False olive 48
Feathertop grass 323
Fever tea 182
Fine-leaved verbena 266
Finger grass 324
Fire lily 190
Fishbone cassia 122
Flamethorn 162
Flannel weed 160
Flax-leaf fleabane 42
Fluitjiesriet 336
Fluweelgras 322
Fluweelklipels 306
Fountain grass 317
Four o'clock 164, 226
Fragrant false garlic 34
Fynblaarverbena 266

Gallant soldier 100
Gansgras 108
Garden setaria 319
Geelaandblom 166
Geelaasblom 96
Geelbergvygie 160
Geelbiesie 130
Geelbokbaard 120
Geelinkblom 176
Geelkransaalwyn 150
Geelopslag 104
Geelplakkie 126
Geelsewejaartjie 112
Geelstinkklawer 140
Geeltulp 150
Geeluintjie 274
Geelvuurlelie 94
Gekleurde euphorbia 296
Gemsbok bean 124
Gemsbokboontjie 124
Geneesblaarboom 264
Gewone haakdoring 162
Gewone kafferboom 206
Gewone paspalum 325
Gewone wildevy 300
Giant carrion flower 96
Giant spear grass 320
Giant turpentine grass 329
Gifappel 264
Gifblaar 294
Gifbol 148
Gifbossie 180
Gladdetongblaar 304
Goat bitter apple 264
Golden beard grass 328
Golden setaria 319
Gombossie 236
Goorappel 306
Goose grass 325
Gouebaardgras 328
Grasklokkie 218
Graslelie 190
Green wattle 162
Grey sour grass 315
Groenwattel 162
Grootblaarrotsvy 300
Grootrooiblom 236
Grootslymuintjie 278
Grysappeltjie 124
Guarri 56
Guinea grass 335
Gum grass 333
Gunpowder plant 198
Gwarrie 56

Haarbossie 182
Haaskos 230
Hair-bell 218
Hairy trident grass 331
Hairy wild lettuce 118
Hanekam 230
Harige drieblomgras 331
Harige gifbossie 180
Harige skaapslaai 118
Harpuisboom 36
Harpuisbos 100
Hartjiesgras 333
Heart seed love grass 333
Herringbone grass 326
Heuningbossie 140
Highveld cabbage tree 288
Highveld white vygie 76
Hongerbos-senecio 104
Hottentot's bread 270
Hottentot's tea 112
Hottentotsbrood 270
Hottentotstee 112
Hound's tongue 198
Hoëveldse kiepersol 288
Huilboom 124

Ink plant 86
Inkberry 170
Inkblom 86

Jaagsiektebossie 136
Jakkalsbos 56
Jerusalem cherry 88
Jeukbol 298
Jongosgras 325

Kafferdissel 42
Kafferlelie 218
Kaffertulp 148
Kaffir lily 218
Kakiebos 108
Kalmoes 288
Kandelaarnaboom 132
Kankerroos 118
Kannabas 238
Kappertjieblaar 116
Karee 286
Karkoer 128
Kasuur 172
Katbos 70
Katdoring 70
Katpisbossie 130, 204
Katstert 176, 282
Katstertgras 318
Katstertmannagras 319
Kerrieblom 180
Khadi-root 260
Khadivygie 224
Khadiwortel 260
Khaki weed 108
Klapperbossie 136, 222
Kleefgras 306, 333
Kleinmannagras 317
Kleinperdepram 84
Kleinrolgras 338
Kleinskraalhans 42
Kleurbossie 296
Klewerige appelliefie 178
Klimop 80
Klipdagga 278
Klipgras 314
Klipmelkbossie 132
Kliptaaibos 288
Klitsgras 320
Knapsekêrel 40, 108
Knopkruid 100
Koekbossie 160
Koorsbossie 64
Kopseerblom 188
Kosmos 40, 192
Kraal spike thorn 50
Kraalpendoring 50
Krimpsiektebossie 126
Krismisblom 202
Kruisbessie 238
Kruitbossie 198
Kwaggaballetjies 160
Kweek 324

Lablab bean 212
Lablab-boontjie 212
Laloentjie 128
Lance-leaf waxberry 302
Langbeenpaspalum 326
Langklits 188
Lantana 238, 282
Lantern flower 150
Lanternblom 150
Large cocklebur 118
Large witchweed 236
Large-fruited bushwillow 292
Large-leaved rock fig 300
Lavantelkoorsbessie 130
Lavender fever-berry 130
Laventelbossie 182
Leendertz's yellow vygie 160
Lekkerbreek 166, 226
Lighted matches 222
Lightning bush 130
Lucerne 252
Luisboom 264
Lusern 252

Maagbitterwortel 194
Maagbossie 180
Mealie crotalaria 136
Meidebossie 178
Melkbol 204, 302
Melkbos 96
Melkdissel 120
Melkgras 132
Melktou 96
Mexican poppy 78
Mielie-crotalaria 136
Mierbossie 36
Milk thistle 120
Milkweed 96
Misbredie 286
Mispel 306
Mistletoe 308

Moederkappie 266, 302
Moepel 84
Monkey's tail 90, 266
Mooinooientjie 198
Morning glory 200, 250
Moth catcher 38
Motvanger 38
Mountain aloe 278
Mountain bristle grass 337
Mountain karee 286
Mountain medlar 306
Mountain nettle 182
Mountain red top 336
Muistepelkaroo 248
Muisvoëlkomkommer 128

Naaldebossie 60, 216
Naboom 132
Nagblom 166
Nana-berry 286
Nanabessie 286
Narrow-heart love grass 334
Narrow-leaved plantain 78
Nastergal 88
Natal panicum 335
Natal red top 337
Natalse rooipluim 337
Nentabos 202, 272
Notsung 280

Old man's beard 327
Oldwood 174
Olieboom 88, 262
Olienhout 76
Olifantsoor 60
Olifantsvoet 224
Olifantswortel 164
Oorpynhoutjie 78
Opstandingsplant 224
Orange River lily 190
Ossetongblaar 198
Otterbossie 48
Ouhout 174
Oulandsgras 333

Padda-lepel 34
Painted euphorbia 296
Pampas grass 332
Pampasgras 332
Papkuil 282
Parsley tree 288
Patrysblom 66
Patrysuintjie 150
Pearl acacia 164
Peeling plane 166, 226
Pendoring 50
Perdeblom 120
Perdegras 338
Pêrelakasia 164
Perskwasbossie 246
Pienkaandblom 226
Pienkheide 204
Pienksalie 220
Pigweed 286
Pincushion grass 317
Pineapple flower 298
Pinhole grass 322
Pink heath 204
Plakkie 202
Platvoetaasblom 270
Ploegbreker 206
Pluimbossie 232
Pluisbossie 44
Poison apple 264
Poison bulb 188
Poison leaf 294
Pompon tree 238
Poprosie 44, 196
Porcupine huernia 270
Potato creeper 264
Pretty lady 198
Prickly malvastrum 158
Pronkgras 317
Purperwinde 200, 250
Purple nutsedge 274
Purslane 172
Puzzle-bush 252
Pyjama flower 66

Raasblaar 292
Raisin bush 180
Ramenas 122
Randjiesgras 337
Rank wag-'n-bietjie 162
Rankklits 242
Ranksuring 170
Rasperdisseldoring 98
Rat's-tail dropseed 320
Red autumn grass 318
Red bushwillow 292
Red clover 214
Red grass 331
Red ivory 304
Red paintbrush 190
Red sunflower 272
Red-hot poker 154
Red-leaved rock fig 300
Resin bush 100
Resin tree 36
Resurrection plant 224
Reuse-aasblom 96
Reuseterpentyngras 329
Rhodes grass 323
Rhodes-gras 323
River bushwillow 292
River pumpkin 296
River red gum 76
Rivierpampoen 296
Rock dagga 278
Roerkruid 114
Rolling grass 338
Rooi-ivoor 304
Rooi-opslag 282
Rooiaarbossie 188
Rooiblaarrotsvy 300
Rooiblom 236
Rooibos 292
Rooigras 331
Rooiherfsgras 318
Rooiklawer 214
Rooikwas 190
Rooiuintjie 274
Rose evening primrose 226
Rosyntjiebos 180
Ruikbossie 262
Rusperbossie 198
Ruspergras 316
Russet grass 330

Saffraanbossie 236, 280
Sagewood 248
Saliehout 248
Sambokbos 116
Sand apple 306
Sand olive 308
Sandlelie 72
Sandmelktou 38
Sandolien 308
Satansbos 264
Saw-tooth love grass 334
Scottish thistle 194
Sedge-leaved broom grass 335
Seepbos 304, 308
Seeroogblom 188
Sekelbos 164, 224
Sekelgras 326
Sering 258
Sesbania 276
Sickle bush 164, 224
Sigorei 246
Silky bushman grass 330
Silver wattle 162
Silverleaf bitter apple 264
Silwerblaarsuikerbos 232
Silwerwattel 162
Sjambok bush 116
Skaamblommetjie 298
Skotse-dissel 194
Slangkop 46
Slanguintjie 278, 298
Slangwortel 230
Slootopdammer 104
Slymuintjie 66
Smalblaarwasbessie 302
Smalhartjiesgras 334
Small evening primrose 166
Small knobwood 84
Smelter's bush 108
Smelterbossie 108
Smooth dock 304
Snake root 230
Snotterbelletjie 48
Soap bush 304, 308
Soetdoring 162
Sooibrandbossie 260
Sorrel 228
Sour grass 315
Sourplum 302
Sow thistle 120
Spaanse knapsekêrel 100
Spanish blackjack 100
Spear grass 316
Speelwonderboom 44, 196
Spider-leg 160
Spider-wisp 48
Spiderweb grass 323
Spike thorn 50
Spindlepod 198
Spine-leaved monkey orange 300
Spinnerakgras 323
Spiny sida 160
Spotted knotweed 230
Spring stars 192
St John's wort 146
Stamvrug 176
Starvation senecio 104
Stekeltaaiman 160
Sticky bristle grass 320
Sticky everlasting 110
Sticky gooseberry 178
Stingelgras 330
Stinkkruid 114
Stippelgras 322
Sugarbush 232
Suikerbos 232
Sumach bean 164
Suring 228
Suurbuffelsgras 335
Suurgras 315
Suurkomkommer 128
Suurpruim 302
Swartbas 56
Swartbasbloekom 224
Swartsaadgras 321
Swartsaadmannagras 318
Swartteebossie 42
Swartwattel 162
Sweet-thorn 162
Sybossie 104
Sydissel 120
Syringa 258

Taaibos 288
Taaiman 160
Taaipol 320
Taaisewejaartjie 110
Tall paspalum 326
Tandpynwortel 94
Teesuikerbossie 62
Terblansbossie 74, 156
Terpentyngras 328
Thatch grass 329
Thorn apple 88, 262
Tinderwood 90
Tonteldoosbossie 102
Tontelhout 90
Transvaal milkplum 176
Transvaal red milkwood 84
Transvaal silverleaf 232
Transvaal stone plant 160
Transvaal sumach 308
Traveller's joy 80
Tree euphorbia 132
Tree fuchsia 280
Treurwilger 308
Trident grass 331
Triraphis 338
Tropical richardia 84
Tropiese-richardia 84
Tsamma 128
Tuin-setaria 319
Turpentine grass 328
Tweevingergras 322

Vaalboontjie 142
Vaalsuurgras 315
Vaalteebossie 110
Vaderlandswilg 292
Varkkos 172
Varkstertgras 321
Veergras 327
Veldsambreeltjies 200
Velvet bushwillow 292
Velvet grass 322
Velvet rock alder 306
Verfblommetjie 176
Vermeerbos 102
Vieruurtjie 164, 226
Vingerblaarertjie 214
Vingergras 324
Vingerhoedblom 228
Vingerpol 132
Visgif 252
Vleibloutulp 254
Vleilelie 190
Vlieëbos 76, 252
Vlieëpisbossie 146
Volstruiskos 70
Voëlent 74, 308
Voëltjiebos 136
Vuurhoutjies 222
Vuurlelie 190
Vuurpyl 154

Water hyacinth 260
Water parsnip 94
Water plantain 34
Watercress 46
Waterhiasint 260